Supplanting the Postmodern

Supplanting the Postmodern

An Anthology of Writings on the Arts and Culture of the Early 21st Century

Edited by
David Rudrum and Nicholas Stavris

Bloomsbury Academic
An imprint of Bloomsbury Publishing Inc

BLOOMSBURY
NEW YORK • LONDON • NEW DELHI • SYDNEY

Bloomsbury Academic

An imprint of Bloomsbury Publishing Inc

1385 Broadway	50 Bedford Square
New York	London
NY 10018	WC1B 3DP
USA	UK

www.bloomsbury.com

BLOOMSBURY and the Diana logo are trademarks of Bloomsbury Publishing Plc

First published 2015

© David Rudrum and Nicholas Stavris, 2015

Library of Congress Cataloging-in-Publication Data

A catalog record for this book is available from the Library of Congress.

ISBN: HB: 978-1-5013-0687-7
       PB: 978-1-5013-0686-0
       ePub: 978-1-5013-0688-4
       ePDF: 978-1-5013-0689-1

Typeset by RefineCatch Limited, Bungay, Suffolk

For Alice
and
for Suzy

Contents

Acknowledgements

First and foremost, our thanks go to Haaris Naqvi and Mary Al-Sayed at Bloomsbury for taking on this project and helping us see it through to completion. We would also like to thank Robert Eaglestone for his initial encouragement and enthusiasm for the idea of such a book, which persuaded us that this was a project worth undertaking.

Much of the funding that made it possible to pay for permission to reprint many of the writings anthologised herein came from the generous research budget of the School of Music, Humanities and Media at the University of Huddersfield. We are particularly grateful for this financial support, as without it we would have had to settle for a much less ambitious anthology.

We acknowledge with due thanks the respective publishers for permission to reprint the following writings:

'Epilogue: The Postmodern … in Retrospect' from Linda Hutcheon, *The Politics of Postmodernism*, 2nd edition, Copyright © 2002, Routledge. Reproduced by permission of Taylor & Francis Books UK.

'Beyond Postmodernism: Toward an Aesthetic of Trust' by Ihab Hassan, from *Beyond Postmodernism: Reassessments in Literature, Theory, and Culture*, ed. Klaus Stierstorfer, Copyright © 2003, Walter de Gruyter. Reproduced with permission.

'Auto-Modernity after Postmodernism: Autonomy and Automation in Culture, Technology, and Education' by Robert Samuels, from McPherson, Tara, ed., *Digital Youth, Innovation, and the Unexpected*, pp. 219–40, © 2008 Massachusetts Institute of Technology, by permission of The MIT Press.

Material from *Post-Postmodernism: or, The Cultural Logic of Just-In-Time Capitalism* by Jeffrey T. Nealon, Copyright © 2012, the Board of Trustees of the Leland Stanford Jr. University. All rights reserved. Used with the permission of Stanford University Press: http://www.sup.org

Material from *Performatism, or the End of Postmodernism* by Raoul Eshelman, Copyright © 2008, Davies Group. Reproduced with permission, all rights reserved.

Material from *Hypermodern Times*, by Gilles Lipovetsky, trans. Andrew Brown, Copyright © 2005, Polity. Reproduced with permission. This book was first published by Grasset in 2004 under the title *Les Temps Hypermodernes*, and we are particularly grateful to Ellen MacDonald-Kramer of Polity for securing the permission of the original publisher.

Material from *The Passing of Postmodernism: A Spectroanalysis of the Contemporary,* by Josh Toth, reprinted by permission from the State University of New York Press, © 2010, State University of New York. All rights reserved.

Material from *Postmodernism: What Moment?* ed. Pelagia Goulimari, Copyright © 2007 Manchester University Press. Reproduced with permission.

Material from *Digimodernism: How New Technologies Dismantle the Postmodern and Reconfigure our Culture* © Alan Kirby, 2009, and Continuum US, an imprint of Bloomsbury Publishing Inc. Reproduced with permission.

Altermodern Manifesto and material from *Altermodern,* by Nicolas Bourriaud, © Tate 2009, reproduced by permission of Tate Trustees.

'Notes on Metamodernism' by Timotheus Vermeulen and Robin van den Akker, from *Journal of Aesthetics and Culture,* Vol. 2, 2010, is reproduced here thanks to the commendable open access policy of that journal. We regret that it was not possible to include the many images that accompanied the original article, nor the abstract with which it began. For the terms of creative commons license governing further use of this text, see http://creativecommons.org/licenses/by/4.0/

'Introduction: A Wake and Renewed?' by Neil Brooks and Josh Toth, republished with permission of Rodopi, from *The Mourning After: Attending the Wake of Postmodernism,* eds. Neil Brooks and Josh Toth, 2007; permission conveyed through Copyright Clearance Center, Inc.

We are personally grateful to Vlad Strukov for his kind permission to reprint Steven Connor's 'Postmodernism Grown Old'. This chapter was originally published in Maria Popova and Vlad Strukov (eds.) *Cul'tura 'Post': on the Crossroads of Culture and Civilization,* Voronezh, Voronezh UP, 2004, pp. 55–73.

We are similarly indebted to Alan Kirby for his permission to reprint his article 'The Death of Postmodernism and Beyond', from *Philosophy Now,* Issue 58, November/December 2006.

We thank Charles Thomson and Billy Childish for permission to reprint 'The Stuckist Manifesto' and 'Remodernism'. Both are available at http://www.stuckism.com, and in in *The Stuckists: The First Remodernist Art Group,* ed. Katherine Evans (London: Victoria Press, 2000).

Introduction

David Rudrum and Nicholas Stavris

As dead horses go, the notion of postmodernity is certainly one of the most heavily flogged in recent cultural memory. Philosophers and sociologists, critics and theorists, artists and writers alike have spent the better part of half a century formulating definitions of it; arguments for and against it; analyses and interpretations of it; historical, economic, sociological, and political contextualizations of it; textbooks about it and introductions to it; and even the occasional spirited refutation of its very existence. All in all, the ink expended on discussing postmodernity – alternatively 'postmodernism' or 'the postmodern', according to each commentator's preference – has flowed from so many diverse and far-flung tributaries that tracing the headwaters of the raging torrent's source became all but impossible quite some time ago.

But this river is no longer in spate; the flood has subsided. Not only is there markedly less ink given over to the discussion of the postmodern in the early twenty-first century than there was in the late twentieth, but such discussions of it as are written today seem impelled with increasing regularity to the conclusion that postmodernism is rapidly becoming a thing of the past. Works of contemporary art and literature seem ever less amenable to analysis by criticism emphasizing postmodernist modes and traits. Philosophers and theorists are no longer as inspired by the question of modernity's aftermath – some of them (Zygmunt Bauman or Jacques Rancière, for instance) are conspicuously retreating from the notion of postmodernity. Perhaps the artists and writers who do not baulk at being tarred with the postmodernist brush were always few, but their number is apparently decreasing. The postmodern river, it would seem, is drying up.

How to account for this downturn in what was the most hotly contested cultural debate of the latter part of the twentieth century? If we may stretch this fluvial metaphor tauter still, its aptness resides in what happens to mighty rivers as they near the end of their journey: they slow down, as their swift currents lose their force under the weight of the sediment they have swept along with them; and they lose their way, bifurcating and fragmenting into the confusingly forked paths of a delta. With apologies to T.S. Eliot, they end not with a splash but a trickle. This is more or less exactly what has happened to the question of postmodernity in the early twenty-first century. In its early stages, postmodernism surged swiftly and noisily over rapids and maelstroms: it loudly courted controversy in its exuberant formulations and proclamations, and the debates it sparked were always heated, often acrimonious. Think, for example, of Barthes on the death of the author, Foucault on the disappearance of man, Derrida on the non-existence of the *hors-texte*, Baudrillard on the loss of the real, or Lyotard on the demise of grand narratives: all these sets of rapids and maelstroms were negotiated within just fifteen years of each other, and some took a good couple of generations before the whitewater abated. As John McGowan puts it in his essay in Part One of this volume, the stakes in these debates were so high that sometimes it seemed as if 'nothing less than the West's soul hung in the balance'. However, the cultural commentator looking at the same river today would not recognize those heady days in its current stagnated, sluggish state. The reasons behind this seem to us to resemble the factors that cause the slowing down of any other mature river.

On the one hand, 'the postmodern' has become so broad a concept that its breadth, like that of a river, slows it down by dispersing it. This breadth has become so all-encompassing that, as a term, it can now be applied to more or less anything, and so describes essentially nothing. Moreover, like a river accumulating silt, the idea of the postmodern has picked up so much cultural baggage that its critical focus has been irretrievably swamped. For examples of this, reading Steven Connor's essay in the first part of this anthology will lead one to reflect that whereas the term 'postmodernism', when applied to architecture, meant turning one's back on modernist minimalism and re-embracing, albeit ironically, a return to certain kinds of ornamentation, the same term when applied to dance is generally taken to mean turning one's back on modernist ornamentation in order to embrace a (confusingly) postmodernist minimalism: the same term, then, is used to describe two currents flowing in apparently opposite directions.

A similar ambivalence that verges on contradiction can be found in the irony that, while certain strains of the postmodern can trace their source to the anarchism that flung up barricades in May 1968, the idea of the postmodern now informs contemporary debates in legal theory and jurisprudence. The terms 'postmodern' and 'postmodernist' have simply become too broad – too inclusive, too all-embracing – to function effectively as critical or descriptive terms. As Klaus Stierstorfer puts it, 'Postmodernism as a whole may have become too blunt a tool to be useful in debating many of the most hotly contested issues today'

(Stierstorfer 2003: 9). In other words, if postmodernism was once a mighty flowing river, it now seems to lack a clear current or a direction and so, leading apparently nowhere, it scarcely resembles a river at all. It is a spent force, and many critics and theorists – including some of its erstwhile champions – appear to be giving up on it altogether. Some are even publicly renouncing it. In the telling words of Linda Hutcheon, who did more than most for the currency of postmodernism, and whose writings open this collection, 'it's over'.

On the other hand, and at the same time, the slowing down and stagnation of postmodernism have been intimately related to a number of new developments. Dating from the *fin de millénaire* years to the present, a number of offshoots of the postmodern have been striking out in a multitude of new directions from it, and some of these directions seem to run athwart the main postmodern currents. Coinages with such striking names as 'altermodernism' and 'automodernism', 'metamodernism' and 'hypermodernism', 'remodernism' and 'digimodernism', 'performatism' and 'renewalism' have been mooted by cultural theorists and critics, and sometimes by artists themselves, in order to diagnose or champion ways in which the art, literature, and culture of the twenty-first century involve important differences and new departures from the mainstream of postmodernism. (Incidentally, that it is possible, and perhaps even unavoidable, to talk of 'the *mainstream* of postmodernism' is telling in itself. Time was this phrase would have been self-contradictory.) While some of these coinages are at pains to distance themselves as much as possible from the postmodernism that preceded them, others are more willing to accept that their formulations follow on from those of a now-defunct postmodernism, taking them in new directions. These new directions, however, are many and varied, and sometimes at odds with one another. If we may be permitted one last stretching of the river metaphor, we might think of them as collectively constituting a 'delta effect'. That is, as the flow that was once postmodernism slows to a halt, it diverges and splits into multiple channels, with different streams striking out along different courses, forming the delta of the once-mighty postmodern river.

The shape of this anthology is in large measure based on these two tendencies. Its first part contains writings that, in various ways and from various angles, explore the idea that postmodernism is in decline, or simply is no more. We have borrowed the apt phrase 'The Sense of an Ending' as a title to this part, since it describes so effectively a widespread intuition that the postmodern moment is now over, give or take the singing of a few proverbial fat ladies. The title is borrowed from a recent prize-winning novel by Julian Barnes, itself borrowing it in turn from Frank Kermode's classic 1967 study, which explores the importance of the trope of apocalypse to narrative fiction. The double origin of this title could, perhaps, be taken to illustrate some of the complications involved in arguing that postmodernism is over and done with: on the one hand, the fact that one of Britain's foremost writers of postmodern fiction was awarded the Man Booker prize for *The Sense of an Ending* in 2011 might suggest that postmodernism is not altogether out of favour just yet; on the other hand, that he chose a title redolent of apocalyptic anxieties might suggest that one of the foremost postmodern novelists shares the suspicion that the end of an era has finally come. In effect, this ambiguity sums up the findings of many of the writings in this part of the book: postmodernity is not an easy thing to draw a line under, because its legacy still has a persistent influence, and so identifying the watershed moment at which it ended is all but impossible. Hence, Linda Hutcheon's retrospective phrase 'gone forever but here to stay' is probably a more judicious verdict than the bald assertion that the postmodern is over and done with.

Asserting that the postmodern is over and done with, however, instantly gives rise to the inevitable question: what's next? If we no longer live in the postmodern era, what kind of an era are we now living in? The second part of this anthology consists of a range of writings that seek to formulate answers to this question. Most of them attempt to diagnose or describe tendencies in our culture that are distinct from postmodernism: they are thus mostly interventions in criticism. Some, however, *call for* an art that will bring into being a successor to postmodernism: thus, there are two manifestos included herein. What is shared in these different kinds of writing is the need to coin a term to name what comes after the postmodern. The suggestions mooted in these writings are as inventive as they are many and varied. Hence, we have given the title 'Coming to Terms with the New' to this part of the anthology, to underscore the twofold endeavour of on the one hand forming and articulating a clear understanding of what follows postmodernism, and on the other hand finding a term or set of terms with which to name or describe it.

Each of the entries in the two main parts of this book is prefaced by a short introduction, in which we outline the central ideas, point out the main similarities to and/or differences from some of the other positions found in the anthology, and suggest a few possible strengths and limitations to the insights presented in each piece. Thus, there is no need for this introduction to spend overmuch time in exegesis or synthesis of the individual extracts and writings that follow.

Instead, we present here two brief overviews of some of the problems and challenges posed in articulating the sense of postmodernism's ending, and in coming to terms with what follows it.

The sense of an ending

From September 2011 until January 2012, London's Victoria and Albert Museum ran a well-attended exhibition, billed as the world's first major retrospective show on the phenomenon of postmodernism. Focusing largely on architecture and design, and touching upon visual art, film, and music, it conveyed to a very large public the clear message that postmodernism had run its course. Entitled *Postmodernism: Style and Subversion, 1970–1990*, its neatly bookended dates may have aroused some academics' suspicions, and it must be said that the curatorial team did not appear to have expended as much effort on communicating how and why postmodernism had ended as they did in tracing its origins (see Adamson & Pavitt 2011). Nevertheless, such an ambitious show at such a prestigious venue could by itself be adduced as evidence of a clear sense of postmodernism's ending.

Analysing the end of postmodernism, though, proves to be a much harder task than proclaiming it. Problematically, there does not seem to be a neat term with which to encapsulate the idea that postmodernism is finished. To speak of the 'ending' of postmodernism is to moot the idea of an 'end' – as does Raoul Eshelman's subtitle in Part Two. Anyone versed in the rudiments of the postmodern could instantly object here that this idea is out of place, since postmodernism rejected the thought of closure more than almost any other. Postmodern artworks and postmodern interpretations of artworks alike were supposed to resist closing finalities, and the deep-seated postmodern critique of teleology itself ought to have taught us to regard such talk of an 'end' with suspicion. In postmodernist terms, the *sense* of an ending is all we ever have – the end itself is another matter.

Alan Kirby's article in this section opts for what is probably the next most obvious term – 'the death of postmodernism'. However, as we will see in Part Two of this collection, Josh Toth has been quick to point out that postmodernism might better be thought of not as dead but as *un*dead, since it keeps returning to haunt us. Drawing on Derrida's writings about ghosts and specters in *Specters of Marx*, he points out that the postmodern appears to have survived its own death, because it simply will not be laid to rest. According to Toth, while we could not say that postmodernism is alive and well, it is certainly living an afterlife and, like a revenant, it comes back to haunt the culture of the next generation. One could argue, indeed, that the various postmortems, epitaphs, obituaries, and requiems, of which those anthologized here are only a representative few, are actually a means of prolonging postmodernism's cultural (after)life. So, while talk of the 'death' of postmodernism is perhaps less problematic than talk of the 'end' of it, neither term can quite offer the sense of a finishing line that they argue for – and perhaps, as we shall shortly suggest, this is just as well.

A more popular option has been to use a preposition, such as 'beyond' or 'after' postmodernism. The vocabulary involved in such discussions serves to highlight how enslaved to grammar criticism can be. 'After' postmodernism has become a very popular phrase, in use since at least the early 1990s, when it entitled a season of symposia at the Stuttgart seminar in cultural studies. Since then, it was used in 1997 at a major conference at the University of Chicago; in 2001 as the title of a collection of essays on contemporary fiction edited by José Lopez and Gary Potter; in 2007 as that of a special issue of the journal *Twentieth-Century Literature*; and as a phrase it has cropped up in passing in numerous essay and chapter titles over the past decade or two. But this preposition is arguably not fit for purpose: in the first place, it implies a sense of historical periodization, which may sit well with Fredric Jameson's conception of the postmodern, but rather less so with Jean-François Lyotard's. Second, and more problematically, the historical sense it implies carries with it an assumption of history as involving sequentiality, chronology, and straightforward succession. The postmodern conception of history, of course, repudiated this understanding of how history works: from Hayden White to Graham Swift, one of the most salient lessons of postmodernism was to be wary of narrativizations of the past, especially those involving a linear or chronological account of it. (In this respect, *pace* Alan Kirby's article [Kirby 2010a], it is arguably unhelpful to conceive of the writings in Part Two as 'successors' to the postmodern.) And finally, of course, the idea of 'after' was itself always already present in the 'post' of 'postmodernity', so the phrase 'after postmodernism' is arguably tautologous.

The solution opted for by Klaus Stierstorfer in his 2003 volume, and by Ihab Hassan in his contribution to it included herein, is to spatialize the temporality implied by the preposition 'after', by adopting 'beyond' in its stead. But this solution has its problems too: in order to speak of what lies 'beyond postmodernism', one would surely need to have mapped out a territory, so that it was clearly demarcated. That is, one can only locate the regions 'beyond postmodernism' once one has already drawn a line around it. The obvious objection to this preposition would be that no such clear delineation of postmodernism has yet been achieved, because it is a notoriously loose concept. But a more grammatically minded objection would take this point further by pointing out that 'beyond postmodernism' actually *presupposes* a boundary or end to it – and that is begging the question. Thus, neither of these prepositions offers a very promising choice of tree to go barking up.

Many of the commentators in this part of the anthology are all too aware of the problems and challenges involved in debating, or even formulating, the issues involved in the demise of postmodernism. Few of them regard it as a *fait accompli*. Indeed, we have kept out of this section on purpose a multitude of discussions and analyses that oversimplify the matter by taking postmodernism's demise as a given or self-evident fact. The causes assigned to the downfall of the postmodern by the writings in this section are many and varied, but none of them is straightforward: Jeffrey T. Nealon identifies changing economic patterns as driving the move away from postmodernism, though he admits that this move amounts to an 'intensification' of postmodernism rather than a repudiation of it. Linda Hutcheon underscores the role of the cultural and educational establishment in institutionalizing the once vital subversive force of the postmodern; however, a somewhat contrasting view is offered by John McGowan, who argues that the intellectual urgency of postmodernism abated after the end of the cold war, and that a decline in theoretical ambition – perhaps itself concomitant with the declining influence of the academy in society since the 1960s, though McGowan does not make this point outright – is to blame for postmodernism's stagnation. Both Hutcheon and McGowan agree that the roles played by institutions of education and culture are in large measure behind this decline; each takes a different view of how this happened; but, like Nealon, neither of them regards the postmodern as straightforwardly over and done with. Nor does Steven Connor, who argues that the idea of the 'postmodern' was porous enough to absorb, by a kind of theoretical osmosis, an ever broader variety of subject matters, meanings, and contexts – or, to reverse the metaphor, to filter into and permeate new fields of discussion. In the process, both the term and the concept 'postmodernism' were twisted into new shapes, so rather than seeing postmodernism as dead or dying, Connor suggests it might better be conceived of as alive and evolving. A somewhat dimmer view is taken by Ihab Hassan, who sees recent history as evidence that a postmodern condition of contingency and plurality has sadly failed to materialize. He argues that the contemporary arts now tend towards articulations of the values of truth, sincerity, spirituality, and authenticity rather than the postmodern shibboleths of irony and relativism. His argument, it will be seen, anticipates several of the formulations in Part Two, as does that of Alan Kirby, who argues that the postmodern has been superseded by a new set of aesthetics and values ushered in by the digital age.

Perhaps this would be the opportune moment at which to explain the title of the anthology as a whole – *Supplanting the Postmodern*. On reflection, we felt that the efforts of the critics and theorists in Part One were better encapsulated by the participle form of a verb in the present tense than with a noun such as 'end' or 'death', or a preposition like 'after' or 'beyond'. As will be seen from the previous summaries, few of the writings herein are simple coroners' verdicts proclaiming the death of the postmodern. Rather, these analyses demonstrate that calling time on postmodernism is still a work in progress: hence, *Supplanting the Postmodern* rather than *Postmodernism Supplanted*. As for the choice of verb – to supplant – this relates largely to the writings in Part Two, which in most cases clearly set themselves up as new cultural paradigms taking the place of the postmodern. However, its relevance to the debates in the first part of the anthology resides in its etymological and phonetic similarity to the Derridean idea of the *supplement*. Derrida's *Of Grammatology*, it will be recalled, highlights the contradictory nature of our understanding of the supplementary: a supplement can *add to* what it supplements; but it can also (and contrariwise) supersede, outmode, or *replace* it. Since it appears to us that the jury in the coroner's court is still out on this matter – that the debate around the death of postmodernism is at its most incisive when it refuses to regard the case as closed, and that some accounts of postmodernism's demise involve its pursuit by other means – we submit that most of the writings in this section partake of the condition of the Derridean supplement. That is, many of the arguments around whether postmodernism has been replaced, or whether the time has come to replace it, in fact end up adding to it.

For the most part, we have chosen to keep out of this anthology writings that seek to nail down the precise moment, event, or date when the postmodern era finally ceased. We have done so because the overwhelming majority of such assessments seem to us to involve an oversimplification of the issues involved, and in many cases raise more questions than they answer. Whether the suggested date is that of a major historical event (the fall of the iron curtain in 1989 or the terrorist attacks of September 11, 2001 being frequently mooted as obvious landmarks), or the passing of an iconic figure (for example, Brooks and Toth point to the death of Samuel Beckett, also in 1989), or the appearance of an iconic new cultural artifact that appears to cut the cord attaching it to postmodernism – it does not seem likely to us that any one particular event could encapsulate all that is at stake in the claim that postmodernism is finished. Moreover, such claims tend to carry with them the implications that first, it is clear what 'postmodernism' means; second, its meaning is stable and unitary; and third, the proposed finishing moment is a good fit for it – that is, the event neatly encapsulates both the essence of the postmodern and the clear evidence of its downfall. In our experience, the third point is unlikely to be true because the first two are manifestly false, and so the concept of postmodernism would be poorly served by including too many writings in this vein. Furthermore, we have tried to keep to a minimum the inclusion of writings that simplistically equate the sense of an ending with a view of either the triumph of postmodernism, or the vanquishing of it. These two sets of exclusions are, in fact, related, because many of the writings we have kept out exhibit both these tendencies simultaneously.

Consider the case of that *annus mirabilis*, 1989, when the Soviet bloc imploded, and the walls between East and West came crashing down in spectacular fashion. There is a widely held view, represented in this anthology by John McGowan, and by Neil Brooks and Josh Toth, that this was the moment when it became evident that postmodernism was essentially over. But there is no consensus as to *why* this moment sounded the knell of postmodernism. Instead, there is a clear contradiction. On the one hand, the end of the cold war can be read as postmodernism culminating in a final victory: the grand narrative of Soviet-style Marxism had been dramatically jettisoned, the formerly communist countries rushed to embrace postmodernist culture (especially pop music and architecture), and it seemed telling that the key reforms that had made this possible were labelled *Glasnost*, often translated as 'openness' – a very postmodern virtue. On the other hand, though, if the idea of the postmodern had entailed rejecting the values of the Enlightenment (such as the Rights of Man) and had been suspicious towards utopian impulses, then the events of 1989 can be read as a rebuttal of it: here was evidence of an ongoing faith in the supposedly metaphysical concepts of freedom, human rights, and democracy – one, moreover, that was unashamedly utopian, and that bore many of the hallmarks of a grand narrative. Furthermore, with the world left with only one superpower, the years that followed 1989 saw the West embark on a journey of globalization and neo-imperialism that belied postmodernism's avowed championing of multiplicity and diversity. So the fall of the iron curtain in 1989 is clearly a landmark event in the history of the postmodern, but what exactly it landmarks – whether success or failure, triumph or defeat, the end of the story or the start of a new chapter in it – is unclear.

The same contradictions bedevil smaller scale events, too. Minsoo Kang has suggested that postmodernism was finished on 18 June 1993, at the premiere of John McTiernan's movie *Last Action Hero*, starring Arnold Schwarzenegger. Alan Kirby recently made a similar suggestion in relation to the final instalment in the Wachowksi brothers' *Matrix* trilogy, *The Matrix Revolutions* (see Kirby 2010b), which came out on 5 November 2003. In both cases, it is agreed that the release of a Hollywood action movie (and in neither case is it a particularly good or memorable movie) signalled the final curtain for postmodernism. Once again, their reasons seem to contradict each other: Kang argues that *Last Action Hero* demonstrated clearly how postmodernism's classic devices of irony, parody, metafictional self-awareness, and ontological play between different levels of reality and fictionality, had finally been appropriated by mass culture to such an extent that postmodernism had become too pervasive to distinguish it from anything else. Alan Kirby is less clear as to why *The Matrix Revolutions* spelled the end of postmodernism, but the reasons seem fairly self-evident: the film launches a wholesale retreat from the flirtations with postmodernism's theories of simulation that were so prominent in the trilogy's first instalment, and replaces these ideas with a hackneyed resolution to a typical action movie, involving a messianic figure bringing peace to the world, his arms spread out in a cruciform shape as he dies to save humanity and to set us free. So in 1993, postmodernism had come to an end because its success was so total it had engulfed even Made-in-Hollywood family entertainment, but a decade later, it came to an end because any intellectual impact it may have had on Hollywood was finally negligible.

Obviously, certain kinds of contradiction are helpful, productive, and even necessary in generating debate. However, we find contradictions such as these to be rather less so, because they are born simply of taking too narrow a view. Accordingly, this anthology has been kept relatively free from bald verdicts on postmodernity's success and failure, and from attempts to pin down some particular event that might constitute postmodernism's apocalypse. Instead, we have presented an array of writings that explore the issues involved in less simplistic terms. Perhaps what is most telling about this part of the book is the number of contributions from canonical champions of postmodern theory: Linda Hutcheon, Steven Connor, and Ihab Hassan helped shape our understanding of postmodernism throughout its formative years, yet in recent years their views towards it appear to have changed dramatically. The juxtaposition of the writings of such established commentators with newer voices, such as that of Alan Kirby, is designed to incorporate perspectives on the sense of postmodernism's ending that contrast with each other in more fruitful ways.

Coming to terms with the new

There is, in fact, a word already in common use to designate whatever comes trailing behind in the aftermath of postmodernism. That word is, of course, 'post-postmodernism'. It is a term favoured by Jeffrey T. Nealon in Part One of this anthology, though even he begins his definition of it by calling it an 'ugly word'. In our view, *pace* Nealon, the best that can be said for this word is that it is 'a vile term consecrated by Wikipedia' (Kirby 2009: 40). Its lack of specificity renders it worse than useless: it does not enable even basic distinctions between, for example, following behind postmodernism in order to pursue its revolution in other directions or by other means; arguing that postmodernism is dead and buried, whether in whole or in part; and departing from the postmodernist agenda in order to forge trailblazing new departures from it. Its meaning is even more vague and elusive than that of the postmodernism it purportedly supplants, and hence nothing but confusion and conceptual muddle can be expected to follow from it. Should this term catch on, it is an inevitability that, sooner or later (and probably sooner rather than later), some critic or artist anxious about sounding out-of-date will coin the term 'post-post-postmodernism' to supplant it. The idea of 'post-postmodernism' plunges headlong into what, almost three decades ago, Paul de Man predicted would be 'a bottomless pit' (de Man 1986: 139). 'It is like the *Nouvelle Revue Française*, the *Nouvelle Nouvelle Revue Française*, the New Criticism, the New New Criticism, etc.' (de Man 1986: 139), he wryly observed.

De Man, however, was speaking not of post-postmodernism, but of the idea of postmodernism itself. And so one may – rightly – feel that the term 'post-postmodernism' is an unimaginative and uninspiring coinage: it suggests either that the sense of departure from the postmodern is too vague and unclear to be labelled neatly and accurately, or else that critics and theorists lack the perception or inventiveness to identify its characteristics in a terminological nutshell. But it should be remembered that the very same charge has repeatedly been brought against postmodernism itself. That, certainly, was de Man's view: 'the notion of postmodernity becomes a parody of the notion of modernity,' he said (de Man 1986: 139). And so, if we feel that the term 'post-postmodernism' fails to designate the nature of whatever it is that has apparently supplanted the postmodern, one should bear in mind that some of the blame can be laid at the door of the postmodern, for its terminological failure to differentiate itself more clearly from the modernism it supplanted. As Zygmunt Bauman has put it, 'The term [postmodernism] "cleared the site", but once ground-clearing jobs are done the bulldozers need to be removed lest they block the start of building works ... It is high time to arrive at more "positive" concepts, referring to what our realities *are*, instead of what they have ceased to be' (Bauman & Tester 2007: 26). Bauman – who, like Linda Hutcheon, Ihab Hassan, and Steven Connor, was once a leading explicator of the postmodern, but has more recently been given to finding a replacement for it – is critical of 'the purely negative function of the "postmodernity" concept', which 'said what social reality was *no longer* but [which] kept silent or sounded neutral about what it was instead' (Bauman & Tester 2007: 25–6). The term 'post-postmodernism' is doubly vulnerable to Bauman's criticisms. 'How long can you go on listing the has-been traits?' he asks. 'We get tired of buzzwords' (Bauman & Tester 2007: 25–6) – and though Bauman, like de Man, is speaking of the postmodern here, it is hard to avoid the conclusion that post-postmodernism is nothing more than such a buzzword. In Bauman's terms, it is just another 'negative' coinage that fails to assign any positive identity to what it (putatively) designates.

So it is not surprising that even Tom Turner, author of the first book to use the word 'post-postmodernism' in its title, concedes that 'post-Postmodernism is a preposterous term', and that we should 'hope for something better' (Turner 1996: 10). Tellingly, he issues the following piece of rather equivocal advice: 'Let us embrace post-Postmodernism – and pray for a better name' (Turner 1996: 10). Linda Hutcheon (below) articulates a similar view, though she is even more forthright on the need for a better name: in the essay that follows this Introduction, her final analysis is that 'Post-postmodernism needs a new label of its own, and I conclude, therefore, with this challenge to readers to find it – and name it for the twenty-first century'.

Turner's prayer and Hutcheon's challenge have certainly been answered. Over the past decade or so, there has been a steady stream of imaginative proposals for a neologism that would supplant 'postmodernism'. Presented herein is a selection of some of the leading contenders, arranged in roughly chronological order, from 1999 to the present: remodernism, performatism, hypermodernism, auto-modernism, renewalism, altermodernism, digimodernism, and metamodernism. Surveying them as a whole, three things become immediately apparent. First, there does not appear to be a simple 'smoking gun' – a single trait or property that all can agree is central to the culture that follows that of postmodernity, and that clearly betokens postmodernism's demise. Second, one is struck by the broad range of art forms, media, and genres that are discussed here, and how many different kinds of contemporary artworks and artifacts are amenable to critical analyses that resist, repudiate, or rebut postmodern ideas, themes, or characteristics. Third, it is telling that the authors of these writings are drawn from a multitude of different academic (and some non-academic) fields and backgrounds.

To take these points in order: the lack of any identifiable single quality inherent in all these critical positions is hardly a problem because, in the first place, there was never a single quality inherent in all things postmodern either and moreover, as Wittgenstein might have put it, we would do better to pay attention to what he calls 'family resemblances' (Wittgenstein 1968: §67) than 'to think that there must be something in common to all' (Wittgenstein 1965: 17). Put simply, when looking at a family portrait, we might notice 'various resemblances between members of a family', such as 'build, features, colour of eyes, gait, temperament, etc. etc.' (Wittgenstein 1968: §67). It is not necessary for all the members of the family to possess all these features in order to speak of a family resemblance. It is not even necessary for any member of the group to possess all of them. What is important is rather the 'network of similarities overlapping and criss-crossing: sometimes overall similarities, sometimes similarities of detail' (Wittgenstein 1968: §66).

Looked at in this way, a survey of the 'overlap and criss-cross' amongst the writings in this part of the anthology yields four principal resemblances: (i) Most of the writings anthologized in Part Two challenge, reject, or debunk the postmodern insistence that the human subject, and subjectivity in general, is a myth; (ii) Many of the positions included here emphasize the importance of sincerity and authenticity over postmodern irony, of faith and spirituality over postmodern scepticism, of the beautiful as against the postmodern sublime; (iii) A number of them regard the unprecedented technological changes brought about by the new digital age to constitute a decisive departure from the postmodern; (iv) Some of the writings stress the homogenizing role of globalization in putting an end to the postmodern predilection for difference, diversity, plurality, multiplicity, alterity, variety, otherness, and so forth. With all this said, however, it is worth pointing out that none of the writings in this section explicitly advances all four of these points at once. Rather, these themes emerge because of the range of overlapping arguments: as in Wittgenstein's family resemblance analogy, exploring the network of similarities that unfolds amongst the members of the group yields a more fruitful range of results than searching for one property common to all. Hence, the collective significance of these writings is greater because they are making different yet overlapping claims – certainly greater than it would be if they were all making virtually indistinguishable assertions.

A similar point could be made about the range of subject matter discussed in these writings. Remodernism, for instance, is preoccupied with painting, while altermodernism foregrounds rather less traditional forms of the fine arts. Metamodernism, too, has much to say about visual art, but is just as interested in architecture. Renewalism's principal emphasis is on narrative fiction, while performatism attempts to survey pretty much all of these fields, and takes on board film, too. Digimodernism focuses mostly on audio-visual media – film, TV, and radio – but reads them alongside new electronic developments such as the World Wide Web and internet chatrooms, an interest shared by automodernism. It will be seen from this brief summary that almost all the principal forms of art and popular culture fall within the ambit of the various critics and theorists whose work has been included here. True, there has been a marked neglect of poetry, and music, theatre, and dance might also appear somewhat overlooked (though Alan Kirby's analysis of the supplanting of rock music by electronic dance music would have been well worth including had there been space). But on the whole, the fact that so many different aspects of culture and the arts would appear to bear interpretations that are not easily recuperable within a postmodern framework can in itself be taken to suggest the sheer extent to which postmodernism is being abandoned or supplanted.

The same could also be said of the contributors to this anthology. Some (Billy Childish and Charles Thomson) are artists. The rest are academics. Some of these are critics, though of different disciplinary provenances (Nicolas Bourriaud is an art critic; Josh Toth a literary critic). Others are more closely attuned to the social sciences, such as sociologist Gilles Lipovetsky. Robert Samuels, though his background is in literature, publishes on debates about educational theory and pedagogy as much as he does on debates about literary texts. All in all, then, it would appear that the need to come up with a term to name the supplanting of the postmodern is being felt across a broad cross section of the arts, humanities, and social sciences. Moreover, this need is being felt not just across the academy, but around the world: the contributors to this section hail from Britain, the United States, Canada, France, Germany, and the Netherlands. Once again, the breadth of this consensus is suggestive.

However, surveying the geographical provenances of the writings in this section yields a clear pattern: as is perhaps to be expected, the terrain mapped out by these attempts to supplant the postmodern overlaps almost exactly that of the postmodern itself. Just as classic postmodern theory and culture stemmed largely from North America and Northern Europe (with the United States and France well represented), so too do the writings in this part of the anthology, and the cultural concerns they describe. Postmodernism was always vulnerable to the charge that it was an essentially Western phenomenon: it looks as if (*pace* Bourriaud's altermodernism) its aftermath will be too.

It would be simple to draw a Jamesonian conclusion from this: the rise and fall of postmodernism could very well appear to be intertwined with the fate of Western (and especially American) capitalism. Indeed, this is precisely what Jeffrey T. Nealon argues in Part One. He is not alone in this respect: the opening sentences of Timotheus Vermeulen and Robin van den Akker's 'Notes on Metamodernism' explicitly relate the cultural currents they describe to a number of specifically Western concerns, particularly economic ones: fears about sustainability and the environment, and about the economic depression that has blighted Europe and America in the early twenty-first century. To these we could probably add Alan Kirby and Robert Samuels's concerns about the onset of digitalization, and Bourriaud's interest in globalization: all these views are in large measure responses to developments in the structure of Western capitalism, and in Western culture's responses to them. Thus, the argument would run, in the years when the West's cultural Other was the Soviet Union, postmodernism flourished as an alternative to totalitarian models of thought and art. After the cold war, in a world dominated by just one neo-imperialist superpower, it comes as no surprise to read that Jameson's verdict is that 'it is simply globalization as such which is the other face of postmodernity and offers the most reliable access to all its other embodiments' (Jameson 2007: 215). (Extrapolating from this position, now that the West's principal cultural Other is no longer Soviet-style communism but radical Islam, it is telling that attempts to reclaim what is meant by the 'spiritual' are broadly afoot in such coinages as remodernism, performatism, renewalism, and metamodernism. Certainly, this is a preferable alternative to Samuel Huntington's 'Clash of Civilizations' thesis.)

Whether strictly Jamesonian or not, however, this view has obvious limits. It is not enough to say that both postmodernism and whatever terms supplant it are Western-centric: that insight is not new, and in the case of Bourriaud's altermodernism, it is not strictly true, either. What is missing from this diagnosis – and it is, perhaps, the single most glaring omission from all these attempts to describe the culture of the early twenty-first century – is that it is no longer correct to regard the West, and specifically America, as the world's only superpower. The remarkable rise of a Chinese superpower seems to portend that any globalization of the world's culture is unlikely to be a solely Western-dominated tendency. So if the Jamesonian method of analysing cultural change in terms of the West's socioeconomic history is sound, then Jameson's observation that globalization has become the new face of postmodernism will probably turn out to be an insight with a limited shelf-life. In other words, if it is true that the rise and fall of postmodernism and of the culture that follows it are shaped by the economic fortunes of the American superpower and its Western allies, then there is a sizeable oversight in all the eight positions collected in Part Two of the anthology. Whatever set of ideas or terms ultimately comes to supplant the postmodern, it seems likely that it will have to train its eyes further to the East in order to describe the global culture of the century to come accurately.

To sum up, then, what are we to make of the aftermath of the postmodern, and of these various new terms, each claiming, in their different ways, to supplant it? 'Overall', Kirby has observed, 'the (subjective) sense of an ending is more impressive than the (objective) promotion of a beginning' (Kirby 2009: 44). We would put the matter slightly differently. Just over a decade ago, when Klaus Stierstorfer edited the volume *Beyond Postmodernism: Reassessments in Literature, Theory, and Culture*, there were still a number of contributors refusing to concede that postmodernism was finished, and several more whose 'reassessments in literature, theory, and culture' remained deeply indebted to the postmodernism they claimed was outmoded. The same could be said in 2007, when Pelagia Goulimari edited a similar volume entitled *Postmodernism: What Moment?* However, with the twenty-first century now well into its second decade, we believe that the sense of an ending that Kirby found 'subjective' is no longer so: it is an overwhelming fact. The rush to distance the contemporary from the postmodern has accelerated dramatically and palpably. Indeed, Kirby seems to have sensed this acceleration too. When discussing the successors to postmodernism in his book *Digimodernism*, he felt they 'seem to jostle like impatient listeners at the reading of a will' (Kirby 2009: 44). Just one year later – and it should be pointed out that during this year, Nicolas Bourriaud, Robert Samuels, and Josh Toth, as well as Kirby himself, had each published a book endeavouring to supplant the postmodern – he had changed his tune somewhat: 'Increasingly, these theories feel less like ambitious rivals hoping to inherit postmodernism's estate before the body is even cold than pieces of a jigsaw puzzle whose final picture is still unclear' (Kirby 2010a: np).

This is a judicious observation: the new beginnings collected in this anthology have some way to go before they have established themselves sufficiently to be called 'objective', to use Kirby's term. They remain tentative yet intriguing formulations, which collectively hold out great promise, but individually often sound somewhat impressionistic. Needless to say, we do not venture to predict which of these movements will develop into a fully-fledged school of thought of the magnitude that the postmodern had. (On balance, we rather suspect that a term to finally supplant the postmodern has yet to be coined. Another, closely related suspicion is that the variety of contrasting positions collected in this book suggests that the postmodern is not likely to be supplanted by a single catch-all term.) Nor, let it be understood, should the inclusion of any of the writings herein be interpreted as lending them our endorsement. (For whatever it may be worth, one of the editors is enthused by metamodernism and hypermodernism, while the other alternates between a digimodernist cultural pessimism and an automodernist ambivalence.) Thus, as will be seen from the final section of this book, each of the editors draws a somewhat different conclusion from the writings it contains: indeed, our conclusions are in some ways at odds with each other, as is no doubt fitting given the range of contrasting positions in this anthology.

Just over a decade ago, Klaus Stierstorfer wrote that 'No consensus could be established on the specific forms and themes which distinctly pointed "beyond" postmodernism' (Stierstorfer 2003: 3). In the final analysis, this verdict still stands, though for something like the opposite reason – most of the neologisms herein have been coined during the intervening decade, so that the issue is no longer a lack of alternatives to the postmodern, but a multitude of them. As we have seen, a number of clear tendencies can be diagnosed amongst these positions. So it would be an exaggeration to say that what will supplant the postmodern is anyone's guess. But that does not mean it is possible yet to crown postmodernism's heir apparent. Doubtless, some readers will find it disappointing that this Introduction does not conclude with an answer to the question of what postmodernism will be supplanted by. We share this disappointment, for reasons that are roughly those given by Stanley Cavell in response to a different question:

> A familiar answer is that time will tell. But my question is: *What* will time tell? That certain departures in art-like pursuits have become established (among certain audiences, in textbooks, on walls, in college courses); that *someone* is treating them with the respect due, we feel, to art; that one no longer has the right to question their status? But in waiting for time to tell that, we miss what the present tells.

(Cavell 2001: 188)

Given this sense of cultural urgency, the principal purpose of this anthology is not to indulge in prophecies about what the future will look like once the postmodern has receded into cultural memory, but rather to enable our readers to answer the question 'What supplants the postmodern?' for themselves.

References

Adamson, Glenn and Jane Pavitt (eds) (2011), *Postmodernism: Style and Subversion, 1970–1990*, London: V&A Publishing.

Barnes, Julian (2011), *The Sense of an Ending*, London: Vintage.

Bauman, Zygmunt and Keith Tester (2007), 'On the Postmodern Debate', in Pelagia Goulimari (ed.) *Postmodernism: What Moment?*, 22–31, Manchester: Manchester University Press.

Cavell, Stanley (2001), *Must We Mean What We Say? A Book of Essays*, New Edition, Cambridge: Cambridge University Press.

De Man, Paul (1986), *The Resistance to Theory*, Minneapolis: University of Minnesota Press.

Goulimari, Pelagia (ed.) (2007), *Postmodernism: What Moment?*, Manchester: Manchester University Press.

Hoberek, Andrew (ed.) (2007), 'After Postmodernism: Form and History in Contemporary American Fiction.' Special Issue of *Twentieth-Century Fiction*, 53 (3): 233–420.

Jameson, Fredric (2007), 'Postscript', in Pelagia Goulimari (ed.) *Postmodernism: What Moment?*, 213–16, Manchester: Manchester University Press.

Kang, Minsoo (2005), 'The Death of the Postmodern and the Post-Ironic Lull', in *The Post-Ironic Lull: A Show and a Discussion*, exhibition catalogue, St Louis: UMSL Galaxy.

Kirby, Alan (2009), *Digimodernism: How New Technologies Dismantle the Postmodern and Reconfigure Our Culture*, London: Continuum.

Kirby, Alan (2010a), 'Successor States to an Empire in Free Fall', *Times Higher Education Supplement*, 27 May 2010, available at http://www.timeshighereducation.co.uk/411731.article

Kirby, Alan (2010b), Twitter feed (https://twitter.com/Digimodernist), Tweet posted 4 August 2010.

Lopez, José and Gary Potter (eds) (2001), *After Postmodernism: An Introduction to Critical Realism*, New York: Athlone.

Stierstorfer, Klaus (ed.) (2003), *Beyond Postmodernism: Reassessments in Literature, Theory, and Culture*, Berlin and New York: Walter de Gruyter.

Turner, Tom (1996), *City as Landscape: A Post-Postmodern View of Design and Planning*, London: Chapman & Hall.

Wittgenstein, Ludwig (1965), *The Blue and Brown Books: Preliminary Studies for the 'Philosophical Investigations'*, New York: Harper Torchbooks.

Wittgenstein, Ludwig (1968), *Philosophical Investigations*, trans. G.E.M. Anscombe, Oxford: Basil Blackwell.

Ziegler, Heide (ed.) (1993), *The End of Postmodernism: New Directions. Proceedings of the First Stuttgart Seminar in Cultural Studies 04.08.–18.08.1991*, Stuttgart: M & P Verlag für Wissenschaft und Forschung.

Exploring this Anthology

All of the texts anthologized in this book are prefaced by brief introductions that summarize their main points and indicate some of their strengths and weaknesses. Comparisons and contrasts with other writings included herein are also suggested briefly, where appropriate. However, because the anthology is divided into two main parts – one charting the downfall of postmodernism and the other exploring its aftermath – its structure might lead a casual reader to regard these two sets of debates as separate from one another. To help forestall this possibility, here are some suggestions for reading each of the texts of Part One in conjunction with texts from Part Two.

Linda Hutcheon's writings share small-scale connections with a variety of the texts in Part Two. Her puzzling claim that postmodernism is both over and ongoing is borne out by similar arguments in renewalism and metamodernism; her nod towards the role of information and communication technologies in supplanting the postmodern is extrapolated in automodernism and digimodernism; and her mention of globalization as a factor in this process has an amount in common with altermodernism.

Ihab Hassan's essay, in attempting to reclaim the concepts of 'spirit' or 'spirituality' and to reassert their importance, can be read (to slightly differing extents) alongside the various formulations of remodernism, performatism, and metamodernism. His call for a reassessment of the category of realism matches similar calls in the project of renewalism.

Steven Connor provides a concise historical overview of the origins and development of postmodernism, partly through a study of its usage as a term. This may seem to have little in common with the various efforts to supplant it in Part Two, yet Connor's conclusion overlaps with one of the key contentions of both renewalism and metamodernism: they all concur that postmodernism is not simply over and done with, because it still has a persistent influence over its aftermath.

Alan Kirby's account of the death of postmodernism can most obviously be read in conjunction with his writings on the concomitant rise of digimodernism. Another, subtly different perspective of the role of technological change in supplanting the postmodern is set out by Robert Samuels in his writings on automodernism. Gilles Lipovetsky's notion of hypermodernism offers a more measured version of Kirby's scathing views on the effects of consumerism on contemporary culture.

John McGowan's essay would best be read alongside *all* the writings in Part Two, though it shares common ground with none of them. This may sound unhelpful, so perhaps an explanation is required: the essay can be compared with none of the writings in Part Two because McGowan focuses more on performing an autopsy on postmodernism than on supplanting it; yet it would best be read alongside all of them because McGowan describes, in effect, the kind of plate to which a worthy successor must step up.

Jeffrey T. Nealon contends that postmodernism has been supplanted by economic forces, because globalization is a more intensified phase of capitalism than what Jameson optimistically designated 'late capitalism'. Nealon's critique of globalization can be read as a contrast or challenge to Nicolas Bourriaud's more sanguine view of it, as per his writings on altermodernism. For a position that chimes more closely with Nealon's, see Gilles Lipovetsky's formulation of hypermodernism: its emphasis on the effects of rampant consumerism corroborates Nealon's emphasis on the economic.

Part One

The Sense of an Ending

1

Epilogue: The Postmodern … in Retrospect *and* Gone Forever, But Here To Stay: The Legacy of the Postmodern

Linda Hutcheon

In the 1980s and 1990s, Linda Hutcheon's work on the postmodern helped to define the field, and established her in the front rank of expert commentators upon it. The following extracts, however, written in the first decade of the twenty-first century, revisit the topic of postmodernism with the benefit of hindsight. In an epilogue written for a new edition of her classic text The Politics of Postmodernism, *Hutcheon penned an oft-cited turn of phrase that sums up the view from this vantage point bluntly: 'Let's just say: it's over.'*

Postmodernism, for Hutcheon, owed much of its success to its status as a counter-discourse. Accordingly, it forged alliances with various movements in identity politics, most notably feminism, but also postcolonialism and queer theory. But postmodernism's very success led to its rapid institutionalization: it attained a canonical status within the structures of higher education and the culture industries that did not sit well with its rhetoric of subversiveness, and that in turn alienated its erstwhile support base in oppositional politics.

The second of Hutcheon's texts nevertheless explores the ongoing relevance and persistence of the postmodern. While postmodernism's failure to engage directly with political questions of agency and its preference for deconstructive scepticism over constructive debate may seem frustrating, she argues – in a classically postmodern 'both/and'-style argument – that postmodernism nevertheless serves as a valuable and irreplaceable opening into the demystifying of contemporary culture, which furthers the critique of its politics and its representations.

As an aside, it is noteworthy that Hutcheon suggests that the new media and communications technologies of the digital age, together with the tendency towards globalization (these two not being wholly unrelated), have wrought changes that have transformed the world and the culture postmodernism sought to describe. This argument is expanded by other critics later in this section: Alan Kirby elaborates on the effect of digitalization in supplanting the postmodern, and Jeffrey T. Nealon explores the impact of globalization. Interestingly, the same ideas underpin some of the formulations explored in Part Two: automodernism and digimodernism emphasize the role of digital technologies in the outmoding of postmodernism, while altermodernism flags up the role of globalization.

The extracts are from Linda Hutcheon, 'Epilogue: The Postmodern … in Retrospect' in *The Politics of Postmodernism*, 2nd edition (London and New York: Routledge, 2002), pp. 165–7 and pp. 180–1; and 'Gone Forever, But Here to Stay: The Legacy of the Postmodern' in *Postmodernism: What Moment?*, ed. Pelagia Goulimari (Manchester: Manchester University Press, 2007), pp. 16–18.

Epilogue: The Postmodern … in Retrospect

'What was postmodernism?'

John Frow's 1990 question is just as relevant today, in our new millennium, as it was when initially asked – in other words, just after *The Politics of Postmodernism* was first published. While Frow was already using the past tense, I can't help noticing that I resolutely stayed with the present tense in writing the previous chapters – a reflection, no doubt, of my sense of excitement: the postmodern was in the process of defining itself before my very eyes (and ears). Today, our perspective is inevitably going to be different. Despite attempts to move 'the post-modern critique forward' (Allan 1998), to generalize it into a 'theory of the contemporary' (Connor 1989), or to pluralize it into the more descriptive postmodernisms (Altieri 1998), the postmodern may well be a twentieth-century phenomenon, that is, a thing of the past. Now fully institutionalized, it has its canonized texts, its anthologies, primers and readers, its dictionaries and its histories. [...] We could even say it has its own publishing houses – including this one. A *Postmodernism for Beginners* (Appignanesi 1995) now exists; teachers' guides proliferate. For over a decade, diagnosticians have been pronouncing on its health, if not its demise (see, for a sampling, McGowan 1991; Rose 1991; Zurbrugg 1993; Morawski 1996), with some of the major players in the debate weighing in on the negative side: for people like Terry Eagleton (1996) and Christopher Norris (1990; 1993; 1994), postmodernism is finished, passé; indeed, for them it's a failure, an illusion.

Let's just say: it's over. What we have witnessed in the last ten or fifteen years and what I'd like to explore in this epilogue is not only the institutionalization of the postmodern, but its transformation into a kind of generic counter-discourse (Terdiman 1985) of the 1990s, overlapping in its ends and means (but by no means interchangeable) with feminism and postcolonialisrn, as well as with queer, race and ethnicity theory. What these various forms of identity politics share with the postmodern is a focus on difference and ex-centricity, an interest in the hybrid, the heterogeneous, and the local, and an interrogative and deconstructing mode of analysis. Each one of these, however, has had its own specific artistic and social history; each too has had a different politics, as we shall see. Postmodernism in both fiction and photography [...] could be said to have been born of the particular confrontation between realist referentialism and modernist reflexivity, between the historical and the parodic, or the documentary and the intertextual. But this particular confrontation ended in a typically postmodern truce: no 'either/or' decision was required; the more inclusive 'both/and' prevailed. That very inclusivity, however, became the mark of its potentially complicitous critique and the beginning of the problems identity politics would have with the postmodern.

Since the focus of this study was on artistic practices and on the critical discourses used to analyze them – in other words, on their reception – postmodernism could not simply be treated as a matter of style: it inevitably also involved the ideology of representation, including self-representation. It was over the issue of the access to and means of self-representation that the feminists and the postmodern first met in the 1980s; it would be over this same issue that the postmodern would make the acquaintance of the postcolonial (and others) in the 1990s. These fortuitous meetings worked not only to hone postmodern theory's focus, but also to increase its reflexive awareness of its pragmatic limitations in actual interventionist arenas. Of necessity, then, the definitions offered of the postmodern have continued to proliferate, and Brian McHale's early (1987) query – 'whose postmodernism?' – still has to be answered before this complex phenomenon can be addressed in any sensible way. But this is perhaps as it should be – in a decentered postmodern context. Homi Bhabha used the idea of 'acting from the midst of identities' (1997: 438) to describe his response to the problematic and agonistic state of hybridity that many live today because of race. But if we add creed, gender, sexual choice and class, we can see that postmodern theorists – like all others – are bound to theorize (and thus to theorize differently) from a state of multiple identities. As Edward Said has put it: 'No one has ever devised a method for detaching the scholar from the circumstances of life, from the fact of his involvement (conscious or unconscious) with a class, a set of beliefs, a social position, or from the mere activity of being a member of society. These continue to bear on what he does professionally' (1979: 10). They continue to bear on what *she* does too, of course.

Even if the postmodern is over today, it is likely safe to say that it has persisted nonetheless as a 'space for debate' (Malpas 2001: 1). This is true whether the focus is, as in this book, on postmodernism as an aesthetic phenomenon or on postmodernity as a general social condition. What studies of both of these angles of vision share is the impact of poststructuralist theory (for an extended analysis of this sharing, see Bertens 1995); in addition, everything from communications technology to multiculturalism inevitably spills over from the general culture of postmodernity into the particulars of aesthetic postmodernism. Yet, the use of the term 'the postmodern' blurs the distinctions between the two, and much of the work of the last decade has consciously decided to allow (or produce) that blurring. Because of a mutual focus on 'culture', it is admittedly hard to draw the line between discussions of postmodernism in the arts and postmodernity in social or political terms. Yet such distinctions (and their disciplinary correlates) may be worth attempting, however artificially and provisionally, in order to get a clearer sense of developments and changes in the different realms over the last 15 years.

[. . .]

I have never felt comfortable moving from a predetermined theoretical stance to its 'application' in the analysis of texts; in (perhaps perverse) reverse order, I've always sought to theorize from – to learn from – texts. Therefore, my interest has not been in the producer, but in the text and its reception in the world. The problem, I discovered, is that when parody is involved – as it so often is in postmodern fiction and photography – we inevitably posit intentionality in our very designation of a text as parodic: at the very least, when we call something a parody, we *infer* that someone intended this to be a parody of something else (see Hutcheon 1985: 84–99; 1995: 116–40). This act of interpretive inference is not, however, a retrograde act, even in a poststructuralist and textualized theoretical universe; it is simply the particular form that the readerly/viewerly hermeneutic engagement takes when parodies are brought to bear upon parodied texts. And arguably it is through understanding what is at stake in such hermeneutic activities that postmodernism as a *textualized* phenomenon can be seen to have worldly implications and consequences. When texts are placed together in a parodic relationship – Salman Rushdie's *Midnight's Children* and Laurence Sterne's *Tristram Shandy*, for instance – it is not only their formal connections that are brought to our attention; instead, the similarities of form point to the ironized differences of both content and form. This is where the satiric power of ironic juxtaposition comes into play; this is how Rushdie can articulate both his (postmodern) ambivalence about his cultural debt to a British aesthetic tradition and his (postcolonial) contestation of British imperial domination – cultural, historical, and political. As Roland Barthes once put it: 'To parody a well-known saying, I shall say that a little formalism turns one away from History, but that a lot brings one back to it' (1973: 112).

While in *The Politics of Postmodernism: History, Theory Fiction*, I argued this position in much more detail, I now find myself once again wondering if times have changed, if the postmodern is indeed over. Why? It seems to me that our concepts of both textuality and worldliness are in the process of changing – likely forever. Electronic technology and globalization, respectively, have transformed how we experience the language we use and the social world in which we live. For many, these changes are simply other manifestations of postmodernity (Kroker 1992; Kariel 1989). But what if we considered these as the first signs of what will come *after* the postmodern? The intertextual, interactive aesthetic suggested by hypertextuality is related to the postmodern, to be sure, but is it the same thing? What if postmodern parody were merely the preparatory step to a 'Net' aesthetic, utopianly defined as a 'nonlinear, multivocal, open, nonhierarchical aesthetic involving active encounters' (Odin 1997: 599)? And what about the visual as well as verbal dimensions of electronic creation? British novelist Jeanette Winterson has announced that her current project is a series of on-line texts commissioned by the BBC – to be combined and presented as a single drama at the end.

Given all these changes, it seems appropriate to end the epilogue of a book on postmodern politics with these kinds of questions, for I am convinced that the answers we might come up with will have profound political implications for both the textual and the worldly dimensions of our culture in the future. The postmodern moment has passed, even if its discursive strategies and its ideological critique continue to live on – as do those of modernism – in our contemporary twenty-first-century world. Literary historical categories like modernism and postmodernism are, after all, only heuristic labels that we create in our attempts to chart cultural changes and continuities. Post-postmodernism needs a new label of its own, and I conclude, therefore, with this challenge to readers to find it – and name it for the twenty-first century.

References

Allan, Kenneth (1998), *The Meaning of Culture: Moving the Postmodern Critique Forward*, Westport, Conn: Praeger.

Altieri, Charles (1998), *Postmodernisms Now: Essays on Contemporaneity in the Arts*, University Park, Penn: Pennsylvania State University Press.

Appignanesi, Richard (1995), *Postmodernism for Beginners*, Cambridge: Icon Books.

Barthes, Roland (1973), *Mythologies*, trans. Annette Lavers, London: Granada.

Bertens, Hans (1995), *The Idea of the Postmodern: A History*, London and New York: Routledge.

Bhabha, Homi (1997), 'Minority Maneuvers and Unsettled Negotiations', *Critical Inquiry*, (23) 3: 431–59.

Connor, Steven (1989), *Postmodernist Culture: An Introduction to Theories of the Contemporary*, Oxford: Blackwell.

Eagleton, Terry (1996), *The Illusions of Postmodernism*, Oxford and Cambridge, Mass: Blackwell.

Frow, John (1990), 'What Was Postmodernism?' in Ian Adam and Helen Tiffin (eds), *Past the Last Post: Theorizing Post-Colonialism and Post-Modernism*, Calgary: University of Calgary Press, 139–59.

Hutcheon, Linda (1985), *A Theory of Parody: The Teachings of Twentieth-Century Art Forms*, London and New York: Methuen.

Hutcheon, Linda (1995), *Irony's Edge: The Theory and Politics of Irony*, London and New York: Routledge.

Kariel, Henry S. (1989), *The Desperate Politics of Postmodernism*, Amherst: University of Massachusetts Press.

Kroker, Arthur (1992), *The Possessed Individual: Technology and Postmodernity*, London: Macmillan.

Malpas, Simon (2001), *Postmodern Debates*, New York: Palgrave.

McGowan, John (1991), *Postmodernism and its Critics*, Ithaca, NY: Cornell University Press.

McHale, Brian (1987), *Postmodernist Fiction*, London and New York: Methuen.

Morawski, Stefan (1996), *The Troubles with Postmodernism*, London and New York: Routledge.

Norris, Christopher (1990), *What's Wrong with Postmodernism: Critical Theory and the Ends of Philosophy*, Baltimore: Johns Hopkins University Press.

Norris, Christopher (1993), *The Truth about Postmodernism*, Oxford: Blackwell.

Norris, Christopher (1994), *Truth and the Ethics of Criticism*, Manchester: Manchester University Press.

Odin, Jaishree K. (1997), 'The Edge of Difference: Negotiating between the Hypertextual and the Postcolonial', *Modern Fiction Studies*, 43 (3): 598–630.

Rose, Margaret A. (1991), *The Post-Modern and the Post-Industrial: A Critical Analysis*, Cambridge: Cambridge University Press.

Said, Edward W. (1979), *Orientalism*, New York: Vintage.

Terdiman, Richard (1985), *Discourse/Counter-discourse: The Theory and Practice of Symbolic Resistance in Nineteenth-Century France*, Ithaca, NY: Cornell University Press.

Zurbrugg, Nicholas (1993), *The Parameters of Postmodernism*, Carbondale, Ill: Southern Illinois University Press.

Gone Forever, But Here To Stay: The Legacy of the Postmodern

Two opposing impulses clashed in the late twentieth-century writing of the cultural history of the postmodern. On the one hand, as John Frow asked so presciently in 1990, 'what was postmodernism?' Terry Eagleton and Christopher Norris were among the many who confirmed the past-ness of the tense by declaring the postmodern not only over but also a failure. On the other hand, in 1998 Charles Altieri forcefully articulated the sense many others retained of the astounding plural-ness and abiding present-ness of the phenomenon in his title *Postmodernisms Now*. At the century's end, this position suggested, postmodernism was still alive and indeed thriving.

What about now, in the twenty-first century, in the brave new world of globalization, diaspora, electronic technology? Is any kind of helpful or even heuristic historical perspective possible yet? With the benefit of hindsight, we can certainly look back and watch the usage of the word 'postmodern' spread across domains, from architecture to literature and philosophy, and from there to other art forms and other 'human sciences'. We can see that the final decades of the last century witnessed the institutionalization of the postmodern in the academy, the publishing and movie industries, the art gallery, and the theatre, concert, and opera stage. With this institutionalization came what can only be called a generalization of postmodernism into a kind of generic counter-discourse, but paradoxically one well on its way to becoming a discourse, a *doxa*.

At this point we can observe that other competing counter-discourses – those of identity politics, in particular – clearly sensed trouble. Fearing the absorption of their own specific interventionary oppositional agendas into those of some generic category called postmodernism and deeply suspicious of the postmodern's apparent lack of a theory of political agency, feminists in the 1980s were among the first to attack postmodernism's complicitous form of critique, its tendency to deconstruct cultural monoliths but never to reconstruct. As Seyla Benhabib put it, postmodernism 'in its infinitely skeptical and subversive attitude toward normative claims, institutional justice and political struggles, is certainly refreshing. Yet it is also debilitating' (1992: 15). Ajay Heble took up this critique to argue that, for oppositional critics, the value of postmodern theory's suspicion of truth-claims and its denaturalizing and demystifying impulses had been compromised by its very institutionalization (1996: 78). Postmodernism's deliberate open-endedness, its 'both/and' thinking, and its resolute lack of resolution risked immobilizing oppressed people, he argued. As postcolonial theorists insisted (echoing feminists before them), it can be hard to achieve activist ends (with firm moral values) in a postmodern world where such values are not permitted to be grounded, where no utopian possibility is left unironized.

Where does this leave the postmodern politically today? Is it dead or alive? The answer is: 'yes'. In other words, 'both/and' is more appropriate than 'either/or' in addressing this issue. In the twenty-first century too, all evidence points to the realization that it is no longer enough simply to focus attention on ex-centricity, marginality, and difference as part of a demystifying process – though that may still be considered a crucial first step to action. Nevertheless, there are others – Elizabeth Ermarth, among them – who wish to remind us of the *potential* that still lies in what she calls the 'generous impulses of postmodernity' in the political arena:

> the postmodern condition re-opens political options that the culture of modernity has increasingly suppressed by its search for unity, rationality, and non-contradiction. Postmodernity acknowledges and even features precisely the inescapability of contradiction, of unmediatable difference; it shifts emphasis from rational resolution to negotiated contradiction in ways that have profoundly political implications.
>
> (2001: 39)

Le postmodernisme est mort; vive le postmodernisme!

References

Altieri, Charles (1998), *Postmodernisms Now: Essays on Contemporaneity in the Arts*, University Park, Penn: Pennsylvania State University Press.

Benhabib, Seyla (1992), *Situating the Self: Gender, Community, and Postmodernism in Contemporary Ethics*, New York: Routledge.

Eagleton, Terry (1996), *The Illusions of Postmodernism*, Cambridge, MA and Oxford: Blackwell.

Ermarth, Elizabeth (2001), 'Agency in the Discursive Condition', *History and Theory* 40 (4): 34–58.

Frow, John (1990), 'What Was Postmodernism?' in Ian Adam and Helen Tiffin (eds),
    Past the Last Post: Theorizing Post-Colonialism and Post-Modernism, Calgary:
    University of Calgary Press, 139–59.
Heble, Ajay (1996), 'New Contexts of Canadian Criticism: Democracy, Counterpoint,
    Responsibility' in Ajay Heble, Donna Palmateer Pennee and J.R. (Tim) Struthers
    (eds) *New Contests of Canadian Criticism*, 78–97, Peterborough, ON: Broadview.
Norris, Christopher (1990), *What's Wrong with Postmodernism: Critical Theory and the
    Ends of Philosophy*, Baltimore: Johns Hopkins University Press.

2

Beyond Postmodernism: Toward an Aesthetic of Trust

Ihab Hassan

In the 1970s and 1980s, Ihab Hassan's work was a seminal influence in the diagnosis of postmodernist tendencies in post-war literature. His stature as a figure in the canon of postmodern literary criticism is immense. In this essay, however, Hassan steps back from some of the orthodoxies and platitudes that have become common currency in the debates around postmodernism, in order to ask what might lie 'beyond' it.

Hassan begins by observing that one of the strongest and most important of impetuses behind the advent of postmodernism was a sense of crisis in identity – that is, a deep-felt need to assert plurality, multiplicity, and diversity in the categories and terms used to describe our identities. This identity crisis, however, has not resulted in the hoped-for respect for difference, otherness, and alterity so optimistically envisaged by postmodernists: rather, it has tended increasingly to manifest itself in the forms of tribalism, fundamentalism, the 'clash of civilizations', and even genocide. Hence, as monolithic 'catch-all' identities were, in postmodern fashion, broken down into numerous micronarratives, the sense of a public sphere was accordingly abandoned, and with it, the ground on which civil society is based, which in turn only hastened the breakdown into ever smaller, more 'self'-centred identities.

In the face of this fallout from postmodernism, Hassan argues the need for a sense of 'planetary civility'. He attaches great importance to re-establishing the concepts of trust and truth – trust being the precondition for a society founded on the mutual respect of difference. Where postmodernism jettisoned the notion of 'truth' altogether, Hassan asserts the importance of retaining a pragmatist notion of truth, one which nevertheless remains compatible with the postmodern critique of universal truth. Without some yardstick of truth, he believes, it becomes impossible to uphold shared values such as human rights, or to work together to save the environment.

Hassan's early work on postmodern literature did much to highlight its playful use of experimental narrative devices, and indeed its metafictional undermining of narrative itself, resulting in a tendency towards scepticism, unreliability, and uncertainty. Here, however, he revisits this view: scepticism about reality is not a strategy that is conducive to a sense of respect for others' identities or for the planet at large. Instead, Hassan describes a need for literature to return to some form of realism in order to do justice to the ethical claims of our increasingly complicated and fraught world. Such a realism needs, however, to be grounded in pragmatism rather than in dogmatism: it is to be a realism grounded on trust as much as on truth, and on subjectivity and identity rather than on external reference. In a nutshell, Hassan is suggesting that postmodernism's path from relativism to nihilism needs to be retrodden, so that a better way of accommodating multiple truths can be found than the postmodern denial of truth itself.

What is remarkable about Hassan's essay – and one of the main reasons for its inclusion in this volume – is the extent to which its vocabulary matches or anticipates that of so many of the movements set out in Part Two. Nicolas Bourriaud's description of altermodernism, for example, stems from a similar intuition that postmodernism's ultimately insular emphasis on micro-identities has, in the era of globalization, been supplanted by a new sense of planetary negotiation between identities. Where Hassan upholds the importance of realism in contemporary literature – 'fiduciary realism', as he calls it – Josh Toth sees 'neo-realism' (which he sometimes calls 'dirty realism') as vital in reconnecting us with the sense of reality abandoned by postmodernism: this task is, for Toth, a fundamental aspect of renewalism. Hassan decries the postmodern flight from any talk of 'spirit' or 'spiritual values'; so do Billy Childish and Charles Thomson, who claim that what they call remodernism aims at a new spirituality in art.

Thus, though Hassan is all too aware that his essay sounds like something of an embarrassing climbdown – a retreat from postmodern relativism to the safer, more familiar, staid terrain of humanism – his is in fact one of the more prescient discussions, antedating and perhaps predicting many of the formulations found in Part Two.

The extract is Ihab Hassan, 'Beyond Postmodernism: Toward an Aesthetic of Trust' in *Beyond Postmodernism: Reassessments in Literature, Theory, and Culture*, ed. Klaus Stierstorfer (Berlin and New York: Walter de Gruyter, 2003), pp. 199–212.

Beyond Postmodernism: Toward an Aesthetic of Trust

and we know at heart how
beauty surely binds,
binds us to otherness
in the sweet jigsaw of creation.

Chris Wallace-Crabbe, 'Beauty: An Ode'

Introduction

My theme is the evolution of postmodernism, or rather, our own evolution in postmodern times. Since I owe readers clarity and concision, which have all but abandoned us in academe, let me focus the issue at the start. What lies beyond postmodernism? Of course, no one knows; we hardly know what postmodernism was.

But questions have a way of inveigling an answer. I will offer a double response in the form of two major intertwined themes: postmodernism expands into geopolitical postmodernity while seeking to become a postmodernism not of suspicion but of trust. The braided strands of this proposition may define the cultural code of our moment. How?

What was postmodernism?

Let us step back for a moment. What was postmodernism in the first place? I am not at all certain, for I know less about it today than I did some thirty years ago. No doubt, that is because I have changed, postmodernism has changed, the world has changed, and historical concepts, unlike Platonic Ideas or geometrical forms, suffer the tyranny of time. Of course, postmodernism was born in strife and nursed in contention; it still remains moot. Lock ten of its foremost proponents in a room, and watch the blood trickle under the door. Hype and hyperbole, parody and kitsch, media glitz and ideological spite, the sheer, insatiable irrealism of consumer societies all helped to turn postmodernism into a conceptual ectoplasm. I cite – from an essay called 'From Postmodernism to Postmodernity' – four current exemplars of the phenomenon, nearly at random:[1]

1. Frank Gehry's Guggenheim Museum in Bilbao (Spain), Ashton Raggatt McDougall's Storey Hall in Melbourne (Australia), and Arata Isozaki's Tsukuba Center (Japan) qualify as postmodern architecture. They depart from the pure angular geometries of the Bauhaus, the minimal steel and glass boxes of Mies van der Rohe, mixing aesthetic and historical elements, flirting with fragments, fantasy, and even vulgarity.
2. In a recent encyclical, titled '*Fides et Ratio*', Pope John Paul II actually used the word postmodernism to condemn extreme relativism in values and beliefs, acute irony and skepticism toward reason, and the denial of any possibility of truth, human or divine – in short, from the Church's point of view, incipient nihilism.
3. In cultural studies, a highly politicized field, the term postmodernism often surrenders to postcolonialism, the former deemed historically feckless, being 'unpolitical' or, worse, not political in the right way. Postcolonialism is deemed a serious concept, postmodernism a light one.
4. In Pop culture, postmodernism – or PoMo as Yuppies call it insouciantly – refers to a wide range of phenomena, from Andy Warhol to Madonna, from the colossal plaster Mona Lisa I saw advertising a *pachinko* parlor in Tokyo to the giant, cardboard figure of Michelangelo's David – pink dayglo glasses, canary shorts, a camera slung across bare, brawny shoulders – advertising Kon Tiki Travel in New Zealand.

What do all these have in common? The answer is familiar by now: fragments, hybridity, relativism, play, parody, pastiche, an ironic, sophistical stance, an ethos bordering on kitsch and camp. So, willy nilly, we have begun to gather a family of words applying to postmodernism; we have begun to sketch a context, if not a definition, for it. More ambitious readers can consult Hans Bertens' *The Idea of the Postmodern*, the best and fairest introduction to the topic I know.[2]

But who needs definitions nowadays, anyway? The desert grows, the desert grows, Nietzsche growled only yesterday, and our mouths now parch with de-definition, with disbelief. Still, rather than construct bizarre tables, contrasting modernism with postmodernism, as certain critics have done, I propose to engage postmodernism in ways that may lead us through it, beyond it.

The equivocal autobiography of an age

In 1784, Immanuel Kant asked, in a celebrated essay, '*Was ist Aufklärung?*'. The question was taken up by Michel Foucault, though we do better to ask ourselves, in terms of this particular occasion, '*Was ist Postmodernismus?*'. How could we ever share the historical poise of the punctual thinker of Königsberg? Versed in suspicion, inward with incredulity, votaries of decenterment, pluralist, pragmatic, polychronic, we can hardly privilege our moment as Kant privileged the Enlightenment. Instead, we betray an abandon of belatedness, a delirium of reflexivity, a limitless anxiety of self-nomination. Who am I, who are we – is that not the chorus of the moment? Perhaps postmodernism can be defined, after all, as a continuous exercise in self-definition. Or perhaps we can simply call it the equivocal autobiography of an age.

This is not altogether flip: two pivotal points are at issue here. One regards the hermeneutic seductions of postmodernism in developed societies. The other relates to the crisis of identity, driving geopolitics in the postwar era (I will return to that idea in discussing *postmodernity*). Let me begin with the former.

Autobiography, as we all know, is a verbal interpretation – not simply recollection, not simply construction – of a life. So is postmodernism a collective interpretation of an age. More than an artistic style or historical trend, more than a personal sensibility or zeitgeist, postmodernism is a hermeneutic device, a habit of interpretation, a way of reading all our signs under the mandate of misprision. I simply mean that we now see the world through postmodern-tinted glasses. Rabelais? Look at all those excesses of parody and pastiche, all those paratactical lists. Sterne? Please, don't be obvious. Jane Austen? See all those self-reflexive ironies, those subtle deconstructions of squirearchy not to mention phallocracy. And so it goes (as Vonnegut would say). Moreover, it's all true, or at least partially true. But not even a *fatwa* would induce me to consider Rabelais, Sterne, and Austen postmodern or, preposterously, pre-postmodern.

Certainly, we read history from the vantage of the present; certainly we write history as narratives, tropic and revisionary. But this gives us no license to cannibalize our past to feed our flesh. History, too, has its pragmatic truth, its otherness, which refuses assimilation to our needs, our desires. History, too, requires our tact, our respect, our trust: I mean that measure of intuition, empathy, and self-discipline enabling every cognitive act.

I hope you do not think I have lost myself in the labyrinths of postmodernism. Words like truth, trust, tact are key to the idiom of this paper, and I will return to them, repeatedly. For the moment, however, I wanted simply to suggest that postmodernism could be understood as a kind of autobiography, an interpretation of our lives in developed societies, linked to an epochal crisis of identity, the other pivotal point.

A global crisis of identity

What, then, is that global crisis of identity? Look everywhere, the evidence chills the blood, boggles the mind. Fortunately, some sane and readable books, like Michael Ignatieff's *Blood and Belonging* and Amin Maalouf's *In the Name of Identity*, help us to awake from this particular nightmare of history.[3] The latter work is especially pertinent here, though I can summarize its generous argument only in the baldest terms.

Maalouf calls for the acceptance of multiple and dynamic identities, without prejudice to any; he rejects, in all of us, a single, static, essential self, 'deep down inside', coercing other allegiances. And he insists on respect, reciprocity, non-exclusiveness, in the exacerbated traffic between fields of cultural force, anthropological zones, estates of personal being. Still, since modernity is so often perceived as 'the hand of the stranger' in many cultures, the shadow of suspicion, indeed of outraged rejection, falls on the West, especially on the United States. In this nexus, a free spirituality, loosely attached, or even unattached, to the need to belong, may prove salutary. Maalouf concludes by enjoining us to act and to dream:

> We must act in such a way as to bring about a situation in which no one feels excluded from the common civilization that is coming into existence; in which everyone may be able to find the language of his own identity and some symbols of his own culture; and in which everyone can identify to some degree with what he sees emerging in the world about him, instead of seeking refuge in an idealized past.[4]

That is, indeed, the practical dream of a pluralist postmodernity. But how is that crisis of identity relevant to postmodernism itself? And how do I distinguish between postmodernism and postmodernity?

In the past, I resorted to a neologism, 'Indetermanence', to interpret postmodernism. I meant to designate two decisive antithetical, but *not* dialectical, tendencies: indeterminacy and immanence.[5] Since then, the double process of 'localization' and 'globalization', as every CEO now glibly says, has become dire. What I had hinted has become the daily grist of our news: I mean the sundry movements of secession, decolonization, separatism, on the one hand, and the fluent imperium of high-tech, media capitalism, on the other – cargo cults here, satellites there, the Taliban in one place, Madonna everywhere. In sum, cultural postmodernism has mutated into genocidal postmodernity (witness Palestine, Bosnia, Kosovo, Ulster, Rwanda, Chechnya, Kurdistan, Sri Lanka, Sudan, Afghanistan, Tibet . . .). But cultural postmodernism itself has also metastasized into sterile, campy, kitschy, jokey, dead-end games or sheer media hype.

To these changes, the world responded with vast changes of its own, changes that I describe as postmodernity.

From postmodernism to postmodernity

This brings me to the first, braided theme of this essay: namely, the expansion of postmodernism into postmodernity. It is as if the breaks, the indeterminacies, of the former have turned into tribalism (postcolonial factions), and the immanences of the former have accelerated world interactions (globalization). I say 'as if' because I distrust large and symmetrical explanations.

In any case, the horrendous facts of postmodernity invade our lives continually: diasporas, migrations, refugees, the killing fields, a crisis of personal and cultural values seemingly without parallel in history. Therefore, we may be forgiven to conclude: a specter is haunting Europe *and* the world – the specter of Identity. Can we wonder that its ghostly steps lead everywhere, from the jungles of the Philippines to those of Peru, from the ruins of the World Trade Center to the wastes of Gaza, from the tenements of Belfast to the mosques of Kashmir?

Some will proffer socio-economic explanations, the inequities of north and south, west and east, which feed the iniquities of the world. Some will adduce vast conflicts of civilizations, which, since 9/11, have given Samuel P. Huntington renewed plausibility. And some will cite sociobiology, the 'epigenetic rules' of E.O. Wilson or the 'mass soul' of Elias Canetti, hard-wired in our species.[6] Yet none of these facts suffices alone, as Amin Maalouf would agree.

Beyond postmodernism, beyond the evasions of poststructuralist theories and pieties of postcolonial studies, we need to discover new relations between selves and others, margins and centers, fragments and wholes – indeed, new relations between selves and selves, margins and margins, centers and centers – discover what I call a new, pragmatic and planetary civility. That's the crux and issue of postmodernity.

But how establish this civility without borders? Needless to say, short of omniscience, short of omnipotence, I find no answer to this query. But I can try to put certain ideas, certain words, into play, words that we have forgotten in academe, words that need, more than refurbishing, reinvention. I mean words like truth, trust, spirit, all uncapitalized, in addition to words like reciprocity and respect, sympathy and empathy, so central to *In the Name of Identity*. Here twines the second strand, or major theme, of the essay.

Truth and trust

If truth is dead, then everything is permitted – because its alternatives, now more than ever, are rank power and rampant desire.

True (pun intended), we no longer share an absolute, transcendent or foundational Truth. But in daily life, we distinguish well enough between truth and falsehood, from little white lies to darker deceptions. It is repugnant to pretend that the atrophy of transcendent truths licenses self-deception or justifies tendentiousness – truth is not *pravda*.

Truth is a single phoneme, but it carries the curse of miscellany, of sundry semantemes. There is traditional truth: what myth and tradition hold to have been always so. There is revealed truth: what a divine, sacred, or supernatural authority declares as true. There is the truth of power: what a tyrant proclaims, believe it or die. There is the truth of political or social or personal expediency: it would be good for the party, or for the community, or for my own interest, to assume such to be the case. There is truth as correspondence: in naïve science and empiricism. There is the more sophisticated truth of scientific falsification: a theory is held true until disproven. There is truth as coherence: in the arts, especially music, in mathematics and logical systems. There is the truth of a poetic intuition: for instance, Yeats's quip that we 'can refute Hegel but not the Saint or the Song of Sixpence'. There is subjective truth: what you intensely feel or experience or desire becomes incontrovertibly so. There are probably other kinds of imbricated truths, and they all revert to some underlying axiom or belief.

William James knew this nearly a century before Rorty or Derrida. In *Pragmatism*, he acknowledges the fecund diversity of truth, a truth, he says '*made*, just as health, wealth, and strength are made, in the course of experience'.[7] But this is *not* an invitation to cynicism, self-interest, or ideological mendacity. For at the heart of James's own philosophical practice is an idea of *trust: truth rests not on transcendence but on trust.* This fiduciary principle is epistemic, ethical, and personal all at the same time, since our trust must also depend on another's trust, and our faith, James remarks in *The Will To Believe*, 'is faith in someone else's faith, and in the greatest matters this is most the case'.[8] Hence the self-defeating character of radical relativism, of extreme particularism, which denies reciprocity, denies both empathy and obligation.

Epistemic trust flows, in Western cultures at least, from evidence, logic, dispassion, trial, doubt – from intuitions and speculations, too, that can earn our unselfish assent. Altruism, like self-criticism, is conducive to trust. Such trust, I have said, is fragile. 'How can one and the same identical fact experience itself so diversely?' James asks in *A Pluralistic Universe*.[9] And in the end – I repeat, *in the end* – he answers that our 'passional natures' must decide '*between propositions, whenever it is a genuine option that cannot by its nature be decided on intellectual grounds*'.[10] But these 'passional natures', I wonder, have they no cognizance of broader restraint, a larger reference?

The question reclaims maligned universals. Both social determinism and cultural constructionism find them anathema. Yet universals, not Platonic but empiric, abound. For instance: languages; human emotions; marks of status; ceremonies of birth, marriage, and death; gods, spirits, taboos and their rituals; not to mention socio-biological imperatives like the sixty-seven cross-cultural practices Wilson lists in *Consilience*.[11] Human beings are not a *terra nullius* colonized by myriad systems of signs. Human beings also create themselves and recreate their environments, and chance and aeons of biological evolution help shape their lives. To hard-core cultural constructionists, I say: browse Matt Ridley's *The Genome Project* or Steven Pinker's *The Blank Slate* to see the intricacies of 'nature' and 'nurture', no longer separable in their interactions.[12] In sum, human beings not only vary infinitely; they also share a portion in the infinite.

Pragmatic or 'soft' universals need not alarm us; they enable both individual and collective judgments. Without them, the U.N. Declaration of Human Rights would vaporize; without them, Amnesty International would whistle in the wind; without them, jurists at the Hague would sit in an empty court; without them, Greenpeace or the Kyoto Protocols would founder in the Pacific. In short, without qualified generalizations, no appeal to reason, freedom, or justice can stand; no victim can find redress, no tyrant retribution.

I am aware of the arguments against Truth (capitalized), from Nietzsche to Derrida. Nietzsche offered the best challenge, first in his youthful essay on 'Truth and Lying in the Ultra Moral Sense', then in his posthumous *Will to Power*. Truth, he said in the earlier essay, is 'a mobile army of metaphors';[13] truth, he later declared, is an aspect of the 'will to power', thus a *'processus in infinitum*, an active determining'.[14] But the Truth he pretends to rout is not pragmatic; it is universal.

William James, we have seen, also abandons the transcendental view of truth, opening it to our 'willing nature', nudging it toward a 'noetic pluralism', a process more than state, subject always to contestation. Still, his view makes place for a will to truth, as strong in certain human beings – the great saints, artists, scientists, intellectuals – as the will to power or the will to believe. Does not Oedipus embody, beyond a shady Freudian complex, that miraculous will to truth – what interest can it possibly serve? – that implacable will to truth, at the cost of self-destruction, entailing blindness, bringing a deeper, luminous sight?

Oedipus here is apt. Truth, I have said, rests on trust, personal, social, cognitive trust. But what is trust? Roundly, I answer: more than consensus, trust depends on self-abnegation, self-emptying, something akin to *kenosis*. It requires dispassion, empathy, attention to others and to the created world, to something not in ourselves. But, ultimately, it demands self-dispossession. That is why truth and trust remain spiritual qualities – not simply psychological, not merely political, but, above all, spiritual values.

At the mention of spirit, some may grit their teeth. So, put spirit aside, if you must; I will not insist on a willing suspension of disbelief. Consider another line of thought. The humanities, by the very nature of their epistemologies, can not resist the incursions of history and politics, ideology and illusion. *But that is precisely why the humanities must not yield to their promiscuous incursions*, which would degrade knowledge, deface evidence, defeat answerability. Truth does matter, as we know from Solzhenitsyn's Nobel Lecture (a single truth is more powerful than all the weapons of the world, he claimed);[15] as we have rediscovered in the Sokal Affair. Truth matters, and the 'calm sunlight of the mind', as Susan Haack put it in her wise *Manifesto of a Passionate Moderate*.[16] We may be all biased, as the jejune slogan goes, but we are not all biased about the same things, or to the same degree, or in the same manner, nor, *above all*, do we all comply with our biases invariably. Discriminations here are the life-blood of thought, nuance is mind. If nothing else, let us recover the truth of tact and nuance, the trust of intellectual courtesy, which tacitly assumes self-control, if not outright *kenosis*.

Realism and the Aesthetic of Trust

I come at last to the aesthetic, to the literary question, in my subtitle: 'Toward an Aesthetic of Trust'.

As you know, Beauty is back in the work of Elaine Scary, Wendy Steiner, Charles Jencks, among others – and I am immensely cheered. But I will consider the aesthetic here from another ambit, that of realism. Realism, you cry, in 2003, *realism*? A moment ago, I spoke of trust as a quality of attention to others, to the created world, to something not in ourselves. Is that not the premise of realism?

Realism is no light matter: it touches the inviolable mystery of mind's relation to the world. It refers us to the enigma of representation, the conundrum of signs, the riddle of language, the chimera of consciousness itself. So let us step gingerly here.

Elsewhere, I have presumed to remark on realism in science, philosophy, painting, photography, and literature, concluding that realism, despite its cunning, is a convention built on answerable faith – something like Santa Claus.[17] Ernst Gombrich summed it up in *Art and Illusion* with wondrous concinnity: 'the world', he said, 'can never quite look like a picture, but a picture can look like the world'.[18]

And in literature? We all know the epochal work of Erich Auerbach, a Teutonic hymn to mimesis. But a reader of that work may well conclude that the great scholar regards the loss of mimesis in modernism with acute ambivalence. The 'uninterpretable symbolism' in the works of Joyce and Woolf; the 'multiple reflection of consciousness' leaving the 'reader with an impression of hopelessness', 'something confusing, something hazy [...] something hostile to the reality which ... [the works] represent'; the 'atmosphere of universal doom' and implied 'hatred of civilization'[19] – Auerbach finds all these distressing in modern literature. At the same time, he fairly recognizes that in the work of Virginia Woolf 'random occurrence' can yield 'something new and elemental ... nothing less than the wealth of reality and depth of life in every moment to which we surrender ourselves without prejudice'.[20]

I am not sure that Saul Bellow or John Updike would disagree with Auerbach. I am not sure that younger writers, like David Malouf (this the Australian not the French Maalouf now) or Salman Rushdie or Vargas Llosa or Michael Ondaatje would disagree either. I am not sure that certain qualified postmodernists would fail to recognize the price literature has paid in renouncing realism altogether. Hence, the innovative, not to say magical, realism in such novels as Malouf's

Remembering Babylon, Rushdie's *Midnight's Children*, Vargas Llosa's *The Notebooks of Don Rigoberto*, Ondaatje's *Anil's Ghost* (which the author claims to be an accurate description of life in Sri Lanka, a claim similar to that of Garcia Marquez about life in his native Colombia).

The critical point here is that literary realism, though it may not suffice, remains indispensable; its discontents spill into, indeed inform, other genres. Myself, I believe that Virginia Woolf's strictures against certain realists – Mr. Wells, Mr. Bennett, Mr. Galsworthy, as she called them with withering courtesy – still stand. They are 'materialists', she wrote in *The Common Reader*, by which she meant that 'they write of unimportant things; that they spend immense skill and immense industry making the trivial and the transitory appear the true and the enduring'.[21] That has ever been the banal flaw of realism. Yet Woolf herself had great faith in the possibilities of the novel, and in the same essay, 'Modern Fiction', she reminds us that there is no limit to the novel's horizon, 'and that nothing – no "method", no experiment, even the wildest – is forbidden, but only falsity and pretense'.[22]

Only falsity and pretense are forbidden: these words lead to my penultimate section.

On spirit and the void

Falsity and pretence stand nearly antithetical to truth and trust. Hence my interest in what I will call fiduciary realism, a postmodern aesthetic of trust. Such an aesthetic would assume 'negative capability' (Keats), but would go farther toward self-emptying; as in Shakespeare, Kafka, or Beckett, it would become acquainted with Silence, with the Void. For Nothing (Nothingness) is the other face of fiduciary realism. Emily Dickinson expressed it stunningly:

> By homely gifts and hindered words
> The human heart is told
> Of nothing –
> 'Nothing' is the force
> That renovates the World –[23]

She might have said as well: 'That renovates the Word'. For a realism of faith must know that Silence or Absence is the ground of language, the ground of Being itself. This idea, surely central to both modernism and postmodernism, makes us all acolytes of the void. This intuition, central again to postmodernism, surely engages spirit as I understand it. But how do I understand, if not define, spirit?

For the last time, I need to step back a little, in order to see past, beyond, postmodernism. By the late eighties, I have said, I began to wonder how postmodernism could recreate its best self. Could it take a spiritual turn? Could the materialist ideologies of the moment open or crack? And what would spirit mean in our intellectual culture of disbelief? Certainly, it would not mean atavism, fundamentalism, or occultism; it may not mean adherence to orthodox religions – Christianity, Judaism, Hinduism, Islam – though it would not exclude them.

I did not answer these questions, though I made a stumbling start in an essay titled 'The Expense of Spirit in Postmodern Times'.[24] There, with some encouragement from figures as diverse as Friedrich Nietzsche, William James, and John Cage, I envisaged a postmodern, spiritual attitude compatible with emergent technologies; with geopolitical realities (population, pollution, the growing obsolescence of the nation state); with the needs of the wretched of the earth; with the interests of feminists and minorities and multicultural societies; with an ecological, planetary humanism; and perhaps even with millennial hopes. I could so envisage the prospects of a postmodern spiritual attitude, without occult bombinations or New Age platitudes, because spirit pervades a variety of secular experiences, from dreams, creative intuitions in art or science, and a sense of the sublime, to extraordinary, visionary states, including the gift of seeing the eternal in the temporal, an apprehension of primal relations in the universe. Indeed, spirit echoes even in geopolitics, as in current debates on the idea of Forgiveness with regard to genocides (see the references to Ricoeur, Derrida, Morin, Kristeva, among others, in a recent issue of *PMLA*).[25]

Dictionaries offer many senses of 'spirit'. These usually center on something fundamental to human existence yet intangible, an activating principle, a cosmic curiosity, a meaning, often religious or metaphysical in character, shading into the ethical yet irreducible to it. This bedrock meaning is not obsolete; for as Saul Bellow noted in his Nobel Lecture of 1976, when distraction increases, so does the desire for essentials.[26] Can that desire be alien to our spiritual impulses? Is it not alive still in the work of another Nobelist, Seamus Heaney, who spoke of poetry as a 'matter of angelic potential, a motion of the soul', and of 'tilting the scales of reality towards some transcendent equilibrium'?[27] Yet spirit does not offer invariable solace. As mystics know – I am *not* one – spirit is exigent; it has its harshness, its clouds of unknowing, its dark nights of the soul. It may begin in agnosticism and end in despair. This is particularly true in postmodern times, times of irony, suspicion, nihilism. Yet even nihilism, at its best, can serve as a penultimate form of lucidity. Thus, as I have insisted, a postmodern spiritual attitude may become deeply acquainted with *kenosis* – self-emptying, yes, but also the self-undoing of our knowledge in the name of something more fundamental than deconstruction: that is, in the name of Reality.

I have no space here to elaborate this concept of unknowing, of cognitive undoing or nescience, a kind of intellectual *via negativa*. I need only repeat that fiduciary realism – a postmodern realism, if any – demands faith and empathy and trust precisely because it rests on Nothingness, the nothingness within all our representations, the final authority of the Void.

Conclusion

My path has been sinuous. Perhaps I can make some amends by carrying forthrightly the argument to its conclusion, a quasi-utopian conclusion, I admit.

What lies beyond postmodernism? In the larger scheme, postmodernity looms, postmodernity with its multiple crises of identity, with its diasporas and genocides, with its desperate negotiations between local practices and global procedures. To call this condition simply postcolonial is to misperceive our world. For colonialism and its afterglow cast only a partial light on our condition; colonialism is not the whole of our history. In this regard, I regret that prominent postcolonial critics have sometimes chosen to tap the vast, often justified, resentments of our moment instead of bringing to it fresh, equitable, and true discernment.

We, in our literary professions, must turn to truth, truth spoken not only to power but, more anguished, truth spoken to ourselves. This cannot be sectarian, self-serving truth, which appeals only to partisans and subverts trust.

Trust, I have claimed, is a spiritual value, inward with self-dispossession, and in its postmodern form, familiar with the void. For only through nihilism is nihilism overcome. Our second innocence is self-heedlessness, and beyond that, 'unknowing'. In the Japanese *Hagakura*, there is a shocking statement, inviting meditation, not explication: 'This man has worth. In the highest level, a man has the look of knowing nothing'.[28] I, for one, would trust such a man. I would also trust Voss, in Patrick White's shattering novel by that name, who at the end of his spiritual agonies in the Australian desert cries: 'Now that I am nothing, I am, and love is the simplest of all tongues'.[29]

Does love have a place in an essay on postmodernism? It does. A postmodern aesthetic of trust, I have argued, brings us to a fiduciary realism, a realism that redefines the relation between subject and object, self and other, in terms of profound trust. Are we not close here to something deeper than empathy, something akin to love? Are we not broaching, beyond realism, Reality?

An aesthetic of trust is, ultimately, a stance toward Reality, not toward objects. At the *far limit*, such a stance demands identification with Reality itself, dissolution of the distinction between the I and not-I. Emerson said it famously in 'Nature': '[…] all mean egotism vanishes. I become a transparent eyeball. I am nothing, I see all'.[30] That is the horizon, infinitely far, attainable only by the elect, toward which fiduciary realism tends.

I repeat: it is a *horizon*, seen and perhaps imagined but never reached. But in the sublunary world we inhabit, fiduciary realism must content itself with humbler aims. It needs only acknowledge its debt to spirit, its wide attentiveness, its intuition of *kenosis*. Such an intuition may also assuage the trials of postmodernity, the clamors of identity – sages say, the solution to identity is, get lost – thus linking our two themes, cultural postmodernism and global postmodernity. Identities created by an assured way of being in the world flow toward ultimate mysteries, sometimes called sacred, beyond the horizons of their assurance. And they can do so without benefit of dogma – church, mosque, temple, shrine – because spirit finally empties itself out of its own forms. But even that acknowledgment may put on postmodernists too great a demand. Perhaps it will suffice, on any good day, for fiduciary realism, to follow the advice of David Malouf in *Remembering Babylon*:

> [T]he very habit and faculty that makes apprehensible to us what is known and expected dulls our sensitivity to other forms, even with the most obvious. We must rub our eyes and look again, clear our minds of what we are looking for to see what is there.[31]

Rub your eyes, rub them, please, without undue reflexivity, and without prejudice to Creation. That is my charge to postmodernists, which I hope is neither nostalgic nor utopian.

Notes

1 Ihab Hassan, 'From Postmodernism to Postmodernity', *Philosophy and Literature* 25, 1 (April 2001), 1–13.

2 Hans Bertens, *The Idea of the Postmodern* (London, New York: Routledge, 1995).

3 Michael Ignatieff, *Blood and Belonging: Journeys Into the New Nationalism* (New York: Farrar, Straus & Giroux, 1993); Amin Maalouf, *In the Name of Identity: Violence and the Need to Belong*, tr. Barbara Bray (New York: Arcade Publishing, 2001).

4 Maalouf, *In the Name of Identity*, 163.

5 See Ihab Hassan, 'Culture, Indeterminacy, and Immanence' in id., *The Postmodern Turn. Essays in Postmodern Theory and Culture* (Columbus, OH: Ohio State UP, 1987), and the 'Postscript' in id., *The Dismemberment of Orpheus* (Madison, WI: U of Wisconsin P, 1982).

6 Elias Canetti, *Auto-da-fe* (New York: Seabury Press, 1978); E.O. Wilson, *Consilience: The Unity of Knowledge* (New York: Random House, 1998).

7 William James, *Pragmatism* (New York: Meridian Books, 1955), 143.

8 William James, *The Will to Believe and Other Essays in Popular Philosophy* (New York: Dover Publications, 1956), 9.

9 William James, *A Pluralistic Universe* (Cambridge, MA: Harvard UP, 1977), 94–95.

10 James, *The Will to Believe*, 11.

11 Wilson, *Consilience*, 160–61.

12 Matt Ridley, *The Genome Project* (New York: HarperCollins, 1999); Steven Pinker, *The Blank Slate* (New York: Viking, 2002).

13 Friedrich Nietzsche, 'Truth and Falsity in an Ultramoral Sense' in Geoffrey Clive (ed.), *The Philosophy of Nietzsche* (New York: New American Library, 1965), 508.

14 Friedrich Nietzsche, *The Will to Power*, tr. Walter J. Kaufmann, R.J. Hollingdale (New York: Random House, 1967), 298.

15 Aleksandr Solzhenitsyn, *The Nobel Lecture on Literature*, tr. Thomas P. Whitney (New York: Harper & Row, 1972).

16 Susan Haack, *Manifesto of a Passionate Moderate: Unfashionable Essays* (Chicago: Chicago UP, 1998), 5.

17 Ihab Hassan, 'Realism, Truth, Trust: Reflections of Mind in the World' in id., *Symbolism and Third Text* (forthcoming).

18 E.H. Gombrich, *Art and Illusion: A Study in the Psychology of Pictorial Representation* (Princeton, NJ: Princeton UP, 1972), 395.

19 Erich Auerbach, *The Representation of Reality in Western Literature*, tr. Willard R. Trask (Princeton, NJ: Princeton UP, 1953), 551.

20 Auerbach, *The Representation of Reality*, 552.

21 Virginia Woolf, *The Common Reader* (London: The Hogarth Press, 1951), 187.

22 Woolf, *The Common Reader*, 194.

23 R.W. Franklin (ed.), *The Poems of Emily Dickinson*, Variorum Edition (Cambridge, Massachusetts: The Belknap Press of Harvard UP, 1998), III, 1413.

24 Ihab Hassan, 'The Expense of Spirit in Postmodern Times: Between Nihilism and Belief', *Georgia Review* 51, 1 (Spring 1997).

25 *PMLA* 117, 2 (March 2002).

26 Saul Bellow, *It All Adds Up: From the Dim Past to the Uncertain Future* (New York: Viking Penguin, 1994).

27 Seamus Heaney, *The Redress of Poetry* (New York: Farrar, Strauss, and Giroux, 1995), 192–93.

28 Tsunetomo Yamamoto, *Hagakure: The Book of the Samurai*, tr. William Scott Wilson (Tokyo, New York, London: Kodansha International, 1979), 26.

29 Patrick White, *Voss* (New York: Viking, 1957), 291.

30 Ralph Waldo Emerson, 'Nature' in id., *Essays and Lectures* (New York: Library of America, 1983), 10.

31 David Malouf, *Remembering Babylon* (New York: Vintage, 1994), 130 (italics in the original).

3

Postmodernism Grown Old

Steven Connor

Like Linda Hutcheon and Ihab Hassan, Steven Connor is the author of works that stand in the very front rank of discussions of postmodernism. His book Postmodernist Culture *is one of the most authoritative overviews of the subject, while his* The Cambridge Companion to Postmodernism *is one of the most accessible. The extract below also offers an overview: it is something of a brief historical outline of the numerous permutations that the idea of postmodernism and, no less importantly, the usage of the term, have undergone since their advent in the 1970s.*

Connor astutely charts a number of subtle but important shifts that postmodernism has undergone since its first coinage. At first something of a neologism used variously by Charles Jencks to describe the architectural flight from modernism, by Ihab Hassan to characterize post-war literature, and by Jean-François Lyotard to map the changing nature of knowledge in the late twentieth century, postmodernism began with a number of specific, localized meanings, often used to describe a style, school, or genre. By the end of the 1980s, though, postmodernism had evolved into a far more grandiose term, regularly used to designate something along the lines of a contemporary worldview, or mindset, or zeitgeist, or even a new historical period.

However, where Hutcheon regards postmodernism in this sense as a thing of the past, and Hassan is eager to look beyond its retrospectively apparent limitations, Connor's approach is more measured. Rather than opting for a strategy of proclaiming the end of the old order or diagnosing the emergence of the new, Connor prefers to demonstrate how the meanings designated by the terms 'postmodern', 'postmodernism', and 'postmodernist' have never been securely fixed. Rather, they have if anything been in more or less constant flux, evolving as they come into contact with new contexts and take on new content.

Thus, from the 1990s onwards, postmodernism as a term or concept began to gain ground in some surprising areas: for example, religion, legal studies, and ethics. These developments were surprising because throughout most of postmodernism's life cycle, debates in such areas would have seemed incongruous to postmodern sensibilities to say the least. It is a far cry, for instance, from the anarchism of 1968, which is often said to have engendered the postmodern, to debates in jurisprudence. Similarly, if, in some usages, postmodernism was synonymous with a secular 'anything goes' attitude of moral relativism, then its relevance to debates in religion or ethics might not have been immediately obvious at an earlier stage in its history. Nevertheless, at the close of the twentieth century, there was an upsurge of interest in the work of the philosopher Emmanuel Levinas – a thinker whose work is primarily concerned with ethical and religious themes – which breathed new life into debates around postmodernism.

According to Connor's final analysis, then, it is simply not possible to make any definitive pronouncements about the fate of postmodernism. It may evolve or mutate as it comes into contact with new ideas and forces, such as the globalization or digitalization of culture. It may dissipate and fizzle out as its ambit grows so broad as to become more or less meaningless. Or it may be revitalized as it adapts and takes on new significances and relevances, much as it has regularly done throughout its half-century history.

The extract is Steven Connor, 'Postmodernism Grown Old', in *Cul'tura 'Post': At the Crossroads of Cultures and Civilizations*, eds. Maria K. Popova and Vladimir V. Strukov (Voronezh: Voronezh State University Press, 2005), pp. 55–72.

Postmodernism Grown Old

'Finished, it's nearly finished, it must be nearly finished', Hamm promises himself at the beginning of Beckett's *Endgame*. But in chess, from which the play takes its title, the end of the game does not come after it, or signal the fact that it is no more. The endgame is not the end of the game, but the game of ending which forms part of it, and may be looked towards from the beginning. There are strategies for managing the end of the game, including ways of deferring that ending, which are not after the game but part of it. Surely, the first thing to be said about postmodernism, at this hour, after three decades of furious business and ringing tills, is that it must be nearly at an end. And yet postmodernism has shown an extraordinary capacity to renew itself in the conflagration of its demise. 'There's nothing like breathing your last to breathe new life into you', as another Beckett character says. Playing the game may become identical with playing the game out. One is compelled to begin almost any synoptic account of postmodernism with such sunset thoughts, even as, in the very midst of one's good riddance, one senses that the sweet sorrow of taking leave of postmodernism may be prolonged for some time yet. One might almost say that the derivative character of postmodernism, the name of which indicates that it comes after something else – modernism, modernity, or the modern – guarantees it an extended tenure which the naming of itself as an *ex nihilo* beginning might not. You can only credibly inaugurate a new beginning for a short so long, whereas you can carry on succeeding upon something almost indefinitely, catching continuing success from your predecessor's surcease. Like Shelley's famous fading coal of inspiration, the weakening of postmodernism itself can be turned into the same kind of regenerative resource as the weakening of modernism itself. Might postmodernism have solved the problem of eternal life? We should remember from Swift's Struldbrugs that eternal life is a monstrosity without the promise of eternal youth.

I will here distinguish four different stages in the development of postmodernism: accumulation; synthesis; autonomy and dissipation. In the first stage, which extends through the 1970s and the early part of the 1980s, the hypothesis of postmodernism was under development on a number of different fronts. Daniel Bell and Jean Baudrillard were offering new accounts of consumer society, Jean-François Lyotard was formulating his views about the waning of metanarratives, Charles Jencks was issuing his powerful manifestos on behalf of architectural postmodernism, and Ihab Hassan was characterizing a new sensibility in post-war writing, all of them, apart from Baudrillard, more-or-less programmatically employing the rubric 'postmodernism'.

At this stage, it was a genuine puzzle for anyone trying to get a secure fix on the term 'postmodern' to make the different sorts of argument applied to different kinds of object line up. Perhaps the principal problem was how to synchronize the arguments of those who claimed that the societies of the advanced West had undergone fundamental changes in their organization, and who therefore seemed to be characterizing a shift from modernity to postmodernity, with those who thought that they discerned a shift in the arts and culture of these societies from a distinctively modernist phase to a distinctively – or indistinctly – postmodernist phase.

From the middle of the 1980s onwards, these separate accounts began to be clustered together – most notably in the superb synopsis and synthesis provided in Fredric Jameson's landmark essay 'Postmodernism: or the Cultural Logic of Late Capitalism' (Jameson 1991: 1–54). Gradually, what came to seem important was not the aptness of the explanations of particular varieties of postmodernism, as the increasingly powerful rhymes that different accounts of the postmodern formed with each other. Indeed, it seemed to be a feature of the postmodern itself that parallelism became more important and interesting than causation. This was also the period of the most vigorous syncretism in thinking of the postmodern. Jameson's essay opened the way for a number of synthesizing guides and introductions, which were followed by anthologies of postmodern writing, such as those of Thomas Docherty, Patricia Waugh, Charles Jencks and Margaret Rose.

The effect of this was that, by the end of the 1980s, the concept of the 'postmodern' was ceasing to be used principally in the analysis of particular objects or cultural areas and had become a general horizon or hypothesis. I was an amateur astronomer as a boy and I remember being told that the way to make out the elusive colour of a faint star was not to look directly at it, but to look just to its side, since this allowed the image to fall on a part of the retina that is more sensitive to colour. I don't know if this is true of star-observation (it certainly never worked for me), but it seems to have begun to be true for spotters of the postmodern during this second period, when it seemed that, if one wanted to pin down the postmodernist features of some unlikely object of analysis, war, say, or prostitution, or circus, the thing to do was not to look directly at your target, but at what lay in its periphery. Postmodernism was the practice of critical distraction (literally being 'drawn aside'). Postmodernism arose from the amalgamation of these many deflections or diagonal gazes. It evoked a horizontal lattice-work of connections between different postmodernisms, rather than a discontinuous series of 'vertical' diagnoses of specific postmodernisms. As kinship patterns among postmodernists became more important than patterns of descent, 'analogical' postmodernism took the place of 'genealogical' postmodernisms (Connor 1992: vii–viii), but synthesis brought its own problems. It seemed clear that important changes had taken place in politics, economics and social life, changes that could broadly be characterized by the two words delegitimation and dedifferentiation. Centrist or absolutist notions of the state, nourished by the idea of the uniform movement of history towards a single outcome were beginning to weaken. It was no longer clear who had the authority to speak on behalf of history. The rise of an economy driven from its peripheries by patterns of consumption rather than from its centre by the needs of production produced much more volatile and unstable economic conditions. These erosions of authority were accompanied by a breakdown of the hitherto unbridgeable distinctions between centres and peripheries, between classes and countries. Given these changes, it seemed to many reasonable to assume that equivalent changes would take place in the spheres of art and culture. The problem was that this very assumption drew from a model in which there was enough of a difference between the spheres of politics, economics and society on the one hand and art and culture on the other for the spark of a specifiable relation to be able to jump between them. During the early twentieth century, relations between the two spheres were thought of as tense, if not downright antagonistic, with many assuming that art and culture needed to be protected from the 'culture industry' and both traditional and Marxist critics agreeing on the need for art to maintain an antagonistic distance from the market and prevailing norms.

Some accounts of postmodernism depended on the argument that not only had the conditions of social and economic organization changed, but so, as an effect of those changes, had the relations between the social and economic and the artistic-cultural. Drawing on the early work of Baudrillard, Fredric Jameson saw that, rather than subsisting in a state of fidgety internal exile, the sphere of culture was in fact undergoing a prodigious expansion in an economy driven by sign, style and spectacle rather than by the production of goods. The plucky attempts of commentators to legislate terminologically between these realms, insisting, as I myself attempted to do in my book *Postmodernist Culture*, on the difference between 'postmodernity' on the one hand and 'postmodernism' on the other were in fact the secondary effect of a more fundamental coalescence, in which politics and economy had become culturized, and postmodernity had itself become postmodernist. It is perhaps for this reason that the 1980s saw such a proliferation of variants in the word itself. How one capitalized or hyphenated the word – 'post-modern', 'Post-Modern', 'postmodern', or 'Postmodern' – seemed to many to matter a great deal, along with whether one chose to refer to 'postmodernism', 'postmodernity' or simply 'the postmodern'.

During this second, syncretic phase, another subtle shift began to take place in the word 'postmodernism'. This word was now a name not only for the way in which new attitudes and practices had evolved in particular areas of society and culture – in architecture, in literature, in patterns of economic or political organization – but also for the characteristic discourse in which such things were discussed. 'Postmodernism' named all those writers who gave houseroom to the postmodern hypothesis and all the writing they did about it. At this period, it did not seem possible even to discuss the existence of the postmodern without being drawn into its discourse. Genealogies of specific postmodernisms in politics, society and the arts were followed by genealogies of the discourse of postmodernism, such as Hans Bertens's *The Idea of the Postmodern* (1995). By the 1990s, the 'post' idea had achieved a kind of autonomy from its objects. At this point, the argument about whether there really was such a thing as postmodernism, which had driven earlier discussions of the subject, started to evaporate, since the mere fact that there was discourse at all about the subject was now sufficient proof of the existence of postmodernism – but as idiom rather than actuality. Postmodernism became the name for the activity of writing about postmodernism. The postmodern became a kind of data-cloud, a fog of discourse, which showed up on the radar even more conspicuously than what it was supposed to be about. Thus postmodernism had passed from the stage of accumulation into its more autonomous phase. No longer a form of cultural barometer; postmodernism had itself become an entire climate.

Having expanded its range and dominion hugely during the first period of separate accumulation in the 1970s and the syncretic period of the 1980s, the idea of the postmodern began for the first time to slow its rate of expansion during the 1990s. In this decade, 'postmodernism' slowly but inexorably ceased to be a condition of things in the world, whether the world of art, culture, economics, politics, religion or war, and became a philosophical disposition, an easily recognisable (and, increasingly dismissible) style of thought and talk. By this time, 'postmodernism' had also entered the popular lexicon to signify a loose, sometimes dangerously loose relativism. Now, its dominant associations were with postcolonialism, multiculturalism and identity politics. So where postmodernism had expanded its reach in academic discussion, it had shrunk down into a casual term of abuse in more popular discourse. Postmodernism had become autonomous from its objects.

One of the earliest commentators on postmodernism, Daniel Bell, made the suggestion that something like a postmodern condition arose when the utopian ideals and life-styles associated with modern artists began to be diffused among populations as fashion, life-style and consumer 'choice'. It is common to construe some kinds of artistic postmodernism as a reaction against the canonization of modernism, in institutions like the Museum of Modern Art in New York. There were some, like Leslie Fiedler, who welcomed the loosening of the grip of modernism, in favour of a more popular sensibility. But this was not a view held by many early formulators of postmodernism. Rather, they were inclined to emphasize the difficulty, the challenge and the provocation of postmodernist art. Lyotard's argument that the postmodern represented the acknowledgement of unrepresentability without the retreat into the consolation of form, could easily be read as a confirmation of modernist principles. Indeed, Lyotard was inclined to see postmodernism as the reactivation of principles that had flared up first in modernism.

The well-known tendency of many of the thinkers and theorists associated with postmodernism to focus on modernists (Lacan on Joyce, Derrida on Mallarmé, Foucault on Roussel) might have offered support for the view that early postmodernist formulations were attempting to reinstate something like the heroic refusal of modern life that constituted artistic modernism. Where the modernity refused by modernists was the modernity of urban transformation, mass production and speed of transport and communications, the modernity refused by postmodernists was that of consumer capitalism, in which the world forcibly wrenched into new material forms by modernity was being transformed by being immaterialized, transformed into various kinds of spectacle.

So far, I have been describing postmodernism as though it were itself merely a descriptive project, the attempt simply to get the measure of the new prevailing conditions in art, society and culture. But from its beginning, postmodernism has always been more than a cartographic enterprise; it has also been a project of renewal and transformation.

As postmodern studies began to proliferate, more complex relations began to arise between description and allegiance, or between postmodernism conceived as a condition, and postmodernism conceived as a project. During the 1980s, it was still possible to separate out the question of whether there was such a thing as postmodernism from the question of whether one was or was not generally for it. The work of Fredric Jameson may be seen as maintaining the fragile equilibrium between description and recommendation, which is why that work has been read in so many different ways: as a stern critique of postmodernism; as a subtle preservation of the project of the modern through strategic accommodation to the postmodern; and as a full-scale capitulation to postmodernism.

One might adapt one of Jameson's own favourite strategies and permutate the possibilities according to which the credence and approval accorded to the idea of the postmodern can be combined. The range of possibilities would be as follows: 1) One could believe in postmodernism and be all for it. This was the position adopted by Charles Jencks and Jean-François Lyotard. In fact most of those who wrote about the postmodern condition in the 1970s were broadly in favour of it, or at least saw the postmodern as an irresistible necessity. 2) One could believe in postmodernism but be against it. This was the position influentially set out by David Harvey, in his *The Condition of Postmodernity* (1980) and carried forward recently by critics like Paul Virilio (1997). 3) One could not believe in postmodernism and (one supposes for that very reason) not be for it. This was the position occupied by most of the early critics of the 'postmodern turn', as well as of Marxist cultural critics who believed that postmodernism was a snare and a delusion which mystified the real bases of domination and gave up prematurely on modernity, identified as this can be with the project of human emancipation from error and oppression inaugurated in the Enlightenment. The most influential proponent of this view was Jürgen Habermas, in his *The Philosophical Discourse of Modernity* (1987).

An interesting feature of such permutations is that they often generate a merely abstract possibility, that is required for the logical integrity of the model, but cannot be expected to have any real-world existence – a sort of -1^2 or similar mathematical fiction. In the case of this model, the phantom position is that which would both dispute the possibility of postmodernism and yet be in favour of it. But even this Carrollian position seems to have found an advocate. In *We*

Have Never Been Modern, Bruno Latour argues that modernity, which he prefers to call 'The Modern Constitution' (Latour 1993: 13), arises from the coordination of two absolutisms: 1) the absolute separation of human culture from nonhuman nature, and 2) the absolute separation of present from past. The Modern Constitution arises out of the sense of the sharp separation of nature and culture, and the forms of knowledge they produce and are addressed by. Nature produces science, the knowledge of how things are in themselves. Culture (language, society, politics) produces the social sciences, discourses of morality, politics, psychology, etc. Modernity is characterized by the sense that there is no relation between these two kinds of object and two kinds of knowledge, indeed, the sense that they should be kept rigorously distinct. Modernity thus 'invents a separation between the scientific power charged with representing things and the political power charged with representing subjects' (Latour 1993: 29). The originality of Latour's argument is that the very moment that modernity invents this distinction and starts to hold itself in being by means of it (the beginning of the 'scientific revolution' in the seventeenth century), is the moment at which the middle ground, of objects and forms and ideas and practices, lying between the inhuman realm of nature and the human realm of culture, begins to proliferate. More and more 'things' get drawn into social life, which will become more and more dependent upon and liable to be transformed by what it draws from and does with nature. Where modernity supposes a stark division between subjects and objects, cultures and natures, Latour proposes that we pay attention to what, borrowing a phrase from Michel Serres, he calls 'quasi-objects', which crowd into, and then start to crowd out, the space between nonhuman nature and human culture.

Latour then moves his argument towards the question of temporality. He shows that the first absolutism, the absolute separation between inhuman things and human cultures, is mapped on to a second, the absolute temporal distinction between past and present: 'The asymmetry between nature and culture then becomes an asymmetry between past and future. The past was the confusion of things and men; the future is what will no longer confuse them' (Latour 1993: 71). Despite their many antagonisms, modernism (free love and free indirect style) and modernization (telegrams and tanks) depend upon two principles: the sense of the uniform passing of time and the sense of the homogeneity of the present moment, or self-identity of the 'now'. 'Modernizing progress is thinkable only on condition that all the elements that are contemporary according to the calendar belong to the same time', Latour declares (Latour 1993:

73). But the multiplication of quasi-objects produces a temporal thickening, a multiplication of times. Latour writes:

> No one can now categorize actors that belong to the 'same time' in a single coherent group. No one knows any longer whether the reintroduction of the bear in Pyrenees, kolkhozes, aerosols, the Green Revolution, the anti-smallpox vaccine, Star Wars, the Muslim religion, partridge hunting, the French Revolution, service industries, labour unions, cold fusion, Bolshevism, relativity, Slovak nationalism, commercial sailboats, and so on, are outmoded, up to date, futuristic, atemporal, nonexistent, or permanent.
>
> (Latour 1993: 74)

His argument is that, since modern society has not in fact purified itself of nature, but implicated itself ever more deeply within it, there is in fact no distinction to be made between modern and premodern cultures. Indeed, there is no such thing as a 'culture': 'The very notion of culture is an artifact created by bracketing Nature off. Cultures – different or universal – do not exist, any more than Nature does. There are only natures-cultures' (Latour 1993: 104). Furthermore, there never have been any cultures in the sense of wholly self-inventing, non-natural phenomena. Hence, since the idea of the modern depends upon the claim that we have freed ourselves, or will free ourselves, from nature, 'we have never been modern'. Postmodernism apprehends the unevenness of times, the mingling of old and new that belongs to the premodern or amodern apprehension, but, clinging to the habits of modern thinking, sees it as a new development in the flow of time, a new kind of 'now'. Our present condition does not represent a postmodern break with ideas of progress. Latour acknowledges that his own 'amodernist' attitudes overlap considerably with those of 'the postmoderns' (they are clearly supposed to know who they are as well as Latour does), but attempts also to distance himself from them:

> The postmoderns are right about the dispersion; every contemporary assembly is polytemporal. But they are wrong to retain the framework and to keep on believing in the requirement of continual novelty that modernism demanded. By mixing elements of the past together in the form of collages and citations, the postmoderns recognize to what extent these citations are truly outdated. Moreover, it is because they are outmoded that the postmoderns dig them up, in order to shock the former 'modernist' avant-gardes who no longer know at what altar to worship. But it is a long way from a provocative quotation extracted out

of a truly finished past to a reprise, repetition or revisiting of a past that has never disappeared.

(Latour 1993: 74)

Latour's objection to postmodernism is that it turns the permanent impossibility of being modern into a postmodern value. This is perhaps the most lasting problem of postmodernism. The more compelling postmodernism seems as an hypothesis, the more it seems that it might be a condition rather than an imperative, and the more beside the point it seems whether or not one chooses to be postmodernist. Choosing to be postmodernist then starts to look like choosing to embrace contingency, when the point about contingency is that it chooses you, for its own (non)reasons.

The most striking difference between modernism and postmodernism is that no guides or introductions of modernism appeared until it was felt to be over. What the incendiary manifesto was to modernism, the fire-fighting 'guide' or 'introduction' has been to postmodernism. The guide appears more democratic than the manifesto, in that it attempts to meet the reader on his or her own ground, but in the pedagogic relation it assumes and establishes, it can also work to maintain a privative distinction between those in the know and those not yet so. The structure of books like my own *Postmodernist Culture: An Introduction to Theories of the Contemporary* (Connor 1989), which tracked the emergence of different kinds of postmodernism from different kinds of modernism, encouraged readers to feel that, in order to understand and participate in the postmodernist break, it was necessary for them to undergo a kind of apprenticeship in modernism. The seemingly paradoxical fact that the affirmation of the postmodern break required such extensive reprise of modernism does not seem so paradoxical after all, if postmodernist theory is seen as having the same uneasy relation to its public as modernism did to its public, and if postmodernism is seen as driven by some of the resentful desire for privilege as modernism. It should therefore not seem so surprising that the postmodernist transformation should have brought about so remarkable and extensive a revival of interest and research in modernism on all fronts.

Modernism had shocked sensibilities and assaulted senses with sex, speed, noise and nonsense. Postmodernist artists have carried on relentlessly shocking and assaulting and provoking as they had done for nearly a century, but added to their repertoire the kinds of defensive attack represented by postmodernist theory. Modernist work was shock requiring later analysis. As T.S. Eliot wrote, referring to something else altogether: 'we had the experience but missed the meaning'. Postmodernist work attempts to draw experience and meaning, shock and analysis into synchrony. Being modernist always meant not quite realizing that you were. Being postmodernist always involved the awareness that you are.

But, if Bell is right that modernism is surpassed by being diffused, so postmodernism may also be suffering the same fate. We have reached a situation in which the idea of postmodernism has both broadened and simplified. As postmodernism became generalized during its third phase during the 1990s, the force of postmodernism as an ideal, or necessary premonition of the good, seems also to have begun to dissipate. Perhaps the very acceptance, grudging or resigned, of the existence of a widespread postmodern condition in society, culture and politics and a postmodern disposition in the arts and culture has meant that it has become more difficult to see postmodernism as something to be invented, or as a project towards which one must bend one's best efforts. We can now, it seems, be postmodernist without knowing it, and without ever having had to pass exams in being modernist. The late 1990s have been characterized by a different kind of guide, which pays attention to postmodernism as a general and popular sensibility. A recent example might be Ziauddin Sardar's *A–Z of Postmodern Life* (2002). Cristopher Nash's *The Unravelling of the Postmodern Mind* (2002), though much less of a pop guide, nevertheless assumes that postmodernism is a sensibility or state of mind, rather than the result of rigorous philosophical or cultural-political deliberation.

Postmodernism shares with modernism a kind of presentism. Other literary-cultural periods in the past have come about when cultures have looked elsewhere, with a renewing attention to other periods, other cultures: the Renaissance and antiquity, Romanticism with its native archaisms and exoticisms, even modernism with its strange mixture of primitivism and zippy contemporaneity. Postmodernism, by contrast, is concerned almost exclusively with the nature of its own presentness. Indeed, one definition of postmodernism might be that condition in which for the first time, and as a result of technologies that allow large-scale storage, access and reproduction of records of the past, the past appears to be included in the present, or at the present's disposal, and in which the ratio between present and past has therefore changed.

Of course, postmodernism shares with modernism its concern with the present, as well as its sense of the long, or enduring present. But modernism's present was undefinable, a vertigo or velocity rather than a habitat. The presentness to which modernism was drawn was a hair-trigger affair, always on the brink of futurity. By contrast, the perpetual present of postmodernism is mapped, scheduled, dense with retrospection and forecast. The present (as of old) is all there is, but now it includes all time. There is nothing absent from this present, which makes it curiously spectral. This means in its turn that the present can start to age, to become old before its time. The present of postmodernism has come to seem like a stalled present, an agitated, but idle meanwhile.

Perhaps the most extraordinary example of the generalization of postmodernist thinking in the rich cultures of the North is in the area of sexuality. If, as Jameson suggests, the world has been taken over by 'culture', then there is a more recent, assimilation of culture in general to the culture of sex. Sex used to be proclaimed to be the secret, forbidden truth of human life. It is now the most manifest, ubiquitous and compulsory truth. Sex can no longer be stopped or avoided. From being the accessory that assisted the packaging and consumption of a range of commodities, sex has become the product that other commodities exist to sell. Sex has come into its own, because sex wants to be more than sex. This is why everything is sex – because sex has become the form and the name of transcendence. Sex has become the only and ultimate quality. Eros has become life. Sex has been subject to economic transaction, to buying and selling as a commodity, for centuries. But what seems to have come about in the last couple of decades is a situation in which sex becomes the very medium in which other exchanges take place. You do not pay for sex with money; you pay for everything in the currency of sex.

And yet, because it is so triumphant, sex may also be forced to be on guard. Because sex has become so ubiquitous, so polymorphously perverse, so mixed-up and mingled with everything else, it fears, we fear, it may lose its meaning. In previous eras, sex had struggled against repression, and it was repression that made it a looming, irrepressible 'it', a force gathering itself beneath and behind repression. Now, having either defeated repression, or recruited it to its own cause, sex may face a larger battle, a battle against an enemy that it itself produces: indifference. Repression energizes and recharges sex: indifference depletes it. Sex could never be defeated while there was repression. Now that it has won, it stands to lose everything in the face of disaffection.

Postmodernism has had different centres of gravity during its successive stages. In 1970, the dominant discipline was postmodernist literature. In 1980, a sort of heyday of postmodernism, architecture would perhaps have slipped into the position of dominant discipline, supplying as it seemed a fund of language and arguments for the other areas of postmodernism. By 1990, after the break-up of the Soviet Union and the revolutions across Europe both confirmed the hypothesis of the unsustainability of historical grand narratives (or their appropriation on behalf of states) and brought to the surface new problems of ethnic and religious diversity, postmodernism became centred not on any one cultural form but in the problems attaching to the plurality of cultures. The postmodern condition no longer seemed a possible future, to be adumbrated allegorically by literary texts, buildings, or other works, but had become a real and urgent predicament. Significant shifts of emphasis have been taking place in postmodern studies over the last decade, especially in the areas of most rapid growth, namely law, religion, science and technology. Often these new formations – deutero-postmodernisms, we might call them – can throw up problems and provocations which do not so readily come to light in postmodernism's more settled provinces. It seems clear, for example, that the new development one can call postmodern legal studies represents not just a form of legal theory arising from deforming entry into the field of law of a body of ideas from elsewhere, but also a series of claims now radiating outwards from law and the disciplines with which it is affiliating itself – art, literature, film – which may make the whole field of postmodern studies begin to resonate at a different frequency. In allowing the unsettling question of justice to breach the closure of a modernist legal theory that had concerned itself almost exclusively with the problem of making law consistent with itself rather than justly responsive to the world within which it functions, postmodern legal theory also makes the question of justice newly compelling in many other areas of postmodern thinking.

Another area of reciprocal influence is in religious studies, or the field of spirituality. In one sense a postmodern scepticism about the grand narrative of increasing secularism makes postmodern theory a natural resource for those concerned to interpret the many different forms of religious belief and practice as something more than survival or regression to the premodern. On the other hand, the very fact that writers on questions of religion and spirituality have been able to draw so tellingly on the work of philosophers and theorists such as Georges Bataille, Hélène Cixous, Michel de Certeau, Luce Irigaray and, most importantly, Emmanuel Levinas and Jacques Derrida discloses the fact that the question of religion has been at work in powerful but unarticulated ways in the discourse of postmodernism for much longer than may have appeared. Postmodernism's characteristic mode of the '–post', the manner of its 'after-thought', provides a model for what has been called 'post-religion' – a kind of spirituality that both comes after and persists in being religion.

Something similar can be seen in the field of performance studies. In one sense, the performing arts can be seen as simply another area in which postmodernism has come to have an important influence – though the slight dislocation of drama and other performing arts such as dance from the mainstream of modernist development at the beginning of the twentieth century has led to odd anachronisms and anomalies in the development of postmodern theories in those areas. For instance, since the characteristic of much modern drama is its heightened and scandalizing realism (Ibsen, Strindberg), one sign of postmodernism in drama is an antirealism (Brecht, Beckett) which actually makes it seem similar to what was happening in arts like painting in their modernist phase. Dance seems clearly to have its modernist moment, in the break made by dancers and choreographers such as Isadora Duncan and Martha Graham from the traditions of classical ballet; but even the most authoritative exponent of postmodernism in dance, Sally Banes, seems to acknowledge that there have been two very different kinds of postmodernism in dance. The first, described in her book *Terpsichore in Sneakers*, is a postmodernism by subtraction, which deliberately strips dance down to its basic principles (and thus confusingly resembles the analytic mode of modernist painting celebrated by Clement Greenberg) (Banes 1987). But her more recent book *Writing Dancing in the Age of Postmodernism* shows that this analytic period has been followed by the much more opulent, richly combinative forms of dance which have proliferated during the 1980s and 1990s, which have sought to enlarge the scope of dance rather than clarify its essence (Banes 1994). The importance of performance to postmodernism lies not in the adjustment of the postmodernist paradigm to existing areas of the performing arts as in such more far-reaching resonance between postmodernism and the idea of performance. This is brought to a focus by the example of what is variously called 'live art', 'performance art' and simply 'performance', which seems so intrinsically a postmodern form that there is no question of there ever having been modernist or premodernist variants of it. In something of the way that the emergence of post-religion allows the retrieval of the force of religious concerns within postmodern thought, so the emergence of postmodern 'performance' allows a delayed recognition of the origin of postmodernism in the apprehension that performance is a general mode of the postmodern: that rather than simply resting serenely in being, art, politics, identity, all act themselves out.

It is through the work of one of the most influential of these anticipatory thinkers, Emmanuel Levinas, that law, philosophy and religion are drawn together in what one might call, if not exactly a new discipline, then at least a powerful crossdisciplinary 'attractor' or centre of gravity. Emmanuel Levinas represents for the postmodernism of the 1990s and beyond what Mikhail Bakhtin was for the postmodernism of the 1980s. Bakhtin's theory of the crowding of every apparently singular voice by a multiplicity of competing or qualifying voices quickly spread from literary studies into film, art history, philosophy and politics. Polyphonic plenitude, the searching out and affirmation of the plurality of different voices, became the leading and defining principle of postmodernism's cultural politics. Just as Goethe is said to have died with the Enlightenment slogan 'Mehr Licht!' ('More Light!') on his lips, so one could imagine postmodernism going to its rest uttering the defiant cry 'More Voices!'.

But the 1990s also saw an unexpected swerve away from this celebratory or festival mood, as a number of writers in different areas began to ask whether the ethical questions which postmodernist thought had been so very good at setting aside dissolving or transcending might not still have a claim. The question being asked in a number of quarters was, could it be possible to found postmodernism not just on the negative claim to go beyond the narrowness of particular value systems but in some more positive value-claim of its own? Postmodernism had proved extremely resourceful in showing the constructed nature of systems of values: but writers in the late 1990s began to ask whether it might not be possible to imagine a postmodernism that would be not just constructionist, but itself 'constructive' (Schiralli 1999; Gelpi 2000).

The remarkable turn, or turn back, to the ethical was accomplished almost entirely through an engagement with the work of the French philosopher Emmanuel Levinas. For Levinas, ethics is not a matter of rules of behaviour, it is a matter of a condition of exposure to others. In encountering 'the other', that exotic creature whose sightings have been reported in so many of the travellers' tales of philosophy from Hegel onwards, there is always a painful intimacy, which nevertheless prevents the other from being taken to be simply a reflection of the ego. The other represents a kind of immediate demand on the self, a demand for recognition and response. Although this demand is ethical, it also demands not to be formalized into structures of knowledge and policies of action, which turn the other into an object of knowledge. It is the attempt to remain responsive to the claims of the other without resorting to the violence of formalization and objectification that characterizes postmodern ethics. Indeed, the ethical turn may reveal a sort of ethical concern that is originary in postmodernism. Just as Levinas declared that ethics is 'first philosophy', so, Robert Eaglestone has suggested: '[p]ostmodernism, implicitly or explicitly, is about ethics before it is anything else' (Eaglestone 2004). In the light of this claim, Lyotard's influential account of the different kinds of exposure before and response to the sublime enacted by modernist and postmodernist works of art might thus become legible as a differential ethics; the modernist work reduces the other to a theme, while postmodernism attempts to preserve the infinity or unapproachability of the other. In recent years the word 'ethics' has come to have the same authority and reach as the word 'text' had during the 1970s and 1980s.

Although postmodern ethics is not a new discipline, it brings about a new coherence or configuration among disciplines, in the same way that women's studies and gender studies and postmodernism itself had done previously. Perhaps indeed, this is the sign of a new period in postmodern studies, in which the great decentring force of postmodernism is turned against itself, to form new centres of interest and alternative forms of organization. The forms of interrogation and argument that might previously have been conducted under postmodernism's roof are now being conducted in the new disciplinary habitats represented by 'body theory', spatial theory, 'globalization' and, most prominent and active of all, studies of cybernetic or digital culture. This may indicate clearly that the frail, travelling coincidence of postmodernism is beginning to fissure. Postmodernism has always itself been sensitive to the wasting and dissolving effects of time, and has always been hospitable to decomposition. 'Nothing like breathing your last to put new life into you', says a Beckett character. Whether what lies in store for a now aged postmodernism is Larkin's 'only end of age' or some revival through dissipation only time, that blabbering telltale, will unfold.

Bibliography

Banes, S. (1987), *Terpsichore in Sneakers: Postmodern Dance*, Middletown, CT: Wesleyan University Press.

Banes, S. (1994), *Writing Dancing in the Age of Postmodernism*, Hanover, NH: Wesleyan University Press; University Press of New England.

Bertens, H. (1995), *The Idea of the Postmodern: A History*, London: Routledge.

Connor, S. (1992), *Postmodernist Culture: An Introduction to Theories of the Contemporary*, Oxford: Blackwell.

Eaglestone, R. (2004), 'Postmodernism and Ethics' in Steven Connor (ed.) *The Cambridge Companion to Postmodernism*, Cambridge: Cambridge University Press.

Gelpi, D. L. (2000), *Varieties of Transcendental Experience: A Study in Constructive Postmodernism*, Collegeville, MO: Liturgical Press.

Habermas, J. (1987), *The Philosophical Discourse of Modernity: Twelve Lectures*, trans. Frederick Lawrence and J. Habermas, Cambridge, Mass: MIT Press.

Harvey, D. (1980), *The Condition of Postmodernity: An Inquiry Into the Origins of Social Change*, Oxford: Basil Blackwell.

Jameson, F. (1991), *Postmodernism: Or, the Cultural Logic of Late Capitalism*, London: Verso.

Latour, B. (1993), *We Have Never Been Modern*, trans. Catherine Porter, New York and London: Harvester Wheatsheaf.

Nash, C. (2002), *On The Unravelling of the Postmodern Mind*, Edinburgh: Edinburgh University Press.

Sardar, Z. (2002), *The A–Z of Postmodern Life: Essays on Global Culture in the Noughties*, London: Vision.

Schiralli, M. (1999), *Constructive Postmodernism: Toward Renewal in Cultural and Literary Studies*, Westport, CT and London: Bergin and Garvey.

Virilio, P. (1997), *Open Sky*, trans. Julie Rose, London: Verso.

4

The Death of Postmodernism and Beyond

Alan Kirby

This essay is perhaps best read alongside Alan Kirby's writings on digimodernism (see Part Two of this book), to which it can be seen as a preface. Its starting point is a forthright indictment of the outdatedness of much of postmodern culture. While Kirby's remarks on the teaching of postmodern fiction in British universities are in basic agreement with Linda Hutcheon's point that a widespread institutionalization of postmodern ideas has stymied and stultified their further development, Kirby goes further still, pointing out that the institutionalized version of postmodernism that is taught today has fallen out of touch with the contemporary culture it purports to describe: films and novels of the twenty-first century are no longer recognizably postmodern.

Kirby presents a straightforward answer as to why this has happened: its origins are to be found in the rise of new media technologies, such as the internet, digital television, and mobile phones. Critics with a postmodern mindset are quick to recognize in these media a range of liberating postmodern attributes, such as interactivity, open-endedness, and non-linearity. However, Kirby argues that this view involves misunderstanding and simplification: hence his use of the term 'pseudo-modernism'.

The apparent interactivity of pseudo-modernism – playing a computer game, voting for a contestant on a TV show, navigating your way through the internet – appears to have fulfilled the postmodern goal of the death of the author. But, according to Kirby, it has not been accompanied by the birth of the reader, so much as the birth of the consumer. *The death of postmodernism, then, lies in the ephemeral and inane nature of pseudo-modernism's consistently vapid products. In short, postmodernism's artistic experimentation has been supplanted by a cultural populism; postmodernism's diversity and multiplicity have been standardized into consumerist moulds; postmodernism's close ties with philosophy have been broken by an untheorized and unthinking embrace of the here and now – which turns out to be filtered and constructed by the consumerism of the new media, too. Just three years after publishing this article, Kirby would go on to suggest that pseudomodernism was merely one aspect of the demise of postmodernism, and that a new term – 'digimodernism' – was needed to designate the profound changes to our experience of culture brought about by digital technology. A selection of his writings on this topic are included in Part Two of this anthology.*

This is clearly the most pessimistic version of the end and aftermath of postmodernism – Kirby regards the present as a 'cultural desert', after all. This pessimism is not shared by most of the positions outlined in Part Two, which have found plenty of cultural value and merit in any number of works of art, literature, film, and architecture of the new digital age, as we shall see. Furthermore, it is manifestly untrue, for example, that architects who design with a mouse instead of a drawing board and clutch pencil create necessarily inferior buildings, while literature seems to be withstanding the invention of the word processor, just as, the protestations of analogue purists notwithstanding, the manipulation of digital images through software has arguably enhanced the art of photography. The cultural impact of digital technology, then, has not been an exclusively pernicious one. Indeed, as we will see in Part Two, Robert Samuels finds in the same new technological changes an enhanced sense of autonomy, which he dubs 'automodernism'. Nevertheless, when we turn from the artifacts of contemporary 'high' culture to those of digital mass culture – reality TV, internet chatrooms, text messaging, computer games – it soon becomes apparent that Kirby has a point.

It is no less clear that, in principle, things don't have to be this way: Kirby hints that once we have become accustomed to the new media, it may be possible to use them more creatively and more sophisticatedly, to generate a digital 'high' culture. But in the meantime, with the cult of instant gratification, the throwaway attitude to anything that is no longer regarded as 'new', and the marketing of technological innovations that frame their novelty as that of a new toy, it is indeed hard to see how the pseudo-modernist media Kirby decries could rise above the ephemeral to create a successor to postmodernism that would achieve lasting cultural significance.

The extract is by Alan Kirby, 'The Death of Postmodernism and Beyond', *Philosophy Now*, Issue 58, November/December 2006 (pp. 34–7).

The Death of Postmodernism and Beyond

I have in front of me a module description downloaded from a British university English department's website. It includes details of assignments and a week-by-week reading list for the optional module 'Postmodern Fictions', and if the university is to remain nameless here it's not because the module is in any way shameful but that it handily represents modules or module parts which will be taught in virtually every English department in the land this coming academic year. It assumes that postmodernism is alive, thriving and kicking: it says it will introduce 'the general topics of "postmodernism" and "postmodernity" by examining their relationship to the contemporary writing of fiction'. This might suggest that postmodernism is contemporary, but the comparison actually shows that it is dead and buried.

Postmodern philosophy emphasizes the elusiveness of meaning and knowledge. This is often expressed in postmodern art as a concern with representation and an *ironic self-awareness*. And the argument that postmodernism is over has already been made philosophically. There are people who have essentially asserted that for a while we believed in postmodern ideas, but not any more, and from now on we're going to believe in critical realism. The weakness in this analysis is that it centres on the academy, on the practices and suppositions of philosophers who may or may not be shifting ground or about to shift – and many academics will simply decide that, finally, they prefer to stay with Foucault (arch postmodernist) than go over to anything else. However, a far more compelling case can be made that postmodernism is dead by looking outside the academy at current cultural production.

Most of the undergraduates who will take 'Postmodern Fictions' this year will have been born in 1985 or after, and all but one of the module's primary texts were written before their lifetime. Far from being 'contemporary', these texts were published in another world, before the students were born: *The French Lieutenant's Woman*, *Nights at the Circus*, *If on a Winter's Night a Traveller*, *Do Androids Dream of Electric Sheep?* (and *Blade Runner*), *White Noise*: this is Mum and Dad's culture. Some of the texts ('The Library of Babel') were written even before their *parents* were born. Replace this cache with other postmodern stalwarts – *Beloved*, *Flaubert's Parrot*, *Waterland*, *The Crying of Lot 49*, *Pale Fire*,

Slaughterhouse 5, Lanark, Neuromancer, anything by B.S. Johnson – and the same applies. It's all about as contemporary as The Smiths, as hip as shoulder pads, as happening as Betamax video recorders. These are texts which are just coming to grips with the existence of rock music and television; they mostly do not dream even of the possibility of the technology and communications media – mobile phones, email, the internet, computers in every house powerful enough to put a man on the moon – which today's undergraduates take for granted.

The reason why the primary reading on British postmodernism fictions modules is so old, in relative terms, is that it has not been rejuvenated. Just look out into the cultural market-place: buy novels published in the last five years, watch a twenty-first-century film, listen to the latest music – above all just sit and watch television for a week – and you will hardly catch a glimpse of postmodernism. Similarly, one can go to literary conferences (as I did in July) and sit through a dozen papers which make no mention of Theory, of Derrida, Foucault, Baudrillard. The sense of superannuation, of the impotence and the irrelevance of so much Theory among academics, also bears testimony to the passing of postmodernism. The people who produce the cultural material which academics and non-academics read, watch and listen to, have simply given up on postmodernism. The occasional metafictional or self-conscious text will appear, to widespread indifference – like Bret Easton Ellis' *Lunar Park* – but then modernist novels, now long forgotten, were still being written into the 1950s and 60s. The only place where the postmodern is extant is in children's cartoons like *Shrek* and *The Incredibles*, as a sop to parents obliged to sit through them with their toddlers. This is the level to which postmodernism has sunk; a source of marginal gags in pop culture aimed at the under-eights.

What's post postmodernism?

I believe there is more to this shift than a simple change in cultural fashion. The terms by which authority, knowledge, selfhood, reality and time are conceived have been altered, suddenly and forever. There is now a gulf between most lecturers and their students akin to the one which appeared in the late 1960s, but not for the same kind of reason. The shift from modernism to postmodernism did not stem from any profound reformulation in the conditions of cultural production and reception; all that happened, to rhetorically exaggerate, was that the kind of people who had once written *Ulysses* and *To the Lighthouse* wrote *Pale Fire* and *The Bloody Chamber* instead. But somewhere in the late 1990s or early 2000s, the emergence of new technologies re-structured, violently and forever, the nature of the author, the reader and the text, and the relationships between them.

Postmodernism, like modernism and romanticism before it, fetishized the author, even when the author chose to indict or pretended to abolish him or herself. But the culture we have now fetishizes the *recipient* of the text to the degree that they become a partial or whole author of it. Optimists may see this as the democratization of culture; pessimists will point to the excruciating banality and vacuity of the cultural products thereby generated (at least so far).

Let me explain. Postmodernism conceived of contemporary culture as a spectacle before which the individual sat powerless, and within which questions of the real were problematized. It therefore emphasized the television or the cinema screen. Its successor, which I will call *pseudo-modernism*, makes the individual's action the necessary condition of the cultural product. Pseudo-modernism includes all television or radio programmes or parts of programmes, all 'texts', *whose content and dynamics are invented or directed by the participating viewer or listener* (although these latter terms, with their passivity and emphasis on reception, are obsolete: whatever a telephoning *Big Brother* voter or a telephoning 6-0-6 football fan are doing, they are not simply viewing or listening).

By definition, pseudo-modern cultural products cannot and do not exist unless the individual intervenes physically in them. *Great Expectations* will exist materially whether anyone reads it or not. Once Dickens had finished writing it and the publisher released it into the world, its 'material textuality' – its selection of words – was made and finished, even though its meanings, how people interpret it, would remain largely up for grabs. Its material production and its constitution were decided by its suppliers, that is, its author, publisher, serializer etc alone – only the meaning was the domain of the reader. *Big Brother* on the other hand, to take a typical pseudo-modern cultural text, would not exist materially if nobody phoned up to vote its contestants off. Voting is thus part of the material textuality of the programme – the telephoning viewers write the programme themselves. If it were not possible for viewers to write sections of *Big Brother*, it would then uncannily resemble an Andy Warhol film: neurotic, youthful exhibitionists inertly bitching and talking aimlessly in rooms for hour after hour. This is to say, what makes *Big Brother* what it is, is the viewer's act of phoning in.

Pseudo-modernism also encompasses contemporary news programmes, whose content increasingly consists of emails or text messages sent in commenting on the news items. The terminology of 'interactivity' is equally inappropriate here, since there is no *exchange*: instead, the viewer or listener enters – writes a segment of the programme – then departs, returning to a passive role. Pseudo-modernism also includes computer games, which similarly place the individual in a context where they invent the cultural content, within pre-delineated limits. The content of each individual act of playing the game varies according to the particular player.

The pseudo-modern cultural phenomenon *par excellence* is the internet. Its central act is that of the individual clicking on his/her mouse to move through pages in a way which cannot be duplicated, inventing a pathway through cultural products which has never existed before and never will again. This is a far more intense engagement with the cultural process than anything literature can offer, and gives the undeniable sense (or illusion) of the individual controlling, managing, running, making up his/her involvement with the cultural product. Internet pages are not 'authored' in the sense that anyone knows who wrote them, or cares. The majority either require the individual to make them work, like Streetmap or Route Planner, or permit him/her to add to them, like Wikipedia, or through feedback on, for instance, media websites. In all cases, it is intrinsic to the internet that *you can easily make up pages yourself* (e.g. blogs).

If the internet and its use define and dominate pseudo-modernism, the new era has also seen the revamping of older forms along its lines. Cinema in the pseudo-modern age looks more and more like a computer game. Its images, which once came from the 'real' world – framed, lit, soundtracked and edited together by ingenious directors to guide the viewer's thoughts or emotions – are now increasingly created through a computer. And they look it. Where once special effects were supposed to make the impossible appear credible, CGI frequently (inadvertently) works to make the possible look artificial, as in much of *Lord of the Rings* or *Gladiator*. Battles involving thousands of individuals have really happened; pseudo-modern cinema makes them look as if they have only ever happened in cyberspace. And so cinema has given cultural ground not merely to the computer as a generator of its images, but to the computer game as the model of its relationship with the viewer.

Similarly, television in the pseudo-modern age favours not only reality TV (yet another unapt term), but also shopping channels, and quizzes in which the viewer calls to guess the answer to riddles in the hope of winning money. It also favours phenomena like Ceefax and Teletext. But rather than bemoan the new situation, it is more useful to find ways of making these new conditions conduits for cultural achievements instead of the vacuity currently evident. It is important here to see that whereas the *form* may change (*Big Brother* may wither on the vine), the terms by which individuals relate to their television screen and consequently what broadcasters show have incontrovertibly changed. The purely 'spectacular' function of television, as with all the arts, has become a marginal one: what is central now is the busy, active, forging work of the individual who would once have been called its recipient. In all of this, the 'viewer' feels powerful and is indeed necessary; the 'author' as traditionally understood is either relegated to the status of the one who sets the parameters within which others operate, or becomes simply irrelevant, unknown, sidelined; and the 'text' is characterized both by its hyper-ephemerality and by its instability. It is made up by the 'viewer', if not in its content then in its sequence – you wouldn't read *Middlemarch* by going from page 118 to 316 to 401 to 501, but you might well, and justifiably, read Ceefax that way.

A pseudo-modern text lasts an exceptionally brief time. Unlike, say, *Fawlty Towers*, reality TV programmes cannot be repeated in their original form, since the phone-ins cannot be reproduced, and without the possibility of phoning-in they become a different and far less attractive entity. Ceefax text dies after a few hours. If scholars give the date they referenced an internet page, it is because the pages disappear or get radically re-cast so quickly. Text messages and emails are extremely difficult to keep in their original form; printing out emails does convert them into something more stable, like a letter, but only by destroying their essential, electronic state. Radio phone-ins, computer games – their shelf-life is short, they are very soon obsolete. A culture based on these things can have no memory – certainly not the burdensome sense of a preceding cultural inheritance which informed modernism and postmodernism. Non-reproducible and evanescent, pseudo-modernism is thus also amnesiac: these are cultural actions in the present moment with no sense of either past or future.

The cultural products of pseudo-modernism are also exceptionally banal, as I've hinted. The content of pseudo-modern films tends to be solely the acts which beget and which end life. This puerile primitivism of the script stands in stark contrast to the sophistication of contemporary cinema's technical effects. Much text messaging and emailing is vapid in comparison with what people of all educational levels used to put into letters. A triteness, a shallowness dominates all. The pseudo-modern era, at least so far, is a cultural desert. Although we may grow so used to the new terms that we can adapt them for meaningful artistic expression (and then the pejorative label I have given pseudo-modernism may no longer be appropriate), for now we are confronted by a storm of human activity producing almost nothing of any lasting or even reproducible cultural value – anything which human beings might look at again and appreciate in fifty or two hundred years time.

The roots of pseudo-modernism can be traced back through the years dominated by postmodernism. Dance music and industrial pornography, for instance, products of the late 70s and 80s, tend to the ephemeral, to the vacuous on the level of signification, and to the unauthored (dance much more so than pop or rock). They also foreground the activity of their 'reception': dance music is to be danced to, porn is not to be read or watched but *used*, in a way which generates the pseudo-modern illusion of participation. In music, the pseudo-modern superseding of the artist-dominated album as monolithic text by the downloading and mix-and-matching of individual tracks on to an iPod, selected by the listener, was certainly prefigured by the music fan's creation of compilation tapes a generation ago. But a shift has occurred, in that what was a marginal pastime of the fan has become the dominant and definitive way of consuming music, rendering the idea of the album as a coherent work of art, a body of integrated meaning, obsolete.

To a degree, pseudo-modernism is no more than a technologically motivated shift to the cultural centre of something which has always existed (similarly, metafiction has always existed, but was never so fetishized as it was by postmodernism). Television has always used audience participation, just as theatre and other performing arts did before it; but as an option, not as a necessity: pseudo-modern TV programmes have participation built into them. There have long been very 'active' cultural forms, too, from carnival to pantomime. But none of these implied a written or otherwise material text, and so they dwelt in the margins of a culture which fetishized such texts – whereas the pseudo-modern text, with all its peculiarities, stands as the central, dominant, paradigmatic form of cultural product today, although culture, in its margins, still knows other kinds. Nor should these other kinds be stigmatized as 'passive' against pseudo-modernity's 'activity'. Reading, listening, watching always had their kinds of activity; but there is a physicality to the actions of the pseudo-modern text-maker, and a necessity to his or her actions as regards the composition of the text, as well as a domination which has changed the cultural balance of power (note how cinema and TV, yesterday's giants, have bowed before it). It forms the twenty-first century's social-historical-cultural hegemony. Moreover, the activity of pseudo-modernism has its own *specificity*: it is electronic, and textual, but ephemeral.

Clicking in the changes

In postmodernism, one read, watched, listened, as before. In pseudo-modernism one phones, clicks, presses, surfs, chooses, moves, downloads. There is a generation gap here, roughly separating people born before and after 1980. Those born later might see their peers as free, autonomous, inventive, expressive, dynamic, empowered, independent, their voices unique, raised and heard: postmodernism and everything before it will by contrast seem elitist, dull, a distant and droning monologue which oppresses and occludes them. Those born *before* 1980 may see, not the people, but contemporary texts which are alternately violent, pornographic, unreal, trite, vapid, conformist, consumerist, meaningless and brainless (see the drivel found, say, on some Wikipedia pages, or the lack of context on Ceefax). To them what came before pseudo-modernism will increasingly seem a golden age of intelligence, creativity, rebellion and authenticity. Hence the name 'pseudo-modernism' also connotes the tension between the sophistication of the technological means, and the vapidity or ignorance of the content conveyed by it – a cultural moment summed up by the fatuity of the mobile phone user's 'I'm on the bus'.

Whereas postmodernism called 'reality' into question, pseudo-modernism defines the real implicitly as myself, now, 'interacting' with its texts. Thus, pseudo-modernism suggests that whatever it does or makes is what is reality, and a pseudo-modern text may flourish the apparently real in an uncomplicated form: the docu-soap with its hand-held cameras (which, by displaying individuals aware of being regarded, give the viewer the illusion of participation); *The Office* and *The Blair Witch Project*, interactive pornography and reality TV; the essayistic cinema of Michael Moore or Morgan Spurlock.

Along with this new view of reality, it is clear that the dominant intellectual framework has changed. While postmodernism's cultural products have been consigned to the same historicized status as modernism and romanticism, its intellectual tendencies (feminism, postcolonialism etc) find themselves isolated in the new philosophical environment. The academy, perhaps especially in Britain, is today so swamped by the assumptions and practices of market economics that it is deeply implausible for academics to tell their students they inhabit a postmodern world where a multiplicity of ideologies, world-views and voices can be heard. Their every step hounded by market economics, academics cannot preach multiplicity when their lives are dominated by what amounts in practice to consumer fanaticism. The world has narrowed intellectually, not broadened, in the last ten years. Where Lyotard saw the eclipse of Grand Narratives, pseudo-modernism sees the ideology of globalized market economics raised to the level of the sole and over-powering regulator of all social activity – monopolistic, all-engulfing, all-explaining, all-structuring, as every academic must disagreeably recognize. Pseudo-modernism is of course consumerist and conformist, a matter of moving around the world as it is given or sold.

Secondly, whereas postmodernism favoured the ironic, the knowing and the playful, with their allusions to knowledge, history and ambivalence, pseudo-modernism's typical intellectual states are ignorance, fanaticism and anxiety: Bush, Blair, Bin Laden, Le Pen and their like on one side, and the more numerous but less powerful masses on the other. Pseudo-modernism belongs to a world pervaded by the encounter between a religiously fanatical segment of the United States, a largely secular but definitionally hyper-religious Israel, and a fanatical sub-section of Muslims scattered across the planet: pseudo-modernism was not born on 11 September 2001, but postmodernism was interred in its rubble. In this context pseudo-modernism lashes fantastically sophisticated technology to the pursuit of medieval barbarism – as in the uploading of videos of beheadings onto the internet, or the use of mobile phones to film torture in prisons. Beyond this, the destiny of everyone else is to suffer the anxiety of getting hit in the cross-fire. But this fatalistic anxiety extends far beyond geopolitics, into every aspect of contemporary life; from a general fear of social breakdown and identity loss, to a deep unease about diet and health; from anguish about the destructiveness of climate change, to the effects of a new personal ineptitude and helplessness, which yield TV programmes about how to clean your house, bring up your children or remain solvent. This technologized cluelessness is utterly contemporary: the pseudo-modernist communicates constantly with the other side of the planet, yet needs to be told to eat vegetables to be healthy, a fact self-evident in the Bronze Age. He or she can direct the course of national television programmes, but does not know how to make him or herself something to eat – a characteristic fusion of the childish and the advanced, the powerful and the helpless. For varying reasons, these are people incapable of the 'disbelief of Grand Narratives' which Lyotard argued typified postmodernists.

This pseudo-modern world, so frightening and seemingly uncontrollable, inevitably feeds a desire to return to the infantile playing with toys which also characterizes the pseudo-modern cultural world. Here, the typical emotional state, radically superseding the hyper-consciousness of irony, is the *trance* – the state of being swallowed up by your activity. In place of the neurosis of modernism and the narcissism of postmodernism, pseudo-modernism *takes the world away*, by creating a new weightless nowhere of silent autism. You click, you punch the keys, you are 'involved', engulfed, deciding. You are the text, there is no-one else, no 'author'; there is nowhere else, no other time or place. You are free: you are the text: the text is superseded.

5

They Might Have Been Giants

John McGowan

Postmodernism, according to John McGowan, was a project with colossal ambitions. Its goals constituted nothing less than a complete reappraisal of the structures of Western thought, together with a wholesale critique of their ethical and political consequences. Despite Lyotard's denunciation of grand narratives, McGowan argues that the postmodern tradition was nevertheless a discourse preaching liberation and emancipation on a grand scale, and he tracks this tendency in the work of a triumvirate of postmodern thinkers: Derrida, Foucault, and Habermas.

New work in the humanities now lacks this sense of drive and scope, claims McGowan, and he argues that the comparative poverty of the scale of its ambition is symptomatic of the demise of postmodernism. The philosophical aspirations of the postmodernists have all but vanished under a steady stream of more measured, more methodical, and more thorough scholarship that is evidentially rather than theoretically oriented. This understated timbre of most recent scholarship in the humanities contrasts starkly with the postmodernists' sense of zeal at shifting intellectual boundaries: McGowan ruefully observes that this zeal now resurfaces only rarely, and when it does, it is mostly in the service of explicitly right wing, reactionary agendas.

The reason for this can be traced to 1989, with the collapse of Soviet power in Eastern Europe, and the fall of the Iron Curtain. Notwithstanding the fraught relationships between postmodernist and Marxist thought, and postmodernism's regular denunciations of totalitarianism in all its forms, the Cold War had conditioned the postmodern generation of theorists to think in terms of (because in the shadow of) a political alternative. Once such alternatives were lacking, it became all but impossible to think of a possibility outside of a hegemonic Western capitalism, and so postmodernism had had its day. Thus, McGowan's postmodernism is a historical period bookended by two revolutions: it was engendered in the failed revolutions of 1968, and sought the same liberation from the Western mindset as the students of Paris and Prague; and it was struck a mortal blow in the successful revolutions of 1989, which seemingly sought a wholesale embrace of the very Western values that postmodernism was predicated on denouncing.

The extract is by John McGowan, 'They Might Have Been Giants', in *Postmodernism: What Moment?*, ed. Pelagia Goulimari (Manchester: Manchester University Press, 2007), pp. 92–101.

They Might Have Been Giants

The postmodernism debate in theory circles can be dated from the publication of Jean-François Lyotard's *The Postmodern Condition* in 1979 to Fredric Jameson's book-length version (finally published in late 1991) of his much-read and much-discussed essays of the mid-1980s.[1] The theoretical debate follows, I will argue, the historical arc from 1968's incoherent but widespread rebellions to 1989's Eastern European revolutions. The term 'postmodernism' is still with us as a vague reference to French theory, historical meta-fiction, and eclectic hybrid forms in architecture and art. But the theoretical debate represented by 'postmodernism' has, for better and worse, passed from the scene. Yes, the academic discourse around postmodernism had some important and interesting relation to the 'culture wars' between traditionalists and progressives that have sullied, if not outright polluted (especially in the USA), public arts policies, efforts at educational reform, and all talk of 'values'. Unfortunately, the culture wars are all too much still with us since they have proved so useful to America's rightist politicians. But the predictable, pro forma efforts by conservative pundits to blame social ills on academic writers they have never read has little to offer us by way of understanding why 'postmodernism' as a concept served to galvanize a group of major thinkers for some ten-plus years fifteen years ago. By confining myself in these remarks solely to the conversation among those thinkers, who were to a very large extent writing about and to each other, I considerably raise my chances of saying something coherent and cogent.

In particular, I am interested in a group of writers who were all born too late to be active participants in the Second World War but were coming of age during that traumatic event – and, especially, in its aftermath of facing up to the death camps and to the atom bomb. Lyotard, Foucault, Derrida, Jameson, Said, Rorty, and Habermas were all born between 1925 and 1935. The important feminist theorists of the postmodern moment are a bit younger: Cixous was born in 1937, Kristeva in 1941, Spivak in 1942.[2] Crucially, the male writers are not baby-boomers and, consequently, were not students during the 1960s. Their work participates in, as well as reflects, both the rise and the collapse of 1960s radicalism, but the connection is hardly direct and certainly not simple. Their intellectual formation came in the 1950s, not the 1960s, and they were not of the student movement even when they allied themselves with it. All of these writers, the women included, come from complex and very specific intellectual and cultural backgrounds that make generational generalizations pointless. Several – the Palestinian Said, the Algerian and Jewish Derrida, the Indian Spivak, and the Romanian Kristeva – are transplants, living and writing in non-native lands, but others – Foucault and Rorty among them – come from the professional upper middle classes.

All of these writers, with the exception of Rorty, were internationally prominent by the time they were forty. Despite claims that their work was obscure, they earned their precocious academic and international reputations by virtue of playing for very large stakes while making those stakes dramatically clear. Nothing less than the West's soul hung in the balance. The postmodernism debate was about the Western tradition's crimes and accomplishments. All of the participants acknowledged the disasters of the Holocaust, of the economic and political colonization of non-white peoples in the non-West, and the secondary status of female and colored persons in the West. At issue was how fundamental the causes for such evils were. Their abiding question was: what went wrong – and where – and why? Specifically, was Western philosophy – its traditional canons of thought, knowledge production, and rationality – and Western political commitments – to rights, equality, and popular sovereignty under the banner of a universalist humanism – root causes of these crimes or a potential source for protesting against or even remedying them? The Enlightenment, especially, came in for criticism. In retrospect, the European attempt to replace divinely ordained hierarchies with polities grounded on popular sovereignty, the rule of law, and universal rights (all justified and underwritten by reason) seemed a disaster. Specific battles were waged over the terms 'reason', 'truth', 'human' and others. But the main battle was clear: what, if anything, of the tradition could be salvaged, could be justified? How fully and completely had the West gone off the rails?

Admittedly, these dramatic questions were asked in very arcane forms, embedded within technical and exegetical discussions of past writers. Academic protocols sometimes overwhelmed the clear articulation of issues. But the accusations of obscurity were greatly exaggerated. The postmodern theorists' struggles with Kant and Hegel offer a case in point. Kant remains the most important exponent of the Enlightenment and liberalism's humanism, while Hegel represents Western thought's recurrent will to totality, its relentless intellectual imperialism. Yet simple condemnation of these two figures is hardly possible, since Kantian reason (not to mention his explorations of the sublime and of judgment in the Third Critique) and Hegelian historicism remain fundamental constituents of how we think and argue. To tangle with such figures and the complexity of their legacy was to address the meanings of the West in a responsible and thorough way, no matter how opaque the discussion might seem to newcomers.

What I want to consider here is why this debate proved so gripping for a short time – and why it seems so much less gripping today. I will focus specifically on Derrida, Habermas, and Foucault, but this troika is meant to stand in for an entire cadre of writers born between 1925 and 1942. We would, undoubtedly, argue about whom to include in this wider group, but I only need you to grant that some, if not all, of the writers I have already named might plausibly fit the profile. They might have been giants. Their work dwarfs those who come after, continuing to set the intellectual agenda even as they are less and less explicitly discussed or even invoked. The academic world has, as it will, moved on. The postmodernism debate in particular is long over. And the 'revolution' that 'theory' promised has either occurred or not. The odd thing is how hard it is to tell. Yesterday's controversies become today's received wisdom. Depending on your angle of vision, everything – or nothing – seems to have changed since 1960, a convenient date for marking a time when the academy and the West in general still seemed safely ensconced in their dogmatic slumbers. Standing at the end of 2004, it makes perfect sense to claim that postmodernism as a theoretical shift of epic proportions never happened. But it is equally possible to claim that intellectual work is utterly different today than it was forty years ago. Was postmodernism a passing fad or are we all postmodern now?

Put that way, I can only reply that the question is ill-framed. I don't think an era or a style hangs together in that way, so that a broad label captures some kind of essential features shared by many particulars. No practice (body piercing), art work (architecture), technological innovation (cell phones), or scientific discovery (genetic engineering) is going to hold the key to who we are – fundamentally, truly, and really. And there is the additional problem that people who are differently situated socially are going to live in the same time period, even use the same buildings and institutions, in very different ways. The lines of force and meaning are more dispersed, more conflictual, more partial than a term like postmodernism conveys.

But the term provides a powerful charge of simplicity and clarity. My naïve question is: why did Derrida, Foucault, and Habermas command so much attention, from such widely dispersed quarters? They wrote books that everyone with any kind of intellectual pretensions in the humanities and social sciences had to read. No one has published a book like that in the last ten years. Why not?

I think it is partly an issue of style. Quentin Skinner had it right when he spoke of a 'return of grand theory'.[3] Charles Taylor wrote: 'Foucault's attraction is partly that of a *terrible simplicateur*'.[4] Dense as their work is, Foucault, Habermas, and Derrida all work from a grand set of contrasts between the premodern and modernity in the first two cases, between Western metaphysics and its shadowy other in Derrida's case. Surprisingly, given the fact that the term 'postmodernism' came to be affixed to their work, neither Foucault nor Derrida pays much mind to postmodernism per se. Habermas is partly responsible for attaching the label to them in his polemic against the postmodernists, *The Philosophical Discourse of Modernity*. But the modernism/postmodernism contrast does fit the spirit of Derrida's and Foucault's habitual reliance on drawing strong, binary oppositions in their work. And, even more fleetingly although certainly hauntingly, the postmodern makes its appearance as a faintly drawn apocalyptic scene on the far side of our current entanglement in the West's tarnished tradition – famously in Foucault's evocation of the 'disappearance of man' at the end of *The Order of Things*.[5]

> If those arrangements were to disappear as they appeared, if some event of which we can at the moment do no more than sense the possibility – without knowing either what its form will be or what it promises – were to cause them to crumble, as the ground of Classical thought did, at the end of the eighteenth century, then one can certainly wager that man would be erased, like a face drawn at the edge of the sea.

This gesture toward a grand-scale historical transformation, one that would usher in a post-human era utterly different from the 'modern' liberal era or the 'classical' era that preceded it, holds out the promise of the 'postmodern' even while refusing to specify what it might look like. Derrida, in his early essays (especially 'Structure, Sign and Play in the Discourse of the Human Sciences' and 'The Ends of Man'[6]), gingerly takes up this question of a transition from one era to another, ending 'Structure' with reference to a 'birth' from which some turn their eyes away – 'those who, in a society from which I do not exclude myself, turn their eyes away when faced by the as yet unnamable which is proclaiming itself and which can do so, as is necessary whenever a birth is in the offing, under the species of a nonspecies, in the formless, mute, infant, and terrifying form of monstrosity' (*Writing and Difference* 293). In his later work, Derrida will be more direct, albeit no more specific, in his repeated invocations of the 'to come' as in his appeal to the 'democracy to come' in *The Politics of Friendship*.[7]

To some extent, all three writers – Foucault, Derrida, and Habermas – aim to overcome dualisms, to avoid contrastive binaries. They each, in their own way, offer an analysis that denies the existence of an 'outside'. For the Foucault of *Discipline and Punish*, power encompasses everything and we must jettison our romantic notions of something or some person standing apart from and independent of power; 'there is no outside'.[8] Similarly, Derrida tells us that we cannot simply step outside of Western metaphysics; deconstruction is a 'trembling' of the structure that will not collapse it entirely and must be ever cognizant of the 'force and efficiency of the system that regularly change transgressions into "false exits"'.[9] Habermas is at great pains in the two volumes of *The Theory of Communicative Action* to prove that every utterance is embroiled in the basic contract that underwrites all language use. But a fundamental contrast between freedom and oppression drives all of their work. Foucault turns in his later work to issues of self-mastery in order to develop a model of power that also offers a modicum of freedom; Derrida always held on to the image of an 'irreducible alterity' even as he despaired of our ability to locate it or to protect it from the 'violence of metaphysics' once we found it.[10] Even as he warns us against delusions of easy escape from 'the system' in 'The Ends of Man', he also tells us that 'a radical trembling can only come from the *outside*' (134). And Habermas's whole project is predicated on distinguishing between the 'distorted' speech acts within oppressive societies and the 'ideal' speech acts of the truly free.[11] This epic struggle between freedom and its opposite is staged in their work and serves as the grand unifying idea that makes their fine-grained details and sophisticated arguments cohere. The clarity of their work stems from the reader's always being able to map the details back to whether here freedom is being advanced or retarded. The standard of measurement (even if only implicit) can always be wheeled into action.

Even where they cannot see victory – or despairingly predict eternal defeat – Foucault, Derrida, and Habermas are passionate moral advocates for alternatives to the prevailing social order. All three provide readers with a key to the world we live in, 'a history of the present', as Foucault put it – one that locates us at the nexus of a series of traceable forces and transformations.[12] In short, they do philosophy of history, as it was practiced in the days when philosophers aspired to reveal the grand patterns that underlay the whole trajectory of the West. And they also do straightforward philosophy, as it was practiced when philosophers aspired to provide the conceptual basis for understanding everything. Neither kind of philosophy had been practiced by someone born in England or America since Hume or Gibbon, with the possible exception of John Dewey. Continental examples were more abundant, with Foucault and Derrida taking up the mantle of Sartre, while Habermas directly follows from Adorno.

The irony, of course, was that Foucault and Derrida, at least, promulgated their grand visions in the name of dismantling what Wittgenstein called 'the craving for generality'.[13] Wittgenstein identifies this craving with, among others things, 'the tendency [which the poststructuralists call essentialism] to look for something common to all the entities which we commonly subsume under a general term' (17); 'our preoccupation with the method of science. I mean the method of reducing the explanation of natural phenomena to the smallest possible number of primitive natural laws' (18); and with 'the contemptuous attitude toward the particular case' (18). Foucault and Derrida's continual assault against essentialism and their focus on particularity and singularity echoes with Wittgenstein's critique.[14] Habermas is a trickier case, arguing for a less magisterial, 'post-metaphysical' philosophy, while still insisting on the necessity for and legitimacy of transcendental claims.[15] Derrida, the most fatalistic of the three, appears to believe that the craving for generality cannot be eradicated, but that it can be controlled by eternal vigilance, by the work of a deconstruction that is never finished.[16] Foucault had greater hopes of finding a new modus vivendi – for intellectual work, for the experience of selfhood, and for living a life.[17] And the price he pays for dismantling coherent identities and sweeping generalizations is that the final volumes of *The History of Sexuality*, endearingly modest, even pedestrian, pale in comparison to the fire of *Discipline and Punish*.[18] Foucault just another scholar working in the salt mines of minutiae? A charming concept, but . . .

Yet it is those final volumes that set the tone of scholarship for the past fifteen years. Except for the diehard Deleuzians (god bless their addled pates), the academics have scurried back into their holes. (Negri and Hardt's *Empire*, with its ungainly mixture of Marx and Deleuze and its grand sweep, is to be honored precisely for its ambitions, no matter what reservations we have about its specific arguments.[19]) Our social theory reading group in Chapel Hill, which brought together twenty to twenty-five people each year to read Spivak or Laclau and Mouffe in the old days, has now dwindled to four or five hardy souls. Whether it's post-colonial theory or Spinoza, we can't find a text busy people can agree they need and want to read. The academics I know are not writing books that engage conceptual frameworks directly. They may, in some cases, think their specific historical work or case histories might nudge received ideas or methodologies in one direction or another, but they write as if they think, as one colleague of mine put it, that change in such matters is very slow and comes from careful examination of a quite particular issue.

I am of mixed mind. The 'might' in my title reflects my sense that much of the postmodernism debate was awfully silly. Caricatures of the West, of various intellectual traditions and positions, and, especially, of the political consequences of holding certain ideas often prevailed. The exasperation that Foucault expressed in 'What Is Enlightenment?' with the tenor of the debate, the simplicities it had introduced, was well justified.

> [W]e must not conclude that everything that has ever been linked with humanism is to be rejected, but that the humanistic theme is in itself too supple, too diverse, too inconsistent to serve as an axis of reflection.... In any case, I think that, just as we must free ourselves from the intellectual blackmail of 'being for or against the Enlightenment', we must escape from the historical and moral confusionism that mixes the theme of humanism with the question of the Enlightenment. An analysis of their complex relations in the course of the last two centuries would be a worthwhile project, an important one if we are to bring some measure of clarity to the consciousness that we have of ourselves and of our past.
>
> (44–5)

As it turned out, the West's future did not hinge on the outcome of our theoretical debates. But while the heightened rhetoric and oversimplifications are easy to mock, the passion, ambition, and dramatic clarity of *The Philosophical Discourse of Modernity, Discipline and Punish*, and *Of Grammatology* still seem titanic when measured against the best the last ten years have to offer. Furthermore, those books oriented us, giving us the large simplifications and moral stakes that our subsequent work set out to clarify, to nuance. Pluralism has its virtues, both intellectual and political, not the least of which is an egalitarianism that makes giants unnecessary. I have no doubt that detailed work, modest in its scope and careful in its conclusions, is more mature, more attuned to scholarship as a communal enterprise. But when I see the ambition that animated the work of my troika only displayed these days by the likes of Steven Pinker and Niall Ferguson, I think the company of a few clumsy, even megalomaniac, giants in the Marx-Nietzsche-Sartre line would be a fine thing.[20]

Currently, only conservatives who want to reaffirm a basic, unalterable human nature (like Pinker) or urge America to adopt wholeheartedly an imperial role (like Ferguson) are thinking big. The left is in retreat in the West – and that makes me think that postmodernism might best be 'periodized' as lasting from 1968 to 1989, with the inevitable academic time lag explaining why it took a while to burst into print and some time after historical events rendered it moot to stop occupying academic imaginations. That year of failed revolutions – 1968 – precipitated the desire for overarching interpretations of the West and for radical, total solutions. Paradoxically, even Lyotard's famous turn away from 'grand narratives' in *The Postmodern Condition* was presented as a radical – and pervasive – break from previous practices. The very notion of postmodernity works against the assertion of historical continuities; it posits a change that alters the very conditions of life and thought. That this revolutionary change was more desired than actual always made the label 'postmodern' problematic. Foucault, Derrida, and even Habermas were all gesturing toward desired, and perhaps impossible because ideal, transformations. Hence all three shied away from proclaiming that some radical break had already been accomplished. Even Lyotard retreated from the notion that we were already postmodern, tying himself into knots over the question of whether 'postmodernism' named a precise historical period or instead stood for an attitude that was present, if submerged, in all eras.[21] Only the dystopian Jameson actually claimed that postmodernism had arrived, was our current reality. In short, the postmodernism debate partook of the revolutionary hopes of 1968 insofar as it was organized around the notion of a complete transformation of a West that was understood as being all of one piece. It was a revolution that had not happened, that was to come.

The year 1989 put an end to all that. Interpreted as the triumph of the West, the fall of communism not only deprived the left of its favorite alternative to Western liberalism but also undermined the thesis that the West was rotten to the core, everywhere and in every time. That the oppressed peoples of Eastern Europe associated the West with freedom made the more extreme denunciations of the West by privileged Western intellectuals look like political naiveté or, worse, bad faith. Between the end of communism and the onset of globalization, the left was put on the defensive, working piecemeal and frantically to protect as many of the threatened components of social democracy as possible. Freed from the implied contrast with socialism and the real presence of a second 'superpower' in the Soviet Union, capitalism embarked on a new round of ruthless exploitation of labor while the USA turned into a swaggering bully. Now it was the right that promulgated – and actually achieved – wide-scale change (although hardly total transformation as envisioned in the most radical dreams and theories of revolution). The change in tone and approach is manifested in one of the last things Derrida wrote before his death. He looks to 'Europe, as a proud descendant of the Enlightenment past and a harbinger of the new Enlightenment to come' to stand as a counterweight to globalization and American imperialism. But he also cautions: 'That doesn't mean that any grand revolution is about to remove the power centres that emerged victorious from the cold war.' The best hope he offers is that 'constant pressure from the counter-globalization movement and ordinary people the world over' will 'weaken' the triumphant and 'force them to reform'.[22]

As I have indicated, I am of two minds about the loss of the grand clarity and flourishes of theory's style at the height of the postmodernism debates. A sensible and sober Derrida is, like a cautious Foucault, a letdown. But surely such sobriety does indicate both the way forward for those who wish to change the West's ways and the slow, complex work any successful reform movement will have to do. There is no magic wand that will make it all disappear, no theoretical analysis or rhetorical bravado that will unlock the door to freedom. Postmodern theory failed if its aim was to deliver a better world. But the passion and wide-reaching vision with which it pursued that goal of a better world was – and remains – exemplary. I am only willing to applaud the current return to careful scholarship that attends to the small continuities and disruptions within a complex, non-unified, and contested Western tradition if such scholars are driven by the grand and passionate desire of the postmodern giants for a freedom that the West still continues to deny to most people, Westerners and non-Westerners alike.

Notes

1   Jean-François Lyotard, *The Postmodern Condition*, trans. Geoff Bennington and Brian Massumi (Minneapolis: U of Minnesota P, 1984); Fredric Jameson, *Postmodernism or, The Cultural Logic of Late Capitalism* (Durham, NC: Duke UP, 1991). The key interventions by Jameson in the mid-1980s were his 'Introduction' to the Lyotard text cited above, and essays in *New Left Review* 146 (1984): 53–92; *Social Text* 15 (1986): 65–88; and in Hal Foster (ed.), *The Anti-Aesthetic* (Port Townshend, WA: Bay, 1983): 111–25. All of these essays, albeit expanded and somewhat revised, are included in the 1991 book.

2   Besides the works by Lyotard and Jameson cited in the previous note,
    representative works particularly relevant to postmodernism by each of these
    writers are Jacques Derrida, *Of Grammatology*, trans. Gayatri Chakravorty Spivak
    (Baltimore: Johns Hopkins UP, 1976); Michel Foucault, *Discipline and Punish*,
    trans. Alan Sheridan (New York: Vintage, 1979); Jürgen Habermas, *The
    Philosophical Discourse of Modernity*, trans. Frederick Lawrence (Cambridge, MA:
    MIT P, 1987); Richard Rorty, *Contingency, Irony, and Solidarity* (Cambridge:
    Cambridge UP, 1989); Edward Said, *Orientalism* (New York: Pantheon, 1978);
    Hélène Cixous, *Coming to Writing and Other Essays*, trans. Sarah Cornell et al.
    (Cambridge, MA: Harvard UP, 1991); Julia Kristeva, *Powers of Horror*, trans. Leon
    S. Roudiez (New York: Columbia UP, 1982); Gayatri Chakravorty Spivak, *In Other
    Worlds: Essays in Cultural Politics* (New York: Routledge, 1988).

3   See Skinner, *The Return of Grand Theory* (Cambridge: Cambridge UP, 1985).

4   Charles Taylor, 'Foucault on Freedom and Truth' in *Foucault: A Critical Reader*, ed.
    David Couzens Hoy (New York: Blackwell, 1986) 82.

5   Michel Foucault, *The Order of Things* (New York: Vintage, 1973) 387.

6   'Structure, Sign and Play in the Discourse of the Human Sciences' in *Writing and
    Difference*, trans. Alan Bass (Chicago: U of Chicago P, 1978) 278–93; and 'The Ends
    of Man' in *Margins of Philosophy*, trans. Alan Bass (Chicago: U of Chicago P, 1982)
    111–36. The original dates of the essays are 1967 and 1968, respectively.

7   Jacques Derrida, 'The Politics of Friendship', trans. George Collins, *Journal of
    Philosophy* 85 (1988): 632–44.

8   *Discipline and Punish* 31.

9   See 'The Ends of Man', esp. 134–36.

10 See the early (1963) essay 'Violence and Metaphysics: An Essay on the Thought of
    Emmanuel Levinas' in *Writing and Difference* 79–153. The phrases 'absolute
    alterity' and 'the absolutely irreducible exteriority of the other' recur throughout
    the essay. For two instances, see 91 and 93.

11 For a succinct account of Habermas's views, see 'A Philosophico-Political Profile',
    trans. Peter Dews, in *Habermas, Autonomy and Solidarity: Interviews with Jürgen
    Habermas*, ed. Peter Dews (London: Verso, 1986) 149–90, esp. 157–66.

12 *Discipline and Punish* 31.

13 Ludwig Wittgenstein, *The Blue and Brown Books* (New York: Harper, 1960) 17–18.

14 See, for example, Foucault's discussion of method in 'What Is Enlightenment?'
    where he writes: 'it seems to me that the critical question today has to be turned
    back into a positive one: in what is given to us as universal, necessary, obligatory,
    what place is occupied by whatever is singular, contingent, and the product of
    arbitrary constraint?' (45). 'What Is Enlightenment?', trans. Catherine Porter, in *The
    Foucault Reader*, ed. Paul Rabinow (New York: Pantheon, 1984).

15 For Habermas's attempt to articulate a 'modest' contemporary philosophy that still retains some ability to offer 'general' and 'transcendent' perspectives, see his essay 'Philosophy as Stand-In and Interpreter', trans. Christian Lenhardt, in *After Philosophy: End or Transformation?*, eds Kenneth Baynes, James Bohman and Thomas McCarthy (Cambridge, MA: MIT P, 1987) 296–315.

16 I have discussed at length Derrida's 'tragic' view that Western metaphysics and its violence cannot be overcome in *Postmodernism and its Critics* (Ithaca, NY: Cornell UP, 1991) 89–121.

17 The essay 'What Is Enlightenment?' is crucial here, but see also 'The Ethic of Care for the Self as a Practice of Freedom', trans. J.D. Gauthier, SJ, *Philosophy and Social Criticism* 12 (1987): 112–31.

18 Do we witness a similar retreat from 'grand' theorizing in the careers of Derrida and Habermas? Yes and no. Habermas has become less transcendental if we interpret (as I am inclined to do) his later work on norms and laws as acknowledging that these societal forms are not universal but tied to specific polities or international agreements/institutions. But it is not clear that he is willing to go that far toward relativism. And I don't quite know what to make of the later Derrida, with his simultaneous *rapprochement* (discussed below) with the European legacy he once scorned and his gestures toward a transcendent and religious call as the basis of his work.

19 Antonio Negri and Michael Hardt, *Empire* (Durham, NC: Duke UP, 2000).

20 Steven Pinker, *Blank Slate: The Modern Denial of Human Nature* (New York: Viking Penguin, 2002); and Niall Ferguson, *Empire: The Rise and Demise of the British World Order and the Lessons of Global Power* (New York: Basic, 2004).

21 See *The Postmodern Condition*, esp. 71–82.

22 Quoted from Derrida, 'Enlightenment Past and to Come', trans. John McGowan, *Le Monde Diplomatique* 6 Nov. 2004, available <http://mondediplo.com/2004/11/06derrida>.

6

Post-Postmodernism: Or, The Cultural Logic of Just-In-Time Capitalism

Jeffrey T. Nealon

If, as Fredric Jameson saw it, postmodernism was essentially an economic condition, then for Jeffrey T. Nealon, so too is post-postmodernism. Jameson argued that, in the late twentieth century, culture was no longer simply an expression of economic forces, nor was it exactly 'determined by' the realm of the economic. Rather, for Jameson, the nature of capitalism meant that it was no longer possible neatly to separate the economic from the cultural, because culture itself was part and parcel of the capitalist economy. Nealon argues that Jameson's diagnosis of the postmodern has become more rather than less prescient and relevant during the thirty years since its publication. His description of post-postmodernism, as he puts it, is an 'intensified' update of Jameson's diagnosis.

The most significant change the world has undergone in the years since Jameson's work was published is, for Nealon, the transition from the era of cold war imperialism to the era of globalized capitalism. Thus, in Nealon's view, the 1980s constituted a watershed: the loss of faith in 'big government', the onset of 'Reaganomics' (the decentralization and deregulation of the economy during the Thatcher and Reagan years), the disappearance of the Soviet bloc leading to the opening up of the world's markets to global capital, and the increasingly ruthless and erratic manoeuvrings of the financial markets have brought about a world in which the once-iconoclastic ideas of postmodernism are now taken as received wisdom. For example, the idea that values are not fixed, but rather are socially constructed or dependent on contexts which are themselves in constant flux, was once a radical new idea in postmodern philosophy, but now is accepted as financial common sense by people shopping around for mortgages or pension plans, as anyone involved in the economic crisis of 2008 (and beyond) will recall.

Contemporary culture, as Nealon sees it, cannot be understood in isolation from the dominant forces of neoliberalism and globalization. Indeed, one could (over) simplify Nealon's argument by saying that post-postmodernism just is the neoliberal project of globalization. Insofar as this project amplifies economic and cultural tendencies already diagnosed by Jameson as integral to postmodernism, Nealon's post-postmodernism involves less a supplanting of the postmodern and more a culmination of it. That is, instead of supplanting or superseding the postmodern, post-postmodernism rather intensifies what Jameson saw as the cultural logic of advanced capitalism.

The obvious commonsensical riposte to Nealon's views would be that if post-postmodernism is simply an intensification of the postmodern rather than a supplanting of it – if 'it's hard to understand today as anything other than an intensified version of yesterday' as Nealon puts it (Nealon, 2012, p. 8) – then why (let alone how) is post-postmodernism distinguishable from postmodernism itself? Such a counterargument is not, however, very propitious, for similar objections were often made in the opposite direction when the term 'postmodernism' was first mooted – namely, that postmodernism was better understood as an intensification of modernism than as a supplanting of it. Indeed, Nealon's view that the postmodern has mutated rather than ended is shared – albeit for different reasons – by other writers in this section, like Steven Connor.

Instead, the single biggest weakness in Nealon's position is that, while it claims to offer an analysis of the era of globalization, it in fact does no such thing: its argument focuses almost exclusively on American culture and economics, and the examples Nealon analyses (such as the Hollywood blockbuster movie and Las Vegas shopping malls described in this extract) seem more or less oblivious to non-American experiences, interpretations, and worldviews. In other words, Nealon's position is symptomatic of a mindset that equates globalization with Americanization, whereas a truly globalized perspective would offer more scope for critiquing his targets.

For instance, the Las Vegas-style gambling Nealon describes, rather than becoming globally ubiquitous (like, say, Coca Cola or Nike) remains illegal and subject to strict punishment in many countries. Perhaps as a result of this, Las Vegas has now become an international gambling tourist destination, attracting visitors from all over the world, yet few (if any) cities outside the USA have looked to replicate it as a model for economic growth, let alone architecture or town planning. Put simply: if Nealon takes the gambling mecca of Las Vegas as a microcosm of global neoliberal post-postmodern culture, then this is a highly problematic claim. Moreover, whilst Nealon's point about the growth of the gambling industry in an economy that glamorizes risk is a judicious observation, nevertheless gambling as an industry does not fit the neoliberal mould: it remains one of the most heavily regulated and state-controlled industries in the world, clearly giving the lie to neoliberal claims that the intervention of the state impairs profitability, and that economic deregulation is a precondition for economic growth.

The years which, according to Nealon, saw the final triumph of American laissez-faire capitalism also saw at least two dramatic phenomena which bucked this trend. In stark contrast to the neoliberal ideology, the European Union's response to the financial downturn of 2008 was to spend hundreds of billions of euros on loans to bail out the faltering economies of its weaker member states – hardly a laissez-faire market-based solution. At the same time, the USA's position as the world's dominant economy began to come under sustained pressure due to the remarkable rise of China as an industrial superpower, showing that, pace Nealon, the world is not (yet) one big American empire. In light of these developments, Nealon's view of globalization, focused so tightly on the depredations of neoliberalism in the American economy, begins to appear rather parochial.

Nevertheless, though the global economy and global culture may be more complex and multifaceted entities than Nealon's analysis suggests, it would be wrong to disregard his argument altogether, or to underestimate the massive impact of globalization and the 2008 financial crisis (the effects of which are still being keenly felt at the time of writing). If his economic analysis has moments of undue pessimism, it also offers a more measured, more carefully argued, more economically grounded view of globalization's role in supplanting the postmodern than (for example) the celebratory declarations of Nicolas Bourriaud's altermodernism (see Part Two).

The extract is from Jeffrey T. Nealon, *Post-Postmodernism: or, The Cultural Logic of Just-In-Time Capitalism* (Stanford: Stanford University Press, 2012), pp. ix–xii; pp. 14–15; pp. 29–42.

Post-Postmodernism: Or, The Cultural Logic of Just-In-Time Capitalism

Preface: Why post-postmodernism?

'Post-postmodernism' is an ugly word. And not in the sense that swear words or racial slurs are ugly, or even in the way that 'rightsizing' or 'outsourcing' are ugly words (which is to say, evasive spin-doctored words that try to paper over something foul). Post-postmodernism is, one might say, just plain ugly: it's infelicitous, difficult both to read and to say, as well as nonsensically redundant. What can the double prefix 'post-post' possibly mean? Insofar as postmodernism was supposed to signal the end of modernism's fetish of the 'new', strictly speaking, nothing can come after or 'post-' postmodernism, which ushered in the never-ending end of everything (painting, philosophy, the novel, love, irony, whatever).

But at the same time, there are a number of things to recommend the title 'Post-Postmodernism' over its undoubtedly more felicitous rivals – such as 'After Postmodernism,' 'The End(s) of Postmodernism,' 'Postmodernism's Wake,' 'Postmodernism 2. 0,' 'Overcoming Postmodernism,' 'Whatever Happened to Postmodernism?,' and so on. For my purposes, the least mellifluous part of the word (the stammering 'post-post') is the thing that most strongly recommends it, insofar as the conception of post-postmodernism that I'll be outlining here is hardly an outright overcoming of postmodernism. Rather, post-postmodernism marks an intensification and mutation within postmodernism (which in its turn was of course a historical mutation and intensification of certain tendencies within modernism).

So the initial 'post' in the word is less a marker of postmodernism's having finally used up its shelf life at the theory store than it is a marker of postmodernism's having mutated, passed beyond a certain tipping point to become something recognizably different in its contours and workings; but in any case, it's not something that's absolutely foreign to whatever it was before. (Think of the way that a tropical storm passes a certain threshold and becomes a hurricane, for example: it's not a difference in *kind* as much as it is a difference in *intensity* – or, more precisely, any difference in kind is only locatable through a difference in intensity.) With its stammering inability to begin in any way other than intensifying the thing it's supposed to supersede, 'post-postmodernism' is a preferred term for suggesting just such a super-postmodernism, hyper-postmodernism, or maybe a 'late postmodernism,' as opposed to the overcoming or rendering obsolete of postmodernism that would be implied by a phrase like 'after postmodernism.' Related and more pragmatic reasons to hang on to the moniker 'post-postmodernism' might be that it has its own Wikipedia entry and that the term has been popping up everywhere from the *New York Times* to literary criticism journals, though it has been used in architectural circles for at least fifteen years.[1]

Indeed, postmodernism has seemingly been lingering at death's door, refusing to pass definitively, for quite some time: John McGowan, author of *Postmodernism and Its Critics* (1991), jokingly suggested to me in the early 1990s that my first book, *Double Reading: Postmodernism after Deconstruction* (1993), would be among the last suggesting that postmodernism was still an ongoing phenomenon. In 1997, John Frow made the fatal tense change official, asking 'What Was Postmodernism?' in his *Time and Commodity Culture: Essays in Cultural Theory and Postmodernity*, though we should note that Brian McHale consciously repeated Frow's titling query in an essay a decade later in 2007, suggesting that there may be something about postmodernism that resists outright overcoming or obsolescence.

But for me the most compelling reason to hang on to the awkward 'post-post' is that (as is clear from my title) I want to position this analysis squarely in the orbit of Fredric Jameson's authoritative work, *Postmodernism; or, The Cultural Logic of Late Capitalism* – which argues, among many other things, that postmodernism is best understood as a historical period of capitalist development rather than (or, really, as the prior ground of) understanding it as a style of artistic practice, a movement within various art and architecture discourses, or even a kind of zeitgeist. In short, I argue throughout that capitalism itself is the thing that's intensified most radically since Jameson began doing his work on postmodernism in the 1970s and '80s. The 'late' capitalism of that era (the tail end of the cold war) has since intensified into the 'just-in-time' (which is to say, all-the-time) capitalism of our neoliberal era.

[...]

Suffice it to insist here in the Preface: my aim is not to render obsolete either postmodernism or any particular analysis of it (as if either were possible) but to intensify, highlight, and redeploy certain strands within Jameson's analyses of postmodernism, and thereby to suggest some further structuring mutations in the relations among cultural production and economic production in the years since Jameson originally produced his magisterial analyses.

[...]

So if I dedicate considerable space to the questions of theory yesterday, today, and tomorrow, I do so to argue that a changed cultural and economic situation (a changed sense of the 'cultural dominant') likewise suggests that we need a new theoretical and methodological toolbox for responding to post-postmodern culture. I fear that if we can't engage robustly with the present, humanities disciplines that are invested in cultural production risk becoming wholly antiquarian archival exercises: Jameson's theory-era *cri de coeur* 'always historicize' is a long distance from what seems to be developing as the new humanities research slogan, 'shit happened.' So I'm interested in revisiting a series of crucial postmodern concepts from the era of big theory (commodity, deconstruction, interpretation, literature, among others) to see what changes have been wrought in their critical effectiveness by the cultural and economic shifts that travel under the name post-postmodernism. Hence, each chapter also attaches to a postmodern keyword that it's trying to intensify, rethink, or redeploy.

Arguing against the contemporary 'death of theory' hypothesis, I want to insist that just as postmodernism was a synonym for theory, so post-postmodernism needs to be as well. If we can say one thing for sure in our uncertain present, it's that the world hasn't gotten any *less* complex over the past few decades. Which, to my mind at least, suggests that in making post-postmodern sense (which is importantly different from postmodern 'meaning') of our situation, it's a very bad time indeed to give up on the discourses of theory. I am following the suggestion of another, more sage Nealon (Christopher) in his reading of Jameson, when he argues that the project of theory in the present is less a continuation of the postmodern 'hermeneutics of suspicion' than it is a toolkit for the construction of a 'hermeneutics of situation,' an intensification perhaps of Jameson's long-standing dream of producing a cognitive map of the present.

[...]

I want to follow Jameson insofar as he suggests we need to do a genealogy of the recent economic past, not so that we can nostalgically recall and celebrate the gains and losses, but finally so we don't delude ourselves into thinking that the oppositional strategies of the past can unproblematically and effectively be imported into the present. (I take this to be the force of the Jamesonian slogan 'always historicize.') If Jameson's two 1984 essays suggest – however subtly – that many left-leaning academics in the mid-'80s were still stuck in an outmoded mind-set of the 1960s, and that an economic analysis was the clearest way to show this, I want to fast-forward that hypothesis into our present. To put my concern baldly, it seems to me that much North American humanities 'theory' of the present moment is essentially stuck in and around 'the '80s'; and perhaps the easiest and most effective way of breaking that spell is to try to think economically as well as culturally about the differences between the two periods.

If we consider only the most obvious example of such present-day theoretical anachronism, Jameson's 'Postmodernism' essay itself remains the touchstone for cultural studies work on the present – it's a perennial syllabus favorite, and it continues to function as a term-setter for debates about economics and culture today. This, it seems to me, is quite odd (and quite un-Jamesonian). Remember that when Jameson's essay was published in 1984, the Berlin Wall was still firmly in place – the cold war was in fact heating up again, with Reagan's new morning in America still dawning; the Dow Jones was struggling to run at 1,200; Paul Volcker's inflation-worried Fed had US interest rates sky high; Japan, it seemed, was the economic power to be reckoned with and feared in the next century (recall that in the industrial Midwest of the mid-80s, people would routinely vandalize Japanese cars and motorcycles – or, for that matter, just take a look at 1982's *Blade Runner* and its Japanized dystopian future); in 1984, Americans were just beginning to talk about AIDS; the first MAC computer – with 286 stunning k of RAM – debuted in North America in January 1984, introduced in a splashy, Orwellian Super Bowl commercial; the Internet – at least as we know it – was still the stuff of science fiction, as was the global ubiquity of cell phones and smartphones. Watching Michael Douglas talk on a billionaire's prize – a portable satellite phone the size of a shoebox – in *Wall Street*, who could have imagined that only two decades later, most middle school students would possess communication technology ten times smaller and a hundred times more powerful?

We live, in other words, in a very different world from the early to mid-80s. Though we still live with the fallout of the 80s, it's clear that the economic component of our 'cultural dominant' is no longer that particular brand of 'postmodernism, or late capitalism.' In fact, the neo-Marxist hope inscribed in the phrase 'late capitalism' seems a kind of cruel joke in the world of globalization ('late for what?'). So among the tasks of periodizing the present, a collective molecular project that we might call *post-postmodernism*, is to construct a

vocabulary to talk about the 'new economies' (post-Fordism, globalization, the centrality of market economics, the new surveillance techniques of the war on terrorism, etc.) and their complex relations to cultural production in the present moment, where capitalism seems nowhere near the point of its exhaustion. Although the hopes contained in the phrase 'the new economy' have all but dried up in recent years, the dreary realities of its market dictates remain very much with us – one hesitates to say permanently, but as far as the eye can see at the present moment. Also, I should note that I take mine to be a diagnostic project: any kind of tentative *pre*scription for treating current ills would have to follow from a thick *de*scription of the symptoms and their genealogical development over time. So it's to that descriptive or diagnostic project that I now turn.
[...]

Hail Caesar!

Perhaps the best site to begin surveying this burgeoning empire of commerce and culture is Caesar's Palace Casino and Hotel, located at the center of the Las Vegas Strip, an appropriately labyrinthine imperial site. If Jameson had a hard time making his way around the Bonaventure Hotel in LA, one shudders to think of the disorientation he'd experience in the 'Forum Shops at Caesar's': an unapologetic overlap of hotel, casino, restaurant, theme park, and shopping mall – all done up in some hyper-postmodern version of the ancient past. Around Caesar's shops are scattered mythological Greek figures like Poseidon, Homer, and the Trojan Horse – all emblems that, we may recall, were already ancient by the time of Plato, some four hundred years before the reign of Augustus Caesar. The statuary rubs elbows with a roaming live Cleopatra and her buff Roman Centurions, all of whom will gladly pose for pictures with Caesar's honored guests.

The Forum Shops are a hybrid of the contemporary suburban mall and the nineteenth-century flaneur's arcade (curiously decked out with ubiquitous Roman aqueducts – flows, everywhere flows). You're ferried into the Forum from the sweltering Strip along a series of covered moving sidewalks – a welcome fit for an emperor. When you want to leave, however, you have to trudge the five hundred yards back to Las Vegas Boulevard like a plebeian – through the Caesar's casino (if you can find the poorly marked exit) and out over the unforgivingly hot acres of blacktop set aside for horseless carriages. While you're there, the 'experience' of the Forum Shops is rounded out by the usual American mall stores (Gap, Victoria's Secret, Abercrombie & Fitch) as well as unusual ones (Burberry, Versace, Cavalli); restaurants launched by ubiquitous uber-chefs Wolfgang Puck and Bobby Flay; and a huge aquarium, which both complements the statuary in 'Poseidon's Fountain' (right next to the Cheesecake Factory in the Roman Great Hall) and serves as a backdrop for one of the rare free shows in Vegas, the 'Fall of Atlantis'.[2]

In Caesar's new empire, the myths of the absolute past and the promises of the deferred future are mishmashed together for easy, intensive, one-stop 'experience' shopping. The heroes of Atlantis, Troy, Greece, and Rome did not die in vain; they perished to help create this new empire of 'freedom' – which, as we all know, means subjective empowerment as consumer choice, the only water fit to satisfy our thirsts. But, one might ask the FAO Schwartz Trojan Horse (which curiously talks, making it an appropriately anachronistic mix of Mr. Ed and the Oracle of Delphi), What do you get for a crowd that has already experienced everything? The answer: more of the same.

Contemporary Las Vegas is not so much a figure for imperialist expansion or assimilation – the old-time 'Fuck you, we're movin' in' Vegas of the Mob and the Teamsters – as it is an ongoing, live experiment conducted to see what happens when a certain imperial project has completed itself, when there are no more lands for Caesar to conquer: 'the place where the wave finally broke and rolled back', as Hunter Thompson (1998: 68) put it. In other words, Las Vegas's current modes of power are no longer primarily deployed in the service of legitimating the enterprise or overcoming an enemy (the government, the middle-American prude, the other casinos); those battles have already been decided. Rather, emergent modes of both corporate and subjective power in Las Vegas are aimed at intensifying what you've already got: expanding market share and deepening the demographic base by deploying new forms of value-added entertainment 'experiences'.

In short, the economic force that's deployed in Las Vegas functions *not* by conquering or assimilating new territory but rather by intensifying new versions of familiar things: for example, Paris (with its own Eiffel Tower), the Venetian (with its replica frescoed ceilings and gondolas in the annexed shopping mall), and New York, New York (the building itself constructed as a faux version of Manhattan, complete with a Statue of Liberty). The wholly rebuilt Aladdin, a posh theme-park version of the eponymous Mob casino, was opened at the dawn of the new century – overtly completing the feedback loop of anachronism by taking the past of Las Vegas itself as the original historical script to be remixed and remastered. (That proved not 'intense' enough a concept, so the Aladdin became the Planet Hollywood Hotel and Casino, with its Hollywood film theme, including movie memorabilia in every guest room – the stars' throwaways serving as the altar relics of privatized capitalism.)

In such settings, you don't so much *consume goods* as you *have experiences* where your subjectivity can be intensified, bent, and retooled. In contemporary Las Vegas, you are offered opportunities for doing work on yourself (experiencing, seeing, feeling) rather than opportunities for confronting, overcoming, purchasing, or otherwise consuming some 'other'. As Michael Hardt and Antonio Negri write, 'In the postmodernization of the global economy, the creation of wealth tends ever more toward ... biopolitical production, the production of social life itself, in which the economic, the political, and the cultural increasingly overlap and invest one another' (2000: xiii). The force of the new globalized economic empire – the empire one spies from Caesar's Palace – doesn't primarily turn outward in an expansive, colonialist, or consumerist assimilation. Now it turns inward toward intensification of existing biopolitical resources. The final product, in the end, is you and me.

And gambling is the logical cornerstone of such an empire, insofar as *risk* is the perfect figure and vehicle for this new economy of intensities. In any endeavor, but especially economic ones, risk of various kinds is irreducible. You can't simply accept or deny risk wholesale; no actor has that kind of control over contingency. Any actor or collective can only *modulate* risk – speed it up or slow it down. Certainly, risk can be canalized – some outcomes made more likely, and some less likely; but risk per se cannot be subsumed or assimilated. Risk constitutes a flow that can't be overcome but one that can be affected only by being intensified – being made greater or smaller, faster or slower. This intensification, to take only the most obvious example, is what's on display when gamblers 'chase' losses: increasing their bets, and their risk, in the hope of getting even.[3]

Such is the logic of intensity, then, on both the global and the subjective levels: in a world that contains no virgin territory – no new experiences, no new markets – any system that seeks to expand must by definition *intensify* its existing resources, modulate them in some way(s). This, in a nutshell, is the homology between the cultural logic of globalization and the economic logic of finance capital, neither of which is dedicated to discovering wholly new sources of human or economic capital: neither is set on cold war goals like seeking out raw materials or new territory to bring into the empire. Rather, the challenge for the globalized logic of finance capital is to find new mechanisms to work on money itself – new modes of risk intensification like derivatives, swaps, futures, currency trading, arbitrage.

On a subjective level of intensities, then, the paradigmatic Vegas casino experience is no longer modeled on the existentialism of Dostoyevsky's *Gambler*: a masculinized, heroic confrontation with a mysterious 'other' (God, fate, chance, destiny, sex, money).[4] Here in Vegas, authenticity is no longer won extensively by challenging such an other but by a more direct, intensive retooling of the self. Even the strictly speaking corporate force in town is not aimed essentially at overcoming the competition. In contemporary biz-speak, the hostile corporate takeover or leveraged buyout (staple of the junk-bond era that provided the money to build the theme-park Vegas) is a distant memory – soooo 80s. 'Mergers' and 'synergy' are the new watchwords of empire.

Caesar, in other words, is not at war with the Flamingo or the Bellagio; they are all merely coexisting provinces within the same essentially peaceable kingdom. As a mundane example of this synergy, note that casino chips in Las Vegas are – unlike competing national currencies – essentially interchangeable: the other big casinos will treat Caesar's chips as the coin of their realm as well, which only makes sense, because you can't spend capital if you don't liquidate it – if you can't morph it into a form where it can immediately flow. Monetary chauvinism – like so many practices of the cold war nation-state – is just plain inefficient. At least since the fall of the Berlin Wall in 1989 and the millennial 'defeat' of Soviet power worldwide, it seems that there is no 'out there' for casino capitalism to vanquish, no dialectical other against which to define or test itself.[5] Such an empire can expand only by intensifying its victory, since there are no new lands to conquer.

Empire of the intensities

Not coincidentally, such a very literal sense of empire's completion pervades another high-profile exercise in Romanesque anachronism at the dawn of the new millennium, Ridley Scott's Academy Award-winning film *Gladiator* (2000). In the opening scene, we're introduced to our protagonist, General Maximus (Russell Crowe, not channeling Charles Olson), who's about to lead his men into the final battle of the Roman Empire's last great campaign, circa AD 180.

Maximus is the favorite general of the reigning emperor Marcus Aurelius (Richard Harris), the last Caesar of Rome's Golden Age. Victory against the 'Germanians', we are told by the opening credits and by Caesar himself, will suture and complete the empire's imperialist expansion. After this battle, which the Romans are sure to win, the peaceable kingdom of Rome's Golden Age will have been wholly forged: there will be no more wars left to fight, no territory left to assimilate.

And seemingly no more movie, no more story to tell. Once this opening battle is over and the empire is secured, what's left to narrate? Audiences seem unlikely to respond favorably to a three-hour chronicle of an aged Caesar and his favorite general playing checkers and reminiscing over libations at the Old Soldiers' Club in Rome. As far as a promising Hollywood plot goes, the bureaucratic management of more-or-less peaceable kingdoms (whether Marcus's management of civil empire or Maximus's desired return to the domestic sphere of the family) hardly seems the stuff of spectacle-laden, epic cinema in the tradition of *Ben-Hur* or *Spartacus*. After seeing Maximus lead his men into the last battle for empire – a sweeping, gory, jump-cut-laden slaughter of the Germanians – do we then look forward to one hundred minutes of Maximus mowing the lawn and ordering the kids to clean up their rooms?

Luckily, Caesar's venal son Commodus (Joaquin Phoenix) steps in to save the plot. Seeing that Caesar distrusts him and favors Maximus – or, worse, that Caesar intends to turn power over to the Senate – Commodus murders his father and ascends immediately to the role of emperor. Aside from the simple motivating force of Commodus's lust for power, the audience can't help noting that Commodus also grasps a complex historical truth: after the defeat of the Germanians, the old emperor has outlived his usefulness. The skills of the father – assimilating and annexing land through warfare – are not the skills required for managing a vast transnational and multicultural empire. As Hardt and Negri write of a parallel in our globalized world, post-cold war politics becomes a matter of regulating 'hybrid identities, flexible hierarchies, and plural exchanges through modulating networks of command' (2000: xii–xiii).

Paradoxically, *Gladiator's* conquering Caesar has no place in the multicultural, global empire that he's brought about – where a kinder, gentler form of coercion, bloodshed, and violence will have to be invented and practiced.[6] Needless to say, neither does Maximus – commander of the tightly ordered and homogeneous world of the Roman legions – have any clue concerning the administration of such an unwieldy and complex new world order. But Commodus has some ideas.

In fact, he's hip to the productive qualities of biopower and the coercions of the culture industry: keep the masses fat and happy by giving them entertainment, he surmises. Bring back the gladiators!

If we enter the world of *Gladiator* at the end of Roman imperialism proper – where the project for the foreseeable future becomes managing diversity rather than assimilating territory – what better tactic than bringing back the crowd-pleasing, heroically nostalgic intensities of gladiator battles? Scott's film – somewhat disingenuously, given its participation in this empire of nostalgia and representation – shows us that like our own colonial cold war, Roman imperialism was indeed brutal; but the film retroactively portrays those days of disciplinary imperialism as honorable, satisfying, and 'real' in some way. We see this trace of authenticity repeated in Maximus's signature trope, deployed throughout the film: he picks up a handful of local soil before entering any battle, thereby cementing his existential bond with the earth and the land – with the forces of nature and the stability of the real.

Certainly *Gladiator* suggests that the imperialist world of the film's opening was a dangerous place – paradoxical, fraught with contradiction. Men had to act and fight for a nationalist abstraction, 'Rome', without really understanding why. But the faux, staged gladiator fights of the post-imperialist empire (those that dominate the rest of the film) will never offer anything close to this kind of authentic subjective heroism. In the end, *Gladiator* shows us a world where the hard-fought battles of imperialism bring about the ancient analog to the slap-fights that festoon twenty-first-century reality TV programs. The eclipsing of Roman colonial expansion leads to an even more sinister kind of image-based totalitarianism: a spectacle economy staged for the amusement and, finally, *control* of the Roman masses – represented as decadent, fickle, Colosseum-bound couch potatoes. If Augustus ruled them with discipline, fear, and grudging respect, Commodus – a sort of Baudrillard in a toga – will amuse them to death.

I take this detour through *Gladiator* for a reason. First, the film quite overtly wants to function as a *Spartacus* (1960) for the new millennium; and like Stanley Kubrick's film, Scott's *Gladiator* offers – among other things – a historical allegory by which we might come to understand, and maybe even resist, the sinister powers of our own day. The most obvious target of Kubrick's film – and the blacklisted Dalton Trumbo's script – was the anticommunist hysteria of 1950s America. The (in)famous scene where dozens, then hundreds, of slaves stand up and pronounce 'I am Spartacus!' functions as a kind of critical inversion and refusal of the US House of Representatives Un-American Activities Committee's practice throughout the 1950s – and, more broadly, the scene functions as a reaction to McCarthyist racial, ethnic, and political intolerance and hysteria in the US. Rather than offer up the names of others – 'name names' – to absolve yourself of guilt, *Spartacus* models a mode of resistance to political blackmail: 'I am Spartacus' could be roughly translated as, 'If freedom of thought and action is the charge, then yes, we are all "guilty", and proud of it. We are all Spartacus – we are all communists, Jews, African Americans, poor people, homosexuals.' In *Spartacus*, we see the slaves standing up to power through solidarity, and in the process the film provides a democratic model of collective action – a united subaltern strategy that promises to confront totalitarian threats of any stripe.[7]

Scott's *Gladiator* likewise uses the model of the ancient Roman Empire to comment on recent events. But, half a century later, Scott's presentation of global capitalism is inexorably different from Kubrick's cold war moment. Rome, for example, is depicted in *Gladiator* as a crowded, multicultural, and transnational city, much like contemporary global metropolises New York, Shanghai, or London. The gladiators, slaves with whom Maximus falls in after his family is slaughtered on the orders of Commodus, uniformly hail from the distant, annexed Roman colonies: the Middle East, Africa, Spain, Germania. And among Scott's contemporary targets seems to be the exposure of a kind of postmodern plantation system, with all the shit jobs of our empire still performed by those from the so-called third world. More directly, however, *Gladiator* attempts to name and critique the globalized urban mass's obsession with media spectacle – the subtle voyeuristic coercions of 'extreme' sports, political spin doctoring, trash talk shows, reality TV, celebrity gossip, millionaire quiz shows, and so on. Like the decadent Romans portrayed in the film, we post-postmodern capitalists are trained by our media masters to watch rather than act, consume rather than do.

Presumably, following the lead of *Spartacus*, *Gladiator* should try to produce a strategy for us, a model for resisting the commodified spectacle that the film so effectively demonstrates. There should be another way mapped – a response that might act as a vehicle for collective resistance, a road to some better place. But, alas, recall that the film is framed by the completion of empire, the literal absence of any such outside. In our world, as in the world of *Gladiator*, there's literally no place else to go: the dominant mode of power has succeeded in covering the known earth. And in the end, *Gladiator* responds to this situation fairly predictably – offering nothing but nostalgia for an older form of domination, longing for the good old days of discipline. Throughout, but especially in the end, the film rather shamelessly lauds the imperialist, masculine labor power of

Maximus and Augustus ('good'!) and excoriates the feminized and incestuous practices of the image-monger Commodus (need I say, 'bad' – even his name suggests heading for the toilet). Indeed, they don't get much more reprehensible than Commodus: incest and the hint of child molesting are bad enough, but this guy's even shown to be a *bad sport*, having fatally wounded a bound and helpless Maximus moments before their final battle in the Colosseum. So Maximus is forced to stumble through – and of course win – the battle while dying from this wound.

After the mutual death of Maximus and Commodus in the Colosseum, the Senate is poised to take power at the conclusion of the film, with Senator Gracchus (Derek Jacobi) as their leader. But this ending gesture toward 'democracy' can't leave savvy, image-saturated movie audiences entirely happy. Senator Gracchus portrays himself as the ancient counterpart of a Kennedy liberal ('Not a man of the people', he reminds us, 'but a man for the people'). However, Camelot hasn't fared so well in revisionary American history: Jack Kennedy was elected president largely because of his slick media savvy (or the 1960 Nixon's lack thereof), and he's remembered these days less for any populist credentials than for having brought about the Cuban Missile Crisis, Vietnam, and a level of White House philandering that would have made Bill Clinton blush. Besides, if audiences recall their high school textbook history, they know what's on the menu for Rome after the Golden Age of Marcus Aurelius: decline and fall. In the end, *Gladiator* suggests that only the reluctant but heroic leadership of someone like General Maximus – an Eisenhower for the ancient world – could have saved the empire: if we liked Ike, we'd have loved Max. But saddled as we are with our own venal, image-obsessed political and corporate emperors, we global capitalists in the United States should expect the same immanent moral and political decline as the Romans.

In *Gladiator*'s vision of the Roman epic film, a strategic mode of resistance to the violent othering of cold war imperialism ('I am Spartacus!') is replaced by a nostalgic mourning *for that very world of imperialism*: 'I wish I could be like the conquering Maximus! But they don't make 'em like that anymore'. *Spartacus*'s collective response is replaced by *Gladiator*'s atomized yearning for individual authenticity. And, needless to say, such a Golden Age of subjective authenticity is always already a thing of the past, an object of commodified nostalgia in late Augustan Rome as well as in contemporary Disneyfied Hollywood.

Taken as a contemporary political and historical allegory of cold war imperialism giving way to an even-more-dangerous, media-saturated globalized capitalism, *Gladiator* leaves us with very little strategic room to move, other than pining for the good old days of imperialism – when you knew who the good guys were, when you could be heroic and authentic, when the blood was real. Resistance to the global flow of fleeting images, the film suggests, can be found only in the intensive authenticity of your own private experience, turned up to Maximus: a quirky individuality that's available – maybe even on sale – at sublime locations like the Forum Shops at Caesar's, as well as mundane sites like your Netflix queue. And seemingly everywhere in between.

In any case, rest assured that it's coming soon – in fact, over and over again – to a theater near you, as virtually all Hollywood films contain a version of this message: resist the system by courting intense experiences, always modulating your own authentic, flexibly specialized subjectivity.

Post-postmodern empire

Of course, this new empire of postimperialist biopolitical production travels under a more recognizable pseudonym, one we read in the paper every day: globalization. In their mammoth book *Empire*, Michael Hardt and Antonio Negri point out that 'Empire is materializing before our very eyes. Over the past several decades, as colonial regimes were overthrown and then precipitously after the Soviet barriers to the capitalist world market finally collapsed, we have witnessed an irresistible and irreversible globalization of economic and cultural exchanges' (2000: xi). It's all one world now, we're told over and over again, by people on the right and the left.

But how exactly is this new world of globalized, triumphant capital different from the old colonial hostilities of the cold war? Is this really a peaceable, postimperialist kingdom? The answer seems to be, yes and no. The new mode of empire's power – as *Gladiator* shows us – is different, but it's no less forceful. Hardt and Negri write, 'Although the practice of Empire is continually bathed in blood, the concept of Empire is always dedicated to peace – a perpetual and universal peace outside of history' (2000: xv).

As Foucault puts forth in his work on disciplinary regimes, iron-fisted mechanisms of regulation are both expensive and inefficient – a lesson that international business learned long before the cold war nation-state did. Foucault argues that the disciplinary apparatus was born gradually alongside imperialist expansion in the seventeenth through nineteenth centuries, and reached its height in the twentieth. As Hardt and Negri explain, 'In a disciplinary society, the entire society, with all its productive and reproductive articulations, is subsumed under the command of capital and the state, and that the society tends ... to be ruled by criteria of capitalist production. *A disciplinary society is thus a factory society*' (2000: 243). For Hardt and Negri, the American New Deal represents the apex of this disciplinary vision of society as a vast but centrally controlled and regulated factory.

By all accounts, however, this kind of Fordist New Deal welfare state has been systematically dismantled by worldwide conservative political hegemony and the rise of the new economy. In a world of cyber-work, e-commerce, wireless communication, distance education, virtual markets, home health care, and the perpetual retraining of flexibly specialized labor, the disciplinary world of partitioning and surveillance (the office, the school, the bank, the trading floor, the mall, the hospital, the factory) seems like it's undergone a wholesale transformation. As Deleuze argues, 'We're definitely moving toward "control"' societies that are no longer exactly disciplinary. . . . We're moving toward control societies that no longer operate [primarily] by confining people but through continuous control and instant communication. . . . In a control-based system, nothing's left alone for long' (1995: 174–75). Deleuze further elaborates on the distinction between discipline and control: 'In disciplinary societies, you were always starting all over again (as you went from school to barracks, from barracks to factory), while in control societies you never finish anything – business, training, and military service being coexisting metastable states of a single modulation, a sort of universal transmutation' of power (1995: 179). So, while societies of control certainly extend and intensify the tactics of discipline (by linking training and surveillance to ever more minute realms of everyday life), they also give birth to an entirely new form of power.

Discipline itself constitutes a form of power different from its predecessors – the sovereign power of the spectacle, the banishment of the leper, or the confinement of the plague victim (see Foucault 1979: 195–200). The panoptic power characteristic of modern discipline acts not directly on bodies but on the body's potential for actions: as Deleuze explains in *Foucault*, 'Force is exercised on other forces' (Deleuze 1988: 35). In short, the Foucauldian power of surveillance doesn't directly mark bodies, as the sovereign power of the scaffold does; it is a (much more efficient and economical) regulatory mechanism – you don't know exactly when you're being watched, so you adapt your behavior at all times to the power of being seen. Such a form of power acts on your actions; its primary target is your 'virtual' possibilities, which in turn more economically regulate your actions.

Surely, surveillance in the globalized world of control has been taken to a new, even more disembodied and therefore efficient state; your Web browser, your DNA, your credit or debit cards, your subway pass, cellphone usage, or credit report all suggest that you are tracked in ways that make the warehousing of bodily traces (like photographs, surveillance tapes, fingerprints, or blood types) seem positively quaint by comparison. If you can't even escape your undergraduate alumni magazine, how can you hope to evade the grip of transnational corporations?

Discipline has been taken to the limit of what it can do; and in this intensive movement, discipline's limit has become a threshold, inexorably transforming this form of power into a different mode, a 'lighter' and even more effective style of surveillance that can only accelerate the already lightning-fast spread of that monstrous form of power/knowledge known as globalization. And Hardt and Negri build their concept of post-postmodern empire precisely on this notion of the waning of disciplinary power and the waxing of the society of control: 'The society of control might thus be characterized by an intensification and generalization of the normalizing apparatuses of disciplinarity that internally animate our common and daily practices, but in contrast to discipline, this control extends well outside the structured sites of social institutions through flexible and fluctuating networks' (2000: 23).

Hardt and Negri suggest that we are witnessing not so much the end of imperialist or disciplinary power, but its intensification and transmutation into another kind of power. At its completion, one might say that the disciplinary power of imperialism doesn't merely halt, but it's forced to work differently, to develop another modus operandi. As Hardt and Negri argue, the present-day empire of transnational capital comprises 'something altogether different from "imperialism"'. They explain:

> Imperialism was really an extension of the sovereignty of the European nation-states beyond their own boundaries. Eventually, nearly all the world's territories would be parceled out and the entire world map could be coded in European colors: red for British territory, blue for French, green for Portuguese, and so forth. Wherever modern sovereignty took root, it constructed a Leviathan that overarched its social domain and imposed hierarchical territorial boundaries, both to police the purity of its own identity and to exclude all that was other.
>
> (2000: xii)

As *Gladiator*'s Romans no longer fight the Germanians and Caesar's Palace is no longer out to slay the Venetian, so the logic of post-postmodern capitalism no longer works primarily according to the rigid disciplinary logics of exclusion, othering, and noncontamination. As GATT, NAFTA, the euro, and the WTO attest, the nation-state no longer functions primarily as a machine 'to police the purity of its own identity and to exclude all that was other'; rather, the nation-state now seeks primarily to hold the door for transnational capital – though, of course, this task regularly requires crackdowns of a terrifyingly 'old-fashioned' disciplinary nature.

Such brutal tactics are still in fact prominently on display wherever global elites – the leaders of the World Bank, IMF, WTO, G20, major political conventions – meet, and where dozens of 'potential' protestors and protest leaders are summarily arrested or banished to far-flung 'free speech zones'. And of course, the War on Terror has brought such first-world barbarity front and center – with 'enhanced interrogation', arrest without warrant, and illegal rendition remaining approved US government tactics long after the George Bush administration has faded into unpleasant memory. And in times of economic downturn, you can still count on xenophobic political scapegoating of immigrants, or so we've seen globally in recent years: Turks in Germany, Muslims in Scandinavia, Mexicans in the American Southwest. In short, simply because the nation-state's primary reason for being has changed, we shouldn't therefore assume that it's been evacuated of its disciplinary power or its investments in confinement. This is especially obvious in the context of the US not only in terms of terrorism, but with its burgeoning prison-industrial complex: throughout the 1990s, the American prison industry boasted growth rates second to only one economic sector – that's right, gambling.[8]

So the emergent economy of globalized control doesn't simply supersede or wholly displace the society of the nation-state's discipline. However, in the world of post-postmodern capital, nationalism's political boosters dream not of purity or overcoming a threatening other but rather of the endless, smooth flow of capital and goods (though not so much people) across boundaries of all kinds. These days, everyone from politicians to CEOs to the Arby's fast-food chain joins in the global refrain 'different is good': and, needless to say, one can't imagine any cold war leader worth his SALT talks saying such a thing. The world of imperialism is, by definition, a world where 'different is bad' – otherness is an obstacle, there only to be excluded, demonized, or assimilated.

But difference in the postmodern world isn't there to be overcome; it's there to be intensified.

The logic of *intensification* is the (non)site where the logic of the individual subject overlaps with the logic of globalization. As the subjective pole of existentialism – with its thematics of alienation, mutually assured destruction, binarized subject/object splits, its heroic confrontations with the other and with death – is inexorably tied to the era of *extensive* imperialism, so the subjective pole of contemporary experience *intensification* is equally tied to the economic and political logic of globalization. The 'flexible and fluctuating networks' of postmodern globalization function according to an intensification of Foucault's notion of productive power, which teaches us that power doesn't hold good unless the subject can take some pleasure or knowledge from its bargain with a dominant mode of power. There has to be something 'in' it for the subject. This is the breakthrough modus operandi of empire, its direct linkage to subjective intensities, the complete 'culturization' of political and economic life. As Hardt and Negri argue, 'The society of control is able to adopt the biopolitical context as its *exclusive* terrain of reference' (2000: 24).

Unlike the discontinuous, desiring subject of Lacanian psychoanalysis (and the nation-state to which that subject was bound), the new globalized subject of empire requires no rigid boundaries to transgress, no central or Oedipal laws by which to orient itself. As Hardt and Negri continue, 'In contrast to imperialism, Empire establishes no territorial center of power and does not rely on fixed boundaries or barriers. It is a *decentered* and *deterritorialized* apparatus of rule that progressively incorporates the entire global realm within its open, expanding borders' (2000: xii–xiii). It is precisely its deterritorialized status – the biopolitical network of intensities – that inexorably links the individual subject to the logics of globalization and capital.

In the end, we may have to admit that *Gladiator*, at some level, has it right: the image-based intensities of the new culture industry *are* the ironic fruits of the West's economic 'victory' in the cold war, the form of power that flourishes in our era of globalized finance capital. Rather than lament the victories of these intensive economies, we had best do some hard thinking about how these economies work, what they can and can't do, and how they might produce results otherwise. Because whether we like it or not, today it seems that Wall Street and Main Street are connected by the intensities we see played out along Las Vegas Boulevard.

Notes

Editors' note: In the interests of internal consistency, the notes in this extract have been re-numbered to make them sequential.

1   See also, in the literary critical context, the essays collected in a 2007 special issue of *Twentieth-Century Literature*, 'After Postmodernism', which essentially try to draw a series of distinctions between the 'high' postmodern novels of, say, Thomas Pynchon, and whatever a newer generation of 'ambitious' writers is doing (Dave Eggers, Jonathan Safran Foer, Zadie Smith, and the like); in architecture, see Turner's 1996 *City as Landscape*. Those working specifically in the wake of Jameson's analyses (and other economic analyses, like David Harvey's) tend to stick to the phrase 'late postmodernism': see especially Wegner's fine book, *Life between Two Deaths* (2009).

　　In the *New York Times*, the adjective 'post-postmodern' functions, just like 'postmodern' did in its day, as a synonym for tragically hip. Just to take the fate of the word in 2010–11 as an example, 'post-postmodern' was used to describe the March 2010 Fashion Week in Paris, to name composers in the wake of Philip Glass (January 24, 2010), and to characterize a modern dance work in which there's no dancing (April 16, 2010). In addition, 'post-postmodern' in the *Times* has modified everything from the experimental music of Jim O'Rourke (November 23, 2010) to the portraits in a Connecticut art show (April 30, 2011) and even the Hollywood blockbuster *Captain America* (July 21, 2011).

2   In the Forum, this special brand of intensive consumerism is linked everywhere to *water*, the condition for life as we know it. This ubiquity of water symbolism also functions as a recurring auto-tribute to the founding of Las Vegas itself, the intensive eruption of life in the godforsaken desert. Following the Romans, who sealed the hegemony of empire with the flow of aqueducts, what could be more unquestionably forceful than controlling water in the middle of a desert? Caesar's is an empire that finds its considerable thirst slaked only by resources – water and money – brought in from elsewhere and endlessly circulated.

3   On the risk society, see especially Beck (1992).

4   In Dostoevsky's *The Gambler*, a true gambler plies his trade against (feminine) abstractions and gambles solely to overcome them, thereby hoping to secure a kind of masculine nobility in an otherwise absurd universe. As the unrepentant gambler holds near the end of the novel, 'As long as I am around [roulette], I have a chance to be a man' (1977: 171).

5   In fact, Mother Russia has come to Las Vegas in the form of the 'Red Square' restaurant, complete with a headless Lenin statue guarding its entrance inside the Mandalay Bay Casino. The original pitch: 'Welcome to the warmer half of Moscow.'

By that we mean Red Square, an original restaurant where you'll discover vodka and caviar fit for a Czar. So forget everything you thought you knew about the frigid Siberian tundra, and enjoy the particular comforts that only the Motherland provides'. The phone message reminds you to 'avoid bread lines' by making reservations early.

Here one might also argue that terrorism represents the 'other' left for casino capitalism to conquer, but the very logic and practice of terrorism is less extensive than it is intensive. (We are reminded time and again that terrorists have no homeland – they are everywhere and nowhere; terrorism is, in Derrida's parlance, not so much an external threat as it is an 'auto-immune disorder' generated internally by contradictions and exclusions in the current ruling world order. See Derrida [2005]).

6   Parallels to Ronald Reagan and Margaret Thatcher are hard to resist here, or at least the broad ideological sense that after the era of the cold warriors, political leadership has given way to media showmanship – with Bill Clinton and Boris Yeltsin blazing a public relations trail that's been well trod by Tony Blair, George W. Bush, Barack Obama, Nicolas Sarkozy, and the like.

7   Even if the strategy is in essence doomed, as it is in *Spartacus*: in the end, slaves are crucified as far as the eye can see along the Appian Way. But that failure is part and parcel of the film's ruling existentialist ethos: one gains authenticity only by facing up to certain death, refusing its power, acting honorably in an absurd universe. Several times Spartacus reminds his followers that 'a free man only dies once, but a slave dies every day'. As Hardt and Negri write in *Empire*, such modernist 'refusal certainly is the beginning of a liberatory politics, but it is only a beginning. The refusal in itself is empty. . . . In political terms . . . refusal in itself (of work, authority, and voluntary servitude) leads only to a kind of social suicide. . . . What we need is to create a new social body, which is a project that goes well beyond refusal' (2000: 204). Note also that Kubrick's film – true to its existentialist ethos of authenticity – closely follows actual historical events, so the film has to end with the revolt's failure and the mass crucifixion.

Scott's *Gladiator* is not so hamstrung by historical 'facts'. There is no Maximus in the historical record; and while Marcus's son Commodus did in fact succeed him (and by nearly all accounts Commodus was a disaster as an emperor), Commodus was not killed by a gladiator, nor did he seem to experience substantial friction with his father. The historical Commodus was in fact elevated to the status of co-emperor during the last years of Marcus's life and reign.

8   Baseball was once euphemistically known as 'the American pastime', but today almost twice as many Americans visit a casino each year as attend a baseball game (Cooper 1997: 28). On the staggering growth of the prison industry and its ties to other sectors of the American economy, see Parenti (2000); and Davis (2000).

References

Beck, Ulrich (1992), *Risk Society*, London: Sage.

Cooper, Marc (1997), 'America's House of Cards', in Jennifer Vogel (ed.) *Crapped Out*, 28–39, Monroe, ME: Common Courage.

Davis, Angela (2000), *The Prison-Industrial Complex*, San Francisco: AK Press.

Deleuze, Gilles (1988), *Foucault*, translated by Sean Hand, Minneapolis: University of Minnesota Press.

Deleuze, Gilles (1995), *Negotiations, 1972–1990*, translated by Martin Joughin, New York: Columbia University Press.

Derrida, Jacques (2005), *Rogues: Two Essays on Reason*, translated by Pascale-Anne Brault and Michael Naas, Stanford, CA: Stanford University Press.

Dostoyevsky, Fyodor (1977), *The Gambler*, translated by Andrew R. MacAndrew, New York: W.W. Norton.

Foucault, Michel (1979), *Discipline and Punish*, translated by Alan Sheridan, New York: Vintage.

Hardt, Michael and Antonio Negri (2000), *Empire*, Cambridge, MA: Harvard University Press.

Jameson, Fredric (1984), 'Periodizing the 60s', in Sohnya Sayres et al. (eds), *The 60s without Apology*, 178–209. Minneapolis: University of Minnesota Press.

Jameson, Fredric (1991), *Postmodernism; or, The Cultural Logic of Late Capitalism*, Durham, NC: Duke University Press. Originally published in *New Left Review* (1984) 146: 53–92.

McHale, Brian (2007), 'What Was Postmodernism?' Electronic Book Review, December 20. http://www.electronicbookreview.com/thread/fictionspresent/tense.

Nealon, Christopher (2009), 'Reading on the Left', *Representations* 108 (1): 22–50.

Nealon, Jeffrey T. (1993), *Double Reading: Postmodernism after Deconstruction*, Ithaca, NY: Cornell University Press.

Parenti, Christian (2000), *Lockdown America*, London: Verso.

Thompson, Hunter (1998), *Fear and Loathing in Las Vegas*, New York: Vintage.

Turner, Tom (1996), *City as Landscape: A Post-Postmodern View of Design and Planning*, London: Taylor and Francis.

Wegner, Philip (2009), *Life between Two Deaths, 1989–2001: US Culture in the Long Nineties,* Durham, NC: Duke University Press.

Part Two

Coming to Terms with the New

7

Remodernism

Remodernism will probably always be associated primarily with the art movement that engendered it: stuckism. Formed in Britain in the late 1990s, stuckism came to be seen as a foil to an increasingly pervasive postmodern orthodoxy epitomized by the Young British Artists group. Postmodernism, in short, seemed to have become part of the British establishment: artworks by the likes of Damien Hirst and Tracey Emin were regular winners of the prestigious Turner Prize, were sought after by prominent collectors such as Charles Saatchi, and were being championed by leading galleries such as the Tate, under the directorship of Sir Nicholas Serota. So, with the twentieth century drawing to a close, giving rise to speculations of the 'end of an era' sort, Billy Childish and Charles Thomson had the perfect set of conditions for declaring the bankruptcy of postmodernism, and proclaiming a successor to it, which they called remodernism.

Where postmodernism embraced theory, giving a central role to the conceptual in art, remodernism re-asserts the importance of the spiritual, understood in a broad sense that might have been familiar to an earlier generation of modernists from Wassily Kandinsky to T.S. Eliot. Remodernism holds the basis of art to be the artist's exploration of his soul, and the expression of his vision of it. Clearly, there is no room in such a conception of art for the postmodern traits of irony, parody, or pastiche; nor for the kind of bricolage *that recycles readymade objects or the artworks of others; nor for postmodernism's tendencies towards minimalism and conceptualism in art. Instead, Childish and Thomson refocus on properties they feel have been devalued by postmodernism: for instance, authenticity, sincerity, beauty, content, and skill. Crucially, they advocate a return to painting, as an antidote to the stuffed sharks, unmade beds, and re-shot films of the Young British Artists.*

As painters, Childish and Thomson called themselves 'stuckists', and announced that stuckism was the first remodernist art group. Their manifesto (below) offers an outspoken rejection of postmodern art in favour of a conception of painting as an artistic voyage of self-discovery and self-expression. It is important to note, however, that stuckism and remodernism are not entirely synonymous: in the years since it was coined, the term 'remodernism' has been deployed in contexts beyond the stuckist emphasis on painting, and has been invoked to describe photography, film, and music, for example (albeit with rather less uptake).

Remodernism's use of the prefix 're-' has given rise to the impression that it is in some way reactionary, retrogressive, or backward-looking – something its proponents have consistently denied, though without refuting the charge in much detail. It is, however, a misunderstanding to regard remodernism as advocating a straightforward return to the values of modernism, as if the interventions of postmodernism could be erased from history and somehow forgotten about, and modern art could just revert to an earlier, simpler aesthetic, resuming business-as-usual as if postmodernism had never happened. Rather, remodernism regards modernism as something ongoing, a work-in-progress whose development has been stymied by attaching the spurious prefix 'post' to it. This view bears some structural resemblances to that of Jürgen Habermas, whose principal objection to the idea of postmodernity is that modernity is still an incomplete project, rather as the stuckists assert that modernism ought not be written off as over and done with.

However, placing the idea of remodernism in dialogue with a thinker like Habermas reveals one of its key weaknesses: Childish and Thomson appear to regard postmodernism merely as a school or style in the visual arts, and one that was a passing fad at that. Obviously, postmodernism in its broader sense was not only endemic throughout all the arts (literature, film, and architecture, for example) but, in its more ambitious moments, claimed to be rooted in deep-seated changes to economic structures (Jameson), in repudiations of the philosophical values of the Enlightenment (Lyotard, Foucault), and even in a critical riposte to the entire tradition of Western metaphysics (Derrida). Problematically, remodernism has nothing to say about any of these dimensions of the postmodern, and little awareness of the broader implications of denouncing postmodernism as such. Despite the energy and vigour of their strident critique of the turn-of-the-century arts scene, remodernism apparently fails to appreciate that what is at stake in the fallout from postmodernism may amount to a chapter in the cultural history of the West's attempts to understand and represent itself. Compared with a target this size, the stuckists' denunciations of Damien Hirst and Sir Nicholas Serota seem comparatively small fry.

Perhaps because remodernism ignores postmodernism's theoretical and philosophical dimensions, by engaging with the postmodern solely as an artistic style or movement, it fails to acknowledge the extent to which terms like 'spirituality' or 'authenticity' have become troublesome. Reasserting such concepts naively – that is, without regard for the postmodern suggestion that spirituality or authenticity might be mediated, or performed, or signified, or constructed in some way – no more refutes postmodernism than Dr Johnson refuted Bishop Berkeley by kicking a stone. In other words, remodernism repudiates postmodernism largely by caricaturing it.

Remodernism nevertheless deserves a good deal of credit for being one of the first to identify a key theme amongst many of the positions that follow: the end of postmodern irony, and the embrace of a sense of sincerity or authenticity in its place. This is also a key theme in performatism, which, like remodernism, seeks to emphasize the spiritual – a step Ihab Hassan might approve of (see his essay in Part One). Metamodernism and renewalism also see similar tendencies at work in early twenty-first-century culture, but they describe their workings in more measured and more intricate ways.

The extracts are by Billy Childish and Charles Thomson, 'The Stuckist Manifesto' and 'Remodernism', in *The Stuckists: The First Remodernist Art Group*, ed. Katherine Evans (London: Victoria Press, 2000), pp. 8–10 and pp. 10–11; both are also available at: http://www.stuckism.com.

The Stuckist Manifesto (est. 1999)

Billy Childish and Charles Thomson

'Your paintings are stuck, you are stuck! Stuck! Stuck! Stuck!'

Tracey Emin

Against conceptualism, hedonism and the cult of the ego-artist.

1. **Stuckism is the quest for authenticity.** By removing the mask of cleverness and admitting where we are, the Stuckist allows him/herself uncensored expression.
2. **Painting is the medium of self-discovery.** It engages the person fully with a process of action, emotion, thought and vision, revealing all of these with intimate and unforgiving breadth and detail.
3. **Stuckism proposes a model of art which is holistic.** It is a meeting of the conscious and unconscious, thought and emotion, spiritual and material, private and public. Modernism is a school of fragmentation – one aspect of art is isolated and exaggerated to detriment of the whole. This is a fundamental distortion of the human experience and perpetrates an egocentric lie.
4. **Artists who don't paint aren't artists.**
5. **Art that has to be in a gallery to be art isn't art.**
6. **The Stuckist paints pictures because painting pictures is what matters.**
7. **The Stuckist is not mesmerised by the glittering prizes**, but is wholeheartedly engaged in the process of painting. Success to the Stuckist is to get out of bed in the morning and paint.
8. **It is the Stuckist's duty to explore his/her neurosis and innocence** through the making of paintings and displaying them in public, thereby enriching society by giving shared form to individual experience and an individual form to shared experience.
9. **The Stuckist is not a career artist but rather an amateur** (*amare*, Latin, to love) who takes risks on the canvas rather than hiding behind ready-made objects (e.g. a dead sheep). The amateur, far from being second to

the professional, is at the forefront of experimentation, unencumbered by the need to be seen as infallible. Leaps of human endeavour are made by the intrepid individual, because he/she does not have to protect their status. Unlike the professional, the Stuckist is not afraid to fail.

10. **Painting is mysterious. It creates worlds within worlds, giving access to the unseen psychological realities that we inhabit.** The results are radically different from the materials employed. An existing object (e.g. a dead sheep) blocks access to the inner world and can only remain part of the physical world it inhabits, be it moorland or gallery. Ready-made art is a polemic of materialism.

11. **Post Modernism, in its adolescent attempt to ape the clever and witty in modern art, has shown itself to be lost in a cul-de-sac of idiocy.** What was once a searching and provocative process (as Dadaism) has given way to trite cleverness for commercial exploitation. The Stuckist calls for an art that is alive with all aspects of human experience; dares to communicate its ideas in primeval pigment; and possibly experiences itself as not at all clever!

12. **Against the jingoism of Brit Art and the ego-artist.** Stuckism is an international non-movement.

13. **Stuckism is anti 'ism'.** Stuckism doesn't become an 'ism' because Stuckism is not Stuckism, it is stuck!

14. **Brit Art, in being sponsored by Saatchi, mainstream conservatism and the Labour government, makes a mockery of its claim to be subversive or avant-garde.**

15. **The ego-artist's constant striving for public recognition results in a constant fear of failure.** The Stuckist risks failure wilfully and mindfully by daring to transmute his/her ideas through the realms of painting. Whereas the ego-artist's fear of failure inevitably brings about an underlying self-loathing, the failures that the Stuckist encounters engage him/her in a deepening process which leads to the understanding of the futility of all striving. The Stuckist doesn't strive – which is to avoid who and where you are – the Stuckist engages with the moment.

16. **The Stuckist gives up the laborious task of playing games of novelty, shock and gimmick.** The Stuckist neither looks backwards nor forwards but is engaged with the study of the human condition. The Stuckists champion process over cleverness, realism over abstraction, content over void, humour over wittiness and painting over smugness.

17. **If it is the conceptualist's wish to always be clever, then it is the Stuckist's duty to always be wrong.**

18. **The Stuckist is opposed to the sterility of the white wall gallery system and calls for exhibitions to be held in homes** and musty museums, with access to sofas, tables, chairs and cups of tea. The surroundings in which art is experienced (rather than viewed) should not be artificial and vacuous.

19. **Crimes of education:** instead of promoting the advancement of personal expression through appropriate art processes and thereby enriching society, the art school system has become a slick bureaucracy, whose primary motivation is financial. The Stuckists call for an open policy of admission to all art schools based on the individual's work regardless of his/her academic record, or so-called lack of it.

    We further call for the policy of entrapping rich and untalented students from at home and abroad to be halted forthwith.

    We also demand that all college buildings be available for adult education and recreational use of the indigenous population of the respective catchment area. If a school or college is unable to offer benefits to the community it is guesting in, then it has no right to be tolerated. We hereby demand the right of creative opportunity for all!

20. **Stuckism embraces all that it denounces.** We only denounce that which stops at the starting point – Stuckism starts at the stopping point!

The following have been proposed to the Bureau of Inquiry for possible inclusion as Honorary Stuckists: Katsushika Hokusai, Vincent van Gogh, Edvard Munch, Karl Schmidt-Rotluff, Max Beckman, Kurt Schwitters.

Billy Childish
Charles Thomson
4.8.1999

Remodernism

Billy Childish and Charles Thomson

Towards a new spirituality in art

Through the course of the 20th century, Modernism has progressively lost its way, until finally toppling into the pit of Postmodern balderdash. At this appropriate time, The Stuckists, the first Remodernist Art Group, announce the birth of Remodernism.

1. **The Remodernist takes the original principles of Modernism and reapplies them, highlighting vision as opposed to formalism.**
2. **Remodernism is inclusive rather than exclusive and welcomes artists who endeavour to know themselves and find themselves through art processes that strive to connect and include rather than alienate and exclude.** Remodernism upholds the spiritual vision of the founding fathers of Modernism and respects their bravery and integrity in facing the travails of the human soul through a new art that was no longer subservient to a religious or political dogma and which sought to give voice to the gamut of the human psyche.
3. **Remodernism discards and replaces Post-Modernism because of its failures to answer or address any important issues of being a human being.**
4. **Remodernism embodies a spiritual depth and meaning and brings to an end an age of scientific materialism, nihilism and spiritual bankruptcy.**
5. **We don't need more dull, boring, brainless destruction of convention, what we need is not new, but perennial.** We need an art that integrates body and soul and recognises the enduring and underlying principles which have sustained wisdom and insight throughout humanity's history. This is the proper function of tradition.
6. **Modernism has never fulfilled its potential.** It is futile to be 'post' something which has not even 'been' properly something in the first place. Remodernism is the rebirth of spiritual art.

7. **Spirituality is the journey of the soul on earth.** Its first principle is a declaration of intent to face the truth. Truth is what it is, regardless of what we want it to be. Being a spiritual artist means addressing unflinchingly our projections, good and bad, the attractive and the grotesque, our strengths as well as our delusions, in order to know ourselves and thereby our true relationship with others and our connection to the divine.

8. **Spiritual art is not about fairyland.** It is about taking hold of the rough texture of life. It is about addressing the shadow and making friends with wild dogs. Spirituality is the awareness that everything in life is for a higher purpose.

9. **Spiritual art is not religion.** Spirituality is humanity's quest to understand itself and finds its symbology through the clarity and integrity of its artists.

10. **The making of true art is man's desire to communicate with himself, his fellows and his God.** Art that fails to address these issues is not art.

11. **It should be noted that technique is dictated by, and only necessary to the extent to which it is commensurate with, the vision of the artist.**

12. **The Remodernist's job is to bring God back into art but not as God was before.** Remodernism is not a religion, but we uphold that it is essential to regain enthusiasm (from the Greek, *en theos*, to be possessed by God).

13. **A true art is the visible manifestation, evidence and facilitator of the soul's journey.** Spiritual art does not mean the painting of Madonnas or Buddhas. Spiritual art is the painting of things that touch the soul of the artist. Spiritual art does not often look very spiritual, it looks like everything else because spirituality includes everything.

14. **Why do we need a new spirituality in art?** Because connecting in a meaningful way is what makes people happy. Being understood and understanding each other makes life enjoyable and worth living.

Summary

It is quite clear to anyone of an uncluttered mental disposition that what is now put forward, quite seriously, as art by the ruling elite, is proof that a seemingly rational development of a body of ideas has gone seriously awry. The principles on which Modernism was based are sound, but the conclusions that have now been reached from it are preposterous.

We address this lack of meaning, so that a coherent art can be achieved and this imbalance redressed.

Let there be no doubt, there will be a spiritual renaissance in art because there is nowhere else for art to go. Stuckism's mandate is to initiate that spiritual renaissance now.

Billy Childish
Charles Thomson
1.3.2000

8

Performatism

Raoul Eshelman coined the term 'performatism' in 2000, in an essay entitled 'Performatism, or the End of Postmodernism'. Over the next few years, he extended the scope, meaning, and application of it by writing studies of contemporary literature, film, art, architecture, and critical theory, before collecting and publishing these essays in 2008, in a book of the same title as his original essay. Performatism shares some of its basic features with the remodernism of the stuckists: both champion authenticity over postmodern irony, both re-accentuate the importance of the artist or author-figure as creator, and both place a return to the spiritual or 'theistic' at the centre of the arts of the (then) new century.

Unlike the stuckists, however, Eshelman's performatism recognizes that there can be no possibility of simply ignoring the postmodern assault on metaphysics and blindly re-embracing faith or belief. Rather, works of performatist art, literature, and philosophy are said to force us to decide in favour of these values by forcing us to decide against postmodern undecidability. Films like American Beauty *and novels like* Life of Pi *do this by offering their readers and viewers a Hobson's choice: although authenticity, morality, and spiritual belief are shown to be artifice, these texts and artworks leave us with practically nowhere else to go (except, perhaps, total nihilism). We therefore find we have been manoeuvred into accepting a performatist 'transcendence', the structure of which superficially resembles that of Moore's Paradox – that famous problem from analytic philosophy which explores the apparently absurd statement that 'I believe [X], but it isn't true'. This interesting refinement contrasts with metamodernism – in which the reader is said to oscillate between deciding in favour of postmodern irony and metamodern authenticity, between a postmodern scepticism and a metamodern faith – and also with renewalism, in which the spectre of postmodernism is said to return to haunt its inheritors.*

Eshelman describes performatism as a 'new monism', which draws inspiration from Erving Goffman's writings on 'frame analysis' and Eric Gans's vision of the origins of language. Both of these appear problematic. Methodologically, there is no reason why Goffman's work – basically, a schematic approach to communication and behaviour influential in the social sciences – could not be applied just as easily to postmodernist texts or artworks as to performatist ones. (Relatedly, many of the terms Eshelman uses to describe performatist works could as easily be applied to postmodern texts: metafictional novels and films are perpetually breaking out of frames, while magical realism often embraces the spiritual or theistic, for instance.) Equally, Gans's anthropology proposes an essentially ahistorical, atemporal, universalist pattern of cultural analysis, yet performatism decries postmodernism's so-called 'posthistorical' perspective, and claims to be a new historical 'epoch' succeeding it. Moreover, Eshelman gives no clear explanation as to why a transhistorical theory of language rooted (or, better, posited*) in the evolutionary prehistory of human beings should have taken on a sudden relevance at the close of the twentieth century.*

Performatism, nevertheless, remains one of the more ambitious of the would-be successors to postmodernism: it aims to designate an epoch rather than a movement or tendency, and it seeks to trace the hallmarks of this new epoch across a very wide range of cultural forms. However, at the risk of deflating many of the claims Eshelman makes for performatism, it might be worth entertaining the possibility that performatism names neither a historical epoch nor a new style of art or literature, but rather a method of interpretation. Just as it makes sense to differentiate between (for example) postmodernist novels and postmodernist readings of novels, so too what Eshelman seems to offer is a series of performatist readings of works that could, in principle, be read through a postmodernist lens just as easily.

The extract is from Raoul Eshelman, *Performatism, or the End of Postmodernism* (Aurora, CO: Davies Group, 2008), pp. ix–xiii; pp. 1–38; pp. 226–7.

'Introduction' *from* Performatism, or the End of Postmodernism

Raoul Eshelman

Some twenty years ago, Andreas Huyssen published an article called 'Mapping the Postmodern'[1] whose cartographic imagery turned out to be ideally suited to describing the problem at hand. At the time, postmodernism was a murky, uncharted terrain whose existence was not acknowledged by many scholars and critics, let alone the general public. Apart from Lyotard's *La Condition postmoderne* (which had just come out in English) and Charles Jencks's *Language of Postmodern Architecture*, there were no book-length treatments of the subject and only a few noteworthy articles and essays. Now, more than two decades later, there is little question about the success of the cartographic venture launched by Huyssen. Students can draw on a well-regarded set of general works by authors like Hassan, Hutcheon, Huyssen himself, Jameson, Jencks, and McHale as well as on a vast body of more specialized studies. Today, few scholars and critics would dismiss postmodernism offhand as a mere fad or style, and you probably could, if so inclined, muster up a fair amount of agreement on a canon of typically postmodern authors and works.

A funny thing happens, though, when you try to use the map today. The reader perusing a novel like Yann Martel's *Life of Pi*, the cineast taking in Jim Jarmusch's *Ghost Dog*, or the pedestrian strolling past the Presidential Chancellery in Berlin[2] would have trouble connecting the standard descriptions of postmodernism with the works of art in question. *Life of Pi*, for example, makes you want to identify with a character who wants to believe in all major religions at once – a monist, faith-based wish not exactly in keeping with the pluralism and skepticism you would expect from a postmodern hero. *Ghost Dog*, for its part, is about a lone hero single-mindedly sacrificing himself in the name of an utterly rigid, hierarchical code of honor – also not exactly a plot device easily accounted for by postmodernist notions of decentered subjectivity and ludic regress. And the Chancellery looks like a sleek anthracite hatbox with windows chiseled into it; it certainly doesn't resemble the playful, eclectically decorated buildings described by Charles Jencks in his classic work on postmodern architecture. Of course, you might want to argue that all these works are all in some way *ironic* – that they are ultimately just citing things alien to postmodernism and then twisting them around in order to renew and extend postmodernism itself. Even if you really believe this argument yourself, though, it's hard not to feel how strained it is. For with this simple formula you can assimilate literally *anything* back into the endless field of the postmodern episteme. The fact remains that, as of today, pulling out your trusty map of postmodernism doesn't always help when explaining contemporary books, films, and architectural objects. There are simply too many narrative strategies and motifs that go unexplained, too many artistic devices that diverge from the expected postmodern patterns.

Given these striking deviations from prevailing postmodern norms, you would think that there would be a groundswell of interest in finding out whether they have something in common or if they might all be leading in a similar direction. The case is quite the opposite, however. In spite of a widely held feeling that both postmodernism and its theoretical adjunct, poststructuralism, are on their way out, there is little or no interest in inquiring about what a succeeding epoch might look like or what other theoretical tools could be used to describe it.[3] This is due not just to plain force of habit, but also to a fundamental assumption about how signs relate to things. In poststructuralism explicitly and postmodernism implicitly, signs are thought to be tacked onto things belatedly, whether through custom, agreement, or happenstance. To achieve an understanding of things you can only go through signs; hence the sign (or, more precisely, the free-floating signifier) is the starting point for acquiring knowledge, not the thing itself. This basic notion, enormously amplified and elaborated in poststructuralist theory, is very difficult to get rid of once you have it. For the alternative to 'going through the signifier' from this point of view is to assume either a mystical union of signs and things – which no one in our secular world does anymore – or to be subject to a partial, usually unconscious failure to recognize that 'there is nothing outside the text', as Derrida puts it. And indeed, the force of this particular argument is hard to refute both in theoretical and practical terms. No one wants to get caught practicing 'metaphysics' – tacitly basing your entire argument on something that is hidden behind or beyond our semiotic frame of reference and that only you are privy to. The result has been a partly hypercritical, partly defensive discourse that tries above all else to minimize its own participation in 'metaphysics' while maximizing everyone else's. Needless to say, this sort of discourse must write off all unified concepts of the sign as old-fashioned, metaphysical bunk.

The broad, practically universal consensus on the untenability of monism has caused us to forget the historic instability of dominant, seemingly unshakeable concepts of sign. A glance at the history of culture shows that there have always been marked alternations between split concepts of sign and monist ones.[4] The prime reason for this seems to be that both sign types have inversely related strengths and weaknesses. Dualist concepts are strong on interpreting signs and weak on describing how things affect us through signs; monist sign concepts do precisely the opposite. At some point the one type begins to exhaust its descriptive and creative possibilities and the opposite one kicks in. Even if you're not a firm believer in neatly marked literary epochs, switches from Romanticism to Realism or from Symbolism to the era of the modernist avant-garde suggest that basic concepts of sign do change, and that it makes a very big difference when they do. Given this historical experience it seems a bit premature to assume that the concept of belatedness is the Last Word in this back-and-forth contest. For to do so you have to assume that the postmodern notion of the sign will be fine-tuned on into posthistorical infinity, but will never, ever again be superseded by a sign that is monist and unified.

As I see it, we are now leaving the postmodern era with its essentially dualist notions of textuality, virtuality, belatedness, endless irony, and metaphysical skepticism and entering an era in which specifically monist virtues are again coming to the fore. For the most part, this process has been taking place directly in living culture, around and outside the purview of academic theory. Although the earliest theoretical expressions of the radical new monism – Eric Gans's *Origin of Language* and Walter Benn Michaels and Steven Knapp's essay 'Against Theory' – came out in the early 1980s, they never made much headway against the prevailing dualist mindset. As far as I've been able to tell, identifiably monist works of literature, film, art, and architecture began to appear with some regularity in the late 1990s; this trend has intensified noticeably since the turn of the century. The development has been most conspicuous in architecture – almost nothing built today resembles Jencks's or Ventura's exemplary structures – as well as in art movies, which are more inclined to innovation than mainstream cinema. In the art world, performatism is ascendant but not yet dominant; in recent years major individual artists have begun to stress unity, beauty, and closure rather than the endless ironies of concept art and anti-art. In literature, the new aesthetic is spreading slowly, as many authors still seem to have poststructuralist narrative theory in the back of their heads while writing. The one area, of course, where a consciousness of the new monism is lacking entirely is in the field of literary theory itself. Aware that the times are a changin', but unable to part with the split concepts of sign developed by master thinkers like Derrida, Lacan, Foucault, and Deleuze, academic critics have widened their perspective to include cultural studies, historicism, gender studies, and postcolonialism. Depending on your standpoint, this has resulted either in an enrichment of the original theories or their degeneration into what one partisan of deconstruction calls 'the theory mess'.[5] However you look at it, though, the concept of sign remains the same. It is split, belated, and devoted to pursuing an endless, irrefutable otherness that is largely of its own making.

The aim of this book is to close the widening gap between theory and the intensifying aesthetic trend towards monism – towards strategies emphasizing unity, identification, closure, hierarchy, and theist or authorial modes of narration. The name I've chosen for the new aesthetic is, for better or worse, 'performatism'. The term refers to a strong performance, which is to say a successful, convincing, or moving attempt by an opaque subject to transcend what I call a double frame.[6] Performatism as I understand it can be defined in terms of four basic categories: ostensivity (a specific type of monist semiotics); double framing (a specific way of creating aesthetic closure); opaque or dense subjectivity; and a theist or authorial mode of organizing temporal and spatial relations.

[…]

Performatism, or the End of Postmodernism (*American Beauty*)

Raoul Eshelman

Performatism may be defined most simply as an epoch in which a unified concept of sign and strategies of closure have begun to compete directly with – and displace – the split concept of sign and the strategies of boundary transgression typical of postmodernism. In postmodernism – as hardly needs to be explained in great detail any more – the formal closure of the art work is continually being undermined by narrative or visual devices that create an immanent, inescapable state of undecidability regarding the truth status of some part of that work. Hence a postmodern building might create its own peculiar architectonic effect by placing an art nouveau swirl next to a modernist right angle, ironically suggesting that it is obligated to both styles and to neither. And, a postmodern novel or movie might present two equally plausible, parallel plot lines that remain undecidable within the confines of the work. Turning to a higher authorial position to solve this quandary is of little help. For the authorial intent behind the work is what is responsible for this inner undecidability in the first place: it simply sends us back to our point of departure. To escape this conundrum, we are forced to turn outside it – to an open, uncontrollable context. Author, work, and reader all tumble into an endless regress of referral that has no particular fix point, goal, or center.

This strategy has a direct theoretical counterpart in Derrida's deconstruction of Kant's *ergon*, the presumed center or essence of the work.[7] Derrida shows that any talk of intrinsic aesthetic value depends on that value being set off from the 'extraneous' context around it by means of a frame. The frame, which at first seems an ornamental afterthought to the painting, reveals itself as its crucial, undecidable precondition; it is that place which is both inside and out, where text and context meet in a way that is both absolutely crucial to the work's makeup and impossible to determine in advance. Any claim that a painting, text, or building is unified and closed can easily be shown to fall into this same trap. Through the frame, the presumed closure of the work is always already dependent on the context around it, which is itself everything other than a coherent whole. Thus even if the work's creator did somehow manage to create a unified effect, it would, through the frame, already be dependent on some aspect of the context around it. Any way you look at it, the prospects for creating a new, autonomous monist aesthetic are nil – at least from the standpoint of the dominant postmodern and poststructuralist mindset.

Performatist framing

Given this basic – and epistemologically well-founded – suspicion of concepts like intrinsic inner space, closure, and unity, how do performatist works go about establishing a new oneness without falling into old metaphysical traps? The answer lies in a new, radical empowerment of the frame using a blend of aesthetic and archaic, forcible devices. Performatist works are set up in such a way that the reader or viewer at first has no choice but to opt for a single, compulsory solution to the problems raised within the work at hand. The author, in other words, imposes a certain solution on us using dogmatic, ritual, or some other coercive means. This has two immediate effects. The coercive frame cuts us off, at least temporarily, from the context around it and forces us back into the work. Once we are inside, we are made to identify with some person, act or situation in a way that is plausible only within the confines of the work as a whole. In this way performatism gets to have its postmetaphysical cake and eat it too. On the one hand, you're practically forced to identify with something implausible or unbelievable within the frame – to *believe* in spite of yourself – but on the other, you still *feel* the coercive force causing this identification to take place, and intellectually you remain aware of the particularity of the argument at hand. Metaphysical skepticism and irony aren't eliminated, but are held in check by the frame. At the same time, the reader must always negotiate some kind of trade-off between the positive aesthetic identification and the dogmatic, coercive means used to achieve it.[8]

The forced, artificial unification of a work takes place using what I call *double framing*. This in turn breaks down into two interlocking devices that I call the *outer frame* (or *work frame*) and the *inner frame* (or *originary scene*). The outer frame imposes some sort of unequivocal resolution to the problems raised in the work on the reader or viewer. A good example of this is the conclusion of *American Beauty*, which is probably the first popular mainstream movie in a rigorously monist mode. At the end of the movie, the hero, Lester Burnham, is murdered and in effect becomes one with nature. Floating over his old neighborhood as an invisible voice, he extols the beauty of his past life and suggests that we, too, will someday come to the same conclusion after we've also died. You don't have to have studied rocket science – or deconstruction – to figure out what's fishy about this kind of argument. The film's director has arbitrarily endowed an ordinary character with supernatural powers and asked us to accept his literal and figurative point of view as the film's authoritative happy ending. As secular viewers we will be disinclined to believe that Lester can really speak to us when he's dead; as critical thinkers we will be skeptical of his claim that the petty world of middle-class America portrayed in the film is really beautiful. However, if you are at all serious about analyzing the movie as it stands, you have little choice but to accept this authorially certified argument as an indispensable part of the film as a whole.

The dogmatic implausibility of the film's outer frame or denouement does two things. It cuts us off – at least temporarily – from the endlessly open, uncontrollable context around it, and it forces us back *into* the work in order to confirm or deny Lester's odd, authoritative assertion about the beauty of life. In such a case we will encounter two basic possibilities. Either some sort of irony will undercut the outer frame from within and break up the artificially framed unity, or we will find a crucial scene (or inner frame) confirming the outer frame's coercive logic. Whether or not a 'lock' or 'fit' develops between outer and inner frame will determine whether we experience a work as a total object of closed identification or as an exercise in endless, ironic regress. Obviously, this opposition between the locked frame and ironic decentering is not a cut-and-dried affair. There is always a certain amount of tension between the fit between the frames and our legitimate metaphysical and ideological skepticism. However, we are now being offered a specific *choice* as to the outcome of a reading or viewing rather than being condemned from the start to a misreading or misprision.

Whereas the outer frame has an arbitrary or dogmatic quality and seems to be imposed from above, the inner frame is grounded in an *originary scene*: it reduces human behavior to what seems to be a very basic or elementary circle of unity with nature and/or with other people. Although this reduction can take place under very different external conditions, I have found that it almost invariably involves some element of what Eric Gans calls *ostensivity*. Since Gans's notion is the most elegant semiotic expression of the new monism, it's worth looking at it in more detail.[9]

Gans posits the existence of an originary scene in which two protohumans, who up to now have no language, become involved in a potentially violent, uncontrollable conflict over some object – something that René Girard calls mimetic rivalry.[10] Under normal circumstances a violent struggle would result, with one protohuman asserting himself over the other by means of physical force. In this particular case, however, one of the potential combatants emits a sound intended to represent the desired object. If the second protohuman in turn accepts this sound as a representation or substitute for the desired object, the sound becomes a sign and the conflict may be temporarily deferred. The two antagonists have transcended their animal status by agreeing on a sign representing and temporarily replacing a bone of contention; through their act of spontaneous agreement they also lay the foundations for all future acts of semiosis, and hence for all culture and ritual. At the same time, because of its violence-deferring power, the ostensive sign acquires a supernatural valence. Its co-creators, who are unable to reflect on their own role in its creation, ascribe it a transcendent origin, or what Gans calls the name-of-God. The point is not whether the sign is *really* of divine origin; it's that the sign *could* be; it marks not only the boundary line between the human and the animal but also between the immanent, real world and an outside, possibly transcendent one. Although empirically unprovable one way or another, the transcendent explanation of the sign remains an originary fact that we, too, as secular individuals have no choice but to take seriously.[11] Finally, in his hypothetical scenario Gans suggests that the originary sign is also perceived as beautiful because it allows us to oscillate between contemplating the sign standing for the thing and the thing as it is represented by the sign. We imagine through the sign that we might possess the thing but at the same time recognize the thing's inaccessibility to us, its mediated or semiotic quality.[12]

[...]

It is revealing to compare the originary monist sign with the notion of double origin common to poststructuralism. A salient feature of the originary, ostensive sign is that it has no meaning. Rather than automatically presupposing a relation with a binary opposite, as deconstructive theory requires,[13] it is a name referring first and foremost back to its own successful performance – the deferral of the imminent, potentially deadly conflict and the founding of language, cult, culture, and beauty. The ostensive sign is a *performative tautology*, a simultaneous, spontaneously generated linguistic projection that works in spite of the obvious conflicts and contradictions contained within it. Thus you could argue with a certain justification that the struggle for the desired object is only deferred, and that the multiple projection marked by the originary sign is ultimately one of mutual self-deceit. And, you could also object that the real work of culture begins only after more complex, semantic signs have been added on to the simple, originary one. All these assertions would be true. However, you would still have to concede that a synthetic, unified, object-focused projection – and not an epistemological aporia – stands at the beginning of all culture and continues to condition each individual act of language.

Although it's possible to muster both paleo-anthropological as well as ethnological evidence for Gans's hypothesis,[14] neither is crucial to my own argumentation. From my specifically aesthetic and historical point of view, the ostensive is quite simply the most elegant and parsimonious monist answer that we have to the notion of dual origin marked by différance and its many terminological cousins. The ostensive sign and the originary scene provide the minimal tool that can help us describe other monist strategies as they cut through the endless regress and irony of postmodern culture and play out new, constructed narratives of origin in contemporary narrative and thematic guises. The ostensive promises to be to the new epoch what différance was to the old one: a minimal formulation of the dominant concept of sign that manifests itself in everything from lowly pop culture to high-flown literary theory.

In the case of *American Beauty*, this originary scene centers around the white plastic bag which is filmed by Ricky Fitts and which later floats through the air during Lester's farewell address. As Ricky's utterances make clear, he sees in the bag nothing less than an embodiment of the divine:

> It was one of those days when it's a minute away from snowing. And there's this electricity in the air, you can almost hear it, right? And this bag was just … dancing with me. Like a little kid begging me to play with it. For fifteen minutes. That's the day I realized that there was this entire life behind things, and this incredibly benevolent force that wanted me to know there was no reason to be afraid. Ever.[15]

It's also important to remember that Ricky shares Lester's complete tranquility of mind as well as his specific way of partaking of the world's beauty in all its plenitude (Ricky: 'Sometimes there's so much beauty in the world I feel like I can't take it … and my heart is going to cave in'; Lester: '[…] it's hard to stay mad, when there's so much beauty in the world. Sometimes I feel like I'm seeing it all at once, and it's too much, my heart fills up like a balloon that's about to burst ...'[16]). Obviously, the scene with the white plastic bag doesn't display literally all the features of the ostensive as described by Gans. Ricky and Jane are lovers and not antagonists, and the plastic bag is only the filmed reproduction of the original which Ricky plays again because he 'needs to remember'.[17] However, the scene still embodies a basic unifying, thing-oriented projection shared by Ricky, Jane and, ultimately, Lester (in fact, you could maintain that Lester actually is the plastic bag, since he becomes one with that animate, divine principle of which Ricky has spoken earlier).

Now, you *could* argue that the plastic bag is nothing more than a cheap token of the consumer culture that is satirized elsewhere in the film and that Ricky is simply projecting his own wishful thinking onto it. In terms of a purely epistemological critique you would even be *right*. The problem remains, however, that within the total frame of the work this wishful thinking is confirmed on a higher, authorial level in Lester's farewell speech as well as in terms of plot, when he passes into an animate, beautiful, and comforting nature. If you insist on rejecting the basic premise contained in both the inner and outer frame, you'll find yourself in an unpleasant bind. You'll have 'exposed' the work on a dispassionate epistemological level but you'll have missed out on the aesthetic mixture of pleasure and anguish derived from identifying with central characters and scenes.

Even the tragic denouement – Lester's murder by Colonel Fitts – doesn't suffice to break up the movie's immanent argumentation. In effect, Colonel Fitts murders Lester because he follows his liberating example – and is then disappointed to discover that Lester isn't a closet homosexual like himself. The problem is not that Colonels Fitts is evil; it's that he doesn't find the right 'fit' within the frame of the movie's world (his violent 'fit' is the flip side of this disappointment). *American Beauty*, like all performatist works I'll be discussing in the following pages, is set towards metaphysical optimism. Even though crucial events in it may be violent or have an annihilating effect on individual characters, both perpetrators and victims have the chance of fitting into a greater, redemptive whole, even if the time and point of entry may be deferred for certain characters.

Performatist subjectivity

Because of its focus on unity, performatism also allows for a new, positively conceived – but not unproblematic – type of subjectivity. As a reaction to the plight of the postmodern subject, who is constantly being pulled apart and misled by signs in the surrounding context, the performatist subject is constructed in such a way that it is dense or opaque relative to its milieu. [. . .] It has a very real counterpart in Erving Goffman's 'frame analysis' which studies ritualized microsituations in everyday life.[18] Like Derrida, Goffman proceeds from an ironic and some times rather cynical metaposition from which he demonstrates the unpredictable and ultimately uncontrollable shifts of reference between different codes or frames (what he calls 'keying'[19]). However, unlike Derrida, Goffman also makes very clear that everyday human interaction is rooted in what one observer called a 'common focus on a physical scene of action'[20] prior to language. For Goffman, language is always anchored in some way in such scenes by means of indexical or deictic signs ('that there', 'this here' etc.) not immediately applicable to other situations. And, unlike the Derridean approach, which begins and ends with a notion of frame-as-paradox, Goffman's is generative and originary: he suggests the existence of 'primary frameworks' out of which develop still further, more complex frames or modulations of those frames. These primary frameworks are especially interesting for performatism because they allow us to make an initial decision about events in reality and render 'what would otherwise be a meaningless aspect of the scene into something that is meaningful'.[21] The frameworks include an explicit sacral dimension, the 'astounding complex', which suggests that the first question we ask about any unusual action or event is whether it might have a supernatural origin.[22] Other primary frameworks relate to 'stunts' (whether an action is a well-executed performance or trick) 'flubs' (whether an action is a mistake) 'fortuitousness' (whether an action is a matter of luck) and what Goffman calls 'tension' (whether an action involving the body has an officially condoned social character or a sexual, proscribed one).[23] The frameworks help us decide, for example, whether the quick upward movement of someone's right arm is a religious blessing, a move in sport, an accident, or a natural reflex.

As Goffman emphasizes, however, several frameworks can come into consideration at any one time, and the transformations of the basic frames or codes – their 'keying' – makes it virtually impossible to limit any action to a fixed, one-to-one relation. Goffman's frames, although not stable points of reference are, however, more than just the accidental, transient incisions in the stream of human discourse envisioned by Derrida. In fact, you could say that they are anchored in reality in a way comparable to Eric Gans's notion of the originary scene, which is based on a spontaneous agreement to defer mimetic rivalry through the emission of an ostensive sign (also a kind of index sign pointing to a concrete, present thing and surrounded by a minimal frame of social consensus). Taken this way, the ostensive scene would provide the originary ground missing from Goffman's theory, which does not try to explain how the 'astounding complex' came about in the first place, or why it is even a *primus inter pares* within its own category.[24] Conversely, Goffman's theory and observations serve to remind us that ritual and sacrality continue to play a key role in everyday life.

Goffman's notion of frames is also useful in thinking about performatist subjectivity and plot development. At first, Goffman's subject might appear to be purely postmodern – the mere effect of a multitude of overlapping and shifting frames not reducible to one single kernel or core. However, the 'Goffperson' is never so consumed by the discourse it uses so much as to lose all sense of orientation or decorum.[25] As Goffman dryly remarks at the beginning of *Frame Analysis*, 'all the world is not a stage'.[26] Just because we slip in and out of complex sets of overlapping roles doesn't mean that we get hopelessly lost in them, or that fact and fiction are *really* equivalent, or that the *possibility* that something can be fabricated means that our everyday faith in it must be vitiated. Our ability to find a firm 'footing' or 'anchoring' (Goffman's terms) in social interaction is possible because, unlike the poststructuralists, Goffman also sees social frames in a ritual, sacral dimension.[27] This is rather different from a commonsense, namby-pamby trust in convention which a poststructuralist would have no problem confirming as a fact of social life. Indeed, Goffman, following Durkheim, goes so far as to say that social interaction hinges on a tacit agreement in everyday interactions to deify individual subjects: 'Many gods have been done away with, but the individual himself stubbornly remains as a deity of considerable importance'.[28] Society, in other words, is held together by individual subjects using frames in a way that both enhances their own 'divine' status and upholds the decorum necessary to allow others to do the same. This Durkheimian theme, which suggests that originary or archaic religion has a social, rather than a cognitive, function, and that secular society's functional underpinnings are ultimately religious, can be found explicitly in monist thinkers like Gans and Sloterdijk and implicitly in many performatist narratives.[29]

By citing Goffman I don't want to suggest that performatist plots are more realistic or sociologically true to life than postmodern ones. Performatist plots are however very often centered on breaches of a frame that lead to a subject's being deified either in the transcendent, literal sense – as in *American Beauty*

– or in a more figurative, social one. One interesting example of the latter is Thomas Vinterberg's Dogma 95 movie *The Celebration*, in which the main protagonist disrupts the frame of a family gathering to accuse his father of having molested him as a child. By sacrificing himself – by placing himself at the center of attention and repeatedly causing himself to be expelled from the family celebration – he eventually brings the other family members over to his side; the father, by now himself demonized, is forced permanently out of the family circle.[30] These cases demonstrate what I call a *narrative performance*: it marks the ability of a subject to transcend a frame in some way, usually by breaking through it at some point and/or reversing its basic parameters (in *The Celebration* the son doesn't replace the father at the center of power; having forced out the patriarch, he opts to remain on the periphery of the family group). A good formal definition of the 'performance' in performatism is that it *demonstrates with aesthetic means the possibility of transcending the conditions of a given frame* (whether in a 'realistic', social or psychological mode or in a fantastic, preternatural one).

At this point, a good deconstructionist would interject that if this is so, then the ultimate proof of a performatist work would be its ability to transcend itself, i.e., to become something entirely different from what it was to begin with. In purely epistemological terms this objection is irrefutable. However, it misses the point. For the new epoch works first and foremost on an aesthetic, identificatory level, to create an attitude of beautiful belief, and not on a cognitive, critical one. If the performance is successful, then the reader too will identify with it more or less involuntarily – even if he or she still remains incredulous about its basic premises. The reader is 'framed' in such a way that belief trumps cognition.

Theist plots

Because of its emphasis on transcending coercive frames rather than continually transgressing porous, constantly shifting boundaries (as is the case in postmodernism), performatism acquires a distinctly *theist* cast. The basic plot common to all theist theologies is that a personified male creator sets up a frame (the world) into which he plunks inferior beings made in his own image; their task is in turn to transcend the frame and return to unify with the creator by imitating his perfection in some particular way. Deism, by contrast, suggests that there is a breakdown of some kind in a unified origin which in turn generates signs whose traces human beings must follow back to their source; the basic plot structure is one of tracking signs in their feminine formlessness and not imitating a transcendent father-figure or phallus. I don't wish to launch once more into the frequently made comparison between postmodernism/poststructuralism and gnosticism or the Cabbala. Rather, I would like to focus on how the new monist aesthetic revives theist myths and reworks them in contemporary settings. Like other such performatist appropriations these are obligated first to the logic of an aesthetic, authorial imperative and only secondarily (if at all) to a dogmatic source. Performatism is an aesthetic reaction to postmodernism's one-sidedly deist bias and not an old time camp meeting.

Since there are countless variants on the main theist plot I'll restrict my remarks to five patterns that have been appearing regularly in the last few years: *playing God; escaping from a frame; returning to the father; transcending through self-sacrifice;* and *perfecting the self.* These plot constructs are almost invariably ironic in the sense that they couple an archaic theist myth with contemporary, secular twists that don't jive well with received dogma. Performatism, in other words, creates a secondary, aesthetically motivated dogma and makes it into the outer frame of a particular work. Although the irony of this dogma is always apparent – its dogmatism is invariably a created, artificial one running counter to tradition – it doesn't vitiate itself or 'cross itself out' by virtue of this contradiction. Rather, as indicated earlier, it points the viewer or reader back into the work itself to inner scenes which in turn create a tautological lock or bind with the fixed outer premise. The difference between postmodern and performatist works is not that one is ironic and the other is not. Rather, it's that performatist irony is internal, circular, or scenic: it keeps you focused on a set, 'dogmatically' defined discrepancy rather than casting you out into an infinite regress of belated misjudgments of what is going on in and around the work.

In terms of plot, *playing God* is perhaps the most direct way of emulating a transcendent, personified source. A fine example of this is the movie *Amelie,* in which the eponymous heroine sets up little, contrived situations that help unhappy people change their lives for the better (or, in one case, to punish a despotic bully). In contrast to what one might expect from religious tradition, this doesn't lead to acts of hubris and abuse of power on the part of Amelie. Quite the contrary: although she is successfully able to help others with her little traps, she isn't able to find true love herself. Only after her friends and co-workers conspire to apply her tactics to her herself is she able to get together with a monist Mr. Right (whose hobby consists of making ripped-up representations whole – he pastes together pictures torn up and discarded by people using automatic photo machines in train stations). Playing God, in other words, only works after a group has imitated the theist creatrix and projected her own strategy back onto herself. The theist, active role is dependent on its acceptance and reapplication by a social collective.

This basic problem of playing God – that even as a self-appointed creator you can't create happiness for yourself and others by fiat – is treated at length in Lars von Trier's Dogma 95 movie *Idiots*. There, a group of young Danes living together in a commune go about their town pretending to be social workers taking care of mentally retarded patients. At first the group's excursions serve little more than to expose the vanity and insecurity of bourgeois existence by transgressing against basic social decorum – a plot device that is still entirely in keeping with postmodernism's favoring of critical simulation over smug projections about what is 'real'. As the movie moves on, though, it becomes clear that the real aim of the group is a kind of radical self-therapy. The ultimate goal proclaimed by the group's messianistic leader is not to shock total strangers by simulating mental retardation at the most embarrassing possible moment – and thus simply to confirm your own otherness – but to do so in your own familial and social sphere. Ultimately, the only member of the group who succeeds in doing this is a shy, insecure young woman who has just lost her baby. By drooling and slobbering like a retarded child at her stiff, unfeeling family's coffee hour she creates an ostensive sign of solidarity with the dead infant while at the same time breaking with the emotional indifference of her insufferable bourgeois family. This transcendent narrative performance aimed at establishing a sense of self – and not the theist imperative per se – is what makes the work performative.

Another well-established theist plot device is *escaping from a frame*, analogous to the task that a monotheist God places before people trapped in the world of His making. The work of art closest to this archetype is undoubtedly the Canadian cult movie *Cube*, in which seven people find themselves placed for no apparent reason in a gigantic labyrinth of cubes which they have to get out of before they starve to death. The only person who succeeds is, significantly, autistic; he is someone who is socially dysfunctional while having the surest sense of his own self. (The positive reduction of subjectivity to a minimal, invulnerable core of selfhood is impossible in postmodernism, where the subject can experience itself only in terms of *other* signs set by an infinitely receding symbolic Other.) This ubiquitous plot device linking transcendence and the overcoming of closed space can be found in a whole slew of works [...]

A more personified, gender-specific variant of the same myth is the plot involving a *return to the Father* (or the *Mother*, as the case may be[31]). As a rule, in performatism we find highly constructed father–son relationships involving a parity or reversal of strength rather than the oppressive, phallic rule of the Father assumed by Lacan and his feminist interpreters. The most notable example of a constructed return is the movie version of *Cider House Rules*, in which the father-figure, Dr. Larch, uses his position as director of an orphanage to set up one of his charges, Homer Wells, as an ersatz-son. Both part ways over a typical theist dilemma – the son thinks that Dr. Larch's practice of performing abortions means playing God in a negative sense. However, both are reconciled after Homer is himself forced to play God and choose between performing an abortion and delivering an incestuously conceived child. Armed with a phony CV concocted by Dr. Larch, who has in the meantime died, Homer completes the cycle and returns to head the orphanage as a new, benevolent theist creator/destroyer.

[…]

Another important performatist plot motif is that of *transcending through self-sacrifice*. In postmodernism, the victim is always the peripheralized other of a hegemonial, oppressive center; the victim more or less automatically acquires moral and epistemological superiority by virtue of its decentered, peripatetic status as the near helpless target of whatever force the center exerts on it.[32] In performatism, victims are once more *centered*; that is, we are made to focus on them as objects of positive identification rather than as markers of endlessly receding alterity and resistance. Here as elsewhere in the new monism, this recentering is itself an eccentric move that is markedly at odds with religious tradition.

Two of the most radical exponents of sacrificial centering are the Dogma 95 directors Lars von Trier and Thomas Vinterberg. In Vinterberg's *The Celebration* it is the suicide of the hero's sister that motivates his own less drastic act of exposing himself to public embarrassment; in this way the absent, absolute victim is once more recentered in a way that makes her sacrifice negotiable with the collective – and allows the expulsion of the morally debased patriarch from its midst. Thus the traditional mediating role of Christ – the hero's name is Christian, in case anyone has missed the point – is expanded to include a unity of male and female working towards the common goal of evacuating a corrupt, exploitative center. Similarly, almost every movie made by Lars von Trier centers around acts of female self-sacrifice. The most drastic example is his auteur tearjerker *Dancer in the Dark*, where we are set up in a deliberately heavy-handed way to identify with the final sacrificial transaction of the heroine – trading off her own life to save the sight of her son. A complete reversal in terms of plot construction is von Trier's no-less dogmatic *Dogville*, where a female victim is able to return to a fatherly center of criminal power – and responds by promptly wiping out her tormentors down to the last man, woman, and child.

As is the case with the father–son relationship, performatism suggests a *reversibility* of center–periphery or victim–perpetrator positions that isn't possible in postmodernism, where alterity leads to victimization and victimization to still more alterity (and where nobody in his or her right mind would even bother to identify with the 'hegemonial' center). Generally speaking, performatism is no less critical of abuses of power in the center than is postmodernism. However, it recognizes the *identificatory* value of sacrificial centering that is completely alien to the ethos of postmodernism, which can only conceive of viable moral positions being established on the run and on the periphery of the social order. Performatism, by contrast, allows for a centering that establishes a proximity between victims and perpetrators – and allows perpetrators, too, to become the object of reader or viewer identification.

[...]

Performatist plots don't necessarily have to tap into Western, monotheist myths. A plot pattern in works drawing on Eastern philosophy and religion is that of *perfecting the self*, usually in the sense of communing with an animate nature or entering or approaching Nirvana. This takes place most explicitly in Jim Jarmusch's movie *Ghost Dog* and Viktor Pelevin's novel *Buddha's Little Finger*,[33] which is arguably the most important work of post-Soviet fiction in Russia to date. In *Ghost Dog* the eponymous hero, a black ghetto dweller, adheres rigidly to the Samurai code of the *Hagakure* requiring absolute obeisance to a 'master'; in this case, circumstances have obligated him to serve a low-level Mafia family member as a hired killer. Even after he has been betrayed by his mafia employers (whom he then systematically eliminates), his strict code of honor doesn't allow him to betray his 'master', who in the end shoots him without the hero offering any resistance. Before deliberately sacrificing himself, Ghost Dog however manages to pass on his code of honor to a small girl who will presumably continue to develop it in a less violent way. Ghost Dog can only develop so far within the confines of a rigidly framed self, which the hero voluntarily gives up after its possibilities have been expended;

his conscious self-sacrifice serves to further the perfection of the world as a whole.[34] At the end of Pelevin's novel, by contrast, the hero and his sidekick leave a burlesque, dually constructed world and enter directly into Nirvana (a plot resolution repeated in many other of his works). Many readers choose to ignore these authoritative monist resolutions and treat his novels and stories as exercises in undecidable postmodern irony. However, it would seem that he is entirely serious in his desire to force readers to adopt a Buddhist mindset – if only within an aesthetic frame that flirts with the possibility of converting the reader in real life.

Theist narrative

Because of their dogmatic posture performatist narratives create certain odd configurations that stand out against the background of both traditional and postmodern story-telling techniques. One of the most curious such devices is first-person authorial narration, an 'impossible' device in which a narrator equipped with powers similar to those of an all-powerful, omniscient author forces his or her own authoritative point of view upon us in what is usually a circular or tautological way.[35] A prime example of this can be found in the narrative structure of *American Beauty*. At the film's beginning we see the bird's-eye view of a small town and hear a detached, almost meditative voice saying: 'My name is Lester Burnham. This is my neighborhood. This is my street. This . . . is my life. I'm forty-two years old. In less than a year I'll be dead'. As the first scene of the film appears, Lester's voice adds: 'Of course, I don't know that yet'.[36] Lester's tranquility is made possible by the holism of the narrative framework, which is oblivious to the difference between implicit author and character – and hence to death itself.

In this way even the evacuation or destruction of characters serves to strengthen the whole; after his murder by Colonel Fitts Lester dissolves into the authorial frame, from which he reemerges to introduce the story from a personal perspective in which he is again murdered. The act of narrating itself becomes a circular, enclosed act of belief that cannot be made the object of a metaphysical critique or deconstruction without destroying the substance of the work itself (*Life of Pi* [. . .] has a similar structure, as does Ian McEwan's *Atonement*[37]). The narrative is constructed in such a way that the viewer has no choice but to transcend his or her own disbelief and accept the performance represented by the film as a kind of aesthetically mediated a priori. This transformation of the viewing or reading process into an involuntary act of belief stands in direct contrast to the postmodern mode of the virtual, where the observer can't believe anything because ontological parameters like author, narrator, and character have been dissolved in an impenetrable web of paradoxical assignations and cross-references (as happens to the hapless private detective Quinn in Paul Auster's *City of Glass*).

In terms of reader response, performatist narratives must create an ironclad construct whose inner lock or fit cannot be broken by the reader without destroying the work as a whole. The performatist narrative, in other words, makes you decide for a certain posture vis-à-vis the text, whereas the no less manipulative postmodern device of undecidability keeps you from deciding what posture to take. The master of this 'idiot-proof' narrative form in performatism is Viktor Pelevin, who revels in tricking readers into assuming positions that turn out to be Buddhist ones forcing them to transcend their everyday secular mindset. Of these, the most insidious is perhaps the (as of now untranslated) short story 'Tambourine of the Lower World'.[38] There the reader, in the course of a rambling monologue on Brezhnev, light rays, mirrors, and death, is encouraged to memorize the curious phrase contained in the title. At the end of the story the narrator reveals that he has constructed a prismatic device activated precisely by this phrase and focusing a mental death ray on the reader; the ray may however be deactivated by sending 1,000 dollars to a dubious-sounding address. Those who treat this threat as a joke are encouraged to 'divide up your time into hours and try not to think of the phrase "tambourine of the lower world" for exactly sixty seconds'.[39] As in most of his other short stories, Pelevin forces the reader to enter involuntarily into the Buddhist project of transcending the material world entirely; in addition, the story demonstrates the impossibility of forgetting a mental image or projection after it has been framed within a short span of time.

Many readers still consider Pelevin to be postmodern because of his narrative playfulness and satirical jabs at post-Soviet society; they also distrust the motives of the real-life author, who undeniably indulges in self-mystification. However, a wealth of stories – including 'serious' ones likes his 'Ontology of Childhood'[40] – makes clear that his focus remains consistently on the Buddhist goal of self-annihilation and not on the eternal regress of the subject common to postmodernism. Thus in the short story 'Hermit and Six-Toes'[41] we are party to a series of mystical dialogues pertaining to life in what seems to be a dismal prison camp. Towards the end of the story we discover however that the two protagonists are chickens who are eventually able to 'transcend' by training themselves to fly out of their pen. Here, as in many other cases in performatism, we are forced to occupy a superior, theist perspective towards 'lower' characters. The manifest ability of these lower characters to transcend is then reflected back onto us as a performative imperative: as a challenge to become something completely different from what we are now. (This device can be found in *American Beauty* as well as the Coen Brothers' *The Man Who Wasn't There* [...])

Obviously, not all performatist narratives depend on these kind of one-shot tricks ascribing impossible acts of transcendence to narrators, characters, and texts. However, even in 'realistic' works we can observe that first-person narrators and central, weak characters tend to become invested with more and more authorial authority as the work progresses – a development that is directly at odds with the tendency of postmodern heroes and heroines to unravel, split up, or dissolve in outside contexts (and with the tendency of the authorial positions accompanying them to do the same). Because the analysis of psychologically motivated narrative in performatism requires a careful consideration of character development as a whole, I'll return to the problem of authorial empowerment of 'weak' characters in more detail in my treatments of individual literary works, most notably Ingo Schulze's *Simple Stories* and Bernhard Schlink's *The Reader* as well as Olga Tokarczuk's 'The Hotel Capital'.

Theist creation in architecture and the visual arts

The theist mode is not only active in narrative, but manifests itself strikingly in architectonic structures suggesting that the omnipotent hand of a higher being is at work – an architect playing God rather than playing hard to get, as is the case in postmodernism. As in performatist narrative, the basic aim of this new kind of architecture is to evoke a constructed or artificial experience of transcendence in the viewer; you are supposed to feel the powerful, preterhuman hand of the architect rather than reflect on the interplay of ornamentally familiar forms, as in postmodernism, or be transformed by a compelling functional principle, as in modernism. [...] Performatist architecture takes individual spatial features or forms that are already familiar from architectural history and uses them in a way that accentuates the possibility of the impossible rather than ironic knowledge of the undecidable. Hence in the new architectures building parts may move (static becomes dynamic), triangular structures are tilted (stable becomes unstable), a glass, purely ornamental facade is placed in front of the real facade (a solid plane dematerializes), or egg or oval shapes are employed (suggesting imperfect originary wholeness rather than rigid geometric functionality). Large chunks may also be sliced out of a building (suggesting the hand of a theist creator); empty frames may imply the act of theist construction as such while transcending the opposition between inside and out. Instead of irony and play we are confronted with a 'saturated', paradoxical experience of sublimity and beauty that forces us to change our intuitive perception of seemingly quotidian 'givens'.[42] Buildings of this kind may seem to point at, topple on, aim at, or otherwise threaten their users even as they suggest the possibility of a transcendent, incomprehensible force at work. Simple, but no longer rigidly geometric forms like ovals or lemon shapes suggest originary harmony and beauty rather than functional, mathematically dictated rigor. These structures can be said to *perform* in the sense that they induce us to experience these sublime feelings using obviously constructed, artificial means. This sublimity is in turn *postmetaphysical*; it is the result of specifically aesthetic, artificial strategies and need not have any specific theological pretensions.

In the visual arts, performatism has developed in reaction to concept art and what is often called anti-art, both of which one-sidedly dominated the art scene from the 1970s well into the 1990s. In a way comparable to that of narrative performatism, performatist art and photography visually bracket off concept and context and force viewers to accept the inner givens of the work at hand. Unlike modernism, where certain qualities such as flatness, abstraction, or reduction were considered essential expressions of beauty, in performatism these inner givens are constructs that are not reducible to any essential qualities. In turn, these constructs are forced on the viewer in such a way that he or she has no choice but to accept their autonomy from a context – which is to say their aestheticity. Vanessa Beecroft's closed, obsessive-compulsive nude performances, Thomas Demand's photographs of evocative cardboard interiors, and the action-packed, but weirdly incomprehensible paintings of Neo Rauch all share this same basic set towards reality. The inner space of the painting/photo/performance creates a new way of seeing or experiencing the world that can at first only be experienced in terms of a constructed aesthetic interior. If accepted by the viewer, this interiority may then be projected back onto the outside contexts around it. Interiority, then, determines context and not the other way around.

[...]

Performatist sex

In performatism there is a markedly different approach to sex and gender than is the case in postmodernism and poststructuralism. Poststructuralist theory, of course, emphasizes the primacy of belated, constructed, heterogeneous sexual role-playing (gender) over preexisting, binarily defined corporeal identity (sex). And, as usual, poststructuralism confronts us with an epistemological critique of essentialism or naturalization that at first glance seems hard to beat. Here we would appear to have two choices. The first is to dissolve sexuality and corporeality into an endless, unstable regress of discursive assignations – the happy hunting grounds of deconstruction and postfeminism. The second is to stipulate exactly what the natural, preexisting features of sexuality would be in every case – an impossible task considering that the very signs we need to do this continually contaminate the presumably natural essence of sexuality with our own belatedly acquired cultural biases. The question arises as to how a monist concept of sexuality is possible that doesn't achieve unity by positing a neat fit between the stable, heterosexually founded binary opposition between male and female.

The key to performatist sexuality lies once more in double framing, in creating an artificial unity that forces us to accept temporarily the validity of peculiar sexual or erotic constructs while making them the focus of our involuntary identification. Here as elsewhere it's useful to take a quick look at postmodern theory and practice before turning to the alternative offered by performatism. In postfeminist theory (as exemplified by Judith Butler), a dominant, heterosexual field of power is thought to project its unified, hegemonic imperative onto subjects presenting heterogeneous substrates not reducible to a simple binary scheme of male/female. Due to the sheer force exerted by the hegemonic matrix resistance to this compartmentalization can take place only in weak, by definition unsuccessful performances that manage to turn some of the dominant system's coercive energy against itself without really placing it in doubt. The real discursive achievement is located less in the performance itself (which is a function of the dominant power matrix) than in a melancholy, metaphysically pessimistic metaposition that unflinchingly records the insufficiency of simulatory resistance while at the same time touting it as the only possible means of undermining the 'heterosexual matrix'. Ali Smith's *Hotel World* [...] has made this postfeminist metaposition into its main narrative premise.

Performatism as I understand it is less an ideological reaction to postfeminism than a strategic one. The point of performatism is not to roll back multifarious gender constellations into good old binary sex, but rather to frame or construct them in such a way that they stand out positively within the framework of the 'heterosexual matrix' (or whatever other dominant power structure happens to be at hand). The main strategy involved in this is *centering the other*. Instead of automatically equating the other with the marginal and the weak, performatism takes otherness and plops it directly into the middle of the interlocked frames I've already discussed above. Thus at the social center of *American Beauty* we find the 'two Jims' – a hearty, healthy, happy gay pair who because of their unified, but plural, gendering can be all things to all characters (they chat about cultivating roses with Caroline and give tips on physical fitness to Lester). Many critics have noted how this positive portrayal of a gay partnership amidst manifestly unhappy heterosexual marriages parodies middle-class suburban values. However, from a performatist perspective it's even more important to emphasize that the two Jims also overcome the violent tension inherent in what Girard calls mimetic rivalry. As doubles in both name and sexual orientation, one would normally expect the two Jims at some point to incur the wrath of the collective (in Girardian thinking, twins and doubles embody the mimetic, contagious violence which society must constantly seek to assuage by victimizing scapegoats). In this case, though, exactly the opposite is true: the two Jims serve as a model not just for characters like Lester and Caroline but also, it would seem, for Colonel Fitts; the success of their relationship holds forth the promise of a successful 'partnership' between the Colonel and Lester.

[…]

Another quick way of highlighting the differences between postmodernism and performatism regarding sex is to key in on the topic of hermaphroditism. While not exactly a pressing social issue in itself, hermaphroditism has attracted the attention of such prominent theoreticians as Foucault and Butler because it seems to embody the main empirical premise behind postmodernism's concept of gender: namely, that our natural sexuality is a toss-up that a sinister set of encultured norms consistently causes to land on the heterosexual side of the coin. Foucault and Butler, to be sure, disagree on whether Herculine Barbin's hermaphroditism is the 'happy limbo of non-identity'[43] (Foucault) or just another example of one-sided sexuality being forced on a hapless victim (Butler).[44] However, the root idea remains the same: the hermaphrodite is about as close as anyone can get to a state of reified otherness exposing the arbitrariness of prevailing heterosexual norms.[45]

The most programmatic performatist reaction to the postmodern concept of hermaphroditism has up to now been Jeffrey Eugenides' widely acclaimed novel *Middlesex*.[46] Eugenides, who is familiar with Foucault's arguments (and probably also Butler's), switches the frame of reference from one of undecidable, irreducible alterity to one of decidable, albeit defective unity. Eugenides' underage heroine makes a conscious decision to become a male, basing this choice on scientifically founded anatomical data that has been concealed from her by a typically postmodern doctor. Like Lester Burnham, she deliberately becomes a male with a (this time permanently) retracted penis, a man who by the end of the book is capable of loving without penetrating the object of his desire. Additionally, the hero proves to be a person capable of ethnic reconciliation. Of Greek ancestry, he eventually moves to Berlin where he lives amicably among the Turks who had once slaughtered his ancestors and indirectly set off the incestuous relation between his grandparents that led to his anatomical – but not intellectual – dualism.

Rather than appealing to genetically encoded heterosexuality, performatism seeks to transcend sexual difference by resorting to strategies ranging everywhere from chastity to genetic engineering to divine intervention. Instead of acting as a place of liminal undecidability and boundary transgression the body becomes a scene of potential unity, irrespective of the 'input' involved. Thus in Olga Tokarczuk's heavily Jungian novel *House of Day, House of Night*[47] we encounter the figure of Saint Kummernis, who is miraculously endowed with a girl's body and Jesus's head and who dies a martyr's death because of it; in Michel Houellebecq's *The Elementary Particles*[48] the main character succeeds in cloning a unisexed person who overcomes the sexual tension involved in conventional male–female relations. In one of the most absurd performatist plays with sexual identity, in the movie *Being John Malkovich*, a woman who is inhabiting John Malkovich's 'portal' manages to impregnate her girlfriend through the actor and have a child (who can in turn be used as a kind of vessel in which fortunate people can live forever once they have entrance to it). These are not mere gender shifts or weak, refractory 'performances' creating small swirls in the power flow of a mighty heterosexual matrix, but whole, albeit incredible constructions of sexuality aimed at overcoming sexuality's most frustrating and perplexing aspects. These transcendency-breeding frames are, in effect, a logical consequence of the radical dualist constructivism propagated by

Butler. For once you kiss the corporeal world goodbye – once you start constructing gender relations willy-nilly without regard for their genetic or material substrate – there's no reason why you shouldn't go one step further and *reconstruct* these relations as monist ones that once more include the body within them. As long as your unified new construct focuses on transcending sexuality as we know it – and not simply on reinstalling the old binary, heterosexual opposition between male and female – you will be a sexual performatist. Because these monist constructs by definition allow for a secondary pluralism – each whole construct is different in its own way – there is no dearth of possibilities to construct sexuality anew without one-sidedly tipping the scales in favor of homosexuality by default (as does Butler's postfeminism) or heterosexuality by decree (as does traditional Judeo-Christian culture). Performatism holds out the promise of a plurality of sexual preference in which body and soul *both* turn out to matter.

Performatist time and history

Most scholars and critics today will readily admit that writing, film-making, art, and architecture are different today than they were back in, say, 1990, not to speak of 1985 or 1980. None of these observers, however, would dream of suggesting that these differences are epochal in nature – part of a massive paradigm shift fundamentally changing the way we regard and represent the world around us. Instead, in discussions of cultural trends we invariably encounter a kind of one-step-forward, one-step-back attitude towards anything laying a claim to innovation. Since in postmodern thinking every thing New is by definition always already implicated in the Old, it's easy to dispose of performatism – or anything else promising novelty, for that matter – by dragging its individual concepts back into the good old briar patch of citations, traces, and uncontrollable filiations that make up postmodernism. This posthistorical 'yes, – but' attitude is so entrenched in present-day criticism that even such vociferous monist opponents of posthistoricism as Walter Benn Michaels in America and Boris Groys in Germany haven't been able to counter it with positive programs of their own. After introducing a promising monist concept of the new in 2000, for example, Groys has not developed it further.[49] Michaels, for his part, ends a recent polemical book on a note of complete resignation, stating that 'history, as of this writing, is still over.'[50]

Needless to say, I believe that history is nowhere close to being over. At the moment, history is being energetically pump-primed by writers, architects, artists and filmmakers who have – consciously or unconsciously – switched to a monist mindset and are working with frames and ostensivity to inaugurate a new, manifestly unpostmodern aesthetic of temporality. This performatist switch is generating new concepts of time in two crucial areas: in literary history itself and in cinematography, where temporal experience is aesthetically most palpable.

History

Of the varied postmodern concepts of time and history that may be extracted from the writings of Derrida, Foucault, Deleuze, Jameson and others, the most fundamental undoubtedly remains that of *différance* – the state of temporal and spatial undecidability in which, as Derrida cagily puts it, 'one loses and wins on every turn'.[51] In *différance*, as hardly needs to be repeated at length any more, space and time are perceived as mutually conditioning one another from the very moment of their appearance as intelligible concepts in language. Mark a move in time and you'll have created a new spatial position; create a new spatial position and you'll have needed an increment of time to do it. Deconstruction intervenes to disrupt the 'metaphysical' tendency to privilege one over the other and, of course, to destabilize any historical 'ism' that would try to treat a discrete block of time as a 'static and taxonomic tabularization',[52] as Derrida calls it. The net effect, as we know, is a concept of history that is radically posthistorical and radically incremental, since the only thing that can really 'happen' – the only true transcendent event – is the destruction of discourse itself. In the Derridean scenario even the buildup to nuclear war follows the pattern of *différance*, since it's all just discourse – up to the point, at least, where the bombs actually go off.[53] Because there's nothing outside of deconstructive discourse except death, being inside that discourse is, conversely, a kind of key to cultural immortality. And, because that discourse can never be superseded by anything short of death, using any *other* discourse that might come after it would presumably be like *being* dead. The difference between postmodern discourse of this kind and everything else isn't just a matter of how you use signs to convey reality in a certain way: it's a matter of intellectual life and death.

The monist notion of history I am suggesting here is not as deadly serious about its own truth claims as is current theory. Adopting a monist set towards the sign instead of a dualist one doesn't mean that we're going back to a naïve metaphysics deferring to God, History, Truth, Beauty, or some other comforting notion residing outside the purview of our discourse. The belief that material reality should be incorporated into the sign instead of being excluded from it is a recurring feature of human thought that can be observed in Western culture since Antiquity; it is 'true' only inasmuch as large groups of people adopt it for certain periods of time and stick to it until they get tired of it again.

At the same time, the epochal concept of history I would like to develop here is also not as arbitrarily personal as someone like Stanley Fish makes it out to be. People adopt a set towards signs 'with' or 'without' things well before they make the kind of free-wheeling, wildly diverging interpretations that led Fish to pose his famous query 'is there a text in this class?'[54] At some point, everyone decides – usually intuitively – on whether to be a semiotic monist or a semiotic dualist. And, having done so, everyone also tends to stay that way for considerable lengths of time – whether due to a desire for internal consistency or due to sheer intellectual inertia. The issue at hand is not that a few scholars here and there have decided to adopt a monist mindset and apply it for their own personal or institutional ends; it's that writers, moviemakers, and architects *all over* have adopted this mindset and are implementing it in works of art. The changes now occurring in culture are epochal in nature: they represent a fundamental shift in the way we approach the world. However, because of their obligation to postmodern norms, very few critics are in a position to accept that shift as something desirable, and still less to define it as an historical event, rather than as a mere set of incremental changes. This applies no less to those affecting a critical stance towards postmodernism. Although it has by now become fashionable to dismiss postmodernism as exhausted or obsolete, this attitude means nothing if it is not accompanied by a positive alternative position. If you can't define the Other of postmodernism and write, think, and act in terms of that Other then you are – sorry to say – still a postmodernist.

In discussions of epochs it is always tempting to link normative shifts from dualism to monism (and back again) with larger trends in socio-political reality. In the case of postmodernism, the main representative of this materialist line of thought has been Fredric Jameson, who sought to escape the poststructuralist 'prison-house of language' by welding a lucid, highly convincing account of postmodernism onto the *Unterbau* of what he called late capitalism. Unfortunately for Jameson's thesis, late capitalism – its ominous name notwithstanding – has been looking increasingly robust with each passing year. The fact that postmodernism is petering out while global capitalism continues to boom suggests that Jameson's Marxist reading of cultural history is not much more prescient than the deconstructive one: it simply installs never-ending posthistory in the material realm outside the sign.

Given the collapse of socialism and the present lack of any viable alternative to the capitalist mode of production, it is tempting to suggest that the turn towards globalization and the turn towards a monist culture are two sides of the same coin (this is, in fact, the position taken by Eric Gans with his ambitious notion of post-millennialism[55]). Since performatism is a theory of aesthetics – a theory of why we like certain things for no good practical reason – I don't find it necessary to make such far-reaching claims. It is true, of course, that many performatist works treated in this book feed off of problems arising through globalization and/or the collapse of socialism in Middle and Eastern Europe. However, it is also important to remember that there is no urgent practical reason why artists should not keep on thumbing their noses at capitalism using the tried-and-true strategies developed in postmodernism (Ali Smith's *Hotel World* [...] is a good example of a 'classic', politically correct postmodern approach to the subject).

In my view, the main reason for the switch to monism is that creative artists have become tired of recycling increasingly predictable postmodernist devices and have turned to its monist Other to construct alternatives – a move that ultimately knows no ideological boundaries. Hence, in the new monism we find a whole gamut of political positions, ranging from Eric Gans's strident neoconservatism to Arundhati Roy's Chomskian critique of American power politics. The criterion for performatism is ultimately not *whether* you are for or against global capitalism, but *how* you go about formulating your position within it. [...] Roughly speaking, you can make out three positions here: an accommodationist one that seeks to create warmed air pockets of spirituality within the glacial impassivity of global capitalism (Tokarczuk's 'The Hotel Capital', Schulze's *Simple Stories*); a postcolonial one that focuses on creating beautiful unities amidst the moral and political ugliness of the capitalist system (Arundhati Roy's *The God of Small Things*, Jim Jarmusch's *Ghost Dog*); and a terrorist or sublime one, which toys on a fictional level with the possibility of doing away with capitalism altogether (Miloš Urban's *Sevenchurch* and Viktor Pelevin's *Buddha's Little Finger*). Finally [...] Bernhard Schlink's *The Reader* [...] tries to overcome the victimary politics arising out of the Holocaust and open up the possibility of individual subjects advancing in history frame by frame.

Cinematographic time

In aesthetic terms we experience time most intensely in the cinema. Here, too, performatism is changing the way time, space, and the medium of film interact. Up until now, sophisticated viewers have felt most comfortable with the deist notion of dispersed or disjointed time used by postmodernism. Because in deist thinking the spatial markers of divine origin – its signs or traces – are believed to proliferate incrementally and uncontrollably in every which way, the time in which that proliferation unfolds never has much of a chance to develop epic, drawn-out proportions.[56] In (post-)modern deist systems time is either being constantly sliced and diced by space, as in Derrida's *différance*, or removed from chronology and interiorized, as in Bergson's *durée* (which he links with the ability to engage in creative imagination per se). The most ingenious and productive postmodern theory of cinematic time, the one developed by Deleuze in his two 'cinema' books, is more gracious in its attitude towards chronological time – he regards the epic 'movement-image' of pre-war cinema and the 'time-image' of postmodern cinema as different but equal.[57] However, it is obvious that Deleuze's sympathies lie with the neo-Bergsonian 'time-image' that shatters the sensory-motor scheme 'from the inside'[58] and causes time to go 'out of joint'.[59] Deleuze's opposition, which is grounded in an exacting and exhaustive treatment of 80 years of cinematic innovation, would also seem to leave us in a typical posthistorical bind. Either cinema can continue to produce the out-of-kilter time-images typical of the 1970s and '80s or it can fall back into the old sensory-motor patterns of pre-war film – or, even worse, recur to the pedestrian, merely chronological use of cinematic time that has always been a mainstay of popular movies. How can filmmakers create a cinematic time not based on the serial montage of sensory motor images or disjointed, temporal ones?

The answer, once more, lies in framing time in a way that is alien to postmodernism and poststructuralism. The focus is on *creating presence* – which is to say on doing something that the Derridean, epistemological critique of time considers impossible and the normative, Bergsonian-Deleuzian concept of time considers insipid.

Just how does this work? For a start, we are not dealing with a naïve attempt to create a *primary* presence. There is no way that modern-day cinema-goers are going to be shocked, fooled, or cajoled into mixing up reality and its filmic representation. Performatist film does not try to convince us that it is representing reality in a more 'real' or 'authentic' way than any previous cinematic school or direction. Rather, performatist film functions by framing and contrasting two types of time: personal or human time and theist or authorial time. Put more concretely, the performatist film, using the usual coercive means, forces viewers to accept a certain segment of time as a unity or 'chunk' while at the same time providing them with a temporal perspective that *transcends* that temporal unity. The relevant mode here is not epistemological and reflexive, but ontological and intuitive: it is the feeling of being present in a time frame that is qualitatively superior in some way to a previous one.

The most radical example of this is Aleksandr Sokurov's movie *Russian Ark*, which consists of one 87-minute-long, completely uncut shot. While watching the movie, we are made to experience two times. The first is the real time of the cameraman as he slowly moves through the Hermitage museum in St. Petersburg; the second is the 'staged' time of the director as he places a whole series of historical figures and scenes from Russia's czarist past in the path of the passing camera. On the one hand, we plunge with the cameraman into an ever-expanding filmic present corresponding exactly to the real time of the filming procedure (there was no editing and hence no way of shortening or scrambling real time). On the other hand, the *mise en scène* confronts us with characters who can only be interpreted as emblems of transcendent, panchronological time: Peter the Great, Catherine the Great, Pushkin, Nicholas II, and a hodge-podge of other figures taken from Russian history all appear within the same 87-minute sequence. The net effect [...] is that of a quotidian, real time allowing us to participate in a transcendent, suprahistorical one. The key to temporal experience here is the *en bloc* juxtaposition of theist and human time rather than the concatenation of countless time- or motion-saturated frames that forms the basis of Deleuzian film language. Also, needless to say, there's very little point in deconstructing this unreal presentation of historical figures in real time, because even the most simple-minded viewer has no trouble understanding that it's a one-time stunt – an artificial, aesthetic device. *Russian Ark* isn't trying to convince us with cognitive *arguments*; it's trying to make us *believe* by confronting us with a temporal *performance* that we have no way of avoiding – short of not going to see the movie at all.

[…]

Summary

Since my introductory discussion of performatism has covered a lot of ground, it seems helpful to close this chapter by summarizing what I consider to be the four basic features of performatism.

1. The basic semiotic mode of performatism is *monist*. It requires that things or thingness be integrated into the concept of sign. The most useful monist concept of sign I have been able to find up to now is Eric Gans's notion of the *ostensive*. Ostensivity means that at least two people, in order to defer violence in a situation of mimetic conflict, intuitively agree on a present sign that marks, deifies, and beautifies its own violence-deferring performance. This originary ostensive scene, in which the human, language, religion and aesthetics are all made present at once for the first time, is hypothetical. My own, specifically historical interpretation of the ostensive is that it embodies the semiotic mechanism generating the new epoch better than any other competing monist concept. The ostensive, in other words, marks the becoming-conscious of the new epoch. Accordingly, the job of a performatist aesthetics would be to describe the different manifestations of ostensivity in contemporary works of art and show how they make these works appeal to us in terms of monist, no longer postmodern mindsets. This book is devoted to realizing that project.

2. The aesthetic device specific to performatism is *double framing*. The double frame is based on a lock or fit between an outer frame (the work construct itself) and an inner one (an ostensive scene or scenes of some kind). The work is constructed in such a way that its main argumentative premise shifts back and forth between these two venues; the logic of one augments the other in a circular, closed way. The result is a performative tautology that allows the endless circulation of cognitively dubious, but formally irrefutable metaphysical figures within its boundaries. These metaphysical figures are in turn valid only within the frame of a particular work; their patent constructedness reinforces the set-apartness or givenness of the

work itself and coercively establishes its status as *aesthetic* – as a realm of objective, privileged, and positive experience. Because they are easy to identify and debunk, these metaphysical figures force readers or viewers to make a choice between the untrue beauty of the closed work or the open, banal truth of its endless contextualization. Performatist works of art attempt to make viewers or readers *believe* rather than convince them with cognitive arguments. This, in turn, may enable them to assume moral or ideological positions that they otherwise would not have. In terms of reader reception, a performance is successful when a reader's belief pattern is changed in some particular way, and when he or she begins to project that new belief pattern back onto reality.

3.   The human locus of performatism is the *opaque* or *dense subject*. Because the simplest formal requirement of once more becoming a whole subject is tautological – to be a subject the subject must somehow set itself off from its context – performative characters consolidate their position by appearing opaque or dense to the world around them. This opacity is in itself not desirable per se, but rather forms the starting point for possible further development. This development is best measured in terms of whether (or to what degree) a subject transcends the double frame in which it happens to find itself. In narrative genres, this ability of a human subject to transcend a frame is the benchmark of an event or successful performance. In psychological narrative this transcendence is necessarily partial; in fantastic narrative it may be achieved totally. In architectonic and pictorial genres, which are by nature static, we encounter paradoxical states of saturation or impendency that impose the conditions for transcendence on us without actually demonstrating how that transcendence is eventually consummated.

4.   The spatial and temporal coordinates of performatism are cast in a *theist* mode. This means that time and space are framed in such a way that subjects have a real chance to orient themselves within them and transcend them in some way. Because of its obvious constructedness and artificiality, this set-up or frame causes us to assume the existence of an implicit author forcing his or her will upon us as a kind of paradox or conundrum whose real meaning is beyond our ken. In terms of plot, we find a basic conflict between the spatial and temporal coerciveness of the theist frame and the human or figural subjects struggling to overcome it. In terms of spatial representation (in architecture), we find a basic tension between the

architect's attempt to effect transcendence and the physical limitations imposed by the material he or she is using; the expansive theist gesture is always accompanied by a human, limited one.

[...]

Concluding remarks

Performatism in art is not a programmatic movement,[60] a style, or a moral posture (it does not derive its legitimacy from postmodernism being 'bad', 'immoral', or 'arbitrary'). Rather, performatism marks a positive, specifically historical, across-the-board shift to monism in different media and in works of art having otherwise little or nothing in common in the way of subject matter, motifs, or technique. The problem is not so much that contemporary critics have failed to grasp the innovative achievements of individual artists or works of art. There are, as we have seen, numerous perceptive, trenchant analyses of the new, no longer postmodern aesthetic, and there is a widespread feeling that postmodernism is, for better or worse, on its way out. Nonetheless, critics are still loath to take the next logical step and treat these innovations as part of an historical epoch that is irreducible both to postmodernism and to any one of the old monisms like classicism, neo-Kantianism, or the Apollonian. The reasons for this hesitation are in human and institutional terms entirely understandable. For the only way to understand the new epoch *from within* – from its *own* position – is to jettison practically everything that critics have accumulated up to now in the way of analytical and theoretical tools and start again from scratch within the new monist mindset. Unfortunately, there is no way to get around this specifically historical, self-transcending kind of performance. Any reapplication of postmodern concepts to explain postmodernism's historical Other will simply result in a further reification of postmodernism.

Whether the tag 'performatism' will ever be adopted as a name for the nascent epoch is, of course, impossible to say; in a certain sense it is not even crucial to my project. However, there can be little doubt that the things described by performatism – the authorial or theist perspective, the artificial, forced construction of unities, the use of categories rather than concepts, and the set to unified, ostensive signs – are right now the main sources of innovation in contemporary culture and will remain so for some time. What is needed now most in the world of art criticism is a peculiar conflation of Wölfflinian and

Nietzschean virtues: the ability to think in historical, epochal dichotomies and the courage to smash through accustomed patterns of discourse and reenter history via the new monism.

Notes

Editors' note: In the interests of internal consistency, the notes in this extract have been re-numbered to make them sequential.

1 'Mapping the Postmodern', *New German Critique* 33 (1984), 5–52.
2 See the illustration in Chapter Four of this book, 154.
3 Typical of the prevailing attitude in academia is the collection *Beyond Postmodernism. Reassessments in Literature, Theory, and Culture*, ed. by Klaus Stierstorfer (Berlin: Walter de Gruyter, 2003). Most of the book is devoted to critical reassessments of postmodernism that do little more than project postmodernism back onto itself using poststructuralist methodology. A small number of the authors (most notably Ihab Hassan and Vera Nünning) discuss unpostmodern trends toward subjectivity, faith, aesthetics, and ethical solidarity in an approving way. None of them, however, is willing to conceive of, let alone name, an epoch that would lie beyond postmodernism.
4 The notion that literary history is determined by two opposing, alternating styles is of course not new. The tradition I am following can be traced back to such authors as Heinrich Wölfflin in *Renaissance and Barock* (Ithaca: Cornell University Press, 1966 [orig. 1888]) and Ernst Robert Curtius in his *European Literature and the Latin Middle Ages* (New York: Pantheon, 1953). In Slavic studies, the influential notion of a 'primary style' versus a 'secondary style' was first suggested by Dimitrii Likhachev in *Razvitie russkoi literatury X–XVII vekov. Epokhi i stili* [The development of Russian Literature from the 10th to the 17th century. Epochs and styles] (Leningrad: Nauka, 1973) and developed in semiotic and semantic terms by Renate Döring-Smirnov and Igor Smirnov in their *Ocherki po istoricheskoi tipologii kul'tury: . . . realizm – (. . .) – postsimvolizm (avangard)* [Outline of a historical typology of culture: . . . realism (. . .) postsymbolism – (the avant-garde)] (Salzburg, 1982). Within Slavics itself there has been no particular interest in applying epochal models to the cultural development after postmodernism.
5 See Herman Rapaport, *The Theory Mess: Deconstruction in Eclipse* (New York: Columbia University Press, 2001).
6 Obviously, the term isn't to be confused with performance the way that Judith Butler or other contemporary theorists use it. The postmodern performance is by definition weak, split, and doomed to failure before it even starts; the subject in

such conceptions is little more than a belated effect of circumstances far exceeding its control.

7 See his *The Truth in Painting* (Chicago: University of Chicago Press, 1987), esp. 37–82.

8 In this sense, performatism is the opposite of the phenomenological *epokhē*. Phenomenology brackets things to *know* them better; performatism brackets things to *believe* in them better. For more on this see the discussion of Jean-Luc Marion's *Being Given*, Chapter Five.

9 The most recent book-length formulation of this theory is Gans's *Signs of Paradox. Irony, Resentment, and Other Mimetic Structures* (Stanford: Stanford University Press, 1997); see also his *Originary Thinking: Elements of Generative Anthropology* (Stanford: Stanford University Press, 1993) as well as the numerous glosses and additions in his internet journal *Chronicles of Love and Resentment* at www. anthropoetics.ucla.edu/views/home.html

10 See, for example, René Girard, *Things Hidden since the Foundation of the World* (Stanford: Stanford University Press, 1987), 7–9.

11 Gans suggests in his *Originary Thinking* that while the idea of God may be forgotten as society becomes more secular, 'the process of this forgetting can never be concluded. Even if someday not one believer remains, the atheist will remain someone who rejects belief in God, not someone for whom the concept is empty' (42–43).

12 See his discussion, for example, in *Originary Thinking*: 'The pleasure of the esthetic results from the deferral or "drowning" of the prior displeasure – the resentment – generated by unfulfillable desire. The esthetic experience engages the subject in a to-and-fro movement of imaginary possession and dispossession that blocks the formation of the stable imaginary structure of resentment, where the self on the periphery is definitively alienated from the desired object at the center' (118–119).

13 The deconstructionist argument about language origin only works if you assume the existence of binary categories *prior* to language. Compare Jonathan Culler's explanation of this in his *On Deconstruction: Theory and Criticism after Structuralism* (Ithaca: Cornell University Press, 1982): 'If a cave man is successfully to inaugurate language by making a special grunt signifying "food", we must suppose that the grunt is *already distinguished from other grunts* and that the world *has already been divided* into the categories "food" and "non-food"' (96). [The italics are my own.] Culler's explanation suggests two models of language origin. In the first, which is absurd, language would originate through a process of infinite regress. Originary language would be preceded by a still more originary language and so on and so forth. In the second, which is entirely plausible, the

differentiation already exists in human cognition, where it so to speaks sits around waiting for a linguistic correlate to express itself. Unfortunately, this argument is no longer deconstructive, since it assumes the existence of a signified already existing in human consciousness before the signifier. What is really undecidable here is not the origin of the sign itself (which cannot be *known*) but whether there is a pre-existing 'set' in human consciousness towards treating signs and things as unities or dualities. The entire history of culture suggests that both, in fact, are possible, and that the competition between both possibilities is the basis of cultural history.

14 For paleoanthropological arguments see Gans, *Chronicle* No. 52, 'Generative Paleoanthropology', 27 July, 1996 (www.anthropoetics.ucla.edu/views/view52.htm). Gans's hypothesis is also compatible with Mircea Eliade's more general observation that religions must be founded in a sacred, holy place at the center of the world. See his *The Sacred and the Profane: The Nature of Religion* (San Diego: Harcourt, 1987).

15 Alan Ball, *American Beauty* (New York: Newmarket Press), 60.

16 Ball, *American Beauty*, 60 and 100, respectively.

17 Ball, *American Beauty*, 60.

18 See his *Frame Analysis. An Essay on the Organization of Experience* (Boston: Northeastern University Press, 1986).

19 The classic example of 'keying' is the set of signals that transforms fighting into playing for animals (see *Frame Analysis*, 40–82).

20 Randal Collins, 'Theoretical Continuities in Goffman's Work', in *Erving Goffman: Exploring the Interaction Order*, ed. by Paul Drew and Anthony Wooton (Boston: Northeastern University Press, 1988), 51.

21 *Frame Analysis*, 21.

22 *Frame Analysis*, 28–30.

23 *Frame Analysis*, 31–37.

24 The surprisingly good fit between Gans's and Goffman's theories is undoubtedly a result of their common Durkheimian heritage. For more on Goffman's indebtedness to Durkheim see Collins, 'Theoretical Continuities'; for more on Gans's own positive appraisal of Durkheim see his 'The Sacred and the Social: Defining Durkheim's Anthropological Legacy', *Anthropoetics* 1 (2000) (www.anthropoetics.ucla.edu/ap0601/durkheim.htm).

25 For more on this see Collins, 'Theoretical Continuities', 59–60.

26 *Frame Analysis*, 1.

27 Cf. Goffman, *Interaction Ritual: Essays on Face-to-Face Behavior* (New York: Pantheon, 1967), esp. 'The Nature of Deference and Demeanor', 47–95.

28 *Interaction Ritual*, 95.

29 Based as it is on mutually held projections, the Durkheimian tradition is anathema to rigorous deconstructionists as well as other strains of poststructuralism drawing on the illusion-bashing philosophy of Nietzsche. Derrida's own send-up of the Durkheimian projection – his critique of Marcel Mauss's *The Gift* – can be found in Chapter Two of his *Given Time. 1: Counterfeit Money* (Chicago: University of Chicago Press, 1992). See also the discussion of how Jean-Luc Marion reverses this criticism in Chapter Five.

30 According to Girard's scapegoating mechanism, a collective works off its mimetically generated tension by lynching an arbitrarily chosen victim, who is then deified after the fact as the group's saviour. In the case of *The Celebration* the scapegoating mechanism has a moral, rather than simply an energetic origin because the expulsion of the father is justified. Here as in many other cases in performatism, an archaic or originary scene returns outfitted with a constructed, modern-day rationale.

31 This occurs in the black comedy *Dogma*, in which two angels decide to return a God(dess) played by Alanis Morissette.

32 For more on this see Eric Gans's neoconservative critique of what he calls 'victimary politics', e.g., in *Chronicle* Nr. 257, 'Our NeoVictimary Era', 2 March 2002 (www.anthropoetics.ucla.edu/views/vw257.htm).

33 New York: Penguin, 2001.

34 His reading material towards the end of the movie includes *Frankenstein*, suggesting that he is aware of his own monstrosity.

35 Here as elsewhere I've adopted the narratological terminology developed by Franz Stanzel in *A Theory of Narrative* (Cambridge: Cambridge University Press, 1984). Stanzel's opposition of authorial/figural is best suited to describing the homologous relationship between a theist (authorial) creator/creatrix and his or her human (figural) creations. Stanzel himself excludes first-person authorial narration from his well-known tripartite classification scheme.

36 Ball, *American Beauty*, 1.

37 I have treated *Atonement* briefly in 'Originary Aesthetics and the End of Postmodernism', *The Originary Hypothesis: a Minimal Proposal for Humanistic Inquiry*, ed. by Adam Katz (Aurora, Colo.: Davies Group, 2007), 59–82.

38 'Buben nizhnego mira' in Viktor Pelevin, *Sochineniya v dvukh tomakh. Tom I. Buben Nizhnego Mira* (Moscow: Terra, 1996), 362–366.

39 'Buben', 366.

40 In his collection *A Werewolf Problem in Central Russian and Other Stories* (New York: New Directions, 1998).

41 In his collection *The Blue Lantern and Other Stories* (New York: New Directions, 1997), 21–62.

42 For more on these terms as used by Jean-Luc Marion, see Chapter 5.

43 Michel Foucault, *Herculine Barbin. Being the Recently Discovered Memoirs of a Nineteenth-Century French Hermaphrodite* (New York: Random House, 1980), XIII.

44 See the discussion in her *Gender Trouble: Feminism and the Subversion of Identity* (New York: Routledge, 1990), 23–24.

45 In postmodern literature, this principle is exemplified best in Sasha Sokolov's hilarious novel *Palisandriia* (Ann Arbor: Ardis, 1985), in which the hero, after a life of wild sexual and social transgressions, discovers at the end of the book that he was really a hermaphrodite all along.

46 New York: Farrar, Strauss and Giroux, 2002.

47 Evanston: Northwestern University Press, 2003 [Polish orig. 1998].

48 New York: Knopf, 2000.

49 See his *Topologie der Kunst* (Munich: Hanser, 2003), where he ducks the issue completely.

50 Michaels, *The Shape of the Signifier* (Princeton: Princeton University Press, 2004), 182. For a further discussion of Michaels' anti-theory see Chapter Five.

51 *Margins of Philosophy* (Chicago: University of Chicago Press, 1982), 20.

52 See in particular Derrida's 'Some Statements and Truisms about Neologisms, Newisms, Postisms, Parasitisms, and Other Small Seisms', in *The States of 'Theory': History, Art, and Critical Discourse,* ed. by David Carroll (New York: Columbia University Press, 1990), 63–94; here 65.

53 See his 'No Apocalypse, Not Now (Full Speed Ahead, Seven Missiles, Seven Missives)', *Diacritics* 2 (1984), 20–31.

54 See his *Is There a Text in this Class?* (Cambridge, Mass: Harvard University Press, 1982).

55 First introduced in *Chronicle* Nr. 209, 3 June 2000, 'The Post-Millennial Age' (www.anthropoetics.ucla.edu/views/vw209.htm). Gans develops a systematic epochal concept of history prior to post-millennialism in Part Two of his *Originary Thinking,* 117–219.

56 The flip side of the coin is that deist time can also end apocalyptically – see Derrida's 'No Apocalypse, Not Now' or Leibniz's assertion in *Monadology* §6, that the monads can only be created or be destroyed in one fell swoop ('*tout d'un coup*').

57 See Gilles Deleuze, *Cinema 2: The Time Image* (Minneapolis: University of Minnesota Press, 1989), 40.

58 *Cinema 2,* 40.

59 *Cinema 2,* 41.

60 Although performatism was not intended as an artistic program, at least one piece of art work has been inspired by it. Using Apple's text-to-speech software, an

American artist living in Thailand, Dane Larsen, created *Performatist Piece with Embedded Text*. Physically, the piece consists of a black plastic pot filled with raw cotton with an MP3 player inside. Using Apple's text-to-speech software, Larsen set up the MP3 player to read my original essay on performatism ('Performatism, or the End of Postmodernism'). The software's distortion of the original text results in a kind of semi-understandable speech emanating 'magically' from the cotton. The video of the performance can be viewed on Larsen's blog at: http://nofolete.blogspot.com/search?updated-max=2007-01-12T13%3A33%3A00%2B07%3A00&max-results=50

9

Hypermodernism

If postmodernism's objective was to announce the end of modernity, then, according to Gilles Lipovetsky, it is now redundant. Modernity, for Lipovetsky, did not come to an end. Rather, it is undergoing its consummation, and the name Lipovetsky suggests for this new phase of the modern is 'hypermodernity'. Postmodernism was characterized by an essentially liberal impulse – a concerted effort towards deregulation in the aesthetic, philosophical, ethical, and political spheres. But, invigorating though these developments may have been, they have been outstripped by the accompanying trend towards the liberalization and deregulation of the market. The unfettered logic of market forces has put paid to postmodernism's enthusiastic ambitions, and has even crept into the institutions of state, church, and family that withstood many of the onslaughts of postmodernism. The result, says Lipovetsky, is an endemic and unbridled consumerism, giving rise to a cult of excess – hence his choice of the prefix 'hyper-' to designate a culture that is ever demanding more and more. This view is in broad agreement with the position of Jeffrey T. Nealon in Part One, who regards post-postmodernism as deriving from an economic intensification of the power of the market and of consumerism.

This consumerism does not always manifest itself simply as a naked consumerism, but rather as an extreme form of individualism. The hypermodern individual lives a life characterized by flexibility, adaptability, and a demand for continuous improvement, both in the workplace and throughout his or her general life. But Lipovetsky is quick to point out a paradox here: the drive towards flexibility and improvement is something that is demanded of *the hypermodern individual,* as well as *something that the hypermodern individual demands as a consumer. Thus, a contradiction underpins hypermodernity: the sense of freedom, luxury, convenience, and plenitude purveyed by hypermodern culture conditions consumers to demand a more flexible lifestyle (for example), or to consume more luxury goods, while it is this very demand for freedom that imposes more invasive* working patterns on their crowded lives, and also this very demand for consumer goods that constrains their economic behaviour. Thus, hyperindividualism and hyperconsumerism turn out, in hypermodernism, to be different aspects of the same logic.

The hypermodern, however, is not just a new sociological trend that manifests itself in our behaviour and our economics. Lipovetsky suggests that it actually involves a deep-seated transformation in our everyday experience of space and time. This is effected by, for example, the opportunities and pressures of a 24-hour culture, or of 'flexitime' working patterns, and the new possibilities for communication and consumption that are afforded as globalization and digital technologies break down the geographical obstacles to the availability of people and commodities. More than anything else, though, Lipovetsky argues that the hypermodern involves a preoccupation with time, as ever greater demands are made on the present, and as (once again paradoxically) we take refuge from it in the nostalgia for memories from the cultural past, giving rise to a massive upsurge in the heritage industry, or in 'traditional' handicrafts and cookery, or in the current obsession with all things 'vintage' and 'retro'.

A superficial reading of Lipovetsky's prose might yield the impression that it is hallmarked by the very same weaknesses as the classic French theorists of postmodernism that he claims to supplant. That is, his writing displays the same strategy of implying (though not pursuing) surprising connections between seemingly disparate phenomena, the same tendency towards unsubstantiated generalizations, and the same culmination in aphoristic or gnomic summary that one finds in certain unguarded moments of Lyotard, in some of Deleuze's less disciplined work, and throughout most of the writings of Baudrillard. But such a reading is, indeed, superficial: Lipovetsky is in fact a refreshingly undogmatic thinker, who remains genuinely ambivalent and open-minded about both the positive and negative features of the hypermodern era. Hypermodernism's emphasis on individualism may indeed mark a new phase in the pursuit of freedom and self-fulfilment, while its emphasis on consumerism may just as easily lead in the very opposite direction. For Lipovetsky, it is important to take both possibilities equally seriously, rather than to rush to judgment.

Hypermodernism is cited approvingly by Alan Kirby in his formulation of digimodernism, where he argues that both share a grounding in a more or less consonant critique of consumerism. Similarly, Nicolas Bourriaud's altermodernism is rooted in a vision of a new relationship between time and space that redefines contemporary culture. However, it is arguably Robert Samuels's notion of

*automodernism that has the strongest affinity with Lipovetsky's hypermodernism,
because, while recognizing similar patterns in the changing relationship between
space and time that arise from information and communication technologies,
Samuels maintains the same judicious ambivalence about them, seeing in them
both the possibility of enhanced individual autonomy, and the threat they
simultaneously pose to individual freedom and expression, and indeed to culture
and freedom more broadly conceived – an argument very similar in structure to
Lipovetsky's diagnosis of hypermodernity.*

The extract is from Gilles Lipovetsky, *Hypermodern Times*, trans. Andrew Brown
(Cambridge: Polity, 2005), pp. 29–35; pp. 48–53; pp. 56–7; pp. 62–71. Originally
published as *Les Temps Hypermodernes* (Paris: Grasset, 2004).

Time Against Time, or The Hypermodern Society

Gilles Lipovetsky

Around the end of the 1970s, the notion of postmodernity emerged on to the intellectual scene, with the aim of describing the new cultural state of developed societies. First appearing in architectural discourse in reaction against the international style, it was rapidly taken up and used to designate, on the one hand, the shaking of the absolute foundations of rationality and the bankruptcy of the great ideologies of history and, on the other, the powerful dynamic of individualization and pluralization within our societies. Over and above the different interpretations put forward, the idea gained acceptance that we were dealing with a more diverse society, one with less compulsion and less laden with expectations of the future. The enthusiastic visions of historical progress were succeeded by narrower horizons, a temporality dominated by precariousness and ephemerality. Inseparably associated with the collapse of earlier heroic constructions of the future and the concomitant triumph of consumerist norms centred on living in the present, the postmodern period indicated the advent of an unprecedented social temporality marked by the primacy of the here-and-now.

The neologism 'postmodern' had one merit: that of bringing out a change of course, a profound reorganization in the way that advanced democratic societies worked, both socially and culturally. The dramatic rise in consumption and mass communication, the waning of authoritarian and disciplinary norms, the rising tide of individualism, the primary role now accorded to hedonism and psychologism, the loss of faith in a revolutionary future, the disaffection with political passions and militant positions: some name had indeed to be found for the formidable transformation that was being played out on the stage of opulent societies disburdened of the great futuristic utopias of modernity at its inception.

But at the same time, the expression 'postmodern' was ambiguous, clumsy, not to say loose. It was, of course, a modernity of a new kind that was taking shape, not any surpassing of modernity. Hence the legitimate hesitation that people showed with regard to the prefix 'post'. We can add this: twenty years ago, the concept 'postmodern' was a breath of fresh air, it suggested something new, a major change of direction. It now seems vaguely old-fashioned. The postmodern cycle unfolded under the sign of the 'cool' decompression of the social realm; these days, we feel that the times are hardening again, laden as they are with dark clouds. We experienced a brief moment during which social constraints and impositions were reduced: now they are reappearing in the foreground, albeit in new shapes. Now that genetic technologies, liberal globalization and human rights are triumphing, the label 'postmodern' is starting to look old; it has exhausted its capacities to express the world now coming into being.

The 'post' of postmodern still directed people's attentions to a past that was assumed to be dead; it suggested that something had disappeared without specifying what was becoming of us as a result, as if it were a question of preserving a newly conquered freedom in the wake of the dissolution of social, political and ideological frameworks.[1] Hence the success with which it met. That era is now ended. Hypercapitalism, hyperclass, hyperpower, hyperterrorism, hyperindividualism, hypermarket, hypertext – is there anything that isn't 'hyper'? Is there anything now that does not reveal a modernity raised to the nth power? The climate of epilogue is being followed by the awareness of a headlong rush forwards, of unbridled modernization comprised of galloping commercialization, economic deregulation, and technical and scientific developments being unleashed with effects that are heavy with threats as well as promises. It all happened very quickly: the owl of Minerva was announcing the birth of the postmodern just as the hypermodernization of the world was already coming into being.

Far from modernity having passed away, what we are seeing is its consummation, which takes the concrete form of a globalized liberalism, the quasi-general commercialization of lifestyles, the exploitation 'to death' of instrumental reason, and rampant individualism. Previously, the functioning of modernity was framed or shackled by a whole set of counterweights, alternative models and alternative values. The spirit of tradition continued to live on in different social groups; the division of roles between the sexes was still structurally unequal; the Church still held a tight grip on people's consciences; revolutionary parties were promising a different society, freed from capitalism and class conflict; the ideal of the Nation gave legitimacy to the supreme sacrifice of individuals; the State administered numerous activities in economic life. But now, everything has changed.

The society that is coming into being is one in which the forces opposing democratic, liberal and individualistic modernity are ineffectual, in which the great alternative visions have collapsed, in which modernization no longer meets with any strong organizational or ideological resistance. Not all pre-modern elements have evaporated, but they themselves function in accordance with a modern logic that is deregulated and de-institutionalized. Even social classes and class cultures are fading away before the principle of autonomous individuality. The State is on the retreat, religion and the family are being privatized, a market society is imposing itself: the cult of economic and democratic competition, technocratic ambition, and the rights of the individual all go unchallenged. A second modernity, deregulated and globalized, has shot into orbit: it has no opposite, and is absolutely modern, resting essentially on three axiomatic elements constitutive of modernity itself: the market, technocratic efficiency and the individual. We had a limited modernity: now is the time of consummate modernity.

In this context, the most diverse spheres are seeing a rising tide of extremism, in thrall to a boundless dynamic, a hyperbolic spiral.[2] Thus we are witnessing a formidable expansion in the size and number of financial and stock-market activities, an acceleration in the speed of economic operations that now function in real time, and a phenomenal explosion in the volume of capital circulating across the planet. For a long time, the consumer society paraded its own excess and the profusion of its merchandise: this has become even more so, thanks to hypermarkets and shopping centres that are increasingly gigantic and offer a whole plethora of all kinds of products, brands and services. In every domain there is a certain excessiveness, one that oversteps all limits, like an excrescence: witness different technologies and the mind-blowing ways in which they have overthrown the boundaries of death, food or procreation. The same thing can be seen in the images of the body produced in the hyperrealism of porn; television and the shows it broadcasts that play with the idea of total transparency; the Internet galaxy and its deluge of digital streams: millions of sites, billions of pages and characters, doubling in numbers every year; tourism and its cohorts of holiday-makers; urban agglomerations and their over-populated, asphyxiated, tentacular megalopolises. In the fight against terrorism and crime, millions of cameras and other electronic means of surveillance and citizen identification have already been installed in the streets, shopping centres, public transport and businesses: taking over from the old disciplinary and totalitarian society, the society of hypersurveillance is on the march. The frenzied escalation of 'more, always more' has now infiltrated every sphere of collective life.

Even individual behaviour is caught up in the machinery of excess: witness the mania for consumption, the practice of drug-taking in athletics, the vogue for extreme sports, the phenomenon of serial killers, bulimia and anorexia, obesity, compulsions and addictions. Two opposite trends can be discerned. On the one hand, more than ever, individuals are taking care of their bodies, are obsessed by health and hygiene, and obey medical guide-lines. On the other hand, individual pathologies are proliferating, together with the consumption characteristic of *anomie*, and anarchic behaviour. Hypercapitalism is accompanied by its double: a detached hyperindividualism, legislating for itself but sometimes prudent and calculating, sometimes unrestrained, unbalanced and chaotic. In the functional universe of technology, dysfunctional behaviour is on the increase. Hyperindividualism does not coincide merely with the interiorization of the model of *homo oeconomicus*, pursuing the maximization of his own interests in most spheres of life (education, sexuality, procreation, religion, politics, trades union activities), but also with the destructuring of the old social forms by which behaviour was regulated, with a rising tide of pathological problems, psychological disturbances and excessive behaviour. Through its operations of technocratic normalization and the loosening of social bonds, the hypermodern age simultaneously manufactures order and disorder, subjective independence and dependence, moderation and excess.

The first version of modernity was extreme in ideological and political terms; the new modernity is extreme in a way that goes beyond the political – extreme in terms of technologies, media, economics, town planning, consumption, and individual pathology. Pretty much everywhere, hyperbolic and sub-political processes now comprise the new face of liberal democracies. Not everything is dancing to the tune of excess, but nothing is safe, one way or another, from the logic of the extreme.

It is just as if we had moved from the 'post' era to the 'hyper' era. A new society of modernity is coming into being. It is no longer a matter of emerging from the world of tradition to reach the stage of modern rationality, but of modernizing modernity itself[3] and rationalizing rationalization: in other words, destroying 'archaic survivals' and bureaucratic routines, putting an end to institutional rigidities and protectionist shackles, privatizing everything and freeing it from dependency on local conditions, while sharpening competition. The heroic will to create a 'radiant future' has been replaced by managerial activism: a vast enthusiasm for change, reform and adaptation that is deprived of any confident horizon or grand historical vision. Everywhere the emphasis has been placed on the need to keep moving, on hyperchange unburdened of any utopian aims, dictated by the demands of efficiency and the need to survive. In hypermodernity, there is no longer any choice or alternative other than that of constantly developing, accelerating the movement so as not to be overtaken by 'evolution': the cult of technocratic modernization has won out over the glorification of ends and ideals. The less foreseeable the future, the more we need to be mobile, flexible, ready to react, permanently prepared to change, supermodern, more modern than the moderns of the heroic period. The mythology of a radical break with the past has been replaced by the culture of the fastest and the 'ever more': more profitability, more performance, more flexibility, more innovation.[4] It remains to be seen whether this really means blind modernization, technocratic commodity nihilism, a process spinning round and round in a vacuum without aim or meaning.

The modernity of the second sort[5] is the one which, at peace with its basic principles (democracy, human rights, the market) has no credible model to be set against it, and never stops recycling within its own system the pre-modern elements that were once objects to be eradicated. The modernity from which we are emerging negated its other: supermodernity integrates it. No longer the destruction of the past but its reintegration, its reformulation in the framework of the modern logic of the market, of consumption and individuality. When even the non-modern reveals the primacy of the self and functions in accordance with a post-traditional process, when the culture of the past no longer poses any obstacle to individualistic and free-market modernization, a new phase of modernity appears. From 'post' to 'hyper': postmodernity will have been merely a transitional stage, a short-lived moment. It is no longer ours.

These are all major upheavals which invite us to examine a little more closely the way social time is organized so as to govern the age in which we live. The past is resurfacing. Anxieties about the future are replacing the mystique of progress. The present is assuming an increasing importance as an effect of the development of financial markets, the electronic techniques of information, individualistic lifestyles and free time. Everywhere the speed of operations and exchanges is accelerating; time is short and becomes a problem looming at the heart of new social conflicts. The ability to choose your time, flexitime, leisure time, the time of youth, the time of the elderly and the very old: hypermodernity has multiplied divergent temporalities. To the deregulations of neocapitalism there corresponds an immense deregulation and individualization of time. While the cult of the present makes its presence felt ever more sharply, what is the exact shape it is taking, and what are its links with the other temporal axes? How, on this axis, is the relation to future and past articulated? We need to reopen the dossier on social time: more than ever it requires investigation. To go beyond the way postmodernism envisaged these questions, and to reconceptualize the temporal organization that is being put into place: this is the object of the present study.

[...]

Time in conflict, and chrono-reflexivity

As Marx demonstrated clearly, in his masterly analyses, the economy of time is at the basis of the way modern capitalism works. Capitalism endeavours to reduce working time to a maximum even when it poses working time as the source of wealth: it is a system which rests on a major temporal contradiction that excludes man from his own work. These contradictions, as everyone knows, have not stopped growing. Simultaneously, now that everything is centred on the organization of working time, we have shifted from a world marked by an increase in the different kinds of social time, by way of the development of heterogeneous temporalities (free time, consumption, leisure, holidays, health, education, variable working hours, retirement age) that are accompanied by unprecedented tensions.[6] Hence the accumulation of problems in the organization and management of social time, as well as the new demands for flexible hours – for reorganization and greater elasticity, to be achieved by personalized arrangements that encourage people to choose their own timetables. The modern obsession with time is no longer given concrete form merely in the sphere of work, submitted as it is to the criteria of productivity: it has extended into every aspect of life. Hypermodern society appears as the society in which time is increasingly experienced as a major preoccupation, one in which an increasing pressure on time is exerted in ever wider ways.

These temporal contradictions are echoed in everyday life and cannot be explained exclusively by the principle of economy and profitability transposed from production to the other spheres of social life. When we privilege the future, we have the feeling that we are missing out on 'real' life. Should we enjoy pleasures as they come, or else ensure that we will still have enough vitality for the years to come (health, figure, beauty)? Should we give time to our children or to our career? There is not just an acceleration in the rhythms of life, but also a subjective conflict that arises in our relation to time. Class antagonisms have lost their edge, while personal, temporal tensions are growing sharper and more general. It is no longer class against class, but time against time, future against present, present against future, present against present, present against past. What are we to choose as most important, and how can we fail to regret this or that option, when time has been torn away from tradition and made a matter for individual choice? The reduction in working hours, the growth of leisure, and the process of individualization have led to the escalation of themes and conflicts linked to time. The current trend is for singularized time-wars fought in the arena of subjective experience. The objective contradictions of productivist society are now accompanied by a spiral in existential contradictions.

The state of war against time implies that individuals are less and less trapped in the present alone: the dynamic of individualization and the means of information function as instruments of distancing, introspection and an inward-looking attitude.[7] Hypermodernity is not the same as a 'process without subject'; it is inseparable from self-expression, self-consciousness and consciousness-raising among individuals, paradoxically accentuated by the ephemeral action of the media. On the one hand, we are increasingly subjected to the constraints of rapid time, and on the other hand there is a growth in people's independence, and in their ability to make subjective choices and reflect on themselves. In individualized societies, freed from tradition, nothing can be taken for granted any more: the organization of existence and timetables demands arbitration and rectification, forecasts and information. We need to think of modernity as a metamodernity, based on a chrono-reflexivity.

Accelerated time and time regained

One of the most perceptible consequences of the power of the presentist agenda is the climate of pressure that it exerts on the lives of organizations and individual people. Several executives have pointed out what a frenzied rhythm dominates the mechanism of life in a company, now that global competition and the diktats of financial logic are the order of the day. There are ever more demands for short-term results, and an insistence on doing more in the shortest possible time and acting without delay: the race for profits leads to the urgent being prioritized over the important, immediate action over reflection, the accessory over the essential. It also leads to creating an atmosphere of dramatization, of permanent stress – as well as a whole host of psychosomatic disorders. Hence the idea that hypermodernity is distinguished by the way the reign of urgency has become ubiquitous and turned into an ideological matter.[8] The effects induced by the new order of time go far beyond the world of work: they find concrete expression in people's relation to everyday life, to themselves and others. Thus it is that an increasing number of people –women more than men, thanks to the constraints of the 'double day' – complain about being overwhelmed, of 'running to stand still', of being overworked. And now there is no age category that seems to be able to escape this headlong rush: pensioners and children too now have an overloaded timetable. The faster we go, the less time we have. Modernity was built around the critique of the exploitation of working time; hypermodern time registers a feeling that time is being increasingly rarefied. These days, we are more aware of the lack of time than we are of a widening in the number of possibilities entailed by the growth of individualization; we complain less about being short of money or freedom than about being short of time.

But while some people never have enough time, others (the unemployed, or young people in jail) have too *much* time. On the one hand we have the enterprising, hyperactive individual, enjoying the speed and intensity of time; on the other the individual with nothing better to do, crushed by the empty periods of his or her life.[9] It is hardly debatable that our ways of experiencing time are, as this suggests, twofold: what we are witnessing is the reinforcing of new forms of social inequality with regard to time. These new forms should not, however, conceal the global dynamic which, beyond specific groups or classes, has transformed from top to bottom the relationship of individuals to social time. By creating a hypermarket of lifestyles, the world of consumption, leisure, and (now) of new technologies has made possible a growing independence from collective temporal constraints: as a result, individual activities, rhythms and itineraries have become de-synchronized. The reign of the social present acts as a vector for the individualization of aspirations and behaviour, and it is accompanied by out-of-step rhythms and more personalized ways of constructing one's timetable. Individualism has become polarized – as excess or lack – and can assert itself only against the background of this now ubiquitous pluralization and individualization in the way we manage time. In this sense, hypermodernity is inseparable from the breakdown in traditional and institutional frameworks and the growing individualization of our relation to time, an overall phenomenon which, transcending as it does differences of class or group, goes far beyond the world of the victors in the struggle. The new sense of enslavement to accelerated time occurs only in parallel with a greater ability on the part of individuals to organize their own lives.

This is a new relationship to time, one that is also illustrated by consumerist passions. There is no doubt that shopaholics have found, in many cases, a mere second-best, a way of consoling themselves for the miseries of existence, of filling in the emptiness of their present and future. The presentist compulsion to consume and the shrinkage in the temporal horizon of our societies go hand in hand. But is this compulsion merely derivative, a Pascalian diversion, a flight from a world deprived of any imaginable future – one that has become chaotic and uncertain? In fact, the escalation of consumerism is nourished both by existential distress and by the pleasure associated with change, by the desire to intensify and reintensify, without end, the course of daily life. Perhaps this is where the fundamental desire of the hypermodern consumer lies: to rejuvenate his or her experience of time, to revivify it by novelties that present themselves as so many fresh starts. We need to think of hyperconsumption as an emotional rejuvenating experience, one that can start all over again an indefinite number of times. This does not exactly mean that it is Orwell's 'perpetual present' that defines us, but rather a desire for perpetual self-renewal and the renewal of the present. The consumerist fury expresses a rejection of time that has become worn-out and repetitive, a struggle against that ageing of the feelings that ordinarily accompanies our days. It is less the repression of death and finitude than an anguish at the prospect of becoming mummified, repeating one's life and not really feeling alive. To the question 'what is modernity?', Kant replied: growing out of one's state as a minor, becoming adult. In hypermodernity it is just as if a new priority were arising: that of perpetually becoming 'young' again. Our neo-philiac instinct is first and foremost a way of warding off the ageing of our subjective experience: the de-institutionalized, volatile individual, in thrall to hyperconsumption, is the person who dreams of resembling a Phoenix of the emotions.

[. . .]

The past revisited

The 'return' of the future is not the only phenomenon which undermines the idea that the social present has eyes only for itself: the revival of the past that we are witnessing also suggests that we ought to rectify such an idea.

It is undeniable that, in celebrating the pleasures of the here-and-now and the latest thing, consumerist society is continually endeavouring to make collective memory wither away, to accelerate the loss of continuity and the abolition of any repetition of the ancestral. The fact remains that, far from being locked up in a self-enclosed present, our age is the scene of a frenzy of commemorative activities based on our heritage and a growth in national and regional, ethnic and religious identities. The more our societies are dedicated followers of fashion, focused on the present, the more they are accompanied by a groundswell of memory. The moderns wanted to make a *tabula rasa* of the past, but we are rehabilitating it; their ideal was to break away from the grip of traditions, but those traditions have acquired a new social dignity. Celebrating the slightest object from the past, invoking the duties of memory, remobilizing religious traditions, hypermodernity is not structured by an absolute present, it is structured by a *paradoxical present*, a present that ceaselessly exhumes and 'rediscovers' the past.

[...]

Identity and spirituality

The way the past has come back into favour goes way beyond the mimicry of antiques and the cult of heritage and its commemorations. It finds concrete form, with even greater intensity, in the awakening of spiritualities and the new quest for identity. Religious renewal, national and regional demands, the ethnic revival: in all these guises, contemporary societies are witnessing a rise in the importance of guide-lines that point back to the past, a need for continuity between past and present, a longing to find one's roots and discover one's history. Technological and commercial globalization may be bringing about a homogenized temporality, but the fact remains that this occurs in tandem with a process of cultural and religious fragmentation that mobilizes myths and foundation stories, symbolic inheritances, and historical and traditional values.

It is well known how, in several cases, the reactivation of historical memory functions in frontal opposition to the principles of liberal modernity – witness the upsurge in religious trends which reject secular modernity, the neo-nationalist and ethnic and religious movements that lead to dictatorships, wars of identity, and genocidal massacres. The end of the division of the world into blocs, the ideological vacuum, the globalization of the economy, and the weakening of state power have led to the rise of a multitude of local conflicts based on ethnic, religious or national factors, together with separatist movements and wars between communities. Neonationalist and ethnic and religious upsurges, rejecting the pluralism of open societies, cleansing society of all 'heterogeneous' elements, and closing communities in on themselves, are in one place accompanied by the struggle against Westernization, in another by devastating wars, repression and politico-religious terrorism. Is this the reawakening of old demons? But it would be wrong to interpret these phenomena as resurgences or repetitions of the past, whether that past be tribal or totalitarian. Even if people are falling back on an identity politics that means reviving older mentalities, it is unprecedented forms of conflict, nationalism and democracy that are starting to appear. Behind appeals to the preservation of national or religious identity, tyrannies of a new kind are being set up, together with combinations of democracy and ethnicity, frustrated modernization and all-conquering 'fundamentalism' – combinations which Fareed Zakaria quite rightly calls 'illiberal democracies'.[10]

This being so, all movements that rekindle the flame of the sacred or seek for roots are very far from being similar, or from having the same links with liberal modernity. On the contrary, many of them in the West present themselves as having characteristics that are perfectly in accord with a liberal culture in which the individual legislates for his or her own life. Proof of this is provided by those *à la carte* religions, those groups and networks that combine the spiritual traditions of East and West, and use the religious tradition as a means for their adepts to find self-fulfilment. Here there is no antinomy with individualist modernity, since the tradition is handed over to the initiative of individuals, 'cobbled together' in a DIY manner, mobilized for self-realization and integration into a community. The hypermodern age does not put an end to the need to appeal to traditions of sacred meaning: it merely revamps them to give them greater individuality, a wider spread, and a more intensely emotional set of beliefs and practices. With the pre-eminence granted to the axis of the present, we see a rise in the number of deregulated religions and post-traditional identities.

Instrumental rationality is extending its domain, but this eliminates neither religious belief nor the need to refer to the authority of a tradition. On the one side, the process of rationalization forces the grip of religion on social life to weaken more and more; on the other, it re-creates, of its own momentum, demands for religiosity and a need for roots in a 'line of descent of believers'. Here, too, we should beware of seeing new spiritualities as a residual phenomenon, a regression or a pre-modern archaism. In fact, it is from *within* the hypermodern cosmos that the religious domain is reproduced, in so far as the hypermodern generates insecurity, the loss of fixed guide-lines, the disappearance of secular utopias, and an individualist disintegration of the social bond. In the uncertain, chaotic, atomized universe of modernity, new needs for unity and meaning, for security and a sense of belonging, arise: this is a new opportunity for religions. In any case, the march of secularization does not lead to an entirely rationalized world in which the social influence of religion is in a state of continual decline. Secularization is not irreligion; it is also a process which creates a new form of the religious domain in the sphere of worldly autonomy, a religious domain that is de-institutionalized, subjective and focused on the emotions.[11]

This remobilization of memory is inseparable from a new kind of collective identification. In societies ruled by tradition, religious and cultural identity was experienced as something self-evident, received and intangible, excluding individual choices. This is no longer the case. In the present situation, one's sense of identity and belonging is anything but instantaneous, given once and for all: it is a problem, a claim, an object for individuals to appropriate for themselves. Belonging to a community is a means of constructing oneself and saying who one is, a way of affirming oneself and gaining recognition: it is thus, inseparably, a means of self-definition and self-questioning. We are no longer Jewish, Muslim or Basque 'as easily as breathing'; we question our identities, we examine them, we want to appropriate for ourselves something which had hitherto gone without saying.[12] Cultural identity used to be institutional: now it has become open and reflexive, an individual gamble in which the dice can be thrown again and again.

The upsurge of particularist demands means that we need to correct the simplistic readings that reduce hyper-individualism to a frenzy of consumerist and competitive passions. While hyper-individualism cannot be separated from the consecration of private pleasures and individual merit, we are obliged to note that it is equally inseparable from a great increase in demands for public recognition, and also in demands for different cultures to be equally respected. It is no longer enough to be recognized by what we do, or as free citizens equal to everyone else: it is a question of being recognized by what we are in our specificity as part of a community and a history, by that which distinguishes us from other groups. This is the proof, among other things, that modernity of the second kind is not exhausted by the solipsistic torrent of consumerist appetites: in fact, it bears within itself a broadening of the ideal of equal respect, a desire for *hyper-recognition* which, rejecting every form of the contempt, depreciation or sense of inferiority under which one might suffer, demands the recognition of the other as equal in his or her difference. The reign of the hypermodern present is, to be sure, that of the immediate satisfaction of needs, but it is also that of a moral demand for recognition broadened to identities based on gender, sexual orientation or historical memory.

This process of hyper-recognition is not unlinked to a mass society of individualist well-being. It is this society which, in Western democracies, has contributed to a decline in the value placed on the abstract principles of citizenship in favour of poles of identity that are more immediate and particularist in character. In a hyper-individualist society, we invest our emotions in what is closest to us, in links based on resemblance and common origin, since universalist values and great political ideals appear as principles that are too abstract, too general or remote.[13] By destroying revolutionary hopes, and focusing life on private happiness, the civilization of the present moment has paradoxically unleashed a desire for the recognition of the specific identity conferred by collective roots.

It is also the culture of individualist well-being that, by giving a new importance to the need for self-esteem and esteem for others, has made it impossible to accept suffering engendered by collective negative images imposed by dominant groups. In the era of happiness, everything which inculcates a negative image of oneself, or withholds recognition, is deemed illegitimate, and appears as a symbolic form of oppression or violence incompatible with the ideal of full self-realization. Hence the multiplication of demands for reparation in the case of collective offences, the expectation that everyone will be granted public recognition, and the ever-more-frequent clamourings for victim status. While demands for particularist recognition are inseparable from the modern democratic ideal of human dignity, it is, none the less, our presentist civilization which has made 'the politics of recognition' possible,[14] a politics that acts as an instrument of self-esteem, inculcates new responsibilities *vis-à-vis* the past, and fuels the new controversial debates over memory.

The contemporary galaxy of identities is also an opportunity for taking another look at the rich analyses of high modernity put forward by Ulrich Beck. According to this German sociologist, we have moved from a first stage of modernization based on the opposition between tradition and modernity to a second modernization, self-reflexive and self-critical in nature. In this latest phase, it is modernization itself which is considered as a problem attacking the spread of a scientistic mentality as well as the working bases of industrial society. Hence the idea of a new modernity, self-referential in type.[15]

This description is correct, but we need to take it further and make it more general. What we really need to point out is that the second cycle of modernity is not merely self-referential: it is marked by the return of traditional landmarks and of ethnic and religious demands based on types of symbolic heritage that go back a very long way and stem from diverse origins. In other words, all the memories, all the universes of meaning, all the forms of the collective imaginary that refer to the past and that can be drawn on and redeployed to construct identities and enable individuals to find self-fulfilment. Ultra-modern self-consciousness does not merely affect technological risks, scientific rationality or the division of sexual roles, it imbues all the repositories of meaning, all the traditions of East and West, all the different kinds of knowledge and belief, including the most irrational and the least orthodox: astrology, reincarnation, marginal sciences, etc. What defines hypermodernity is not exclusively the self-critique of modern institutions and forms of knowledge, but also revisionary memory, the remobilization of traditional beliefs, and the individualist hybridization of past and modernity. It is no longer a question merely of the deconstruction of traditions, but of the way they are used without any institutional backing, being perpetually reworked in accordance with the principle of individual sovereignty. If hypermodernity is meta-modernity, it also manifests itself in the guise of a meta-traditionality and a meta-religiosity without bounds.

There is no lack of phenomena which might justify a relativistic or nihilistic interpretation of the hypermodern universe. The dissolution of the unquestioned bases of knowledge, the primacy of pragmatism and the reign of money, the sense of the equal worth of all opinions and all cultures – these are all elements which feed into the idea that scepticism and the disappearance of higher ideals constitute a major characteristic of our epoch. Does observable reality in fact suggest that such a paradigm is correct?

While it is undeniable that many cultural landmarks have been displaced, and that a technocratic and commercial dynamic now organizes whole sectors of our societies, the fact remains that the collapse of meaning has not been taken to its logical conclusion, since that meaning continues to deploy itself against the background of a strong and broad consensus about the ethical and political foundations of liberal modernity. Beyond the 'war of the gods' and the growing power of the market, a hard core of shared values continues to assert itself, one which fixes strict limits to the steamroller advance of operational rationality. Our entire ethical and political heritage has not been eradicated: there are still checks and balances that prevent us from accepting the radical interpretation of hypermodern nihilism – in particular, ethical protests and commitments. The new consecration of human rights puts these right at the ideological centre of gravity as an omnipresent organizational norm of collective actions. It is not true that money and efficiency have become the motive force and ultimate aim of all social relations. How, if this were true, could we understand the value accorded to love and friendship? How could we explain the indignant reactions to new forms of slavery and barbarity? What gives rise to new demands for an ethical attitude in economic activity, the media and political life? Even if our epoch is the stage on which are played out the conflicts between a whole variety of different conceptions of the good, it is marked, at the same time, by an unprecedented reconciliation with its basic humanist foundations: never have these enjoyed such an unquestioned legitimacy. Not all values, not all benchmarks of meaning, have been blown apart: hypermodernity is not a question of 'ever greater instrumental performance, and therefore ever fewer values that have the force of obligations', but a technocratic and market-driven spiral that is accompanied by a unanimous endorsement of the common roots of humanist and democratic values.

No one will argue with the fact that the way the world is going arouses more anxiety than unbridled optimism: the gulf between North and South is widening, social inequalities are increasing, all minds are obsessed by insecurity, and the globalized market is reducing the power of democracies to govern themselves. But does this enable us to diagnose a process of world-wide 'rebarbarization' in which democracy is no longer anything more than a 'pseudo-democracy' and a 'decorative spectacle'?[16] This would be to underestimate the powers of self-critique and self-correction that continue to dwell in the liberal democratic universe. The presentist age is anything but closed, wrapped up in itself, doomed to an exponential nihilism. Because the depreciation of supreme values is not limitless, the future remains open. Democratic and market-led hypermodernity has not uttered its final word: it is merely at the start of its historic adventure.

Notes

1   Krzysztof Pomian, 'Post – ou comment l'appeler?', *Le débat*, 60 (1990).
2   On excess as a figure of ultra-modernity, see Marc Augé, *Non-Places: Introduction to an Anthropology of Supermodernity*, tr. John Howe (London: Verso, 1995); Jean

Baudrillard, *Fatal Strategies,* tr. Philip Beitchman and W. G. J. Niesluchowksi, ed. Jim Fleming (New York: Semiotext(e); London: Pluto, 1990); Paul Virilio, *Vitesse et politique* (Paris: Galilee, 1977).

3 Ulrich Beck, *Risk Society: Towards a New Modernity*, tr. Mark Ritter (London: Sage, 1992).

4 Pierre-André Taguieff, *Résister au bougisme* (Paris: Mille et une nuits, 2001), pp. 75–85. See also Jean-Pierre Le Goff, *La Barbarie douce* (Paris: La Découvert, 1999).

5 The cycle that I have called the 'second individualist revolution' is analysed in *Ère du Vide* (Paris: Gallimard, 1983).

6 Roger Sue, *Temps et ordre social* (Paris: PUF, 1994).

7 I am radically opposed to the arguments that see in our temporal regime nothing more than 'impoverishing traps', 'a whirlwind flight', 'the mutilation of duration' that make any distance and any mediation impossible, as well as any 'reversibility of thought'; cf. Chesneaux, *Habiter le temps.*

8 Nicole Aubert, *Le Culte de l'urgence* (Paris: Flammarion, 2003).

9 Robert Castel, *Les Métamorphoses de la question sociale* (Paris: Fayard, 1995), pp. 461–74.

10 Fareed Zakaria, *From Wealth to Power: The Unusual Origins of America's World Role* (Princeton: Princeton University Press, 1998).

11 I am here drawing on the fine studies by Daniele Hervieu-Léger, *Religion as a Chain of Memory*, tr. Simon Lee (New Brunswick, NJ: Rutgers University Press, 2000), and *Le Pélerin et la converti* (Paris: Flammarion, 1999).

12 Dominique Schnapper, *La France de l'integration* (Paris: Gallimard, 1991), pp. 307–10.

13 Bela Farago, 'La démocratie et le problème des minorités nationales', *Le débat*, 76 (1993), pp. 16–17.

14 Charles Taylor, *Multiculturalism and 'The Politics of Recognition': An Essay*, with a commentary by Amy Gutman (Princeton: Princeton University Press, 1992).

15 Beck, *Risk Society.*

16 Taguieff, *Résister au bougisme*, p. 123.

10

Automodernism

One of the more dramatic changes to have taken place in the years since the advent of postmodernism has been the unrelenting rise and rise of digital information and communication technologies. The effect that (for example) mobile phones, the internet, and digital television are having on our culture is seismic, yet it is still only just beginning to be felt. Some commentators believe that these technologies have the potential to effect profound and far-reaching changes, altering even the way we experience space and time.

The question is whether the transformative effects of these new technologies have had an impact on postmodernity, and, indeed, whether they have superseded it in some way. Robert Samuels's answer treads an interesting line that explores the ambiguities and paradoxes involved in the user's experience of digital technologies. In some ways, the experience seems quintessentially postmodern: take, for example, the nonlinear nature of the internet or the multiplicity involved in social networking. Yet, in ways that are perhaps subtler, the technologies modify and even run counter to some of the classic tendencies within the postmodern. Where postmodernism promoted the idea that identities and truths were social constructs, and were conditioned by their time and place, mobile phone technology gives the impression of liberating our identities from time and place, and similarly the anonymity of the internet replaces a postmodern multiculturalism with a (false) impression of universalism, implying the very unpostmodern idea that internet users are really all the same.

Crucially, however, Samuels highlights the ambivalence of the new sense of autonomy that new forms of media confer on their users. Postmodernism, of course, had repudiated the traditional conception of agency and autonomy, but the sense of personal freedom and control imparted by (say) a first person shooter game, or by building a personal playlist of digital music, or by posting one's ideas to the world in a blog, seems to return these concepts to the centre of the user's experience. Samuels is quick to point out that this autonomy may well turn out to be no such thing: the rules of computer games prescribe and proscribe certain forms of play, and the templates for blogs allow only a certain amount of personalization, for instance. Moreover, the model of 'choice' purveyed by the new media is insidiously linked to an unthinking acceptance of market-driven economics, which also seems far removed from some of postmodernism's more trenchant political values. Nevertheless, Samuels is equally clear that we should not simply dismiss this powerful and pervasive re-embrace of a sense of autonomy that has been enabled by the new media, since it seems (potentially, at least) to offer a sense of empowerment, and moreover since it is so widespread and so dramatic a departure from the ideas behind postmodernism. He calls this new departure 'automodernism', to highlight the intermeshing of autonomy and automation that drives it.

Automodernism has many features in common with Alan Kirby's digimodernism, which also sees technology as the driving force behind the flight from postmodernism. Yet Kirby's analysis of the situation involves a somewhat darker assessment than Samuels's carefully argued paradox, offering instead a more pessimistic interpretation of the role of new technologies in dismantling postmodern culture. Hence, Samuels's emphasis on the ambiguous sense of freedom that differentiates the contemporary subject from the postmodern subject might have more in common with Gilles Lipovetsky's analysis of consumer-driven hypermodernism, which also calls attention to a newfound and paradoxical sense of empowerment of the individual – one that, as in Samuels's automodernism, may well turn out to be illusory, but which nevertheless should not be simply dismissed.

The extract is by Robert Samuels, 'Auto-Modernity after Postmodernism: Autonomy and Automation in Culture, Technology, and Education', in *Digital Youth, Innovation, and the Unexpected*, ed. Tara McPherson (Cambridge, MA: MIT Press, 2007), pp. 219–40.

Auto-Modernity after Postmodernism: Autonomy and Automation in Culture, Technology, and Education

Robert Samuels

This chapter argues that in order to understand the implications of how digital youth are now using new media and technologies in unexpected and innovative ways, we have to rethink many of the cultural oppositions that have shaped the Western tradition since the start of the modern era. To be precise, we can no longer base our analysis of culture, identity, and technology on the traditional conflicts between the public and the private, the subject and the object, and the human and the machine. Moreover, the modern divide pitting the isolated individual against the impersonal realm of technological mechanization no longer seems to apply to the multiple ways young people are using new media and technologies. In fact, I will argue here that we have moved into a new cultural period of automodernity, and a key to this cultural epoch is the combination of technological automation and human autonomy. Thus, instead of seeing individual freedom and mechanical predetermination as opposing social forces, digital youth turn to automation in order to express their autonomy, and this bringing together of former opposites results in a radical restructuring of traditional and modern intellectual paradigms. Furthermore, the combining of human and machine into a single circuit of interactivity often functions to exclude the traditional roles of social mediation and the public realm. For educators and public policy makers, this unexpected collusion of opposites represents one of the defining challenges for the twenty-first century, and it will be my argument here that some innovative uses of new technologies threaten to undermine educational and social structures that are still grounded on the modern divide between the self and the other, the objective and the subjective, and the original and the copy. To help clarify what challenges automodernity brings, I will detail ways that new media technologies are shaping how digital youth learn and play, then I will discuss how these automodern technologies challenge contemporary theories concerning education and self-hood, and I will conclude by suggesting different techniques for the integration of old and new media in education and political culture.

A new-media-writing scene

I am sitting with my fifteen-year-old nephew Benjamin as he works on a paper for his ninth-grade English class. Benjamin has Microsoft Word open, and he is also in a chat room with some classmates who are exchanging parts of their own first drafts. Their assignment is to write individually a five-paragraph essay on the novel they have just read in class. To complete this traditional assignment, Benjamin has his book open on his desk, but he also has on his computer screen a list of Web sites that discuss the novel, and his Instant Messaging program keeps on dinging him to warn of another incoming message. Meanwhile, he is downloading a new movie, and he is also playing a multiuser game that includes live chat with people from all over the world. He is thus multitasking at the same time as he is using multiple media to write his paper and entertain himself. If this scene is typical for many digital youth in the developed West, then these students may come to school with a radically different conception of writing and technology than their teachers have;[1] furthermore, this high level of multitasking points to the virtually seamless interplay of work and leisure activities that can be operated on a single personal computer.

This new-media-writing scene not only shows a breakdown of the old cultural opposition between work and play, but it also challenges the structural conflict between self and other. For instance, when I ask Benjamin if he is supposed to work with his friends on this paper, he responds with a quizzical look. From his perspective, like the movies and songs he is file sharing, information and media are always supposed to be shared and distributed in open networks.[2] Moreover, he reminds me that he still has to hand in his own paper, and thus he is only collaborating on the research part of his paper, and he will 'write the real paper on his own'. After I ask him if he is afraid that all of his multitasking will get in the way of him writing a clear and coherent paper, he informs me that he will use his spell and grammar checkers to make sure 'everything looks professional'. Benjamin therefore retains a high level of personal autonomy at the same time that he is sharing information and employing automated programs and templates. In other words, instead of technological automation creating a sense of mechanical alienation and impersonal predetermination, digital youth turn to new media technologies to increase their sense of freedom and individual control.

Moreover, Benjamin and students like him are now quite used to seeing knowledge and research as collaborative processes, while they retain more traditional notions of reading and writing. In fact, the ways Benjamin and his friends copy and paste texts from the Web and then distribute them in chat rooms and e-mails depicts an important transformation in the 'modern' conception of property and individual work: these young adults have become habituated to sharing all different types of media and information with little concern for property rights or plagiarism.[3] It is also important to point out that the way Benjamin jumps from writing agrammatical instant messages to typing extended essayistic prose displays the ability of young writers to transform the style and voice of their composing according to the context and the audience.

One can argue that Benjamin and his friends are using new technologies and media in innovative and unexpected ways, which in turn challenges the traditional educational structure centered on judging the work of the individual student. While many educators would simply castigate these students for cheating, I want to argue that these digital youths are leading the way for a new type of education that might be more effective and productive. For it may be that the types of collaborative activities in which students are engaging outside of school are very much like the types of activities they will be required to perform in the workplace and in their everyday lives when they finish their education. However, schools have for the most part resisted incorporating these digital innovations because the new media stress on collaboration, multitasking, automation, and copying does not fit into the older model of book-centered learning.

Since so many educators, parents, and administrators are locked into the rigid definition of education defined by the testing of memorized knowledge retained by the isolated learner, our educational systems have helped to create a strong digital divide between students' home and school uses of technology. One of the results of this divide is that students who are now used to employing new media in innovative and unexpected ways when they are at home are often alienated from school because these institutions still concentrate on outdated modes of communication and information exchange. Therefore, on a fundamental level, our schools are still structured by the modern celebration of the isolated individual who is rewarded for individual acts of creativity and/or conformity, while our students have embraced a more collaborative and distributive mode of learning and working.

Some educators who have acknowledged this growing divide between students and educational institutions have developed 'postmodern' theories to account for the current undermining of traditional and modern beliefs and practices. However, I will argue below that most of these postmodern theorists have failed to account for the ways digital youth are combining automation with autonomy. In fact, I will posit that we have moved into a new period beyond postmodernity, and it is important for educators to understand how automodernity undermines postmodern theories and educational efforts. Therefore, just as the development of postmodernism was based on a critique of modernism, I will begin my analysis of automodernity by critically examining postmodernity. This analysis of postmodernity is especially important, because in many ways automodernity represents a popular reaction to the postmodern emphasis on social determinism.

Four versions of postmodernity

Before the reader stops reading because of the use of this word, 'postmodern', I would like to posit that this cultural category has many different possible uses: some of them helpful and some of them not. In fact, I turn to this term because it helps us to enter into discussions occurring in many different disciplines about our current cultural order and how new technologies and social movements are changing the ways we think about education and learning. While some people have sought to dismiss the whole idea of postmodernity by labeling it an intellectual fad or a nihilistic radical movement, my intention is to show that postmodernism describes a series of contemporary social transformations.[4] To be more precise, I want to rescue this term from its misuse by arguing that there are in fact four separate forms of postmodernity that have often been confused.

Perhaps the most important postmodern idea is the notion that our world is made of multiple cultures and that we should respect the knowledge and cultures of diverse communities. In fact, multiculturalism is a reflection of the important social movements of the twentieth century, which fought for civil rights, minority rights, women's rights, workers' rights, and political self-determination. Thus, in recognizing the vital values and historical contributions of diverse social groups, multiculturalists have posited that there is no single, universal source for knowledge or truth.[5] Unfortunately, this multicultural idea has often been confused with the extreme postmodernist notion that there are no truths or moral values since everything is relative to one's own culture.[6] This mode of cultural relativism is often a caricature of the more subtle idea that all truths and values are socially constructed. Therefore, a more accurate statement of multicultural relativism and social constructivism is that while there are truths and values in our world, we can no longer assume that they are universal and eternal, particularly when 'universal and eternal' often function as code words for 'white and male'.[7]

Besides multiculturalism and social constructivism, a third mode of postmodernity concerns the cultural model of combining diverse cultures in entertainment and art through the processes of collage, remixing, and sampling. On one level, we can say that all cultures feed off of other cultures; however, some people have rightly claimed that our incessant recombining of diverse cultural representations does not necessarily help us to understand or encounter other cultural worlds.[8] I would add that while this esthetic version of post-modernity is probably the most prevalent, it is also the easiest to dismiss for its tendency to be superficial and short-lived.

Finally, I would like to define a fourth form of postmodernity, which concerns the academic critique of modern culture and philosophy. This mode of academic discourse often comes under the title of deconstruction or poststructuralism and has been attacked for offering the extreme idea that our world is determined by language. But, language can never escape its own domain, and thus ultimately all knowledge and meaning is suspect.[9] While this overly generalized representation of postmodern philosophy can be questioned, what is often missed is the way that this theory of rhetoric has worked to hide the important connection between postmodernity and social movements. After all, what has fueled multiculturalism and the critique of modernity is the rise of collective action around minority rights, civil rights, and women's rights. These social movements of the twentieth century have challenged many of the presuppositions of modern culture, and it is important to not confuse these vital cultural changes with their reflection in various academic fashions. Indeed, many of those most involved with these social movements as activists or theorists have challenged the extreme focus on difference within postmodernism, positing instead a kind of navigation between 'sameness' and 'difference'.

It is also essential to emphasize that if we want digital youth to use new media to engage in the social and public realms, then we must be able to point to the social movements of postmodernity without being caught up in the more extreme forms of academic discourse. In short, while we desire our students to see how culture, knowledge, and subjectivity are influenced by important social forces, we need to avoid the pitfalls of promoting theories that destroy the foundations for any type of stable meaning, argument, or social action. Moreover, as I will stress below, since one of the determining aspects of automodern youth is that their seemingly seamless combination of autonomy and automation often excludes the social realm of cultural differences and collective action, we need to show the importance of the social realm in contemporary, postmodern culture.

Postmodern theories of education and society

In surveying several texts defining postmodernity from the perspective of multiple disciplines, I have found that the one consistent factor in the circumscribing of this historical period is a stress on the transition from the modern notion of Enlightenment reason to an emphasis on the social nature of all human endeavors. Thus, whether one is speaking about the contemporary loss of master narratives, the critique of universal science, the rise of multiculturalism, the downgrading of the nation state, the emergence of the global information economy, the mixing of high and low cultures, the blending of entertainment and economics, or the development of new communication technologies, one is dealing with an essentially social and antimodern discourse. According to this logic, modernity represents the rise of capitalism, science, and democracy through the rhetoric of universal reason and equality. Moreover, the modern period is seen as a reaction to the premodern stress on feudal hierarchy, religious fate, cosmic belief, and political monarchy.[10] This coherent narrative moving from premodern to modern to postmodern modes of social order and collective knowledge can be challenged and debated, but what is certain is that this schema plays a dominant mode in contemporary intellectual history. However, what I would now like to show through an analysis of the representation of modernity and postmodernity in various fields of study is that this prominent intellectual narrative does not help us to account for the major modes of subjectivity and culture employed by digital youth today, which I have labeled automodernity.

In the field of education, the movement from modernity to postmodernity has often been tied to a belated acknowledgment of the multiple cultures that make up our world in general and our educational populations in particular. For example, Marilyn Cooper has argued that the central guiding force behind the development of postmodernism in education is the acknowledgment of cultural diversity:

Postmodernism is, above all, a response to our increased awareness of the great diversity in human cultures, a diversity that calls into question the possibility of any 'universal' or 'privileged' perspective and that thus values the juxtaposition of different perspectives and different voices and the contemplation of connections rather than a subordinated structure of ideas that achieves a unified voice and a conclusive perspective.[11]

By stressing cultural diversity and 'the contemplation of connections', Cooper points to a social and cultural mode of postmodern education challenging the modern stress on universality and unified subjectivity. Therefore, in this context, postmodern theory can be read as a response to multicultural diversity and the juxtaposition of different voices and disciplines in an environment where social mediation trumps universal reason and individual autonomy.[12]

Like so many other theorists of postmodernity, Cooper's understanding of this epoch is based on the idea that our conceptions of what knowledge is have shifted away from the previous modern stress on universal truth and unified individualism:

The transition involves a shift from the notion of knowledge as an apprehension of universal truth and its transparent representation in language by rational and unified individuals to the notion of knowledge as the construction in language of partial and temporary truth by multiple and internally contradictory individuals.[13]

According to this common academic argument, the movement away from the 'modern' conception of knowledge as universal truth pushes people in postmodern culture and education to sift through competing forces of temporary truths, and this destabilized conception of knowledge and truth leads to the undermining of the modern individual of unified consciousness. In turn, under the influences of postmodernism, education and culture become social and nonuniversal.

This social definition of postmodernism is linked by Cooper to the role played by new computer-mediated modes of communication in culture and education: 'in electronic conversations, the individual thinker moves . . . into the multiplicity and diversity of the social world, and in social interaction tries out many roles and positions'.[14] According to this description of electronic discussions, new technologies help to create a situation where individuals enter into a multicultural environment that stresses the social, dialogical, and interactive foundations of knowledge, communication, and education. However, I will later argue that this emphasis on the social nature of new communication technologies does not take into account the contemporary dominance of automation and individual autonomy in the production of automodernity. Moreover, due to their desire to promote a more socially responsible and multicultural society, many educators have made the questionable assumption that networked collaboration equals an acceptance of cultural diversity and social responsibility. Not only do I think that this easy equivalency between new technologies and multicultural awareness is too simple, but I will argue that many new technologies can foster a highly antimulticultural mode of communication and actually inhibit an understanding of or experience of difference.

Another serious problem with the theories stressing a radical shift from modern universal reason to postmodern social mediation is that they are predicated on a strict linear conception of historical development, and this progressive model tends to ignore the continuation of modern and premodern influences in postmodern culture. An example of this common mode of argumentation can be found in the 'new science' idea that we are now witnessing a radical shift in the transition from modern universal knowledge to the postmodern stress on the social construction of truth. Thus, in George Howard's understanding of the conflict between objectivism and constructivism in the natural sciences, we find the postmodern critique of modern universality:

> All across the intellectual landscape, the forces of objectivism are yielding to the entreaties of constructivist thought. But it is rather surprising that even our notion of science has been radically altered by recent constructivist thought. Briefly objectivism believes in a freestanding reality, the truth about which can eventually be discovered. The constructivist assumes that all mental images are creations of people, and thus speak of an invented reality. Objectivists focus on the accuracy of their theories, whereas constructivists think of the utility of their models. Watzlawick (1984) claimed that the shift from objectivism to constructivism involves a growing awareness that any so-called reality is – in the most immediate and concrete sense – the construction of those who believe they have discovered and investigated it.[15]

According to this social constructivist interpretation of the sciences, the modern conception of knowledge as being universal and objective has been challenged by the postmodern notion that knowledge is always an act of interpretation and invention.[16] Furthermore, by seeing science as the formation of shared constructed versions of reality, postmodern scientists often take on a social and anti-individualistic conception of reality.

This contemporary movement in the sciences from the modern individual as a neutral observer to the postmodern social construction of accepted theories is linked to the rhetorical turn in all aspects of current academic culture. In fact, Alan Ryan has made the following argument about how postmodern rhetoric changes our definitions of the self and the very process of recording our perceptions:

> Postmodernism is a label that embraces multitudes, but two ideas especially relevant here are its skepticism about the amount of control that a writer exercises over his or her work, and a sharp sense of the fragility of personal identity. These interact, of course. The idea that each of us is a single Self consorts naturally with the idea that we tell stories, advance theories, and interact with others from one particular viewpoint. Skepticism about such a picture of our identities consorts naturally with the thought that we are at the mercy of the stories we tell, as much as they are at our mercy. It also consorts naturally with an inclination to emphasize just how accidental it is that we hold the views we do, live where we do, and have the loyalties we do.[17]

Here, individual autonomy is seen as something that has to be constantly negotiated and revised, and is thus not a finished product, and this conception of subjectivity feeds into the social definition of postmodernity. However, as my students often posit in reaction to these postmodern notions of social construction, they do not feel that their autonomy and self-hood are being challenged and rendered transitory; in fact, students most often report a high level of perceived individual control and freedom.[18] Furthermore, the conflict between how students experience their own lives and how postmodern theorists describe contemporary subjectivity often works to make students simply reject these academic theories, and this student resistance to theory is one reason why we may want to rethink postmodernism through the development of automodernism.

Thus, as academics are concentrating on critiquing modern notions of universal reason and unified subjectivity, students are turning to modern science and technology to locate a strong sense of individual unity and control. However, I am not arguing here that we should simply reject all postmodern academic theories because they do not match our students' experiences and perceptions; rather, my point is that we should use these students' resistances to better understand how people today are influenced by the technological access to a heightened sense to individual control that can downplay social subjectivity and multicultural differences. Therefore, by seeing what postmodern theories have gotten wrong in the underestimating of virtual subjectivity, we can gain a better idea of what new educational theories need to get right. For instance, in fully articulating both a social and a psychological theory of student subjectivity, we can show why it is important to defend the social realm at the same time that we expose the reasons why new media caters to a psychological downplaying of social mediation.

In fact, what the social or postmodern theory of self-hood tends to neglect is the psychological and virtual foundation of autonomy and subjective unity. It is important to stress that if we examine how the sense of self is developed psychologically, we learn that one first gains a sense of individual identity by looking into a mirror or external representation and seeing an ideal representation of one's body as complete, whole, and bounded. This mirror theory of self-hood (Lacan) teaches us that since we never really see our whole body at a single glance – at least not without several mirrors or cameras – our internal body map is actually an internalized virtual image and not a concrete material fact. In other words, our sense of self is psychological and virtual and not primarily social and material. Moreover, our subjective feelings of autonomy are built upon this imaginary level of self-hood: To have a sense of self-direction, one must first have a sense of self, and to have a self, one needs to first internalize an ideal body map.

Social theories of subjectivity are thus misleading when they claim to depict a generalized undermining of unified subjectivity; yet, these same theories are vital when we want to discuss the possibility of social and cultural change. In the case of automodernity, I will be arguing that the power of new automated technologies to give us a heightened *sense* of individual control often functions to undermine the awareness of social and cultural mediation, and this lack of awareness can place the isolating individual against the public realm. Therefore, when my students reject postmodern theories because these self-denying concepts do not jive with their own self-understandings, we can posit that students and postmodern theories are both failing to distinguish between psychological and social models of subjectivity. In other terms, many of the postmodern theories discussed here stress the social determination of subjectivity, while many contemporary students focus on their sense of psychological determinism, and we need to offer models of education that integrate both perspectives.

However, instead of balancing the social and the psychological, postmodern educators like Lester Faigley posit that the contemporary subject is defined as being multiple, and identity is seen as a process.[19] In turn, this postmodern notion of subjectivity is contrasted with the Enlightenment ideology of subjective unity, coherency, objectivity, individuality, and universal scientific reason.[20] Moreover, for Faigley, postmodern culture and new media technologies challenge these modern ideologies by emphasizing the contingent and social nature of all acts of writing and knowledge construction.[21] It is also important to note that from Faigley's perspective, there is a growing divide between postmodern students and modern teachers in the ways students and teachers tend to understand the functions and roles of writing, technology, and literacy in culture and education. While I do agree with Faigley that new technologies help to build a growing divide between teachers and students in terms of how they conceive knowledge, identity, and media, my conception of automodernity argues that the simple replacement of modern individual unity with postmodern discontinuity fails to see how digital youth are merging the two sides of the modern divide: unified individuality and universal science. For example, in a prize-winning essay from the Global Kids contest on Digital Literacy, we find a digital youth making the following argument: 'Today, almost all the information that humans have gathered over thousands of years is at the tips of my fingers . . . or those of anyone who cares to use this incredible technology' ('From Gutenberg to Gateway').[22] On the one hand, this statement points to a heightened sense of individual control and access, and on the other hand, it highlights a universal notion of information and technology. By stating that 'anyone' can get almost 'any' information from the Web, this writer universalizes both the subject and object of global information distribution. The internet is positioned here as using automation and modern science to enhance the ability of individuals to access all information. Of course, this common conception of universal access of the World Wide Web represses many real digital divides as it presents a universalized notion of individuality, and it is important to note that one possible reason for this rhetorical neglect of differences is that the power of automation tends to render social and material factors invisible.

The same essay indicates a possible source for this common contemporary rhetoric of universal access:

> Of all the media that I use, I have only touched a spoonful of the ocean that is digital media. There are still thousands upon thousands of other sites, games, songs, and other things that I have never used and probably never will use. Every day, though, I find that I need some obscure piece of information, and this new technology allows me to find it. I play games and listen to music, and this helps define what I like and don't like.

This digital youth feels that since there is too much information available on the Web for one person to encounter, then all information must be available: here, information excess leads to a sense of universal access. Furthermore, it is often the automated nature of new media that functions to hide social disparities behind a veil of easy, global access. In turn, this automation and autonomy of access heightens a sense of individual control. Thus, what postmodern critics like Faigley might be missing in their accounts of contemporary digital youth is the power of new technologies to reinforce the imaginary and real experiences of individual autonomy through automated systems. In other terms, even in situations where information on the Web is determined by social mediation, digital youth are able to absorb cultural material into the frames of their individual point of view. As I will argue below, the PC often gives people the sense that they are in control of the information that appears on their screen, just as they are in control of the perceptions that they let into their own consciousness.

Another important clarification to make is the connection between universal science and automation. In the common understanding of modern science and culture, academics and philosophers often claim that science is universal because it does not rely on social or personal beliefs. In fact, a key to Descartes' development of the scientific method is his call to employ universal doubt to undermine all prejudices and approach every object of study with a shared transparent method open to all. Of course, Descartes developed his method as a counter to the dominant religious beliefs of his time, and central to his understanding of science was his investment in the idea of universal reason. While we may want to applaud the democratic and rational foundations of Descartes' universal approach, it is important to also note that this universalizing model of science, which posits the importance of a 'value-free' method, can actually free scientists from ethical and social responsibilities. Furthermore, in the application of modern science through the development of new technologies, we see how automated devices may create a responsibility-free zone where it is hard to locate any responsible ethical subject.

What then often accounts for the connection between universal science and new automated technologies is the shared process of downplaying the role of social contexts in the shaping of science and technology. Within the context of education, science and math are usually taught as if these subjects were purely objective and neutral, and therefore void of any individual or social influences. For example, even when teachers are discussing such issues as genetic manipulation, pharmaceutical intervention, and technological innovation, the knowledge is delivered without concern for ethical and social issues. Here, we see a division between the postmodern stress on social mediation and the modern rhetoric of science as being objective, neutral, universal, and ultimately inevitable.

We can further understand the presence of modern universality in contemporary education by looking at how literacy is defined in many higher education institutions. Thus, in *Reinventing the University: Literacies and Legitimacy in the Postmodern University*, Christopher Schroeder posits that most textbooks and governmental policies present, 'a universalized definition of literacy, as if what it means to be literate can be separated from the contexts in which literate practices are meaningful'.[23] In this critique of the common use of the term literacy, Schroeder affirms the distinction between a functional and a critical understanding of literacy by distinguishing the modern stress on universal neutrality from the postmodern stress on social context. From Schroeder's postmodern perspective, the myth of a universal model of literacy is derived from the ability of powerful vested interests to hide their own particular values behind false claims of universal objectivity. Moreover, Schroeder posits that this rhetoric of universality still dominates the ways our educational systems are structured and the types of literacy that are affirmed in schooling.[24] It is also important to note how this universalizing rhetoric has been adopted by digital youth in their common claims of global access, and therefore a key task of critical literacy studies is to explore with students these rhetorical constructions that function to hide important differences and discrepancies. For instance, when students claim that, 'Anyone can access any information from any place at any time', we need to engage them in a conversation about the role of the word 'any' in falsely universalizing and globalizing a rhetoric of unquestioned equality. In other words, we need to counter a functional model of technological literacy with a critical model of rhetorical understanding.

In fact, essential to Schroeder's analysis of the conflict between functional and critical models of literacy is his claim that the more school literacies are based on de-contextualized, universal models of information delivery, the more individual aspects of culture become the sole purview of experts.[25] Thus, central to the modern organization of education is the dual process of universalizing educational access to school *and* segmenting individual subject areas into separate areas of expertise. Furthermore, from Schroeder's perspective, functional literacy is dominated by the modern ideological interests of white, middle-class America, and these modern values, which are presented as being universal, no longer fit with the majority of contemporary students.[26]

In opposition to the modern stress on universal reason and neutral functional models of literacy, Schroeder affirms that students bring multiple literacies to universities, and these diverse models of social knowledge and learning are most often neglected by our traditional institutions.[27] As many other scholars have argued, postmodern student literacies are shaped by the cultural realms of television, movies, the Internet, and advertising, and not by the modern emphasis on books and reading as the central source of literacy.[28] While I do feel that Schroeder and other postmodern critics are correct in seeing this conflict between older and newer models of literacy, the stress on the modern universality of school-based literacies versus postmodern diversity of student literacies does not account for the spread of globalized media in automodernity. In other terms, new media technologies have absorbed modern universality into the globalized structures of automated systems, which in turn act to hide social mediation and to highlight individual control. Therefore, as I will argue below, auto-modern literacies based on television, advertising, movies and the Internet do not typically function to undermine people's belief in modern universal reason and unified subjectivity; instead, automodern technologies help to provide a greater sense of technological neutrality, universalized information, and individual power, even if this sense may be illusory.

Automodernity

To clarify what I mean by automodernism, I will examine several common technologies that are used heavily by digital youth in the early twenty-first-century globalized Western world: personal computers, word processors, cell phones, iPods, blogs, remote-controlled televisions, and first-person shooter computer games. These technological objects share a common emphasis on combining a high level of mechanical automation with a heightened sense of personal autonomy.[29] In fact, this unexpected and innovative combination of autonomy and automation can be read as the defining contradictions of contemporary life in general and digital youth in particular. Importantly, while automation traditionally represents a loss of personal control, autonomy has been defined by an increase in individual freedom; however, automodernity constantly combines these two opposing forces in an unexpected way.[30]

We can begin our analysis of this strange combination of autonomy and automation in automodernity by analyzing the automobile as the precursor to this new way of being. In fact, the very name of the automobile indicates a technological push for both the autonomy and automation of movement. Moreover, cars represent a truly nonsocial mode of movement that conflicts with the more social modes of public transportation. Thus, in the contemporary car, the driver not only has the feeling that he or she can go where he or she intends, but there is also the development of a heightened sense of personal control and autonomy. After all, in American popular culture, the automobile is one of the central symbols for freedom, mobility, and independence: it is the car that allows the teenager and the angry adult to escape personal alienation and set out for individual autonomy.

The automobile also creates the sense of a personal environment where technology enables a controlled world full of processed air, artificial sounds, and windowed vision. The car may even be experienced as a second body, and even though many people spend so much of their time stuck in traffic, the car retains the virtual and psychological sense of automated autonomy. In fact, by analyzing the cultural and psychological import of the car, we can begin to see some of the limits of the postmodern notion that contemporary society is founded on the social construction of reality, the overcoming of individual unity, and the critique of universal science. For the car, as an early sign of automodernity, is a vehicle for a nonsocial mode of personal freedom combined with a strong belief in the naturalness of scientific technology: Cars are experienced as artificial bodies that combine automation with autonomy and seem to render invisible most forms of social and cultural mediation.

While the automobile appears to be a prime technology of modernity, I would like to posit that it embodies the seeds to automodernity through its integration of privacy and automation and its downplaying of social mediation. In fact, Raymond Williams coined the term 'Mobile Privatization' to indicate how this type of technology, unlike the telegraph, the radio, and the subway, allows for mobility in a personalized and privatized milieu.[31] We can thus posit that the automobile has helped to lay the cultural groundwork for the new stress on autonomy through mechanical automation.

Like automobiles, personal computers indicate a paradoxical combination of individual autonomy and automated mechanics. While some of the postmodern theorists discussed above argue that computers and other modes of new media allow for a high level of social and cultural interaction, and thus these new communication technologies help digital youth to see how the world is based on social mediation and intersubjective communication, we can also understand these machines as central sources for an antisocial sense of personal control and autonomy. Therefore, in the PC, the world comes to me: not only can I bring my office to my home, but electronic commerce and e-mail allow me to escape from the need to engage with people in a public space. This privatization of public interaction echoes the larger political movement to undermine the notion of a modern public realm protected by a centralized government (The Welfare State). In short, the PC has unexpectedly enabled digital youth the freedom to avoid the public and to appropriate public information and space for unpredictable personal reasons. Furthermore, even when students are engaged in collaborative writing online, the power of the PC to personalize culture can turn this social interaction into a privatized experience. Thus, while it may appear that new communication technologies are actually broadening the social realm of digital youths, I am arguing that the ability of the individual user of new media to control the flow and intake of information provides a strong antisocial and self-reinforcing sense of subjectivity. For example, it is clear that students who are participating in an online discussion or chat room are free to read and respond to only the conversations that interest them or cater to their own individual points of view; however, in a classroom discussion, it is much harder for students to only respond to one person or to just respond to their own ideas over and over again.

It is important to point out here that my argument is not that new technologies are replacing the social realm with the private realm; rather, I want to stress that the power of new media to cater to real and imagined feelings of self-direction threatens to hide and render invisible important social and public forces. Therefore, although it is essential to consider the social construction of new technologies and their usages, we need to start off with a heightened attention to and analysis of the subjective and embodied nature of electronic culture in order to understand how new media is being lived and experienced by digital youth. In fact, one way of rereading the initials PC is to think of Personal Culture as a new mode of privatized social subjectivity. The feelings of personal choice and power that digital technologies so powerfully proffer are at least as important objects of investigation and critical reflection as the social networks they may enable. Perhaps the ultimate technology of personal culture is the laptop computer, which functions as the logical extension of the PC, as demonstrated by the way that it gives the individual user the freedom to perform private activities in public. Thus, the laptop may turn any public or commercial space into a private workplace or play space. Since people can take their work and their games with them wherever they go, the whole traditional opposition between workspace and private space breaks down. For example, when one goes to a café, one sees people working with their laptops as if these customers are sitting at home: they have their food, their phone, their newspaper, and other personal items displayed in public. The reverse of the public being absorbed into the private is therefore the private being displayed in public.[32]

Of course, both the privatization of the public and the publicizing of the private are fuelled by the twin engines of autonomy and automation. In this context, subjective freedom is tied to the mechanical reproduction of a set system of technological functions. For instance, one of the central uses for the PC is the employment of various word and image processing programs. These technologies center on the preprogramming of 'universal' templates and systems of scientific order, thus, programs like spell-checker function by automating tasks that individuals traditionally controlled. However, instead of seeing this transfer of responsibility from the individual writer to the machine, most digital youth that I have interviewed feel that this automation gives them more autonomy to concentrate on what really matters. Moreover, as we saw in my initial example of Benjamin exchanging texts with his friends, the automation of the copy and paste functions increases the freedom of the individual writer to move text around and to engage in acts of constant revision. Automation therefore adds to textual fluidity, which in turn, feeds a sense of personal autonomy.

Powering the PC revolution of automodernity are the Internet and the World Wide Web. At first glance, these technological systems appear to represent the epitome of the postmodern stress on multiculturalism, social interaction, and the movement away from the individuated modern self; however, we can read these technologies as actually undermining the social and the multicultural worlds by giving the individual consumer of information the illusion of automated autonomy. In many ways, the digital youth's experience of the Web challenges the postmodern idea that we are constrained by time and space and that our relationships with others are defined by our cultural and social differences and relations. From the perspective of digital youth, all information from any culture and any person is immediately available to any user at any time and from any place. Thus, in cyberspace, temporal and spatial restraints do not seem to matter.

In fact, by reviewing several of the Global Kids essay winners, we find a reoccurring theme concerning this loss of spatial and temporal differences and a growing sense that cultural differences no longer pose a barrier to understanding. For example, in the essay entitled 'From Gutenberg to Gateway', mentioned earlier, the digital youth writes, 'My generation is more understanding of other cultures, simply because we are better informed than our parents were. We play games that prepare us for the world by heightening our awareness and teaching us to solve problems'. According to this writer, new media digital youth are not only more informed about cultural differences than previous generations, but new communication and gaming technologies are training youth for a globalized world. Another essay reiterates this same point about the growing multicultural awareness of globalized digital youth; however, in this writing, intercultural understanding is founded on a denial of differences, 'Since there is no way to tell who people are when they're online, people have to be accepted for who they are. We learn to think about what a person says often times without knowing who said it, thus eliminating any possible bias' ('Digital Media in My Life'). This statement reflects on the fundamental conflict of modern universalism: on one level, universality promotes equal rights and a rejection of prejudices, but on another level, universality can indicate a lack of sensitivity regarding cultural and ethnic differences. Thus, if we are all treated equally, then none of our differences count.

In automodernity, the conflicted nature of modern universals is often repressed below a hyper-modern sense of globalized access and information exchange. Furthermore, as the following quote from the same digital youth essay implies, modern and automodern universality is haunted by the conflicted double legacy of individualism and social conformity:

> Self-reliance and assertiveness are other important qualities gained from the Net. There are Web sites for all sorts of purposes, from fantasy football to free speech. Internet-based self-reliance comes from the independent nature of the computer because it is designed for use by one person. When on the Internet, people decide where to go and what to do entirely on their own, and that idea has been firmly engrained in the minds of this new generation. These thinking characteristics acquired through frequent use of the Internet can be valuable in society, whether taking a stand for a belief, accepting a person's opinion, or setting a goal, are all positive attributes of the way we think, which makes me optimistic about the new generation.

This digital youth rightly proclaims the power of autonomy afforded by the personal computer, and I do not think that we should posit that he is simply being duped by a lure of false individualism. However, what we do need to examine are the possible consequences of this universal model of libertarian self-reliance. One important issue that this same essay brings up is the common connection between individual autonomy and consumerism: 'The way kids are going to function in the world is amazing, particularly as consumers. The Internet provides nearly unlimited options and choices. The vast "information superhighway" gives so many options that it will become necessary to offer customization for every product'. This statement does seem to reflect the notion that while the internet can increase our sense of individual control, it can also function to steer our autonomy into spaces that are controlled by economic interests. Furthermore, this version of autonomy appears to be predicated on the marketing rhetoric of free choice in a frictionless economy, and what we often see in this type of belief is a libertarian equation of free markets, free speech, and personal freedoms.

It is important to examine how this new media mode of libertarian autonomy often calls for a privatization of the public sphere and a use of automation in the pursuit of personal liberty and controlled social interaction. For instance, in the following statement from this essay, the young writer combines together a celebration of the social aspects of multiple-user video games with a denial of cultural and ethnic differences.

> Online multiplayer video games are, contrary to common belief, very social atmospheres where players get to know one another personally. Gamers often group together in clans or guilds to play alongside each other on a regular basis. I've spoken to forty-year-olds with wives and children who still cut out a half-hour each day to play a World War II-based shooting game. One of the greatest aspects of these groups is that no one sees what the other people look like, but they respect each other nonetheless. These guys could have completely different backgrounds, different ethnicities, and totally different religions, but all of these variables dissolve when you are shooting virtual enemies as a team. Clans and guilds are microcosms of the business world in that people must learn to work together to achieve goals systematically.

In reading this passage, I believe that it is necessary to not fall into a simple pro versus con conception of video games and virtual violence; rather, I want to stress that this new model of social interactivity transforms the public realm into a shared space populated by highly autonomous users/consumers. Instead of the public realm being a place of ethnic and cultural conflict and difference, the privatized public realm becomes a space to ignore differences and to focus on commonalities: once again this is both a positive and a negative universalizing gesture.

On one level, we are seeing a growing tolerance of cultural differences, and on another level, these differences are simply being denied. Moreover, as these digital youth essays reveal, this repression of cultural differences is linked to the veiling of temporal and spatial differences. From a critical perspective, we may want to affirm that without the limits of time and space, many modes of otherness begin to disappear and fade beneath a veil of global access. Therefore, while the Web may enable digital youth to encounter multiple cultures and various social relationships, they often experience those interactions through the window and frame of their PC, and in this technological context, all encounters with others become visually boxed into the confines of the screen: here, the frame of the screen serves as a mental container for Otherness.[33] Like a cage at a zoo or a picture frame at a museum, the structure of the framed screen provides a strong sense of limits and borders. Moreover, it is important to stress that it is the individual who decides what to put up on the screen, and this sense of individual control reinforces the feeling of autonomy for the PC user.

Another location of automated autonomy on the internet are search engines, which allow individuals to perform quickly and easily the complicated tasks of locating, sorting, and accessing diverse information. Through automation, search engines, like Google.com, render invisible the multiple methods and technologies employed to scan, for personal reasons, the globalized Web. Furthermore, instead of relying on experts or modern sorting systems, like library card catalogues, automated search engines appear to put the power of cultural filtering into the hands of the autonomous user. Of course, these technological systems have their own inner logic and preprogrammed priorities, but these systemic issues are most often hidden from view.

In fact, one could argue that PCs and the Web work together to hide social and technological determination behind the appearance of autonomous user control. For example, many blogging programs offer highly controlled and limited templates, but these technological restrictions are buried beneath the power of the individual to create his or her own media. Therefore, even though most MySpace sites look the same and have similar content, digital youth often feel that these automated templates provide for a great deal of personal freedom, self-expression, and personal identity. Furthermore, as in the case of other social networking technologies, personal blogs are a great example of the breakdown between the traditional division between the private and public realms, for blogs give every individual user the possibility of distributing private thoughts in a public space. Like personal homepages, these internet sites trace the movement of media control from large social organizations to the fingertips of individual users and producers. Thus, one of the most exciting aspects of these new media modes of information distribution is that instead of people having to rely on large, corporate media outlets for their news and information, private individuals can become their own public media reporters. In fact, this absorption of the public media into the private realm has also resulted in the use of these private blogging sources in traditional journalistic media. Furthermore, in an unexpected twist, broadcast journalists are now searching blogs for news and personal reporting.

While some may say that the use of blogs exemplifies the postmodern emphasis on the social foundations of knowledge production and exchange, I would argue that the PC world of personalized culture absorbs the social construction of information into the autonomous echo chambers of individuated media. In other words, when every user also becomes a producer of media, the multiplication and diversification of potential sources for information increases to such an extent that individual consumers are motivated to seek out only the sources and blogs that reinforce their own personal views and ideologies. Here, the screen truly becomes an automated mirror of self-reflection.

One way to summarize the effects of many of these automodern technologies that I have related to the PC is to look at the iPod. On one level, the iPod is the perfect example of the use of automation to give individuals the autonomy to select and filter information and to absorb a previously public domain into the control of the private individual. We often forget that at one time, music was heard mainly in public settings; however, with the advent of recording technologies, music was freed from its live expression and was allowed to enter into the homes of individuals through shared distribution systems. It is also important to point out that the radio, like the television, is still a public medium, which is most often absorbed into private homes and now automobiles. Yet, on the radio, the selection of songs belongs to someone else, and therefore it caters to a more public and shared reception of music. Likewise, albums combined songs in a particular order that pre-package a predetermined collection of music. However, with the iPod, these public and industry-related restraints are eliminated, and the user is free through automation to create his or her own selection of songs.

Most importantly, the iPod allows people to take music anywhere and to use headphones as a way of cutting off the social world around them. For example,

I often see students in public spaces listening to their iPods and moving and singing to the music as if they were alone in their private bedrooms. Here, we rediscover the loss of the distinction between the private and the public realms. Also, the fact that so many digital youth take their songs from illegal peer-to-peer internet sites shows how the loss of the public realm is coupled with an undermining of certain commercial interests. In a way, individual users are privatizing the music industry by illegally downloading music and creating their own systems of distribution and consumption. Yet, the success of Apple and iTunes points to the ways that the anticorporate mentality of some peer-to-peer file sharers has been quickly absorbed back into a corporate and consumerist structure. The libertarian impulses of the autonomous new media user are thus quite compatible with the production of a new consumer economy. In fact, in many of my students' essays about their uses of new media, they often equate individual freedom with the free market. Of course, what is usually left out of this equation is the idea of a public realm of protected and enacted citizenship.

Automodern convergences

Many people feel that the next stage of technology development will be the combination of the iPod, the PC, the internet, and the cell phone. In this synergistic approach to automodern technology, we see the desire for total mobility and individual autonomy through the use of highly automated systems. One fear is that once all of these new media and technologies are absorbed into the cell phone, individuals will lose all ability to differentiate how to act in public from how to act in private. Already, cell phones make it easy for people to have private conversations in public, and this ignoring of the public often results in a situation where people in a public setting are all having their own private interactions with people who are not in the same physical space.

Another danger is that cell phones tend to make people forget where they actually are physically. For instance, it has been shown that when people drive cars and talk on the cell phone at the same time, they are more prone to accidents because they literally forget that they are driving.[34] Like so many other automodern technologies, cell phones allow people to enter into a technological flow where the difference between the individual and the machine breaks down. In other terms, due to the fluid and immersive nature of these technologies, people forget that they are using them, and in many ways, they become one with their machines.

With the immersive fluidity of cell phones, digital youth often claim that they are addicted to the use of this technology and that they suffer from withdrawals when they are forced to not use these machines. In fact, I often see my students approach my classes while talking on the phone, and then when class ends, they immediately, compulsively get back on the cell. Sometimes, I overhear the conversations these students have between classes, and these communications seem to have no other content than 'checking in' or stating the students' present location. It is as if they do not feel that they exist unless someone else hears about their current presence. Here, autonomy is shown to be dependent on the recognition of others. Furthermore, it is interesting that students often detail the location and the time of their calls as if to show that time and space are still relevant. Thus, as new automodern technologies break with past conceptions of time and space, they also call for a continuous unconscious return to temporal and spatial coordinates.[35]

This need for digital youth to have their autonomy registered by others can also be seen in blogs, Web cams, and online diaries. All of these new technologies point to the desire for people to be heard and seen by people they may not even know. Like public confessional booths, these automodern processes allow for an externalization of interior feelings and ideas. However, unlike past uses of confession by religious orders, psychologists, and police, these types of self-disclosure do not seem to serve any higher public purpose other than the desire for recognition. Moreover, the fact that the audience of the confession is often absent shows how this type of communication reduces the social other to the role of simply verifying the individual's presence. One could argue that the more mass society makes us feel that we are just a number and that our voices do not count, the more we need to simply use technology to have our autonomy registered through automation. For example, one of the appealing aspects of popular television shows like *American Idol* is that they allow for the individual viewer to call in and register his or her own preference and presence. Likewise, CNN news programs often read viewers' e-mail on air and hold constant polls where viewers can voice their own immediate opinions. In this new combination of autonomy and automation, we have to wonder if this is what direct democracy really looks like, or are these uses of personal opinions just a lure to make people feel like they have some control over situations where they really have very little power? From an automodern perspective, this question of whether these new modes of participatory technology produce false or real autonomy and democracy can be seen as irrelevant because automodern digital youth usually do not distinguish between real and virtual identity.

The production of false autonomy in highly automated systems can also be understood through the example of the elevator button, which is supposed to control the closing of the door, but in reality is not usually attached to any real function. When elevator designers were asked why they include this nonfunctioning button, they responded that many people feel out of control and anxious in elevators, and so this button gives them a sense of control and eases their worries. According to Slavoj Žižek:

> It is a well-known fact that the close-the-door button in most elevators is a totally dysfunctional placebo which is placed there just to give individuals the impression that they are somehow participating, contributing to the speed of the elevator journey. When we push this button the door closes in exactly the same time as when we just press the floor button without speeding up the process by pressing also the close-the-door button. This extreme and clear case of fake participation is, I claim, an appropriate metaphor [for] the participation of individuals in our post-modern political process.[36]

For Žižek, automation often allows for a high level of false autonomy and therefore represents a fake mode of social participation. Here, we refind the short-circuiting of the public realm by the automodern combination of autonomy and automation. Therefore, like pushing a nonfunctioning elevator button, instant television polls may only be giving people the feeling that they are participating in direct democracy, while their actual individual power is being diminished.

This high reliance on automation to prove autonomy is connected to an interesting reversal of the modern opposition between the roles of active subjects and passive objects. For example, in modern science, the scientist is supposed to be active and mobile, while the object of study is fixed in time and space.[37] This same opposition can be seen in modern art where the natural object stays rigid on the canvas, as the painter is free to move around. Furthermore, modernity sees technology as a tool or object that is controlled by the active subject. However, in automodernity, all of these relationships are reversed. For instance, in video games, the player's activity is often reduced to the movement of a finger or fingers, while the object on the screen moves around.[38] Likewise, in contemporary physics, the object of study is in constant movement or chaos, while the scientist remains an immobile watcher. Therefore, through automation, autonomy has been projected onto the external object, while the subject remains passive (Žižek calls this 'interpassivity').

Of course, television is really the technological object that first introduced us to this curious reversal between the subject and the object. In fact, when the television was first reviewed at the World's Fair by *The New York Times*, the reporter wrote that this invention would fail because no one would want to just sit in their homes and stare into a box for hours at a time. Yet, this type of autonomous passivity is precisely what the automodern culture is willing to do, and the fact that the television became the first real object of the global village shows that there is almost a universal desire for people to be inactive as they watch activity appear in the realm of their objects.

Not only do televisions and computer games share this reversal of the subject and object relationship, but both technologies represent a global spread of popular culture that denies its own value and meaning. For example, whenever I try to get students to analyze critically the shows they watch or the computer games they play, they insist that these activities are escapes and sources for meaningless enjoyment. From this perspective, culture is a way of escaping society and the burden of thinking. What then has helped this type of technology and culture to spread around the world is that it is essentially self-consuming, and by this term I mean it denies its own import and value.

Connected to the television and the computer game is the remote control, whose very name points to the idea of autonomous, automated control from a distance. As Christine Rosen argues in her essay 'Egocasting', the clicker allows for a sense of total personal freedom:

> The creation and near-universal adoption of the remote control arguably marks the beginning of the era of the personalization of technology. The remote control shifted power to the individual, and the technologies that have embraced this principle in its wake – the Walkman, the Video Cassette Recorder, Digital Video Recorders such as TiVo, and portable music devices like the iPod – have created a world where the individual's control over the content, style, and timing of what he consumes is nearly absolute.[39]

For Rosen, the ability to just turn people off or go to the next channel represents a strong combination of automation and autonomy, which can be seen as being highly antisocial:

By giving us the illusion of perfect control, these technologies risk making us incapable of ever being surprised. They encourage not the cultivation of taste, but the numbing repetition of fetish. And they contribute to what might be called 'egocasting', the thoroughly personalized and extremely narrow pursuit of one's personal taste. In thrall to our own little technologically constructed worlds, we are, ironically, finding it increasingly difficult to appreciate genuine individuality.[40]

From Rosen's perspective, these new technologies not only do not increase unexpected and innovative activities, but they work to get rid of new and unexpected encounters. While I will discuss below different ways that digital youth are now challenging this thesis of ego-centrism in new media, I often think that one reason why students seem to turn off so quickly in class is that they are so used to having so much control over what they see and hear, and yet, like video games, television still provides a highly limited set of possible interactions and activities. While it is common to point to the use of interactivity as the key driving force behind the popularity of computer games for the automodern generation, we often find that the type of interactivity allowed by automated games is highly restricted. Therefore, not only does most of the activity reside on the machine's side, but the activities the machine can perform are all prescripted and form a limited range of actions. In many ways, we are seeing a usage of new media technologies to simultaneously erase and produce individual freedom, while individual freedom is being equated with the free market.[41]

For instance, in order to allow for a high level of preprogrammed interactivity, first-person shooter computer games must replace human interaction with restrictive social stereotypes. However, people still enjoy playing these games and repeating the same scenarios and choices over and over again. While at first glance, this high level of automation and repetition would seem to preclude a sense of personal autonomy, we must see that individual freedom in automodernity often represents a freedom not to do something. Thus, the freedom not to think or not to interact in a social relationship is a highly valued freedom in this cultural order. Likewise, the automodern celebration of free speech is in part derived from the desire to be free from social, political, relational, and traditional restrictions. What is then loved about computer games and contemporary media is that they are often so politically incorrect, and therefore they celebrate the autonomy of the individual no matter how repetitive and reductive the media representation.

Future uses of automodern technologies in education and politics

The challenge for educators and public policy makers in the period of automodernity is to first recognize the dominant combination of autonomy and automation and then employ this new cultural order in a more self-critical and social way. For example, educators can create learning spaces where students engage in creative file-sharing activities; however, these same students need to be given critical thinking tools to reflect on the social and public aspects of their activities. This process will require the development of critical technology studies as a central core to automodern educational systems, and essential to this new form of education will be a constant effort of forming a dialogue between 'old' school and 'new' home models of media and technology. Therefore, instead of simply ignoring how the digital youth are using new media and technologies in unexpected and innovative ways, it is important to first understand these usages, to theorize and analyze their appeal, and then to find ways to employ them in a productive social manner. Ethnographies [...] offer one method of exploring usage; however, traditions in critical theory, rhetoric, and philosophy offer other modes of thinking about the age we inhabit. And, as I've suggested throughout this essay, careful attention to the subject positions crafted by new technologies will also help us refine the theories humanities scholars deploy when explaining the world around them. If, as scholars, our theories help us to discern the world around us, the new relations of self to power emerging in our networked age suggest we need more supple, nuanced theoretical tools. Whether automodernity represents an extension of postmodernity or a break from it, this chapter argues that we are certainly in a moment of shifting relations of self to other that we need to theorize and understand.

One place where new automodern technologies are being reconnected to the public realm is in the development of social networking Web sites and software dedicated to getting people to organize online and meet offline. For instance, Meetup.com provides templates and strategies for creating social networks that engage in particular group activities. According to their Web site, this electronic social network is involved in combining new media technologies with more traditional social and public activities: 'Meetup.com helps people find others who share their interest or cause, and form lasting, influential, local community groups that regularly meet face to face. We believe that the world will be a better place when everyone has access to a people-powered local Meetup Group'. Like

Moveon.org, this site uses technology and media as a facilitator to connect people online and motivate them to meet in person. In fact, I would argue that this structure employs automodern media for postmodern purposes, and therefore these sites show that the privatization of the public realm is not the only possible result of the combination of autonomy and automation. Furthermore, these new social collective sites may point to the future of both democratic education and politics. In starting off with how people are already using new media technologies, these forums for digital connection offer a new hope for a more democratic public realm.

While I have found that most of my digitally minded students tend to use new media social networking sites as another mode of ego-casting popular culture and personal communication, it is possible to help work from students' own interests while also moving them toward more publicly minded online activities. For example, as an experiment in grassroots online social involvement, teachers can have students create social networks dedicated to a particular social intervention. In using their Viewbook or Facebook personal pages, students can transform their social networks into ad hoc, grassroots collectives directed to whatever causes they want to pursue. One place to look at possible projects for digital youth is the book *MoveOn's 50 Ways to Love Your Country*.[42] This text discusses ways new media technologies can be used to enact a wide variety of public action activities, including letter writing campaigns, product boycotts, social petitions, election activism, voting drives, media criticism, political house parties, and community service projects.

Another way of incorporating the unexpected activities of digital youth is to take advantage of the automodern fascination with viral videos. These short digital movies can be used to collect evidence of consumer fraud and political abuse. In fact, throughout the world, young people are using new technologies to document human rights abuses and other social issues. These social activities display the possible roles new media and digital youth can play in the global democratization and social justice movements. If we still believe that teaching is meant to broaden our students' horizons, challenge them to think and behave ethically, and expose them to ideas and worlds they might not otherwise encounter, we must take seriously the ways in which new technologies address and engage them and then use their interests as a platform for ethical engagement with the world.

Returning to my opening example of Benjamin as a multimedia, multitasking student, it is important to begin to reimagine how our institutions can both hold onto past effective modes of teaching and cater to new media methods of learning and new forms of the self. The first step in this process will be to develop a more critical and tolerant view of how new technologies affect all aspects of digital youth. My hope is that this chapter will begin a conversation that steers between the extremes of naïve celebration and pessimistic dismissal of radically ambivalent automodern media. In developing a critical model of new media literacy, we can work to integrate new modes of learning and living into older forms of social interaction. Furthermore, by defending the public realm against the constant threats of privatization, we can open up a new automodern public space.

Notes

1 Lester Faigley, *Fragments of Rationality: Postmodernity and the Subject of Composition* (Pittsburgh, PA: University of Pittsburgh Press, 1992).
2 Robert Samuels, *Integrating Hypertextual Subjects* (Cresskill, NJ: Hampton Press, 2006).
3 James Gee, *What Video Games Have to Teach Us about Learning and Literacy* (New York: Palgrave Macmillian, 2004), 169–198.
4 One of the most popular criticisms of postmodernism can be found in Alan Bloom's *The Closing of the American Mind*; see Alan Bloom, *The Closing of the American Mind* (New York: Simon, 1987).
5 The work of Homi Bhabha has shown a strong recognition of the role of multiple cultures and social movements in the postmodern challenging of modern universalism and European ethnocentrism; see Homi Bhabha, *The Location of Culture* (London: Routledge, 1994).
6 It is hard to cite sources for the extreme form of postmodern relativism since it is often the critics of postmodernism who have defined this extremist position. A strong example of a critic who has insisted on an extreme version of postmodern relativism is Dinesh D'Souza's *Illiberal Education*; see Dinesh D'Souza, *Illiberal Education* (New York: Vintage Books, 1991).
7 Many of the first strong theories of social construction can be derived from Saussure's work in linguistics and Claude Levi-Strauss's work in anthropology. These social science works were imported into the humanities in Jacques Derrida's early work; see Ferdinand de Saussure, *Course in General Linguistics*, eds. Charles Balley and Albert Sechehaye, trans. Wade Baskin (New York: McGraw-Hill, 1966); Claude Levi-Strauss, *The Savage Mind* (Chicago: University of Chicago Press, 1970); Jacques Derrida, *Margins of Philosophy* (Chicago: University of Chicago Press, 1982).

8 One of the earliest theorists to connect collage and cultural re-mixing to postmodernity was Frederick Jameson.

9 While the work of Jacques Derrida has been blamed for ushering the extreme cultural relativism into Western philosophy and literary studies, I would argue that it has often been his followers and imitators who have offered a less nuanced and more generalized mode of postmodern extremism.

10 Zygmunt Bauman, *Modernity and the Holocaust* (Ithaca, NY: Cornell University Press, 1989); Ulrich Beck, *Risk Society: Towards a New Modernity* (London and Newbury Park, CA: Sage Publications, 1992); Jean Baudrillard, *The Transparency of Evil* (New York: Verso, 1993); Frederic Jameson, *Postmodernism: Or, the Cultural Logic of Late Capitalism* (Durham, NC: Duke University Press, 1991); Jeremy Rifkin, *The Age of Access* (New York: Putnam, 2000).

11 Marilyn Cooper, Postmodern Pedagogy in Electronic Conversations, in *Passions, Pedagogy, and 21st Century Technologies*, eds. Gail E. Hawisher and Cynthia L. Selfe (Logan: Utah State University Press, 1999), 142.

12 While it may seem that Cooper's stress on the connection of diverse voices helps to explain my example above of the unexpected use by students of technology for collaboration, I argue here that automodern collaboration should not be confused with the postmodern stress on public and social mediation.

13 Marilyn Cooper, Postmodern Pedagogy in Electronic Conversations, 143.

14 Ibid., 143.

15 George Howard, Culture Tales, *American Psychologist* 46, no. 3 (1990): 187–197.

16 I have found that many students reject this type of argument because they believe that science is neutral and objective and not subject to cultural and historical influences. Students, and many academics, also tend to confuse social constructivism with subjectivism.

17 Alan Ryan, cited in Lawrence W. Sherman in Postmodern Constructivist Pedagogy for Teaching and Learning Cooperatively on the Web, *CyberPsychology & Behavior* 3, no. 1 (Feb. 2000): 51–57.

18 A central reason why students do not feel that their sense of self is being undermined by postmodern society is that the self is a psychological and virtual entity that is not strictly determined by social forces.

19 Lester Faigley, *Fragments of Rationality: Postmodernity and the Subject of Composition* (Pittsburgh, PA: University of Pittsburgh Press, 1992).

20 Ibid., 4–7.

21 Ibid., 8.

22 Essays from the 2006 Global Kids Digital Media Essay Contest can be accessed at http://www.community.macfound.org/crossvolume. This contest asked students from all over the world to write about their diverse experiences using new media (accessed November 12, 2006).

23 Christopher Schroeder, *Re-inventing the University* (Logan, Utah: Utah State University Press, 2001), 2.

24 Ibid., 3.

25 Ibid., 5.

26 Ibid., 6.

27 Ibid., 7.

28 Ibid., 10; Kenneth Gergen, *The Saturated Self: Dilemmas of Identity in Contemporary Life* (New York: Basic Books, 1991); Neil Postman, *Technopoly: The Surrender of Culture to Technology* (New York: Vintage, 1992); Henry A. Giroux, Slacking Off: Border Youth and Postmodern Education, *Journal of Advanced Composition* 14, no. 2 (1994). http://www.henryagiroux.com/online.articles/ slacking.off.htm.

29 A major problem with my analysis is that it tends to hide the real economic divisions in our culture that prevent many young people from having access to the same technologies. However, I still feel that the technologies I will be discussing are used by a majority of students who end up going to college.

30 Throughout the 19th and 20th centuries, the mechanized assembly line is often seen as the ultimate example of how automation alienates people and takes away their sense of personal autonomy.

31 Raymond Williams, *Television: Technology and Cultural Form* (London: Fontana, 1974).

32 Behind this discussion of the privatization of the public realm through technology is an acknowledgment of the political movement to undermine the public realm and the welfare state.

33 I am drawing here from Heidegger's work on the enframing power of technology; Martin Heidegger, *The Question Concerning Technology and Other Essays* (New York: Harper Colophon Books, 1977).

34 In fact, some studies equate the effect of using a cell phone while driving to driving under the influence of alcohol.

35 I stress the unconscious nature of the retention of spatial and temporal concerns because students claim that they are not aware that they often have conversations about their locations in space and time.

36 Slavoj Žižek, 'Human Rights and Its Discontents', 2005, http://www.lacan.com/ zizek-human.htm.

37 Jean Baudrillard's work is the major source for explaining this reversal of the subject and the object in contemporary science.

38 While it may be true that new game designers are trying to make the movements of the player a larger part of games, this movement is still highly restricted.

39 Christine Rosen, Egocasting, *The New Atlantis*, 2005. http://www.thenewatlantis. com/archive/7/rosen.htm.

40 Ibid.

41 All of these trends feed into the neo-conservative and neo-liberal movements to justify the cutting of taxes through the downgrading of public programs and the deregulation of the free market. Since the public realm has been absorbed into the automated activities of the machine, and the private realm has been equated with the free subject of the free market, there is no longer any need to fund public welfare projects.

42 MoveOn, *MoveOn's 50 Ways to Love Your Country* (San Francisco: Inner Ocean, 2006).

11

Renewalism

The relationship between renewalism and the postmodernism it purports to succeed is arguably more complex than that of any of the other positions set out in this book. Rather than asserting that postmodernism has simply died a death, and something new has just been born in its place, Josh Toth (who refined the idea of 'renewalism' in his 2010 work The Passing of Postmodernism, having first mooted the idea in a 2007 book he edited with Neil Brooks), makes it clear that the contemporary continues to be influenced and informed by the postmodern, despite its much-vaunted death.

It is precisely this overused thanatological vocabulary of the 'death' of postmodernism that gives Toth his opening. Drawing on Derrida's later work Specters of Marx, he argues that postmodernism outlives its own death, much like a specter or ghost: it is a 'revenant' – something that keeps coming back to life and returning to haunt the present. (Its afterlife, indeed, is plainly visible: it lives on in the many obituaries, epitaphs, and eulogies written about the death of postmodernism, of which those in Part One are just a handful.) This haunting takes the form of a deconstructive paradox or aporetic impossibility: it is both dead and alive, both past and present at once, meaning that though postmodernism is dead and renewalism has superseded it, the 'wake' of the postmodern is still ongoing – a transitional time that involves both the rejection of the postmodern condition and the pursuit of postmodernism by other means.

Put more simply, Toth argues that shifts between historical periods are seldom sudden and abrupt: instead, there is a good deal of overlap and continuity as they segue into each other. Thus, the passing of postmodernism and the advent of renewalism need not involve dramatic or violent rifts and ruptures. Rather, a process of 'epistemic reconfiguration' takes place, so that the era after postmodernism is brought about more by a change in emphasis. To demonstrate this point, Toth offers renewalist interpretations and readings of what are generally considered to be classic postmodern texts, such as Pynchon's The Crying of Lot 49, or, in more detail, Toni Morrison's Beloved (see below).

As for the characteristics of renewalism itself, Toth is less clear about these than about the spectral relationship between renewalism and postmodernism, perhaps because he sees renewalism as still very much an emergent episteme. Though renewalism does not entail a simplistic return to Enlightenment values such as truth, meaning, and progress, neither does it endorse the dogmatic, hegemonic postmodern repudiation of them. Instead, renewalism tentatively maintains both sets of values in a deconstructive tension with each other that Toth argues is best summed up in a word like 'perhaps'. As for a renewalist aesthetic, Toth suggests that the tendency towards 'neo-realism' or so-called 'dirty realism' in the contemporary novel entails a renewalist eclecticism of narrative forms and styles, together with a deconstructive face-off between postmodern and Enlightenment sets of values. (A similar face-off forms the basis of metamodernism, though Timotheus Vermeulen and Robin van den Akker see its aesthetic realization in neo-romanticism rather than neo-realism.)

This predilection for eclecticism, together with the insistence on a Derridean open-endedness, could arguably be said to rejuvenate the postmodern rather than to bury it. That is, if the death of postmodern ideas was brought about largely by their all-too-dogmatic institutionalization (as described by Linda Hutcheon and others in Part One), then renewalism could just as easily be characterized as a thought-provoking reassessment of their subtlety and complexity, demonstrating that the canonized version of postmodernism is a simplification, and reasserting the vitality of the ongoing project of contemporary postmodernism. (Indeed, on the whole, Toth's book devotes more energy to discussing the persistence of postmodernism than the emergence of renewalism.) Moreover, if the terms with which renewalist texts and artworks are described can just as easily be used of postmodern ones, then the defining characteristics of renewalism may seem in danger of appearing too indistinct, too inconsistent, or perhaps even too chimerical to be practicably useful.

Such criticisms, however, overlook Toth's key point: that it is foolhardy to assume that the postmodern is simply over and done with, and that a new period, or style, or episteme has suddenly supplanted it. Viewed in these terms, the sketchiness of Toth's outline of renewalism is certainly less problematic than some of the suspiciously brusque attempts to consign the postmodern to the dustbin, as in remodernism.

The extracts are from Josh Toth and Neil Brooks, 'Introduction: A Wake and Renewed?' in *The Mourning After: Attending the Wake of Postmodernism*, eds. Neil Brooks and Josh Toth (Amsterdam: Rodopi, 2007), pp. 1–9; and from Josh Toth's *The Passing of Postmodernism: A Spectroanalysis of the Contemporary* (Albany: SUNY Press, 2010), p. 118; pp. 121–45.

Introduction: A Wake and Renewed?

Josh Toth and Neil Brooks

[M]ourning also wants to get rid of the past, to exorcize it, albeit under the guise of respectful commemoration. To forget the dead altogether is impious in ways that prepare their own retribution, but to remember the dead is neurotic and obsessive and merely feeds sterile repetition. There is no 'proper' way of relating to the dead and the past.

Fredric Jameson, 'Marx's Purloined Letter'

In her brief epilogue to the 2002 edition of *Politics of Postmodernism*, Linda Hutcheon seemingly placed the final nail in postmodernism's coffin: 'it's over' (166). According to Hutcheon, 'the postmodern moment has passed, even if its discursive strategies and its ideological critique continue to live on – as do those of modernism – in our contemporary twenty-first-century world' (181). On the one hand, Hutcheon seems to wash her hands of the whole thing. Postmodernism is dead, no more, finished, passed, past. Yet, on the other hand, she seems to suggest that postmodernism persists, that it 'lives on' (at least in part). What does this mean, though? In what way is postmodernism both past/passed and present? What parts of it have managed to 'live on'? Are these parts, these 'discursive strategies' (like parasites), 'living on' something else, some other epochal trend? If so, what new 'episteme' (if we loosely employ Foucault's terminology) carries this burden, this inheritance, this debt? Or, put differently, what new period of cultural production is this that seems (quite necessarily) to be defined by its commitment to an inevitable work of mourning, a work of mourning the passing (on) of an epistemological trend that defined the past 50 years of cultural and theoretical production? What or who, then, is witness, here (now) at this wake of postmodernism?

Of course, Hutcheon has arrived somewhat late to this seemingly on-going wake – or rather, this ongoing *work* of waking, of enduring the wake, of *waking*, of waking *up*.[1] The 'wake' began, it would seem, as early as the mid-eighties. More specifically, and following a writer like Raymond Federman,[2] we might argue that the first symptoms of some terminal epistemological illness became irrefutable on December 22, 1989 – the day Beckett died. In the mid to late-eighties, in fact, a number of events seemed to herald the end of postmodernism as the reigning epistemological dominant: the journal *Granta* published an issue dedicated to American 'dirty realism'; neo-realist writers like Raymond Carver rose in status; Tom Wolfe published his 'Literary Manifesto for the New Social Novel'; Paul de Man's youthful association with National Socialism was uncovered; Donald Barthelme (along with Beckett) died; Derrida seemed to suddenly shift his attention to distinctly ethico-political issues; religious thinkers, like Emmanuel Levinas, began to garner significant critical attention; and the Berlin Wall fell, suggesting the final triumph of capitalism. Although all of these events seemed to signal a (new) period of mourning, the fall of the Berlin wall is, we think, of particular significance.

Given that postmodernism is typically defined by its opposition to all latent utopian impulses, the fall of the last viable political alternative (i.e. the utopian promise of communism) seemingly speaks to the victory and hegemony of a distinctly postmodern, or late-capitalist, ideology. Not surprisingly, then, it is at the very moment when this victory is imminent – that is, when postmodernism seems to have become the very thing it aimed to destroy – that we begin to see signs of an emergent cultural trend, or 'epistemological configuration'. Put differently, the fall of the last overtly utopian discourse seems to effect the dissolution (also) of a postmodern, or hegemonically 'counter-Enlightenment', epoch. In *the wake of socialism*, postmodernism's increasingly dogmatic rejection of all utopian discourses began to seem totalitarian, if not dangerously utopian. The result, it would seem, was a renewed interest in (or an overt willingness to mourn) the utopian, the teleological, the religious, etc. An example of this 'renewed interest' might in fact be Derrida's apparent 'ethical turn'. It seems hardly coincidental that Derrida published (and presumably wrote) his first overtly ethico-political works – i.e. *The Force of Law, The Other Heading, Specters of Marx, Politics of Friendship*, etc – just as the world was experiencing the dissolution of the Soviet Union. As such texts mark the beginning of Derrida's interest in the arena of ethics, justice, and the messianic, we would argue that they represent the first stages of a period of mourning, a period of mourning for viable political/utopian alternatives that marks (more broadly) the dissolution of the postmodern episteme. Simply put, this emergent epoch seems to 'mourn' the apparent loss of the very idealistic alternatives that postmodernism strove to efface. Moreover, and if we recall Derrida's own take on mourning, this period can be defined by its desire to get over – or, rather, to finally lay to rest – that which came before.

Of course, many might view our locating some shift in the zeitgeist with the fall of the Berlin Wall or any other late twentieth-century signifier we might choose as misleading (if not simply erroneous), as the most obvious marker of a new cultural dominant must certainly be the terrorist attacks in New York on September 11, 2001 and the culture of fear they initiated. After all, what has been enabled by those events has done much to shape the way in which postmodernism has been either rejected or re-fashioned. Quite simply, a culture demanding a shared sense of 'moral outrage' doesn't seem reconcilable with a sustained rejection of metanarratives and a demand for stylistic experimentation. So, indeed, if postmodernism became terminally ill sometime in the late-eighties and early-nineties, it was buried once and for all in the rubble of the World Trade Center.

Still, what we want to highlight here is that a particular *work of postmodern mourning* began sometime in the early-nineties; in the nineties critics began making claims about the fact that the 'high-tide' of postmodernism had finally begun to crash[3] and that a new form of realism had begun to emerge in its wake. Indeed, with the 'First Stuttgart Seminar in Cultural Studies' – a conference in 1991 that included writers like Ihab Hassan, John Barth, Raymond Federman, William Gass and Malcolm Bradbury, and that was aptly titled 'The End of Postmodernism: New Directions' – critics began to formally confirm an apparent shift in aesthetic and theoretical focus. Since then, or so it would seem, we have been engaged in a process of mourning, a process that sees us trying to break (finally) with postmodernism – or, at the very least, to break (finally) with postmodernism's apparent solipsism and irresponsibility, its ethical and social vacuity. After all, since the beginning of the nineties, the suggestion has been that, for one reason or another, postmodernism failed and that its demise (via a certain *re*turn to ethics, religious and realism) was inevitable. Put differently, critics (some of whom have contributed to the following collection) have increasingly stressed the fact that the basic imperative that animated postmodernism paradoxically necessitated its demise. This may require some clarification.

In the 1983 *Granta* issue (entitled 'Dirty Realism: New Writing in America'), Bill Buford argued that a 'new' type of realism had emerged in response to the pretensions of postmodernism. While introducing the issue's contributors – such as Jayne Anne Philips, Raymond Carver, Frederick Barthelme and Tobias Wolff – Bill Buford positioned what he referred to as 'dirty realism', in direct contradistinction to both traditional forms of realism and the metafictional devices of postmodernism:

> It is not heroic or grand: the epic ambitions of Norman Mailer or Saul Bellow seem, in contrast, inflated, strange, even false. It is not self-consciously experimental like so much of the writing – variously described as 'postmodern', 'postcontemporary' or 'deconstructionist' – that was published in the sixties and seventies. The work of John Barth, William Gaddis or Thomas Pynchon seems pretentious in comparison.

(4)

The sense we get from Buford is that this new form of realism is a type of realism that remains inflected by the lessons of postmodernism: 'This is a curious, dirty realism about the belly-side of contemporary life, but it is realism so stylized and particularized – so insistently informed by discomforting and sometimes elusive irony – that it makes the more traditional realistic novels of, say, Updike and Styron seem ornate, even baroque in comparison' (4).

This revival of (some type of) 'realism' was further solidified by the American writer Tom Wolfe in his 1989 'Literary Manifesto for a New Social Novel'. Rejecting the claims of postmodernism as decadent and elitist, Wolfe argued that only the realistic novel – i.e. realistic in the journalistic tradition of a writer like Zola – has the ability to be socially pertinent and captivating: 'It is not merely that reporting is useful in gathering the *petits faits vrais* that create verisimilitude and make a novel gripping or absorbing, although that side of the enterprise is worth paying attention to. My contention is that, especially in an age like this, they are essential for the greatest effects literature can achieve' (55). Not surprisingly, Wolfe holds up his own book, *The Bonfire of the Vanities*, as an example of his specific brand of neo-realism, a form of narrative that rejects postmodern strategies as overly and unjustly privileged by academia. By 1989, then, the demise of postmodernism seemed to be, for most, an inevitability. And, by the mid-nineties, the phrase 'after (or beyond) postmodern' was to be found on the cover of any number of critical works.[4]

Of course, and as the above list of significant 'events' suggests, this recent shift in stylistic privilege – from ostentatious works of postmodern metafiction to more grounded (or 'responsible') works of neo-realism – seems to echo the recent ethico-political 'turn' in critical theory, a turn that is, as we suggested above, most obvious in Jacques Derrida's later work on Marxism, friendship, hospitality, and forgiveness. Along with a later Derrida, though, we might also include the likes of Jean-Luc Nancy, Jean-Luc Marion, John D. Caputo and Slavoj Žižek in a list of theorists who seem to have broken 'the postmodern mould'. For the most part, and by turning their attention to issues of community, religion and ethical responsibility, such theorists do not (if we use Žižek's phrasing) fall 'prey to any kind of "post-modernist" traps (such as the illusion that we live in a "post-ideological" condition' (Žižek 1989: 7). In line with this theoretical turn, then, and in the *wake of postmodernism*, a growing body of cultural and literary criticism has dedicated itself to the careful recovery of various 'logocentric' assumptions, assumptions that postmodernism seemed to think it could finally do without. Recent essay collections – such as Jennifer Geddes' *Evil after Postmodernism: History, Narratives, Ethics* and John D. Caputo and Michael J. Scanlon's *God, the Gift and Postmodernism* – might stand (for the moment) as prime examples of this shift in critical concern.

The suggestion is that the narrative and theoretical production that is typically read as the effect of a subversive and nihilistic epistemological trend has been undermined by a new discourse that is no longer compelled to *focus on* (or endorse) the impossibility of the subject (or author) and the need to avoid a grounded, or situated, commitment to the ethical, political and/or religious. In a recent article – i.e. 'Recent Realist Fiction and the Idea of Writing "After Postmodernism"' – Günter Leypoldt succinctly articulates the nature of this 'shift' (especially as evidenced in recent narrative and stylistic rejections of postmodernism). In *The Man Who Wasn't There*, the protagonist, Ed Crane (played by Billy Bob Thornton), after being accused of murder, is defended by an attorney named Freddy Riedenschneider (played by Tony Shalhoub). A satirical representation of the typical postmodern hero, Riedenschneider is so convinced that reality is nothing more than an effect of contingent representations he attempts to defend Crane by arguing that what 'really happened' can never 'really' be known, for 'The more you look, the less you really know'. Riedenschneider, though (and this is Leypoldt's point), loses the case, and Crane is 'really' sentenced to death. As Leypoldt argues, 'Riedenschneider's fixation on uncertainty recalls the playful skepticism of the metafictional tradition, but in contrast to the heroically self-reflexive philosopher narrators of classic postmodernism, he is portrayed as moronic, vain, and ultimately feckless' (2004: 20). For Leypoldt, the presence of a character like Riedenschneider in a Hollywood film speaks to the way in which 'the metafictional and fabulist devices lost their subversive edge and began to seem less interesting, less "progressive"' (2004: 26).

From the perspective of a writer at this wake of postmodernism, then, postmodernism (at least as it was understood in the mid-eighties) has failed.

Its failure is, in fact, two-fold. On the one hand, its self-affirmation as an anti-ideological discourse, a discourse that privileged individualism and solipsism over the illusion of communal bonds, religious faith, ethical claims, and the possibility of communication, seems (quite naturally) to parallel the progress of modernization. Consistent with the trajectory of modern 'avant-garde' movements, postmodernism's value as a subversive discourse ends when its dominance appears evident. Not surprisingly, and as we suggested above, this moment for postmodernism is heralded by many critics of aesthetic production *after postmodernism* by the fall of the Berlin Wall and the end of the Cold War – or, rather, the end of the last viable utopian ideal/impulse. On the other hand, the postmodern withdrawal from public and/or social discourse – that is, the postmodern imperative to be inaccessible, *to expose* as illusory the ideal of shared experience and communal understanding – becomes itself a very public (because dominant) claim. In other words, an aesthetic that aimed to dismantle binary distinctions, that attempted (more specifically) to destabilize the opposition between high and low culture, becomes (itself) a vacuous and in-effectual aesthetic of the elite. It is, after all, the 'elitism' of postmodernism that most critics identify as its most glaring failure. Thus, postmodernism's increasingly emphatic insistence on inaccessibility – on, that is, the utterly private nature of all discourse (or, rather, the futility of the social or public text) – became a dominant ideal, a hegemonic standard in both academia and the artistic community.

Put differently, we might say that postmodernism 'failed' because it *continued to speak*, because it continued to make (and privilege) *truth claims* about the impossibility of making such claims (while, for the most part, failing to overtly articulate the fact that such claims were necessarily and ironically animated by the latent belief that the truth could finally be expressed). In short, postmodernism failed *because it didn't die* (as it should have). Instead, its increasingly loud movement toward silence and/or the absolute denial of objective truth claims became dogmatic, institutionalized and programmatic. Thus recent critical and theoretical work (including much of the following) seems to highlight the past hegemony of high-postmodernism and the need for a form of cultural production that is no longer confined by corrosive and socially impractical imperatives (however paradoxical and self-reflexive such imperatives might have been). In brief, if somewhat crudely, our current work of mourning – and, thus, of 'waking' – is (to a certain degree) a work of *getting over* the apparent hegemony of postmodernism, of postmodern aesthetic and theoretical imperatives, of (perhaps) imperatives generally.

As a result of postmodernism's pervasiveness – or rather, as a result of its hegemony – we see (in works of literature and film like that of the Coen Brothers) a type of mourning, which is also (and of course) a type of resistance. However, this resistance remains, to some degree, postmodern. Indeed, like the theorists mentioned above, the writers and directors whose work defines (what we might think of as) a still emergent period of 'renewalism' seem to carry on a certain postmodern project while (all the while) critiquing elements of that project as ineffectual, irresponsible, dangerous, absurd, 'feckless', etc. That said, and while extrapolating on the suggestions made in the following chapters (and elsewhere), we might view the following as a tentative list of renewalist writers and directors: David Foster Wallace, Jonathan Franzen, Russell Banks, Richard Powers, Lorrie Moore, David Lynch, Sophia Coppola, Wes Anderson, Paul Thomas Anderson, Maxine Hong Kingston, Mark Z. Danielewski, Darren Aronofsky, Nicholson Baker, Dave Eggers, Jared Hess, etc. Obviously, such a list will always be fraught; and we will not attempt to defend the veracity of this particular list here. However, those listed all share a certain affinity with postmodernism; at the same time, though, they all seem to move beyond the parameters of a specifically postmodern project. Many of them, in fact, seem unabashedly nostalgic and 'realistic' (if not, perhaps, openly logocentric, humanistic and/or onto-theological).

Ultimately, then, it would seem that (at the wake of postmodernism) we are not seeing a simple 'knee-jerk' reaction to the dominance of a seemingly nihilist and socially irresponsible cultural trend. Attending the wake of postmodernism is not a matter of blind and reactionary repudiation. As the following essays make clear, postmodernism – or, at the very least, *the ghost of postmodernism* – has much to teach us (yet). What we have inherited from postmodernism cannot be simply denied, or rejected outright. To a certain extent, then, attending the wake of postmodernism is also a matter of *awakening* postmodernism, of *awakening* it to all of those issues postmodernism in its reified form seemed so anxious to circumvent: issues of faith, ethical responsibility, politics, community, etc. As Klaus Stierstorfer recently pointed out in his introduction to *Beyond Postmodernism: Reassessments in Literature, Theory, and Culture* (and as several of the contributors here also suggest), this (re)turn to seemingly pre-postmodern ideologies remains very much tempered by the lessons of postmodernism:

> Whether it is the more universal interest in the possible foundations of a general or literary ethics in a world of globalization, or the more specific and local issues of identities, scholars and writers alike nevertheless continue to find themselves in the dilemma of facing the deconstructive gestures inherent in postmodernist

thought while at the same time requiring some common ground on which ethical agreements can be based. Hence some form of referentiality, even some kind of essentialism is called for.

(2003: 9–10)

In terms of the apparent shift to a type of neo-realism,[5] then, we might say that some form of mimesis is called for – that is, some type of renewed faith in the possibility of what postmodernist narrative has repeatedly identified as impossible: meaning, truth, representational accuracy, etc. But as Stierstorfer suggests, this shift to some type of 'renewalism' is not simply a backlash in response to postmodern cultural production; it is neither a reactionary return to the (ethical) imperatives of modernism nor a revival of the traditional forms of realism and ethical discourse that proliferated in the nineteenth century. What comes after postmodernism, then, is (perhaps) best described if we recall the ethical paradoxes explored by Derrida in his most recent work; this period of renewal, of renewalism, is, in other words, a period of 'faith without faith', of 'religion without religion', of 'mimesis without mimesis', etc, etc. In short, Postmodernism, to a certain degree, persists. We, undoubtedly, continue to mourn. What follows, then, are attempts to understand and negotiate this often difficult (if inevitable and necessary) process of mourning.

Notes

1   A fact, of course, that Hutcheon herself admits: 'For decades now, diagnosticians have been pronouncing on [postmodernism's] health, if not its demise' (2002: 165).

2   See Federman's 'Before Postmodernism and After (Part One)' and 'Before Postmodernism and After (Part Two)', both of which he delivered in 1991 at the 'First Stuttgart Seminar in Cultural Studies' – i.e. 'The End of Postmodernism: New Directions'.

3   Klaus Stierstorfer describes the situation like this: 'in a much-quoted survey Lance Olsen reported an astounding increase in occurrences of the term "postmodern" in American newspapers from 1980 through 1984 to 1987 at a ratio of 2:116:247. In his turn, Hans Bertens charted a "history of the debate on postmodernism from its tentative beginnings in the 1950s to its overwhelming self-confidence in the early 1990s". From the later 1990s onwards, however, this narrative of the progress of postmodernism appears to lose direction. Although no statistical data are

available, the quantity of references to postmodernism in scholarly publications as well as in the daily press seems to decrease, as does the heatedness of the debate' (Stierstorfer 2003: 1).

4 Along with those discussed above, some examples might include: José Lopez and Garry Potter's *After Postmodernism: An Introduction to Critical Realism*; Robert Rebein's *Hicks, Tribes and Dirty Realists: American Fiction After Postmodernism*; and Klaus Stierstorfer's *Beyond Postmodernism: Reassessments in Literature, Theory, and Culture.*

5 For several useful examinations of the emergence and significance of neo-realism after postmodernism please see *Neo-Realism in Contemporary Fiction*, a collection of essays edited by Kristiann Versluys.

References

Buford, Bill (1983), 'Editorial', *Granta 8: Dirty Realism*: 4–5.

Caputo, John D. and Michael J. Scanlon (eds) (1999), *God, the Gift, and Postmodernism*, Bloomington: Indiana UP.

Derrida, Jacques (1992), *The Other Heading*, trans. Michael B. Naas and Pascale-Anne Brault, Bloomington: Indiana University Press.

Derrida, Jacques (1994), *Specters of Marx: The State of the Debt, the Work of Mourning, and the New International*, trans. Peggy Kamuf, New York: Routledge.

Derrida, Jacques (1997), *Politics of Friendship*, trans. George Collins, London: Verso.

Derrida, Jacques (2002), *Force of Law: The 'Mystical Foundation of Authority'. Acts of Religion*, trans. Mary Quaintance, ed. Gil Anidjar, New York: Routledge.

Federman, Raymond (1993a), 'Before Postmodernism and After (Part One)' in *The End of Postmodernism: New Directions. Proc. of the First Stuttgart Seminar in Cultural Studies 04.08.–18.08.1991, dir. Heide Ziegler*, 47–64, Stuttgart: M & P Verlag für Wissenschaft und Forschung.

Federman, Raymond (1993b), 'Before Postmodernism and After (Part Two)' in *The End of Postmodernism: New Directions. Proc. of the First Stuttgart Seminar in Cultural Studies 04.08.–18.08.1991. Dir. Heide Ziegler*, 153–170, Stuttgart: M & P Verlag für Wissenschaft und Forschung, 1993.

Geddes, Jennifer (ed.) (2001), *Evil after Postmodernism: Histories, Narratives, and Ethics*, New York: Routledge.

Jameson, Fredric (1999), 'Marx's Purloined Letter' in Michael Sprinkler (ed.), *Ghostly Demarcations: A Symposium on Jacques Derrida's Specters of Marx*, New York: Verso.

Leypoldt, Günter (2004), 'Recent Realist Fiction and the Idea of Writing "After Postmodernism"', *Amerikastudien/American Studies*, 49 (1): 19–34.

Lopez, José and Gary Potter (eds) (1994), *After Postmodernism: An Introduction to Critical Realism*, London: Sage.

Rebein, Robert (2001), *Hicks, Tribes and Dirty Realists: American Fiction after Postmodernism*, Lexington, KY: UP of Kentucky.

Stierstorfer, Klaus (2003), 'Introduction: Beyond Postmodernisrn – Contingent Referentiality?' in Klaus Stierstorfer (ed.) *Beyond Postmodernism: Reassessments in Literature, Theory, and Culture*, 1–10, Berlin: Walter de Gruyter.

The Man Who Wasn't There (2001), [Film] dir. Joel Coen, USA: Good Machine.

Versluys, Kristiaan (ed.) (1992), *Neo-Realism in Contemporary Fiction*, Amsterdam: Rodopi.

Wolfe, Tom (1989), 'Stalking the Billion-Footed Beast: A Literary Manifesto for the New Social Novel', *Harper's Magazine* 279 (1674): 45–56.

Žižek, Slavoj (1989), *The Sublime Object of Ideology*, London: Verso.

from The Passing of Postmodernism: A Spectroanalysis of the Contemporary

Josh Toth

This emergent period of renewalism abandons the postmodern *need* to expose, above all else, the impossibility of the specter and, instead, works to embrace both the possibility *and* the impossibility of the specter. Renewalism is, I am arguing, defined by an epistemological willingness – or, we might begin to say at this point, *an imperative* – to, as a later Derrida would have it, 'respect the specter'. In works that outwardly continue to employ the stylistic devices associated with postmodernism – works by, among others, Mark Leyner, David Lynch, Toni Morrison, Maxine Hong Kingston, Mark Z. Danielewski, Don DeLillo, David Foster Wallace, Tim O'Brien, and (perhaps) Louise Erdrich and Quentin Tarantino[1] – this 'respect' is played out via a focus on the necessity of the spectral promise and a renewed faith in its impossible possibility. More overt works of neorealism demonstrate this same spectral relationship – albeit in a more obvious manner – while also demonstrating a concerted effort to abandon the metafictional imperative that defined postmodernism. For this reason, neo-realism seems to be indicative of a more general epistemological relinquishment of aesthetic imperatives *as such*.

[. . .]

Let me clarify this. Because a work of high-postmodern metafiction is overtly focused on emphasizing the impossibility of mimesis, it is seemingly confined to two readings: either it forces us to acknowledge the pointlessness of any narrative representation (in which case its persistence as an art form becomes redundant) or it presents itself as the *finally right representation* because it accurately represents 'reality' as an ideological illusion (in which case we are left wondering why one metafictional text is not enough, why one metafictional text isn't simply the final word on all narrative acts as such). In either case, we are left without a reason to move. We are left in a state of paralysis. We are left, that is, in a state of 'mythic', or pure, indecision – in the sense that there is no longer a decision, or narrative act, to make/perform.[2] What a work of neo-realism – or, rather, any of the works that we might identify with this emergent period of renewalism – stresses is thus the very thing that *continued* to animate postmodernism: the necessarily possible *and* impossible nature of the certainly right decision, or narrative act. At the very moment postmodern works of metafiction seem to present themselves as *finally decided* on the impossibility of any finally right decision, they continue to be animated by the very fact (however paradoxical it may sound) that such a decision is impossible. Neo-realism, in short, attempts to 'get over' this paradoxical problem by embracing it – by embracing, that is, the necessity of the spectrological lure: 'What a realist surface manages to quite effectively do is to constantly refuel the viewer's interest and curiosity because of a promise of representation that is ... never fulfilled' (Fluck 1992: 77). Rather than simply rejecting the spectral promise as illusory idealism – and thus, like postmodernism, becoming hegemonically opposed to the very promise that necessarily animates any anti-ideological movement – neo-realism endorses an ethics of indecision; it overtly embraces the need to believe in the spectral promise of the certainly right decision while simultaneously embracing, *à la* postmodernism, its infinite deferral.

A nice example of this 'neo-realist promise' can be found in the opening chapter of Russell Banks' *Continental Drift*. Entitled 'Invocation', Banks' opening chapter seems to outwardly challenge the postmodern rejection of mimesis and the possibility of historical objectivity:

> It's not memory you need for telling this story ... It's not memory you need, it's clear eyed pity and hot, old-time anger and a Northern man's love of the sun, it's a white man's entwined obsession with race and sex and a proper middle-class American's shame for a nation's history ... nothing here depends on memory for the telling.
>
> (1985: 1–2)

In a manner that recalls Carver's minimalist 'dirty realism' – that is, his realistic accounts of middle America, or American 'white trash' – Banks promises the possibility of 'representative experience' yet consistently populates his text with characters and situations that overtly escape complete apprehension. While moments of climax hold out the promise of positive change and shared understanding, they are consistently eviscerated of meaning. At one point, the main character, Bob Dubois (a middle-aged man who frequently cheats on his wife), is dramatically held up by gunpoint while working at a liquor mart. The scene ends with Bob shooting one of his assailants twice and finding the other, with 'shitpants' (Banks 1985: 104), cowering in a storeroom. While this event seems to *change* Bob, the change we see, as well as the event itself, is quickly diffused by a persistent and unchanging narrative flow; the significance of the event – if, we begin to wonder, it had any at all – is slowly lost on the reader (as it is, we could argue, on Bob). As with Carver, then, 'We are . . . constantly moving between a promise of representative experience, its subversion and its subsequent restitution – a movement that is received time and again by [the neo-realist] strategy of recharging the realistic surface of the text with a meaning that cannot be firmly grasped' (Fluck 1992: 78).

In brief, neo-realism seemingly escapes the dogmatism of postmodernism by explicitly embracing *and* deferring the possibility of the referent, of mimesis. By embracing the fact that both realist and metafictional strategies are necessarily animated by a belief, even if latent, that there 'can be, in principle, only one correct version of reality' (Fluck 1992: 69), neo-realism works to escape the postmodern tendency to make a grand narrative out of an 'incredulity' to grand narratives. Neo-realism seems to 'respect the specter' – it seems, that is, to respect the necessity of an animating, yet impossible, ideal – so as to avoid being dangerously compelled to *either* insist upon the possibility that the spectral ideal can become real and in the flesh *or* to emphatically and repeatedly expose such an ideal as impossible. Viewed alongside the more formalistic texts touched on above, neo-realism can thus be understood as symptomatic of an emergent epistemological reconfiguration that can be defined, as I suggested above, by a desire to abandon – or rather, to get over, to lay to rest – all aesthetic imperatives. What is most significant about this apparent return to realism – a realism, we need to stress, that is informed by postmodern formalism – is that it signals the end of metafiction as a privileged aesthetic style while simultaneously identifying *both* itself *and* metafiction as equally contingent and equally relevant 'language games'. More simply, neo-realism or, more broadly, *the literature of renewalism* can be defined as an attempt to *relax the rules*. By overtly acknowledging that all aesthetic imperatives are necessarily animated by, what I have been calling, a certain spectrological aporia, the literature of renewalism works to avoid becoming, like its modern and postmodern predecessors, another hegemonic ideal – which is to say that it works to avoid effacing the necessarily ironic spectrality of the specter. However, as I have suggested throughout, this impulse to 'respect the specter' inevitably becomes a new way of 'dis-respecting the specter'; it becomes, in other words, another imperative, another *mythic decision* that is itself, and in ways it necessarily cannot control, the effect of a certain spectral compulsion, a certain *absolute* belief in a utopian ideal. Before I can fully reapproach this claim from the perspective of emergent modes of narrative, though, it is perhaps necessary to look more closely at this apparent shift from a postmodern to a renewalist aesthetic. Indeed, with the above discussion in mind, and in a rather spiral-like fashion, I would like to clarify the distinctions, cursively identified above, that separate postmodern narrative strategies from the strategies of an emergent renewalist 'episteme'.

The project of renewalism

In Charlie Kaufman and Spike Jonze's film, *Adaptation* – their follow-up to the particularly solipsistic *Being John Malkovich* – Kaufman writes himself into his adaptation of Susan Orlean's book, *The Orchid Thief*. Played by Nicolas Cage, Kaufman *accidentally* becomes the main character of the film, a film that is supposed to be about Susan Orlean (played by Meryl Streep). In a manner that makes Vonnegut's presence in *Breakfast of Champions* look perfectly normal, Kaufman's fictionalized self comes to dominate the film, effacing, at least partially, the source material that is the film's *raison d'être*. Concerned more with the process of adaptation than with the adaptation itself, the film begins, as the end result of what we see Kaufman attempting to produce throughout, in a state of apparent paralysis; feeling a sense of what we might call postmodern responsibility, Kaufman feels compelled to be corrosively self-reflexive. For the fictional Kaufman, an adaptation *must* ostentatiously acknowledge its process of production, as well as the contingent subject-position of the artist that is engaged in that production. A screenplay mustn't simply reaffirm the romantic illusions of stable meaning, final answers, authorial control, and so on. So, instead of the traditional Hollywood romance, or thriller, or whatever, Kaufman produces, well ... nothing. Indeed, apart from credits, the film opens with a completely black screen. We then hear Nicolas Cage, as Kaufman, in a voice-over: 'Do I have an original thought in my head? My bald head?' The answer is, apparently, no. Rather than what Kaufman would consider to be 'an original thought' – or, in other words, the start of the movie – we are given more of the self-critical voice-over: Kaufman tells us that he has a 'fat ass', that he 'needs to fall in love', that he needs to 'learn Russian or something', that he needs to 'be real'. Eventually, the credits include a line stating that the film is, indeed, 'Based on the book, *The Orchid Thief*, by Susan Orlean'; by this point the information seems incidental.

When the film proper finally begins, it doesn't begin with Susan Orlean or John Laroche, the orchid thief who is the subject of Orlean's investigation. The initial sequence occurs on the set of *Being John Malkovich*. The actors and crew – including the 'real' John Malkovich – are milling about, preparing for the next shot. Filmed in documentary style, this initial sequence is presented as authentic 'making-of' footage. In the background, though, Nicolas Cage *as Kaufman* self-consciously tries to get involved. Ignored by actors and crew alike, Kaufman eventually leaves. This confusion of reality (the Malkovich set) and fiction (Cage as Kaufman) sets up the basic conceit of the film: the only 'real' thing Kaufman can write is himself, yet the self he writes is inevitably forced, fictionalized, discursively determined. All Kaufman can do – as a *responsible* postmodern artist – is draw attention to the fact that everything he produces is inevitably caught up in this inescapable paradox.

After the scene on the set of *Malkovich*, we see Kaufman getting the job of adapting Orlean's book. He informs the studio representative – a beautiful young woman – that he doesn't want to write anything that is artificially 'plot driven'. He's not going to write an 'Orchid Heist' movie, or a movie about poppies and drug runners. He's not going to 'cram in sex'. There won't be any car chases or 'characters, you know, learning profound life lessons. Life isn't like that'. However, Kaufman inevitably fails to realize a way out of the romantic archetypes that he repudiates. So he stalls. He gives us Susan Orlean's story, randomly cut in with his own, up to the point when the film studio buys the rights to *The Orchid Thief* and gives him the job of adapting it. At the same time, he creates another character: his own twin brother, Donald, who is writing a screenplay of his own. The screenplay, Donald tells Charlie, is a Hollywood thriller in which a female detective is hunting a male serial killer who feeds his victims to themselves in small bits. The 'big payoff' is that the detective is really the killer. So, in the end, 'when he forces the woman who's really him to eat herself he's also eating himself to death'. Charlie, of course, thinks that Donald is a 'sell-out'. He repeatedly tells Donald, who has been attending a seminar by Robert McKee, that he needs to be more original, that there are 'no rules', that screenwriting seminars are 'bullshit', that 'Anybody who says they have the answer is going to attract desperate people'. Apart from the rule that there are no rules, the basic *postmodern rule*, according to Kaufman, is that the true artist is always on a 'journey into the unknown'. Taking the Lyotardian 'incredulity toward metanarratives' and the imperative to 'make it new' to its extreme, Kaufman's position becomes virtually suicidal, or cannibalistic. His screenplay – that is, the film we're watching – becomes transfixed on his own inability to write a screenplay. For much of the film he sits in front of his computer, trying to write. When he's not trying to write, he's masturbating.[3] Eventually, he decides that the only thing he can do is write about himself. This 'realization' is articulated in another voiceover: 'I have no understanding of anything outside of my own panic and self-loathing and pathetic little existence. It's like the only thing I'm actually qualified to write about is myself and my own self....' This 'epiphany' (of sorts) is followed by a look of excitement on Kaufman's face and an abrupt cut. In the next shot we see Kaufman at home, speaking into a recorder: 'We open on Charlie Kaufman, fat, old, bald, repulsive, sitting in a Hollywood restaurant across from Valerie Thomas, a lovely statuesque film executive. Kaufman, trying to get a writing assignment....' After another cut, Kaufman is in bed. He's still recording himself, but now he's reading from notes: 'Fat, bald, Kaufman pitches furiously in his bedroom. He speaks into his handheld tape recorder and he says: "Charlie Kaufman, fat, bald, repulsive, old, sits at a Hollywood restaurant with Valerie Thomas...."'

In danger of slipping into infinite regress, the film seems to run into a – or rather, *the* – postmodern dead end. Kaufman, once again, begins to despair, and when Donald tells him that he got the idea for his 'trick' ending from a tattoo he saw of a snake biting its own tale – a symbol Kaufman recognizes as the Ourobouros – he realizes that his own work has become pointlessly and dangerously cannibalistic: 'I'm insane. I'm Ourobouros.... It's self-indulgent. It's narcissistic. It's solipsistic. It's pathetic'. At a loss, Kaufman goes to New York and attends McKee's seminar. At the same time, the segments about Orlean become subtly more dramatic; Orlean becomes obsessed with both Laroche and the possibility of seeing a 'Ghost', an elusive and legendary orchid. At the seminar, McKee tells Kaufman that voiceovers are ridiculous and that any attempt to make a film in which 'nothing much happens' will be both boring and unrealistic. Love, murder, sacrifice, pain: these things are occurring everyday. If you're making a movie, McKee tells Kaufman, 'you got to put in the drama'. If Kaufman's film is to be a success, if it is to be relevant at all, it needs 'an ending'. It needs to assume, or embrace, a certain teleological impulse; it needs to animate itself with the promise of an end, a final answer, the truth. Excited, Kaufman has Donald, who begins to function much more obviously as Kaufman's double, come to New York and help with the script. As Donald and Charlie begin to investigate Orlean in the present day, the segments that involve Orlean at the time of writing the *Orchid Thief* begin to take on a different tone. We discover that Orlean despises her passionless marriage and job; she wants to be passionate in the way that Laroche (who continually becomes obsessed with hobbies and then abandons them altogether) is passionate. Moreover, Laroche tells Orlean that he has been trying to find the 'Ghost Orchid' because it produces a drug that 'seems to help people be fascinated' – which is to say that it allows people to believe in a type of telos, a type of animating goal (even if such a telos/goal is impossible). In the narrative present, Charlie and Donald discover that Orlean has become addicted to the Ghost drug, and that, while writing her book, she began an illicit affair with Laroche, who is now mass-producing the drug in Miami. In brief, then: after a drug cartel subplot, a foot chase through a swamp, a car chase in which Donald is killed, Charlie's epiphany that 'you are what you love, not what loves you', and some gratuitous, and crammed in, sex, the film ends with Kaufman telling us, in another voice-over, that he's ready to finish his adaptation: 'It ends with Kaufman driving home after his lunch with [his ex-girlfriend] thinking he knows how to finish the script. Shit, that's a voiceover. McKee would not approve. Well, who cares what McKee says? It feels right. So: Kaufman drives off from his encounter with Amelia filled for the first time with hope'.

On the most superficial level, the shift in narrative strategy that the film – or, rather, Kaufman undergoes – is a compact representation of the current shift I have attempted to articulate above. It is a shift away from the basic imperative that animated, and eventually came to dominate, the postmodern aesthetic: corrosive and ultimately paralyzing self-reflexivity. Indeed, the first part of the film – the acutely metafictional part – functions as a conscious articulation of the postmodern 'failure' I described above. Kaufman's initial need to be self-reflexive, to be responsible, to demonstrate that there is no final 'answer', no possible telos, or end, inevitably forces him to turn on himself. If he is to escape the archetypes and predetermined discourses that his work inevitably perpetuates, he must withdraw *à la* Rorty from all public, or coherent, discourses; he must become utterly and inaccessibly private. At the same time, though (and quite paradoxically), he must enter into public discourse if he is to make his point – which is, ultimately, that all points are contingent and pointless. We see this problem play out most obviously in those moments when Charlie corrects Donald. There are no rules, there is no answer, but 'don't say "pitch"', 'don't say "industry"', art has to be original, new, and so on. Quite simply, the first portion of the film – its paralysis, its inability to 'progress' – can be read as a critique of a postmodern 'ethics of perversity' and, thus, the ostentatious metafiction that postmodernism has always privileged. What Kaufman seems to suggest is that the postmodern aesthetic necessarily leads to silence, paralysis, utterly private self-reflexivity, masturbation in the dark.

John Barth, the postmodern writer *par excellence*, makes a similar point in 'The Literature of Exhaustion.' Using Beckett as an example, Barth notes that silence is the ultimate ideal of any artist who aims to escape the discursive confines in which he or she necessarily works: 'For Beckett ... to cease to create altogether would be fairly meaningful: his crowning work; his "last word". What a convenient corner to paint yourself into' (Barth 1984a: 68). The sense we get, from both Kaufman and Barth, is that this move toward absolute withdrawal is a type of failure.[4] By recalling Lyotard's terms, as well as the above discussion, we can rephrase the problem like this: not only does the imperative to deny all grand narratives become, itself, a type of grand, or hegemonic, narrative, the postmodern recourse to the *petit récit*, or personally contingent narrative, ultimately leads to the denial of all possible communication, or shared understanding. Again, though, this is not to say that postmodernism was wholly blind to this problem.[5] After all, Barth himself seems to be acutely interested in the paradoxical implications of postmodern solipsism.[6] Still, what we see in the work of a writer like Barth is an investment in provisionality that does not yet seem willing to outwardly embrace the possibility of a truth, or ideal, it knows to be impossible. Consequently, in much high postmodernism we see an emphatic movement toward silence and/or paralysis. However, the fact that postmodernism – like the beginning of *Adaptation* – never *really* ceased to move, never *really* dissolved into so many fragments of private incoherence, speaks to its often repressed desire, its faith in the very promise of the telos it worked to expose as impossible. The postmodern desire to claim that history is over, that nothing original can be said, that the Real is an illusion, becomes the very reason to continue writing. As Barth suggests, 'an artist may paradoxically turn the felt ultimacies of our time into material means for his work – *paradoxically*, because by doing so he transcends what had appeared to be his refutation' (Barth 1984a: 71). Along with someone like Baudrillard, then, the postmodern writer is spectrally compelled to write about the pointlessness of writing, or the impossibility of communication or meaning. Silence is always evaded because the promise of an end (a ghost) is neither possible nor impossible. And, as I demonstrated in the previous two chapters, a promise, like a specter, is never here and now, but it is never entirely absent either; if it were absent or if it were here now and, thus, an actuality, it would cease to animate. This spectral paradox of transcending the very refutation that animates the transcendence of that refutation – a paradox we see Kaufman struggling with and finally embracing as an inescapable part of any narrative act – is played out most obviously in Barth's first novel, *The Floating Opera*. A text that we might readily identify as the first work of American postmodernism, *The Floating Opera* is an overtly metafictional piece that articulates its own *raison d'être*, for the text as well as the main character/narrator, by denying the possibility of ever locating a purpose, or meaning, for the text (or character).

Narrated by the lawyer Todd Andrews, *The Floating Opera* begins by questioning its own narrative relevance. Throughout, though, the promise of an end – that is, in this case, the promise of a satisfactory conclusion to, and explanation for, Andrews' story – is repeatedly identified as a type of illusory lure. As Andrews continually insists, this end (which we are always, as Derrida would say, 'awaiting') is never going to arrive. Andrews makes this point most clearly when he decides to explain the novel's title: '*The Floating Opera*. Why *The Floating Opera*? I could explain until Judgment Day, and still not explain completely' (Barth 1967: 13). Significantly, the apparent impossibility of a conclusive answer does not prevent Andrews from offering some sort of explanation. In fact, Andrews goes on to supply us with his reflections on the name of a showboat – *Adam's Original and Unparalleled Floating Opera* – that 'used to travel around the Virginia and Maryland tidewater areas' (Barth 1967: 13). A setting for the final portion of the book, *Adam's Original and Unparalleled Floating Opera* gives Andrews the idea of a large boat on which a play is running continuously. This imaginary boat, Andrews tells us, would 'drift up and down the river on the tide' and audiences would sit along the bank to watch: 'They could catch whatever part of the plot happened to unfold as the boat floated past, and then they'd have to wait until the tide ran back again to catch another snatch of it, if they still happened to be sitting there. To fill in the gaps they would have to use their imaginations' (Barth 1967: 13). Like any work of historiographic metafiction, *The Floating Opera* included, Andrews' 'floating opera' functions as a way of highlighting the illusory nature of narrative coherence: 'Most times the [audience] wouldn't understand what was going on at all, or they'd think they knew, when actually they didn't' (Barth 1967: 13). The promise of full disclosure compels the audience of this 'floating opera', just as it does Andrews as narrator of *The Floating Opera*, to reassemble the fragments, to *re*-member the event. Nevertheless, and as Andrews repeatedly notes, the event always remains absent. By continually highlighting this inevitable and necessary absence, *The Floating Opera* (as text) *perversely* highlights, as Maurice Couturier puts it, the 'impossibility of all true communication between author and reader'. Not surprisingly, then, Andrews, like Kaufman, is driven by a need to justify his work. And it is because of this need to justify his reason for writing that Andrews arrives at his 'final solution', his final *postmodern* answer: 'I awoke, splashed cold water on my face, and realized that I had the real, the final, the unassailable answer; the last possible word; the stance to end all stances.... Didn't I tell you I'd pull no punches? That my answers were yours? *Suicide! ... Suicide* was my answer; my answer was *suicide*' (Barth 1967: 23). What is interesting here is that Andrews is telling us, some sixteen years after his epiphany, that the *final* true answer is suicide – or rather, we might accurately infer, artistic silence. While the entire text is, in fact, an account of the day Andrews planned, and tried, to commit suicide, it is also, as Andrews repeatedly tells us, a story of the day he changed his mind. The text itself, as the impossible attempt to articulate the impossibility of articulating anything, delays the moment of silence that the text anticipates on, or at, its horizon. More simply, the text's desire to expose the impossibility of its own narrative telos remains spectrally animated by the possibility of just such a telos.[7]

At the end of the text, and right before Andrews commits his final act – or, rather, before he performs what Barth would consider to be Beckett's final artistic solution – he finds that he is paralyzed, that he is unable to do anything, suicide included.[8] This paralysis is, significantly, articulated as a narrative problem: 'why explain at all? Why move at all? ... there was no reason to do anything, and I will say that the realization of this worked upon me involuntarily. This is important: it was not that I decided not to speak, but that, aware in every part of me of the unjustifiable nature of action ... I simply could not open my mouth' (Barth 1967: 264). At this moment, the text seems to be in real danger of losing all faith, however latent, in the promise, or specter, of its own narrative end; via the model of the narrator's physical body, this moment exposes the danger of a seemingly inevitable postmodern textual collapse, the absolute cessation of narrative movement. Put differently, this moment seems to be dangerously close to fulfilling the promise of a truly POSTmodern text. It points to the silence – without itself being 'silent' – that would be the effect of any successful rejection of spectral compulsion, of the impossible promise, of what the later Derrida would call the messianic. Ultimately, Barth and Andrews – or perhaps, Barth *as Andrews* – realizes this. Instead of *going through with it*, though, Andrews (like any good postmodern narrator) continues to explain why there is simply no reason why he *shouldn't have gone through with it*. Shocked out of paralysis by the danger in which he has inadvertently placed his illegitimate daughter,

Andrews once again finds a reason to mobilize himself. With this return of 'desire', however illusory he understands it to be, Andrews decides – quite arbitrarily, he insists – to change his mind. He then spends the next sixteen years preparing to do what he knows is impossible: communicate, to himself and to his readers, his reasons for deciding that suicide was the final and only answer *because there are no answers.*[9]

In *the end*, the promise of a final answer, or telos, ironically becomes the animating 'goal' of *The Floating Opera* as a discourse, or narrative act. Like the postmodern texts examined above, *The Floating Opera* highlights the way in which postmodernism, and thus postmodern metafiction, is spectrally compelled to expose the specter as impossible, as an ideological illusion, as the cause of all past discursive hegemonies. As a type of response to this paradox, then, the current narrative 'turn' overtly embraces this animating specter – this specter that postmodernism attempted to exorcise *once and for all* and that, consequently and paradoxically, animated its major narrative strategy. Simply put: because it was intended to exorcise the very thing that animated its exorcisms, the stylistic mode typically associated with the still residual episteme of postmodernism ultimately and necessarily 'failed', becoming the very thing it sought to undermine: an aesthetic, if not an ethical, imperative. This, of course, brings us back to *Adaptation*.

While the initial portion of *Adaptation* seems to expose and, indeed, mock this particularly postmodern problem, the latter portion seemingly functions as a type of solution. Like any narrative mode we might associate with a renewalist episteme, works of 'neo' or 'dirty' realism included, the final portion of *Adaptation* speaks to the way in which, as Robert Rebein puts it, 'contemporary realist writers have *absorbed* postmodernism's most lasting contributions and gone on to forge a new realism that is more or less traditional in its handling of character, reportorial in its depiction of milieu and time, but is at the same time self-conscious about language and the limits of mimesis' (2001: 20). The latter portion of *Adaptation* speaks to the way in which this emergent epoch *after* postmodernism seems to reject postmodernism's stringent focus on anti-foundationalism. What 'renewalist' works like *Adaptation* overtly announce and accept is the fact that the desire to deny the possibility of any stable truth, or grand narrative – that is, the desire to abandon as a dangerous illusion 'the still incomplete project of modernity' – is ultimately animated by some type of (blind) faith, or teleological impulse. Without descending into absolute silence, which itself becomes a type of 'ideal' end, postmodern narrative strategies must, to a certain extent, remain blind to their own teleological, or positivist, contamination if they are to identify themselves as truly POST modern. Kaufman's acceptance of this 'truth' allows him to abandon the implicit and *perverse* ethics of postmodernism and relax his allegiance to its ultimately unsustainable strategies. So, in the end (of *Adaptation*, or of postmodernism generally), we get forms of narrative that revive the possibility of communal understanding, humanism and/or consensus. They renew, in short, the possibility of a 'still incomplete project of modernity', which is to say that they no longer attempt to do without what Jameson would call a latent utopian impulse (and what Žižek understands as the impossible Real) that animated postmodernism in the first place; renewalism, in short, outwardly embraces the necessary and inevitable 'return of the repressed'. It is, I would argue, hardly coincidental that the concept of a Ghost Orchid – that is, an elusive, if not mythical, flower that stimulates compassion and compels action – becomes a major theme in the last half of *Adaptation*. While it might be going too far to suggest an intentional link between the Ghost Orchid and Derrida's theory of the specter, the presence and discussion of the orchid does highlight the distinctly renewalist assumption that we *must* believe in a certain impossible telos, a certain impossible 'Real'. It is this ability to 'hope' – or, perhaps, to gamble – that is finally articulated as the solution to Kaufman's distinctly postmodern dilemma. Quite simply, then, renewalist forms of narrative are defined by an overt willingness to respect the specter, to endorse, in other words, a certain ethics of indecision.

And, significantly, these renewalist forms of narrative are not restricted to any one specific style. While many critics have associated the end of postmodernism with the growing dominance of neo- (or, dirty) realism, the examples above seem to suggest that, whether or not we call them 'neo-realist', the emergent forms of narrative are marked by an overall rejection of past aesthetic imperatives. For the most part, these narratives do indeed seem more 'realistic' – especially as evidenced in the work of overtly 'dirty' realists like Carver and Banks – but I am arguing that such narratives are better defined by the relationship they reestablish with a certain spectral inheritance, a spectral inheritance *passed on* by postmodernism. Rather than just new 'realisms', then, what we see – in the work of writers and/or directors like Leyner, Morrison, Banks, Richard Powers, David Foster Wallace, Lorrie Moore, Danielewski, Lynch, Sophia Coppola, Wes Anderson, Paul Thomas Anderson, Noah Baumbach, Jared Hess, Maxine Hong Kingston, Nicholson Baker, and Dave Eggers – are narrative forms that renew the realist faith in mimesis while simultaneously deferring and frustrating that faith via the irony and stylistics of a now past, or *passed*, postmodernism. For the sake of clarity, let me employ another example: the early work of Nicholson Baker. After all, if Barth's *The Floating Opera* is one of the first overtly postmodern novels, *The Mezzanine* (i.e., Baker's first novel) is one of the first clearly identifiable works of renewalism.[10] Just as Kaufman, in the end, saves his film by abandoning, or relaxing, his postmodern convictions, Baker works to reestablish the possibility of mimesis and universal understanding while remaining wary of the dangers that postmodernism struggled to expose and move beyond. To a degree, then, a novel like *The Mezzanine* continues to be postmodern; but, then again, and as we have seen, postmodernism (for its own part) seemed to anticipate the renewalist sensibilities Baker overtly embraces.

A novel that consists of nothing more than one man's memories concerning the day he bought shoelaces on his lunch break, *The Mezzanine* (via a series of footnotes) repeatedly draws attention to its own textuality and thus the fragmentary and unstable nature of any narrative reconstruction of the past. Moreover, the narrator's (i.e., Howie's) focus on everyday minutia – how he learned to enjoy sweeping, the problem with floating straws, the strange effect of farting in a bathroom stall while your boss washes his hands and talks business with a colleague – functions as a conscious acknowledgment of the absolutely private nature of existence. At the same time, though, Baker's text remains outwardly 'realistic'; it is always coherent, straightforward, and accessible.[11] In fact, the absolutely private thoughts of the narrator become a way of drawing the reader into the text, a way of reaffirming community; the narrator's idiosyncrasies speak to our own idiosyncrasies. While there is little point in the narrator's conclusion that, when paying for groceries, 'the differential in checkout speeds between a fast, smart ringer-upper and a slow, dumb one [is] three transactions to one' (Baker 1986: 117), it is likely that such a conclusion is not unlike other conclusions to which the reader has, somewhat pointlessly, arrived. Like the work of Leyner, this particular brand of narrative is neither a simple rejection of postmodern strategies nor a 'back-lash' return to Lukácsian realism. In other words, critics like Philip Simmons are, to a certain extent, correct when they associate *The Mezzanine* with a 'postmodern historical imagination' (1992: 603). The text is, after all, 'so extremely solipsistic, so limited to the domestic, the personal, and the resolutely mundane, that any larger historical frame ... is gestured at only through the irony of its absence' (Simmons 1992: 603). Still, as even Simmons admits, Baker's text (like, as I suggested above, Leyner's) 'performs the most fundamental comic function of validating our perceptions in unexpected ways' (1992: 611). In the end, the postmodern fragmentation – that is, Baker's willingness to privilege innumerable 'microhistories' (Simmons 1992: 605) over a single grand narrative – is employed in a manner that seems designed to ironically frustrate the postmodern rejection of communal understanding and/or essentially 'human' experience; 'we gain', as Simmons himself suggests, 'a pleasurable shock of recognition' (1992: 611).

Instead of suggesting that Baker works to endorse a 'postmodern historical imagination', then, we might argue, along with a critic like Arthur Saltzman, 'that *The Mezzanine* does not feature the vanquishment of historical nostalgia, as Simmons contends, so much as it alters its course; it does not eliminate depth per se but posits "deep surfaces"' (Saltzman 1999: 27). In a manner that recalls Fluck's discussion of Carver – in particular, his suggestion that neo-realism is defined by a willingness to privilege 'surface knowledge' – Saltzman's take on Baker highlights the way in which a text like *The Mezzanine* can be read as overtly reaffirming the possibility of communication, or communal understanding, while simultaneously deferring the realization of that possibility. What we get, and what makes *The Mezzanine* utterly distinct from a text like *The Floating Opera*, is the promise of a type of communication without communication, an articulation of community without community. *The Mezzanine* readdresses the postmodern denial of shared understanding – of representational accuracy, of mimesis – by identifying its impossibility as the very grounds of its possibility. Like Blanchot's 'community without community' – or, what the later Derrida associates in *The Politics of Friendship* with the term 'lovence', a term that seems to suggest the possibility of connection via disconnection, touching without contact – the communal promise offered by *The Mezzanine* is continually made possible by the impossibility that it will be fulfilled (or, put differently, *finally effaced as promise*). The ruminations of Howie in *The Mezzanine* offer us, as Saltzman puts it, 'contact and privacy simultaneously' (1999: 69). I don't want to suggest, though, that a text like *The Mezzanine* ultimately reaffirms a traditional notion of privacy, and thus a notion of the subject as 'essentially' anterior to the social, or symbolic. Instead, by pointing to the possibility of a type of community without community, a text like *The Mezzanine* seems to present the subject's 'privacy' as an effect of its singularity, but a singularity that, as a theorist like Jean-Luc Nancy[12] would suggest, is singular only insofar as it is simultaneously and paradoxically 'with' others. This 'singularity' is not 'individuality; it is, each time, the punctuality of a "with" that establishes a certain origin of meaning and connects it to an infinity of other possible origins [or "singularities"]' (Nancy 2000: 85). It is in this sense that I agree with Saltzman that the text offers the possibility of 'contact and privacy simultaneously'. The text, in other words, 'renews', as does a work like Leyner's, the possibility of connection *as* disconnection. If we return again to the work of Nancy, we might in fact say that *The Mezzanine* works to suggest that the 'common measure ... is not some unique standard applied to everyone and everything', but rather 'the commensurability of incommensurable singularities' (Nancy 2000: 75). And, I would argue, this paradoxical renewal of the possibility of connection and/or communication (and, thus, of a finally correct and successful representational act, or decision) is even more obviously endorsed in Baker's later, slightly pornographic, novel *Vox*.

Another seemingly minimalist piece, *Vox* also focuses on the mundane and the personal. However, *Vox*, which is nothing but recorded dialogue between a man (Jim) and a woman (Abby) on a 'phone sex' line, is much more overt than *The Mezzanine* in terms of suggesting the utterly private nature of human existence. Jim and Abby spend most of their time telling each other about their sexual habits, habits that tend to be extremely fetishistic and personal. At the same time, though, and as does *The Mezzanine*, *Vox* reembraces a type of sentimental faith in social experience and communal sharing. However, this 'faith' is not naïve in the way that prepostmodern realism is understood as being. Like *The Mezzanine*, or Leyner's *Tetherballs*, *Vox* remains postmodern in terms of its articulation of a type of inescapable solipsism, or 'singularity'. The conversation, after all, takes place on a phone. There is no 'real contact'. Still, as Mikko Keskinen notes, 'In phone sex, bodies are disconnected, but minds are connected by disembodied voices. ... The point in phone sex seems to be to embrace and indulge in the distance rather than to grieve or curse it' (2004: 102). Jim and Abby's quest for the 'real thing' is thus fueled by its impossibility; their desire is, in fact, repeatedly identified as an effect of the impossibility of its fulfillment. What produces their desire is the absence of the Real; its promise, its *possibility*, is the effect of its impossibility. Jim, as we eventually learn, phoned the 'hot line' because he wanted to move beyond the artificial: 'I felt at that moment that I wanted to talk to a real woman, no more images of any kind, no fast forward, no pause, no magazine pictures. And there was the ad' (Baker 1992: 33). What Jim gets, though, is a phone conversation and another night of masturbation. On a certain level, in fact, the entire conversation can be read as Jim's private fantasy: 'Although nominally divided into two voices, two speakers, the novel gives the impression of one narrative voice characterized by wit, wordplay, and stylistic virtuosity' (Keskinen 2004: 111). Once again, then, we are given an overt promise of communication, of a mimetic utterance, that is simultaneously deferred as impossible. Like Fred speaking to himself through his own intercom at the end of *Lost Highway*, Jim's conversation in *Vox* can be read as an articulation of an always and necessarily deferred movement toward the articulation of some 'impossible Real': 'The long-distance call from Abby's place to Jim's is, in this sense, a local one, or even an intercom call: Jim attempts to speak to himself through a thin inside wall – the borderline separating narrative levels – of the house of fiction' (Keskinen 2004: 112).

What I want to stress here is the fact that this 'renewalist' reaffirmation is marked by a certain redeployment of postmodernist strategies, a certain *relaxing of the rules* that seems to have resulted in both the growing relevance of a type of neo-realism and the persistence of narrative strategies that remain outwardly postmodern – or, in other words, metafictional. As the end of *Adaptation* suggests – that is, the return to the metafictional framework with which the film began and Kaufman's realization that he shouldn't adhere blindly to McKee's rules any more than he should adhere to the postmodern rule that all rules must be rejected – this period after postmodernism is defined by a renewed willingness to abandon all imperatives, including postmodernism's. Texts like Baker's thus seem to point to the postmodern 'failure' around which I have been circling since the beginning. As an example of emergent renewalist narratives, Baker's work suggests that postmodernism 'failed' because it refused, or was unable, to acknowledge *clearly* that it ultimately and necessarily reaffirmed the very positivist ideology it claimed to be refuting.

As I have suggested throughout, emergent narrative forms, in a manner that parallels late-phase deconstruction, seem to take into account *outwardly* a certain postmodern failure, or limitation. What these narrative forms suggest – and what a film like *Adaptation* seems to expose, or play out – is that the corrosively self-reflexive works of postmodernism were necessarily haunted by the very specter they attempted to exorcise: the specter of a telos, the specter of positivism, the specter of humanism. In brief, the very specter we see at work in postmodernism is the very same specter the later Derrida locates in Marxism and, in turn, deconstruction: a past revenant, or ghost, of 'emancipatory and *messianic* affirmation, a certain experience of the promise'. And it seems clear that this current narrative 'turn' is marked by an acceptance of the very spectrality of this particular specter, a ghost that ultimately and necessarily haunted postmodernism's desire to exorcise all past ideological revenants. As an apparent reappraisal of the postmodern relationship to the spectral remainder that animated the aesthetic strategy of metafiction, this current movement away from the recent hegemony of postmodern narrative strategies is, in short, the latest attempt to 'deal with' the specter of postmodernism – which is, quite simply, the specter of 'a still incomplete project of modernity', the essential specter haunting both Marxism and deconstruction.

A conclusion . . . *perhaps*

One final example. In Toni Morrison's *Beloved*, the concept of the specter – of the ghost, of the repressed – is pivotal. For this reason, *Beloved* can help us to clarify two distinct yet intimately related concepts. On one hand, the text exemplifies a distinctly renewalist aesthetic; its narrative strategies overtly endorse and embrace the ironic spectrality of the mimetic promise. On the other hand, *Beloved*, like *Hamlet*, offers us a very specific model of the specter, a model that speaks to the very narrative in which it is articulated. And it seems more than a mere accident that the spectral negotiation that determines the plot of *Beloved* comes to highlight the distinctly renewalist negotiation that defines the text's overall aesthetic.

Like all of the renewalist texts discussed above, *Beloved* redeploys a series of overtly postmodern stylistic devices. Most obviously, *Beloved* (like Morrison's later novel, *Jazz*) approaches its central animating event – that is, Sethe's protective, yet brutal, slaughter of her child, Beloved – again and again via a spiral-like series of narrative returns. Indeed, the event is recounted several times and from a series of different perspectives. As in O'Brien's texts, this repetition comes to suggest the impossibility of the certainly accurate narrative act, the certainly right narrative decision. However, and as we see in a text like O'Brien's *The Things They Carried*, the event's essential inexplicability (or, rather, the specter's essential spectrality) becomes the very thing that animates the narrative act. Ryan P. McDermott puts it like this:

> The 'unspeakable scene(/seen)' of *Beloved* is not only an unwittingly productive critical construction – it is symptomatic of the novel's own desire to break and yet preserve the fungibility of its pervasive silence through the production and reproduction of the image outside of the symbolic order of language. As such, the 'unspeakable scene' works a structural device that both appeals to and frustrates our attempts to translate this silence into narrative.
>
> (2003: 77)

The promise of complete narrative apprehension is made possible by the fact that the event – or rather, the impossible 'Real' – continually resists narrative apprehension. We see this paradox – that is, the paradox that the impossibility of the certainly right narrative act allows for the possibility of such an act – in Sethe's own circular attempts to tell her story: 'Sethe knew that the circle she was making around the room, him, the subject, would remain one. That she could never close in, pin it down for anybody who had to ask' (Morrison 1988: 163). Like O'Brien's narrators, though, Sethe empathically yields to the belief, however contradictory it may be, that her story and, thus, the reality of her trauma can be made manifest; she yields to the belief that, eventually, she will no longer be haunted by the past. Put differently, and in a manner that speaks to the ethical imperative that defines renewalism, Sethe determinedly and ironically opposes the paralysis of narrative indecision (i.e., the effect of knowing that no finally correct decision is possible) with the certainty of indecision (i.e., the belief that there is, indeed, an absolutely correct decision). This ethics of indecision is doubly stressed via the actual event that Sethe, among others, repeatedly tries to apprehend/understand. The text's emphatic willingness to undergo 'the ordeal of indecision' is, in short, mirrored by the impossible decision with which Sethe was faced: to kill her children or to let them be taken as slaves. As deplorable as her ultimate decision might appear *prima facie*, the fact that she makes a decision *at all* can be read as a clear endorsement of the ethical imperative animating the entire text: the ethical imperative that any decision or narrative act *must* endure both aspects of indecision, that any decision *must*, respect both the possibility and the impossibility of the spectral promise.

Of course, this 'ethics of indecision' – or rather, this apparent endorsement of the renewalist imperative to respect the specter – is also mirrored by the text's theme of revenants, of ghosts. The narrative, after all, begins with the assertion that Sethe's house is haunted; Sethe and Denver (Sethe's other daughter) live in a house 'palsied by the baby's fury at having its throat cut' (Morrison 1988: 5). From the very beginning Sethe and Denver are invested in the possibility of some type of exorcism and/or conjuration. In the initial pages of the text, in fact, we are told that 'Sethe and Denver decided to end the persecution by calling forth the ghost that tried them so' (Morrison 1988: 4). What is important to note here is that the desire to call forth (i.e., 'to conjure') the spirit is intimately tied to a desire to explain things *once and for all*, to make the baby (Beloved) understand *at last*. 'If she'd only come', Sethe asserts, 'I could make it clear to her' (Morrison 1988: 4). To begin with, then, Sethe is animated by the promise that the specter can be made manifest and, thus, that the traumatic event can be finally and accurately related. But, in the beginning at least, this promise is continually deferred and Sethe and Denver continue to be haunted. However, when Paul D, an ex-slave with whom Sethe was once held captive, returns and performs a type of exorcism on the house, Sethe and Denver seem to get their wish. The promise is, in short, fulfilled; and, for a time, everything seems better. The sense we get is that Paul D's presence allows Sethe to repress her trauma, to believe that it's finally over, to believe that it has been reckoned with *at last*. Paul D frees Sethe from her responsibility – from, especially, the responsibility of her decisions both past and present. Not surprisingly, though, and in a manner that speaks to the spectrological argument I have been employing throughout, Paul D's exorcism is followed almost immediately by the manifest appearance of Beloved. The suggestion is that the utter rejection of the ghost's presence is tantamount to an utter rejection of its absence; in either case, the ironic spectrality of the specter is effaced. An exorcism is, after all, always also a form of conjuration. Still, combined with Paul D's presence, Beloved's manifestation as an adult woman seemingly liberates Sethe *once and for all*. However, we are slowly brought to the realization that Beloved's manifestation and, thus, *the absence of the ghost* is a dangerously seductive reality, a reality that slowly and quite necessarily tears the makeshift family apart.

Eventually, both Denver and Sethe begin to sense the dangerous effects of Paul D's exorcism/conjuration; they both seem to realize that the ghost continually promised and opened up certain possibilities *because* those possibilities remained deferred. While Denver admits that her and Sethe's attempts to 'reason with the baby ghost … got nowhere' and that, in the end, 'It took a man, Paul D, to shout it off and take its place for himself', she also comes to realize that 'she preferred the venomous baby' (Morrison 1988: 104). Likewise, Sethe begins to lament the loss of the ghost, while simultaneously falling prey to the comfort that Paul D and Beloved seem to offer:

> Alone with her daughter in a haunted house she managed every damn thing. Why now, with Paul D instead of the ghost, was she breaking up? getting scared? needing Baby? The worst was over, wasn't it? She had already got through, hadn't she? With the ghost in 124 she could bear, do, solve anything. Now a hint of what had happened to Halle and she cut out like a rabbit looking for its mother.
>
> (Morrison 1988: 97)

Significantly, this troubling train of thought is interrupted by the pleasure of a massage that Sethe is, at the time, receiving from Beloved: 'Beloved's fingers were heavenly. Under them and breathing easy, the anguish rolled down. The peace Sethe had come there to find crept into her' (Morrison 1988: 97). Still, and regardless of the apparent comfort that Beloved and Paul D seem to offer, the dangerous absence of the ghost and/as the presence of Beloved becomes increasingly evident; we are even led to believe that Beloved may be intent on harming Sethe. What I want to highlight, though, is the fact that, with Beloved *finally present*, Sethe slowly loses the reason to explain herself, to tell her story, to make (in short) decisions about the representative acts that define her past. Beloved, after all, knows what happened. She was there. She is, we might say, the manifestation of the event itself.

As McDermott suggests, 'Beloved's reincarnation can ... be read as a materialization of the visual trace that eludes appropriation into the sphere of narration – the latter being the condition which makes the visual trace not fully recoverable and consequently outside the bounds of historiographic discourse' (2003: 79). This materialization becomes a comforting, if problematic, *presence* for Sethe: 'Sethe's own investment in the newly returned Beloved – more pointedly, in Beloved's bodily presence – becomes a way of compensating for the failure of language to account for this lost object' (McDermott 2003: 79). I would like to take this suggestion a bit further, though. By finally 'compensating for the [necessary] failure' of the narrative act, Beloved's presence – or rather, *the presence of the event itself* – annihilates the possibility of all future narrative acts. Beloved's presence doesn't, as we might expect, exacerbate the weight of Sethe's responsibility – that is, her future responsibility to make narrative decisions about her past; instead, Beloved's presence (like, to a certain extent, Paul D's) strips Sethe of all (narrative) responsibility. Consequently, Beloved's presence strips Sethe of her authority and her control:

> Then the mood changed and the arguments began. Slowly at first. A complaint from Beloved, an apology from Sethe.... Wasn't it too cold to stay outside? Beloved gave a look that said, So what? Was it past bedtime, the light no good for sewing? Beloved didn't move; said, 'Do it', and Sethe complied. She took the best of everything – first ... and the more she took, the more Sethe began to talk, to explain, ... Beloved wasn't interested. ... Sethe pleaded for forgiveness, counting, listing again and again her reasons ...
>
> (Morrison 1988: 241–42)

Paul D's exorcism and/or conjuration of the specter – for, as we have already seen, the two are ultimately synonymous – leaves Sethe in a state of mythic indecision; she no longer has a reason to get her story right, to tell it *in truth*. The story has become, for all intents and purposes, manifest, and its presence leaves no room for other possible accounts. All Sethe can do is apologize (to Beloved) or forget (with Paul D). Either situation, though, can be read as an effect of the ghost's absence. Without the ghost, without the possibility *and* the impossibility of finally apprehending the moment of Beloved's death, without the possibility *and* the impossibility of forgiveness, Sethe loses both the ability and the need to make decisions about her own story. More simply, Morrison's distinctly renewalist text suggests, via its own narrative strategies and its employment of a specific model of the specter, that without the ghost, without the ironic spectrality of the specter, there is no ordeal of indecision and, thus, no possible decision, no possible responsibility (narrative or otherwise).

This renewalist endorsement of spectrality, or narrative indecision, becomes particularly explicit when, in the concluding portions of the novel, the women in Sethe's community finally come together to perform what *seems to be* a second and final exorcism. At this point, though, Beloved is no longer the ghost that haunted 124. She has become real: *in the flesh*. For this reason, we should avoid referring to this communal act as an exorcism. If anything, it is the exact opposite of an exorcism. The community seemingly comes together to insist upon Beloved's spectrality, her status as ghost. The women reject her material presence *so as* to reaffirm her possibility *and* her impossibility as a ghost of the past. And while we are told that, afterward, the community 'forgot her like a bad dream' (Morrison 1988: 274), it would be a mistake to assume that she is finally expelled. After the community confronts her *presence*, Beloved, as Roger Luckhurst astutely notes, '*remains*' (1996: 249). Or better: *her remains* persist. The community reopens the possibility of remembering the dismembered past by performing a ritualized act of forgetting, by *dematerializing* Beloved, by insisting upon her essential spectrality. Once this ritual act is performed, Derridean indecision once again becomes possible. Paul D is told that, 'Maybe', Beloved 'disappeared', *maybe* she 'exploded', *maybe* she is 'hiding in the tress waiting for another chance' (Morrison 1988: 264). Once again, no one knows with certainty what happened; and, in the absence of certainty, the process and possibility of making 'sense out of the stories' (Morrison 1988: 267) is renewed. By coming together to insist upon her impossibility, the community makes possible the act of making narrative decisions about Beloved (and all the past traumas with which she is associated).

The conclusion of *Beloved* stresses the impossible possibility of exorcising the past *finally*, of remembering *or* forgetting. Because 'It was not a story to pass

on' the community works to forget Beloved. But, because 'This is not a story to
pass on', Beloved's spectral 'footprints' necessarily continue to 'come and go, come
and go' (Morrison 1988: 275). The novel thus concludes with an almost audible
call to 'respect the specter'. Even the slippage in this line that repeats *without
repeating* – 'It was not a story to pass on' *and* 'This is not a story to pass on' – is
utterly spectral in nature. It demands a reading that can never be settled, or
decided upon. One meaning ('to forget') is wholly present only when the other
('to remember') is wholly absent. The condition of absolute meaning is here the
condition of its impossibility. As a result, Beloved works to 'pass on' *and* 'pass on'
the very specter of a telos that animated postmodernism. On the one hand,
Morrison's text accepts, or 'passes on', postmodernism's rejection of the modernist
compulsion to conjure this specter into being *once and for all*; on the other,
Beloved clearly moves beyond, or 'passes on', the postmodern imperative to
utterly deny the possibility of the specter's materiality, its potential as a promise
of an ideal future still 'to come'. *Beloved*, in short, outwardly works to suggest that
the impossibility of social justice, authentic experience, and/or true and final
decisions need not prevent us from sincerely struggling for such things. What we
see, then, as I said above, is that only in the absence of absolutely just decisions
(and/or narrative acts) are any decisions (and/or narrative acts) possible.

Put differently and, *perhaps*, in conclusion, *Beloved*'s distinctly renewalist
imperative to respect and endure the 'ordeal of indecision' is, if we follow Derrida,
an ethical call to embrace the spectral contingency of the 'perhaps'. In *Politics of
Friendship*, and while elaborating on the ethical implications of the specter
(implications that he began to address overtly in *Specters of Marx*) Derrida
spends an entire chapter reading, enumerating, and interpreting Nietzsche's use
of the word 'perhaps'. The question Derrida wants to answer is this: what does
this 'perhaps' suggest about the possibility and the impossibility of friendship, of
an ethical and finally true understanding of the other? Derrida, of course (and
while reading Nietzsche's own discussions of friendship alongside the famous
Aristotle quote, 'O friends, there are no friends'), comes to suggest that the
frequency of the term 'perhaps' in Nietzsche's work can be read as symptomatic
of a type of promise. This promise is, as are most things for Derrida, twofold. On
the one hand, this promise promises the veracity of what has been said while
simultaneously rejecting the certainty that a promise typically seems to afford:
'there will come, *perhaps*; there will occur, perhaps, the event of that which
arrives (*und vielleicht kommt*), and this will be the hour of joy, an hour of birth
but also of resurrection' (Derrida 1997: 28). This promise promises, like the ghost

that originally haunts Sethe, that the event will become manifest. It promises the absence/manifestation of the ghost, *perhaps*. In terms of Morrison's text, this promise could be said to promise the true narrative representation of the event, *perhaps*. The perhaps thus defers the possibility of the promise while simultaneously opening up, yielding to, hoping for, the possibility that the deferral is only temporary, that 'there will occur, perhaps, the event of that which arrives' – that there will occur, that there *can* occur, a finally right decision, a finally right narrative and/or interpretive act. On the other hand, this promise promises the perhaps itself; it promises the possibility that we can, finally, accept the 'dangerous' irony of the perhaps:

> What is going to come, *perhaps*, is not only this or that; it is at last the thought of the *perhaps*, the *perhaps* itself. The *arrivant* will arrive *perhaps*, for one must never be sure when it comes to *arrivance*; but the *arrivant* could also be the *perhaps* itself, the unheard-of, totally new experience of the *perhaps*. Unheard-of, totally new, that very experience which no metaphysician might yet have dared to think.
>
> (Derrida 1997: 29)

For Derrida, the future to come is the future of the perhaps. It is the future of the specter, of that which is *and* is not, that which we know we can never know yet somehow believe we will know . . . *perhaps. Perhaps*, then, we might argue, the future is already here and now? Doesn't Derrida, after all, position himself as the philosopher to come? Indeed, Derrida argues for a future of the 'perhaps' *as* a philosopher of the perhaps: 'the thought of the "perhaps" *perhaps* engages the only possible thought of the event' (Derrida 1997: 29, my emphasis). Furthermore – and assuming that the above analysis is, to a degree, accurate – are not these narratives *after* postmodernism, are not these narratives of renewalism, narratives of the perhaps? Are these not narratives that seemingly embrace the spectrality of the specter, narratives that embrace the necessary possibility of the impossible? Yet, if this is true – if, that is, the future of the perhaps is now – does it not suggest, quite paradoxically of course, that the *perhaps* is, itself, an impossibility? Does not this apparent claim (and imperative) to achieve the perhaps – to respect, that is, the specter – efface the ironic danger of the perhaps, the ironic danger of the specter's spectrality? Aren't we once again in the domain of certainty; are we not, once again and quite necessarily, forcing the ghost to become manifest/absent? We might argue, in fact, that it is not a simple accident that, in his endorsement of this future of the perhaps,

Derrida occasionally drops the 'perhaps': 'there is no more just category for the future than that of the "perhaps"' (1997: 29). What happened, here, to the perhaps? Why is this promise of the perhaps no longer, itself, a condition of the perhaps, a condition of epistemological doubt? Let me rephrase the question: what is implied by the fact that, when it comes to a renewalist ethics of indecision, a decision is no longer necessary? After all, the suggestion (as we just saw in a text like *Beloved* and as we are seeing, again, via a look at Derrida's later work) seems to be that, when it comes to the ordeal of indecision, we have no decision. The ordeal of indecision *must* be endured:

> The possibilization of the impossible possible must remain at one and the same time as undecidable – and therefore as decisive – as the future itself. What would a future be if the decision were able to be programmed, and if risk [*l'aléa*], the uncertainty, the unstable certainty, the inassurance of the 'perhaps', were it not suspended on it at the opening of what comes, flush with the event, within it and with an open heart?
>
> (Derrida 1997: 29)

In a claim like this, has not the specter, like Beloved, once again and, perhaps, quite necessarily obstructed us with its apparent manifestation/absence?

What I am trying to suggest by way of a tentative conclusion – a conclusion, *perhaps*, of the 'perhaps' – is this: by positioning itself as a narrative/theoretical strategy that no longer feels compelled to reject, as dangerously impossible, the spectral promise that drives all narrative acts, by defining itself as a narrative strategy that no longer insists on any single type of narrative strategy, this emergent discourse of renewalism slips quite necessarily, *perhaps*, into the same spectral trap that lead postmodernism to its apparent demise. The very specter that is seemingly 'dealt with' in this shift away from a postmodern stylistic imperative *necessarily* returns at the very moment it is thought to be, finally, placed to rest. Most obviously, this specter continues to haunt the claim that what we are witnessing at the end of postmodernism is 'an improvement' that manages to successfully 'lay to rest' the spectrally determined imperatives of postmodernism, that manages to bring our mourning to an end. Yet this specter of positivism must always 'pass on'. Certainly, postmodernism has 'given up the ghost'. And, *certainly*, it would seem that this ghost has *passed on* to a much more welcoming home, a home of the gamble, a home of the perhaps; but the new imperative to respect the specter, to embrace the dangerous irony of the perhaps – an imperative we see in this emergent fiction, as well as in the later work of theorists like Derrida – suggests that the specter is once again being denied, or *passed on*, that it is once again compelling us in ways we cannot control. In brief, what I think we need to note (especially now, at the swell of this new epistemological tide) is that this spectral relationship does not cease to be a problem – that is, a source of teleologies and/or absolutes – simply because we claim to recognize it, to accept it. It is, I am arguing, *necessarily impossible to respect the specter*. This seems to be implicit in the teleological imperative that we *must* respect the specter, that we *must* endure the ordeal of indecision. For to say this is to locate another *final answer* and thus to deny the impossibility of such a solution – the impossibility that the specter represents in the first place. So, what we begin to see in this strange moment of passing, in this strange and ongoing period of mourning, is the fact that the specter works to produce work, if it works at all, because it compels us to destroy it, to efface its spectrality, to disrespect it *as specter*, to always and forever *pass on it*.

Notes

Editors' note: In the interests of internal consistency, the notes in this extract have been re-numbered to make them sequential.

1   Such a list is, of course, tentative, and a careful examination of each author would be necessary before we could identify their individual works as definitively 'renewalist'. However, apart from Tarantino and Erdrich and the authors that I have already discussed above, the writers that make up the remainder of this list have been identified elsewhere as (in one manner or another) complicit with a certain shift away from postmodernism: in 'Writing Fiction in the 90s', Malcolm Bradbury identifies Toni Morrison, along with Alice Walker, as moving beyond postmodern aesthetic imperatives; Alfred Hornung makes similar claims in 'POSTMODERN-POSTMORTEM: Death and the Death of the Novel'; in 'Mood Swings' (discussed above) Hayles and Gannon claim that Danielewski's work participates in a 'mood swing' from postmodernism to, what they identify as, an 'aesthetic of ambient emergence'; Don DeLillo is mentioned by Winfried Fluck (in an article discussed below) as a writer that, while stylistically postmodern, is engaged in a type of writing that can be categorized along with the work of Raymond Carver; and Christopher Den Tandt makes analogous claims about DeLillo, while extending his analysis to the work of Kingston, in his 'Pragmatic Commitments: Postmodern Realism in Don DeLillo, Maxine Hong Kingston and James Ellroy'.

2 Of course, postmodernism never resulted in a state of paralysis. This is, I am arguing, the very failure to which renewalist forms of narrative respond. Because it strove to finally reject the ideal of mythic indecision (or, put differently, the material possibility of the specter) postmodernism necessarily and paradoxically strove toward such a state of indecision. What the persistence of postmodernism demonstrates, though, is that the rejection of either pole of indecision is impossible. Had postmodernism been successful in its aesthetic endeavor, it would have ceased to move; it would have become absolutely silent. The failure of postmodernism to carry through on its various threats to commit suicide is thus symptomatic of the impossibility of *a discourse* that is uncontaminated by the irony of indecision – which is to say, the spectrality of the specter.

3 To a degree, then, the initial portion of Kaufman's film seems to echo and, perhaps, mock the extreme solipsism of high postmodernism. Indeed, Kaufman's continual inability to get his plot 'moving' directly mirrors a text like Barth's ostentatiously metafictional 'Title'. Like Kaufman, the writer of/in 'Title' (i.e., the tenth story in *Lost in the Funhouse*) is paralyzed by his awareness of the futility of writing: 'I think she comes. The story of our life. This is the final test. Try to fill in the blank. Only hope is to fill the blank. Efface what can't be faced or else fill the blank. With words or more words, otherwise I'll fill in the blank with this noun here in my prepositional object. Yes, she already said that. And I think. What now. Everything's been said already, over and over; I'm as sick of this as you are; there's nothing to say. Say nothing' (Barth 1969b: 102).

4 The suggestion seems to be that a text evades artistic failure by continually emphasizing its inevitable failure as a meaningful text. Speaking of Borges' short allegory, 'Pierre Menard, Author of the Quixote', Barth points out that Menard 'writes a remarkable and original work of literature, the implicit theme of which is the difficulty, perhaps the unnecessity, of writing original works of literature. His artistic victory, if you like, is that he confronts an intellectual dead end and employs it to accomplish new human work' (Barth 1984a: 69–70). According to Barth, then, 'the literature of exhaustion' is, quite simply, an original articulation of exhaustion or narrative futility. Ultimately, though, this becomes another aesthetic dead end. Like, we might say, de Manian deconstruction, the literature of exhaustion incessantly works to expose the same ironically *finite* truth *again and again*: the infinite inexhaustibility of apparently exhausted works of art and modes of aesthetic production. As Barth suggests, 'it is a matter of every moment throwing out the bath water without for a moment losing the baby' (Barth 1984a: 70).

5 Of course, Hutcheon succinctly addresses this problem in her *Poetics*. Hutcheon, though, argues that, because it was, for the most part, willing to admit 'that no narrative can be a natural "master" narrative', postmodernism was able to

successfully 'challenge narratives that do presume "master" status, without necessarily assuming that status for itself' (Hutcheon 1988: 13). While I agree with Hutcheon that postmodern metafiction, at least initially, seemed to negotiate this paradox, I would argue that its eventual dominance as an aesthetic imperative exposed such a negotiation as impossible (which it is). As I suggested in chapter 1, even Hutcheon's claim that postmodernism can evade assuming the status of a master narrative necessarily positions it *as* a master narrative – that is, as a form of narrative that can *finally* evade becoming a metanarrative.

6 Given Barth's status as one of the quintessential postmodern writers, the fact that he seems to question what I have identified as a distinctly postmodern move toward aesthetic silence is somewhat problematic. Shouldn't a postmodernist celebrate an ambition like Beckett's? There are, I think, two ways to look at this dilemma. On the one hand, Barth's early work, including 'The Literature of Exhaustion', articulates the very 'failure' I have been attempting to describe throughout. What we see in Barth's work, and as I demonstrate in more detail below, is a type of ethical imperative to articulate the illusory nature of such an imperative. Even for a postmodernist (and this is, perhaps, the most obvious symptom of a postmodern 'failure'), the state of paralysis to which the work of Beckett points seems irresponsible. The postmodernist is compelled to continually voice the utopian ideal of such silence. As we saw with Vonnegut, this is a compulsion to articulate a type of 'ethics of perversity'. Not unlike Vonnegut, Barth identifies the 'felt ultimacies of our time' as a cause for celebration, a reason *to write*: 'By "exhaustion" I don't mean anything so tired as the subject of physical, moral, or intellectual decadence, only the used-upness of certain forms or the felt exhaustion of certain possibilities – by no means a cause for despair' (Barth 1984a: 64). On the other hand, though, Barth's awareness of the problematic paradox animating postmodernism – its strange ability to continue *speaking toward silence* – anticipates the subtle shift we see in his later work. As I pointed out in an earlier note, critics like Thomas Carmichael have identified a certain 'return of the Real' in Barth's later work. Suggesting a connection between Barth and the Žižekean 'art of the ridiculous sublime', such criticism highlights the way in which a late-Barth comes to embrace a form of literature, which he continues to call postmodernism, that is uncannily similar to the forms of renewalist narrative I have been attempting to categorize. By the time Barth publishes 'The Literature of Replenishment' he has begun to outwardly anticipate a type of literature that will 'somehow rise above the quarrel between realism and irrealism, formalism and "contentism"' (Barth 1984b: 203). Calling for a type of ideal aesthetic unity – a type of unity that seems to echo the linking of the disciplines that Habermas' views as the aim of a 'project of modernity' – Barth seems to rewrite his earlier claims regarding what constitutes postmodernism.

In fact, he seems to find in his earlier criticism and fiction suggestions that this was what he was intending all along. And, I would argue, he is quite right to do so. As Carmichael argues, 'What Barth's 1967 prescription finally urges is a synthesis of narrative self-consciousness and the conventions of realistic representation, and if we substitute modernism for the former and premodernism for the latter, we have a clear anticipation of the program that Barth advances for postmodernism in his 1980 essay, "The Literature of Replenishment", with the significant difference that in the later essay this synthesis is no longer couched in the rhetoric of a heroic avant-garde' (1994: 330). Put differently, the later Barth, like the later Derrida, is very much engaged in a certain shift *away from* the postmodern episteme he helped to define. Like Derrida, the later Barth, like the literature of renewalism generally, can be understood as simply shifting his emphasis, pointing to something that was necessarily present (albeit ignored, or denied) all along. With Derrida, the shift is most obvious in his outward acceptance of the necessity of the quasi-transcendental; in Barth, we see it in his much more overt insistence that postmodernism necessarily had to have 'it both ways'.

7   We might think of this paradox, as a critic like Chris Conti does, as an effect of a type of 'double-directed' discourse. Following Bahktin, Conti seems to suggest that the confessional mode assumed by a narrator like Andrews is symptomatic of 'the structure of a double-directed discourse [that] betrays the need for an audience precisely – and paradoxically – at the moment the narrator's independence from others is declared' (2004: 542). The sense we get from Conti is that Andrews' affirmation of nihilism and/or suicide is always and necessarily caught up in the very thing it aims to refute: the need for, or possibility of, validation: 'Todd seeks to justify more than parlor nihilism, though this might be all that remains of his ideology in the end; he seeks, rather, to justify suicide as an authentic choice and a positive act. In short, he wants to display suicidal nihilism as an affirmation of life' (Conti 2004: 541). As with the 'ethics of perversity' we see advocated so blatantly in the work of Vonnegut and Acker, Andrews' need to assure himself, and his readers, that an authentic or positive act is an ideological illusion becomes the very reason for his endlessly deferred suicide. In other words, Andrews' narrative (which can be read as an effect of his hesitation, or doubt) speaks to the impossibility of being certainly right about the impossibility of being certainly right. Andrews' narrative, like Andrews himself, persists because it/he is necessarily caught up in the paradox of 'indecision'.

8   I should note that I am, here, referring to the original 1956 version of *The Floating Opera*, the version Barth altered so as to satisfy his publishers. Barth eventually published a 'restored' version of the text in 1967, but in that particular version Andrews does not experience the moment of paralysis discussed above. While the

1967 version is apparently the novel Barth *wanted* published, I find the idea of Andrews' paralysis too significant to ignore (especially as the theme of paralysis is central in Barth's second novel – i.e., *The End of the Road*). For this reason, I am basing my discussion on the 1956 version, not the 1967 one.

9   This structure is, to a certain degree, repeated in *The End of the Road* and *Giles Goat-Boy*. In *The End of the Road* – the counterpart to *The Floating Opera* – the main character, Jacob Horner, is also subject to moments of absolute paralysis: 'I left the ticket window and took a seat on one of the benches in the middle of the concourse to make up my mind. And it was there that I simply ran out of motives, as a car runs out of gas. . . . There was no reason to do anything' (Barth 1969b: 74). After sitting immobile for an entire night, Horner is approached by a doctor who runs an 'immobilation farm'; and, after undergoing 'mythotherapy' – a process in which he is encouraged to believe in, and restructure, the fictional stories that define his existence – Horner begins a strange relationship with a seemingly 'liberated' couple. Another 'confessional', Horner's story, like Andrews', ultimately becomes an attempt to validate the claim that no claim or decision can be deemed 'valid'. The text itself thus becomes a contingent act of mythotherapy, a narrative that is animated by a spectral desire to invalidate all reasons for being, or acting, or deciding, or whatever. The existence of Horner's narrative, though, ultimately speaks to a latent faith in the teleological claim that intentional 'myth making' is the *only* 'ethical' thing we can *decide* to do. This same inverted code of 'ethics' seems to be the basic conceit of a text like *Giles Goat-Boy*. Playing with the idea of a prophesized messiah – that is, the GILES – *Giles Goat-Boy* continually teases the reader with the possibility that George, the 'Goat-Boy', will fulfill his destiny and become the Grand Tutor. Of course, in typical postmodern fashion, the messianic promise is denied as a dangerous illusion; George's efforts, after all, to 'tutor' inevitably end up causing more harm than good. By the end, when George seems to have finally become Grand Tutor (although a certain ambiguity continues to frustrate our ability to make claims about his messianic status), we realize that the entire narrative has been told years after the events described by a disillusioned and skeptical George. Still claiming to be Grand Tutor, George suggests that he has ultimately failed, that his 'lessons' only resulted in two dogmatic and opposed ideologies and that he believes the narrative he has just recorded is a futile attempt to explain something that cannot be explained: 'And thus it is – empowered as it were by impotence, driven by want of motives – I record this posttape' (Barth 1966: 756). The sense we get is that George *is* the *Grand Tutor*, but only insofar as he understands and preaches the impossibility of articulating the Truth, only insofar as he continually identifies his messianic role as being *without meaning or purpose*: 'I had been sought out, in my obscurity, by journalism-majors with long

memories, who asked whether I still maintained that I was the Grand Tutor. . . . I had replied yes, I was the Grand Tutor, for better or worse, there was no help for it; yes I knew what studentdom was pleased to call "the answer", though that term – indeed the whole proposition – was as misleading as another (and thus as satisfactory), since what I "knew" neither "I" nor anyone could "teach", not even my own "tutees"' (Barth 1966: 759). Like Andrews and Horner, then, George is identified as a type of postmodern saint, an individual who has finally realized and accepted the impossibility of a final answer, a mimetic text, a telos. At the same time, though, each of their narratives is spectrally animated by the promise that an absolute and final rejection of the promise *is possible*.

10 For this reason, it is not surprising that, as Arthur Saltzman notes, the *Washington Post* 'deemed' *The Mezzanine* 'the most daring and thrilling novel since John Barth's 1955 [*sic*] *The Floating Opera*' (Barbara Fisher Williamson as qtd. in Saltzman 1999: 15).

11 As Søren Pold puts it, 'In *The Mezzanine*, . . . one can also find a thorough awareness of the medium of print, and the novel can also be categorized as belonging to Realism' (2004: 141). In other words, Baker demonstrates 'a media consciousness that is simultaneously postmodern and realistic' (Pold 2004: 152).

12 I should note that Nancy's various, and fairly recent, theories of community, and 'being with', echo and run parallel to Derrida's later more overtly 'renewalist' work. We might, then, easily identify Nancy as a theorist of renewalism.

References

Baker, Nicholson (1986), *The Mezzanine*, New York: Vintage.

Baker, Nicholson (1992), *Vox*, New York: Random House.

Banks, Russell (1985), *Continental Drift*, New York: Harper & Row.

Barth, John (1966), *Giles Goat-Boy: Or, the Revised New Syllabus*, New York: Fawcett. First published 1966.

Barth, John (1967), *The Floating Opera*, New York: Avon. First published 1956.

Barth, John (1969a), *The End of the Road*, New York: Bantam. First published 1958.

Barth, John (1969b), *Lost in the Funhouse*, New York: Bantam.

Barth, John (1984a), 'The Literature of Exhaustion', in *The Friday Book: Essays and Other Nonfiction*, 62–76, New York: Putnam. First published 1969.

Barth, John (1984b), 'The Literature of Replenishment: Postmodernist Fiction', in *The Friday Book: Essays and Other Nonfiction*, 193–206, New York: Putnam. First published 1980.

Bradbury, Malcolm (1992), 'Writing Fiction in the 90s', in Kristiaan Versluys (ed.), *Neo-Realism in Contemporary Fiction*, 13–25, Amsterdam: Rodopi.

Carmichael, Thomas (1994), 'Postmodernism Reconsidered: The Return of the Real in John Barth's *Sabbatical* and *The Tidewater Tales*', *Revue Française d'Etudes Américaines*, 17 (62): 329–338.

Conti, Chris (2004), 'The Confessions of Todd Andrews: Double-Directed Discourse in *The Floating Opera*', *Studies in the Novel*, 36 (4): 533–551.

Den Tandt, Christopher (2003), 'Pragmatic Commitments: Postmodern Realism in Don DeLillo, Maxine Hong Kingston and James Ellroy', in Klaus Stierstorfer (ed.), *Beyond Postmodernism: Reassessments in Literature, Theory, and Culture*, 121–142, Berlin: Walter de Gruyter.

Derrida, Jacques (1997), *Politics of Friendship*, trans. George Collins, London: Verso.

Fluck, Winfried (1992), 'Surface and Depth: Postmodernism and Neo-Realist Fiction', in Kristiaan Versluys (ed.), *Neo-Realism in Contemporary Fiction*, 65–85, Amsterdam: Rodopi.

Hayles, Katherine N. and Todd Gannon (2007), 'Mood Swings: The Aesthetics of Ambient Emergence', in Neil Brooks and Josh Toth (eds), *The Mourning After: Attending the Wake of Postmodernism*, 99–142, Amsterdam: Rodopi.

Hornung, Alfred (1992), 'POSTMODERN-POSTMORTEM: Death and the Death of the Novel', in Kristiaan Versluys (ed.), *Neo-Realism in Contemporary Fiction*, 87–110, Amsterdam: Rodopi.

Hutcheon, Linda (1988), *The Poetics of Postmodernism*, London: Routledge.

Keskinen, Mikko (2004), '*Voces Intimae*. Electro-Erotic Speech in Nicholson Baker's *Vox*', *Critique*, 45 (2): 99–114.

Luckhurst, Roger (1996), ' "Impossible Mourning" in Toni Morrison's *Beloved* and Michèle Roberts' *Daughters of the House*', *Critique*, 37 (4): 243–260.

McDermott, Ryan P. (2003), 'Silence, Visuality, and the Staying Image: the "Unspeakable Scene" of Toni Morrison's *Beloved*', *Angelaki*, 8 (1): 75–89.

Morrison, Toni (1988), *Beloved*, New York: Knopf. First published 1987.

Nancy, Jean-Luc (2000), *Being Singular Plural*, trans. Robert D. Richardson and Anne E. O'Byrne, Stanford: Stanford University Press.

Pold, Søren (2004), 'Novel Media: On Typographical Consciousness and Marginal Realism in Nicholson Baker', in Simonsen, K-M., Ping Huang, M., Rosendahl Thomsen, M. (eds), *Reinventions of the Novel: Histories and Aesthetics of a Protean Genre*, 137–153, Rodopi, Amsterdam.

Rebein, Robert (2001), *Hicks, Tribes, and Dirty Realists: American Fiction after Postmodernism*, Lexington: University Press of Kentucky.

Saltzman, Arthur (1999), *Understanding Nicholson Baker*, Columbia: University of South Carolina Press.

Simmons, Philip E. (1992), 'Toward the Postmodern Historical Imagination: Mass Culture in Walker Percy's *The Moviegoer* and Nicholson Baker's *The Mezzanine*', *Contemporary Literature*, 33 (4): 601–24.

12

Altermodernism

The essence of Nicolas Bourriaud's vision of altermodernism involves, at its root, a fusion of the aesthetic of postmodernism with the culture of globalization. The model of multiculturalism infused into the postmodern by the postcolonial thought of the 1990s has, for Bourriaud, been supplanted by a new mode of 'viatorization', characterized by the traversing and criss-crossing of geographical and cultural space. The altermodern is conceived as a new form of modernity, the defining feature of which is a tendency towards creolization, as the art of the globalized age takes the form of a journey between cultures and inevitably assumes a polyglot sensibility. This was the key contention of Bourriaud's prestigious exhibition 'Altermodern', which he curated for the Tate triennial show in 2009. The manifesto below served as a kind of 'mission statement' for the exhibition, and the essay describing the altermodern is taken from the catalogue accompanying the show.

Bourriaud is certainly right that the ascent of globalization has had a profound impact on the formation of art, thought, and culture in the years since Jameson and Lyotard set out to plot the co-ordinates of the postmodern. Moreover, his verdict that, in their current theoretical states, neither postmodernism nor postcolonialism is well equipped to describe or evaluate the changes wrought by globalization is a provocative yet judicious assessment. Bourriaud is by no means the first to point out that postmodernism, formed as a critical response to a modernism whose canon was dominated by white Europeans and Americans, developed in its stead a canon no less dominated by white Europeans and Americans. Altermodernism, however, offers an alternative that eschews what Bourriaud regards as the straightforward essentialism that underpins the simplistic model of cultural relativism (such as that often labelled in the Anglophone world as the much-maligned 'political correctness') that inflected the postmodernism of the 1990s.

Bourriaud's altermodernism may well strike some critics of globalization as misguided: reading Jeffrey T. Nealon's writings on post-postmodernism in Part One will yield a rather less optimistic vision of the role of globalization in supplanting the postmodern. Furthermore, if 'globalization' is regarded as synonymous with

'Americanization', and viewed as the foisting of a homogenizing culture onto the rest of the world as a means of opening up new markets for global capitalism to exploit, then Bourriaud's vision of 'viatorization' is likely to appear as so much wishful thinking, and moreover an option that is wholly unavailable to most of the peoples exploited by globalization. On the other hand, though, there is nevertheless a politics of resistance to altermodernism, whereby the diversity of the world's cultures is highlighted and championed as a means of combating the seemingly unstoppable march of globalization.

In the context of a debate about the aftermath of postmodernism, though, what is most striking about Bourriaud's altermodernism is the extent to which its conceptual vocabulary echoes, or even replicates, that of the postmodernism it claims to supplant. Bourriaud's image of the artist as 'nomad' recalls instantly the thought of Gilles Deleuze and Felix Guattari (the latter an influence on Bourriaud's celebrated work Relational Aesthetics); his description of contemporary culture as an 'archipelago' borrows the term Lyotard uses to describe the multiplicity of language games; his use of the term 'archive', to which a section of Bourriaud's exhibition was dedicated, is indebted to Derrida's usage of this term; and the metaphor of 'border crossings' deployed throughout the exhibition recycles one of the more hackneyed clichés of pseudo-postmodern scholarship. Moreover, it is unclear how Bourriaud's notion of 'creolization' differs from the key concept of 'hybridization' that is already on offer in well-established theories of postcolonialism and postmodernism. Indeed, Bourriaud's characterizing the contemporary artist as an 'exile' – another of the exhibition's key terms – harks back even further, recalling the vocabulary of early twentieth-century modernism.

Yet the central contention of altermodernism – that the world of contemporary culture entails a different experience of space and time from that envisaged by postmodernism – is hard to refute, and indeed is shared by some of the other formulations in this book, such as Robert Samuels's automodernism. Indeed, Bourriaud sometimes uses cyberspace as a metaphor for contemporary culture, which hints at a stronger connection between these two positions. Furthermore, Gilles Lipovetsky's emphasis on the heightened sense of individualism engendered by consumerist culture might equally lend support to Bourriaud's description of the contemporary subject as a 'homo viator'.

Altermodern Manifesto: Postmodernism is Dead

Nicolas Bourriaud

A new modernity is emerging, reconfigured to an age of globalization – understood in its economic, political and cultural aspects: an altermodern culture.

Increased communication, travel and migration are affecting the way we live.

Our daily lives consist of journeys in a chaotic and teeming universe.

Multiculturalism and identity is being overtaken by creolization: Artists are now starting from a globalized state of culture.

This **new universalism** is based on translations, subtitling and generalized dubbing.

Today's art explores the bonds that text and image, time and space, weave between themselves.

Artists are responding to a new globalized perception. They traverse a cultural landscape saturated with signs and create new pathways between multiple formats of expression and communication.

The Tate Triennial 2009 at Tate Britain presents a collective discussion around this premise that postmodernism is coming to an end, and we are experiencing the emergence of a global altermodernity.

Travel, cultural exchanges and examination of history are not merely fashionable themes, but markers of a profound evolution in our vision of the world and our way of inhabiting it.

More generally, our globalized perception calls for new types of representation: our daily lives are played out against a more enormous backdrop than ever before, and depend now on trans-national entities, short or long-distance journeys in a chaotic and teeming universe.

Many signs suggest that the historical period defined by postmodernism is coming to an end: multiculturalism and the discourse of identity is being overtaken by a planetary movement of creolization; cultural relativism and deconstruction, substituted for modernist universalism, give us no weapons against the twofold threat of uniformity and mass culture and traditionalist, far-right, withdrawal.

The times seem propitious for the recomposition of a modernity in the present, reconfigured according to the specific context within which we live – crucially in the age of globalization – understood in its economic, political and cultural aspects: an altermodernity.

If twentieth-century modernism was above all a western cultural phenomenon, altermodernity arises out of planetary negotiations, discussions between agents from different cultures. Stripped of a centre, it can only be polyglot. Altermodernity is characterized by translation, unlike the modernism of the twentieth century which spoke the abstract language of the colonial west, and postmodernism, which encloses artistic phenomena in origins and identities.

We are entering the era of universal subtitling, of generalized dubbing. Today's art explores the bonds that text and image weave between themselves. Artists traverse a cultural landscape saturated with signs, creating new pathways between multiple formats of expression and communication.

The artist becomes 'homo viator', the prototype of the contemporary traveller whose passage through signs and formats refers to a contemporary experience of mobility, travel and transpassing. This evolution can be seen in the way works are made: a new type of form is appearing, the journey-form, made of lines drawn both in space and time, materializing trajectories rather than destinations. The form of the work expresses a course, a wandering, rather than a fixed space-time.

Altermodern art is thus read as a hypertext; artists translate and transcode information from one format to another, and wander in geography as well as in history. This gives rise to practices which might be referred to as 'time-specific', in response to the 'site-specific' work of the 1960s. Flight-lines, translation programmes and chains of heterogeneous elements articulate each other. Our universe becomes a territory all dimensions of which may be travelled both in time and space.

The Tate Triennial 2009 presents itself as a collective discussion around this hypothesis of the end of postmodernism, and the emergence of a global altermodernity.

Nicolas Bourriaud

Altermodern

Nicolas Bourriaud

A collective exhibition, when based around a theoretical hypothesis, needs to establish a balance between the artworks and the narrative that acts as a form of subtitling. It needs to develop a space–time continuum where the curator's voice-off, the statements of the artists, and the dialogues woven between the artefacts can co-exist. This hybrid arrangement is best compared with the production of a film, and cinematographic metaphors provide the clearest introduction to an event like *Altermodern*. According to Wim Wenders, analysing the relationship between image and narrative in the cinema, 'the narrative resembles a vampire attempting to drain the image of its blood'.[1] His observation could belong in any manual of the curator's ethics. It seems to me that the fundamental question that exhibitions ought to be repeatedly asking concerns the interpretation of forms: what is the message they convey today? What is the narrative that drives them? We have an ethical duty not to let signs and images vanish into the abyss of indifference or commercial oblivion, to find words to animate them as something other than products destined for financial speculation or mere amusement. The very act of picking out certain images and distinguishing them from the rest of the production by exposing them is also an ethical responsibility. Keeping the ball in the air and the game alive: that is the function of the critic or the curator. Wenders pursues his reasoning by opposing text and form: 'Images are highly sensitive, rather like a snail, which retreats into its shell when you touch its horns. They don't want to work like a horse, carrying or fetching things – messages, meanings, arguments or morals. Yet that is precisely what a story demands'.[2] A fair riposte to the German director would be that this contradiction has its limits, since images are neither so naive nor so devoid of meaning, and that to believe in their basic 'purity' is an equally dangerous delusion. When a camera registers them, doubtless they are 'pure' in the sense he intends, but as soon as they are projected and shared they assume a host of meanings, and the battle begins anew. Every exhibition is the record of such a battle.

'The figure in the carpet' (the tale of an exhibition)

Usually an exhibition begins with a mental image with which we need to reconnect, and whose meanings constitute a basis for discussion with the artists. The research that has preceded the Triennial 2009, however, had its origins in two elements: the idea of the archipelago, and the writings of a German émigré to the UK, Winfried Georg Sebald. The archipelago (and its kindred forms, the constellation and the cluster) functions here as a model representing the multiplicity of global cultures. An archipelago is an example of the relationship between the one and the many: It is an abstract entity; its unity proceeds from a decision without which nothing would be signified save a scattering of islands united by no common name. Our civilization, which bears the imprints of a multicultural explosion and the proliferation of cultural strata, resembles a structureless constellation, awaiting transformation into an archipelago. We should add that the modernism of the twentieth century, and today's mass cultural movements, amount to agglomerations that we could describe as 'continental'.

As for Sebald's writings – wanderings between 'signs', punctuated by black and white photographs – they appear to me as emblematic of a mutation in our perception of space and time, in which history and geography operate a cross-fertilization, tracing out paths and weaving networks: a cultural evolution at the very heart of this exhibition. The two concepts – the archipelago and Sebald's excursions – do not intertwine arbitrarily: they represent the paths I followed led by my initial intuition: that of the death of postmodernism as the starting point for reading the present.

The term 'altermodern', which serves both as the title of the present exhibition and to delimit the void beyond the postmodern, has its roots in the idea of 'other-ness' (Latin *alter* = 'other', with the added English connotation of 'different') and suggests a multitude of possibilities, of alternatives to a single route. In the geopolitical world, 'alterglobalization' defines the plurality of local oppositions to the economic standardization imposed by globalization, i.e. the struggle for diversity. Here we are back with the image of the archipelago: instead of aiming at a kind of summation, altermodernism sees itself as a constellation of ideas linked by the emerging and ultimately irresistible will to create a form of modernism for the twenty-first century. Why is this imperative necessity? The historical role of modernism, in the sense of a phenomenon arising within the domain of art, resides in its ability to jolt us out of tradition; it embodies a cultural exodus, an escape from the confines of nationalism and identity-tagging, but also from the mainstream whose tendency is to reify thought and practice. Under threat from fundamentalism and consumer-driven uniformization, menaced by massification and the enforced re-abandonment of individual identity, art today needs to reinvent itself, and on a planetary scale. And this new modernism, for the first time, will have resulted from global dialogue. Postmodernism, thanks to the post-colonial criticism of Western pretensions to determine the world's direction and the speed of its development, has allowed the historical counters to be reset to zero; today, temporalities intersect and weave a complex network stripped of a centre. Numerous contemporary artistic practices indicate, however, that we are on the verge of a leap, out of the postmodern period and the (essentialist) multicultural model from which it is indivisible, a leap that would give rise to a synthesis between modernism and post-colonialism.

Let us then call this synthesis 'altermodernism'. It cannot be placed *after* the modernist phenomenon any more than after this aftermath: it does not 'overtake' anything, any more than it 'harks back' to a previous period. There is no question of a return to the principles or the style of twentieth-century modernism, nowadays the object of a revival far from our preoccupations. If today we can envisage a form of modernism, this is only possible starting from the issues of the present and assuredly not by an obsessive return to the past, whatever its attributes.

Altermodernism can be defined as that moment when it became possible for us to produce something that made sense starting from an assumed heterochrony, that is, from a vision of human history as constituted of multiple temporalities, disdaining the nostalgia for the avant-garde and indeed for any era – a positive vision of chaos and complexity. It is neither a petrified kind of time advancing in loops (postmodernism) nor a linear vision of history (modernism), but a positive experience of disorientation through an art-form exploring all dimensions of the present, tracing lines in all directions of time and space. The artist turns cultural nomad: what remains of the Baudelairean model of modernism is no doubt this *flânerie*, transformed into a technique for generating creativeness and deriving knowledge.

Thus the exhibition brings together three sorts of nomadism: in space, in time and among the 'signs'. Of course, these notions are not mutually exclusive, and the same artist can simultaneously explore geographical, historical and socio-cultural realities. We need to be clear that nomadism, as a way of learning about the world, here amounts to much more than a simplistic generalization: the term enshrines specific forms, processes of visualization peculiar to our own epoch. In a word, trajectories have become forms: contemporary art gives the impression of being uplifted by an immense wave of displacements, voyages, translations, migrations of objects and beings, to the point that we could state that the works presented in *Altermodern* unravel themselves along receding lines of perspective, the course they follow eclipsing the static forms through which they initially manifest themselves.

Thus Simon Starling relocates a piece of furniture designed by Francis Bacon from one continent to another by radio waves. Katie Paterson transmits moments of silence from the Earth to the Moon and back, and we are placed in telephone communication with the melting of a glacier. Tris Vonna-Michell, whose exhibit comprises the narrative of a planetary drift, conceives of his exhibitions as linked series. Darren Almond teleports the bus shelters of Auschwitz into a gallery, photographs Chinese landscapes, or sets off to film the Great Wheel of Chernobyl frozen into immobility at the moment of the nuclear disaster. Franz Ackermann invents the age of painting with GPS. Joachim Koester follows the route of the Hashishins in Iran after retracing Kant's daily walks in Könisberg or – as related in *Dracula* – Jonathan Harker's trek in the Carpathians. Rachel Harrison's inspiration to invent a kind of formal anthropology comes from one of Charles Darwin's voyages on the *Beagle*. Walead Beshty passes exposed film stock through airport X-ray scanners, or captures the cracks occurring in Perspex sculptures as they travel to exhibitions in Fedex boxes. Subodh Gupta exports commonplace utensils from India; reassembled as digitized images, they take on a significance that transcends cultural divides. Pascale Marthine Tayou employs colonized forms of African art to suggest the parameters of a truly globalized culture. The tendency of these works is to emphasize the fact that, in this era of the altermodern, displacement has become a method of depiction, and that artistic styles and formats must henceforth be regarded from the viewpoint of diaspora, migration and exodus.

These differing modes of displacement indicate, more generally, a *fragmentation* of the work of art. No longer can a work be reduced to the presence of an object in the here and now; rather, it consists of a significant network whose interrelationships the artist elaborates, and whose progression in time and space he or she controls: a circuit, in fact. Seth Price, in an essay defining the theoretical issues of his work, refers to the 'collective authorship' and 'complete decentralization' that define our new cultural framework, to arrive at the conclusion that 'distribution is a circuit of reading', and that the artist's task 'becomes one of packaging, producing, reframing and distributing'.[3] Put another way, we could say that every artist manifests themself on their individual *wavelength*, especially by that progressive repetition of formal elements we used to call *style*. And this personal wavelength conveys in its emanations signs that are both heterogeneous (belonging to differing registers or cultural traditions) and heterochronic (borrowed from differed periods). Thus with *Feature*, Shezad Dawood has made a film that juxtaposes elements lifted from the western and the 'gore movie' in a narrative framework where Samuel Beckett has a fresh encounter with Buster Keaton. In an equally fantastical vein, Marcus Coates applies the archaic methods of shamanism to the contemporary world, seeking out 'animal spirits' to cure social problems in Israel or the Galapagos Islands. What is cutting-edge in these frolics is not the summoning-up of the past to express the present; it is the visual language with which this business is transacted – that of travelling and nomadism. There are no longer cultural roots to sustain forms, no exact cultural base to serve as a benchmark for variations, no nucleus, no boundaries for artistic language. Today's artist, in order to arrive at precise points, takes as their starting-point global culture and no longer the reverse. The line is more important than the points along its length.

Strictly speaking, then, the exhibition assembles works whose compositional principle relies on a chain of elements: the work tends to become a dynamic structure that generates forms before, during and after its production.[4] These forms deliver narratives, the narratives of their very own production, but also their distribution and the mental journey that encompasses them. Loris Gréaud, for instance, produces electroencephalograms of his own brain as he thinks about an exhibition; this is transformed into a computer programme, then into light emissions and finally into electrical impulses releasing vibrations in the exhibition hall – before, as likely as not, being used somewhere else. Lindsay Seers ceaselessly re-edits the documentary of her life, from her childhood in Mauritius to life in London, in installations that explore the origins of the photographic image.

As they follow the receding perspectives of history and geography, works of art trace lines in a globalized space that now extends to time: history, the last continent to be explored, can be traversed like a territory. In Sebald's *The Rings of Saturn*, the narrator journeys on foot across the landscapes of England's East Coast. He travels through various layers of time, mingling the past, the imaginary and the future. He ploughs through the works of Sir Thomas Browne in search of the burial-place of the philosopher's skull, comments on Rembrandt's *Anatomy Lesson of Dr Tulp*, meets Joseph Conrad en route to the Congo, recalls a film about herring-fishing, muses on ethnic cleansing in the Balkans or great naval battles and their pictorial representation, before discussing Chateaubriand and introducing us to the history of silkworm culture. The narratives are embedded in images or encounters, and Sebald constructs a kaleidoscope of fragments that reflect the footsteps of history. Later, Tris Vonna-Mitchell wrote a piece meant for a website dedicated to Sebald: 'That was in 2003, and through this serendipitous moment, the work started off as a text or prose piece, and just unfolded into this labyrinth of associations and narratives. Three years after this, I went back through my computer files and I saw those documents and photographs, these tunnels and web searches . . . and the project still goes on'.[5]

The journey format, as it appears so frequently in the works of today's artists, goes hand in hand with the generalization of hypertext as a thought process: one sign directs us to a second, then a third, creating a chain of mutually interconnected forms, mimicking mouse-clicks on a computer screen. With Nathaniel Mellors, Olivia Plender, Ruth Ewan or Spartacus Chetwynd, references to the past are coordinated according to a system of cognitive logic. To understand the present means carrying out a kind of rough-and-ready archaeological investigation of world culture, which proceeds just as well through *re-enactments* as through the presentation of artefacts – or again, through the technique of mixing. For example, Ewan installs a giant accordion from an Italian museum; it plays old revolutionary songs to accompany the reproduction of archival documents. Chetwynd, in the same work, can scramble Milton, Marx and Sesame Street; one of the constant features of her oeuvre is a playful use of forms not considered as relics of the past but as living tools that we need to grasp in order to create new narratives. In a similar way, Peter Coffin extracts the narrative potential of existing works of art by employing an audiovisual setup that parasitically appropriates their meaning and puts them to work as fictional characters.

These journeys in time result in a modification of the way in which signs are indexed with their period. In the case of Charles Avery; the artist produces not only signs, but also the context that gives them coherence, through the narrative of an imaginary world: he is the explorer of a universe inside which the idea of contemporaneity is abolished in favour of a voluntary confusion of eras and genres. Olivia Plender's comic-format book on the life of a fictitious artistic genius in 1960s London and her explorations of the archives of utopian communities or magic circles utilize forms not really belonging to any recognisable *present*. And Matthew Darbyshire links different landmarks from periods chronologically far apart, connecting for instance architecture of Stalin's era, fragments of Tate Britain and the facelifting of British public buildings, his aim being a transhistoric meditation on contemporary space. As for David Noonan's images, they seem to originate from a parallel world, once again defying precise localization. These works peregrinate through time and space, released from the fetishistic obsession with contemporaneity. Most probably this is why they are better at describing our present, both heterochronic and heterotopic.

Credit crunch: Postmodern comes out of mourning

The terms 'modern', 'postmodern' or 'altermodern' do not define styles (save as ways of thinking), but here represent tools allowing us to attribute time-scales to cultural eras. In order to understand why the collapse of the globalized financial system in Autumn 2008 appears to mark a definite turning-point in history, it is necessary to re-examine modernism from the point of view of world energy consumption.

In an enlightening text published in 2004, Peter Sloterdijk defined the modern way of living as a 'fast-burn culture', a specific condition of civilization in the era of a 'superabundance of energy'. 'Today', he continues, 'our lifestyle still depends upon being able to squander stocks of fossil fuels. In other words, we have gambled on a sort of explosion. We are all fanatical believers in this explosion, worshippers of this rapid liberation of a massive quantity of energy. I get the impression that the focal point of today's adventure films – "action movies" – is that other primitive symbol of modern civilization: the explosion of a car or a plane. Or rather, of a huge fuel tank that is the archetype of the religious movement of our times'.[6] This relationship between modern life and the explosion appears both literally and metaphorically throughout the twentieth century; from the Futurist eulogizing of war to the 'sudden liberations of great quantities of energy' in the performances of the Gutai group or the Viennese Actionists, not to mention the fragmented forms of Dadaism, the self-destructive machines of Jean Tinguely or the 'blown-up' imagery of pop art.

It is significant that the appearance of the term 'postmodern' coincided exactly with the 1973 oil crisis, the event that caused the entire world, for the first time, to realize that reserves of fossil fuels were limited: the end of Sloterdijk's 'superabundance'. In other words, our future was all of a sudden mortgaged. It is also no accident that the term 'postmodern' became current in the second half of the 1970s, popularized first by the architect Charles Jencks and then by the philosopher Jean-François Lyotard. Jencks's ideas constituted a criticism of modernism in architecture, notably the functionalism of the Bauhaus or Le Corbusier, whilst Lyotard sought to lay down a new paradigm (essentially epistemological) that would extend the life of modernism. Postmodernism thus developed in the wake of the energy crisis and the ending of the boom that the French call the 'thirty glorious years' (1945–75), just as a fit of depression succeeds a traumatic loss: that of the ideologies of carefree superabundance and progress, technical, political or cultural. The oil crisis of 1973 could well represent the 'primitive scene' of postmodernism in the same way as, according to Sloterdijk, oil gushing from a well symbolizes twentieth-century modernism. The latter was the fateful moment when the economy was founded on an unlimited confidence in the availability of energy, and culture on an infinite projection into the future. These were the two principles swept away by the oil crisis, and whose disappearance gave birth to what we call the postmodern.

Since the crisis of 1973, the economy has never again been based on the exploitation of raw materials. Capitalism has since disconnected from natural resources, reorienting itself towards technological innovation – the choice of Japan – or 'financiarization', the route adopted at the time by the United States. And now, when the economy is cutting its ties with concrete geography, culture for its part is divorcing from history; two parallel processes tending towards the abstract.

In the view of Bernard Stiegler, here resuming the essential thread of Jean-François Lyotard's theories on the 'libidinal economy', capitalism functions through the channelling of desires; yet, he adds, 'desire underwent a downward tendency', forcing the system to 'exploit instinctive impulses', all real passions having disappeared among alienated individuals who had lost control of their own lives.[7] After exhausting the consumer's desires, capitalism was thereafter reduced to exploiting his reflexes and gut reactions; sustainable sources of energy had dried up, just as with the oil crisis. In art, this assault upon our instincts was translated as a rapid rotation of works and the ascendancy of the sensational and the spectacular: those aimed simply at releasing a vast quantity of (non-renewable) energy at first sight. Gustav Metzger, master of the energy-burst, self-destruction and ecological disaster, has found his true place in this tableau of our times; a believer in the continuous development of culture, his work anticipates the evolution of capitalism and its culture, assembling the elements of a form of modernism capable of outliving the cult of the explosion.

I wrote earlier that postmodern culture had its roots in the idea of the end of history; more precisely, it posits the end of history considered as a linear narrative. In this respect, Lyotard defines the postmodern as the end of 'grand narratives', future scenarios that history is fated to fulfil, like a film-maker following a pre-defined script. The disappearance of these 'metanarratives' (Marxism, in particular) ushers in a culture of improvisation and time-loops: if there is no more script, we have henceforth to react to a 'context', or deal in short-term measures. Forms are no longer indexed to a narrative defining them as belonging to precise historical moments, but rather embedded in the 'text' of culture, with no reference save to themselves. Palimpsests, pastiches, textuality … Signs have lost all contact with human history and are self-generating in an infinite Brownian motion, a labyrinth of signs.

It seems difficult, in retrospect, to define the postmodern otherwise than as a period of pause and levelling, brief as befits a historical moment entirely determined by the one before – a marshy delta on the river of time. We can now identify those last twenty-five years of the 1900s as an interminable 'afterwards'; after the myth of progress, after the revolutionary utopia, after the retreat of colonialism, after the battles for political, social and sexual emancipation. As a theory, postmodernism has developed in reaction to a teleological view of the world, a vision we find both in the historicism of a critic like Clement Greenberg – for whom the history of art presented itself like a train en route toward the realization of an idea – and in the various politico-aesthetic utopias that typified the century of the avant-garde. This, however, would be to reduce modernism to its most immediately 'progressist' aspect: its identification with ambitions for political change and the most radical artistic movements, i.e. those anxious to excise everything superfluous and return to the root of things. In fact, in the cases of Marcel Duchamp, Robert Filliou, On Kawara or Gordon Matta-Clark, we would have considerable difficulty in discerning the slightest tendency in this direction; their vision of history was not 'progressist', but apprehended time in all its complex and multiple dimensions. With each of these four artists, any movement towards the past – symbolism with Duchamp, Oriental philosophy with Filliou and Kawara, archaeology with Matta-Clark – was superimposed upon another towards the future, making them precursors of our heterochronic time. As for Robert Smithson, whose visual meditations on the notion of entropy or the concept of 'ruin in reverse' still remain so influential among the new generation of artists, he appears to be the first truly postmodern artist in that he anticipates and directly confronts the question of modernity *in relation to energy sources*: his entire corpus forms the narrative of a classic 'oil crisis'.

Postmodernism is the philosophy of mourning, a long melancholic episode in our cultural life. History having lost its direction and ability to be read, nothing remained but to come face to face with an immobilized space-time in which, like reminiscences, arose mutilated fragments of the past: the 'museum's ruins', as Douglas Crimp labelled postmodernism in 1980.[8] This purely depressive attitude profoundly impregnated the first postmodern period, characterized as it was by the borrowing of identifiable forms of art history and the theme of the 'simulacrum', an image that substitutes itself for reality within reality itself. Grieving for a lost reality . . . Crimp defined the image as 'an object of desire, the desire for the signification that is known to be absent'.[9] Frederic Jameson, in his seminal essay on postmodernism, sees its dominant trait as schizophrenia, or, to be more exact, one of the most destructive effects of it – the loss of the mind's ability to perceive time as something ordered, an incapacity to organize experience as a collection of coherent and meaningful sequences, leading to the abandonment of the attempt in favour of a fascination with a kaleidoscopic present.[10] For Slavoj Žižek, depression proves to be 'a perfectly postmodern posture', for it 'allows us to survive in a globalized society while keeping faith with our lost "roots"'.[11] Finally, according to Freud, one of the symptoms of depression associated with mourning is a process that induces the patient to adopt certain characteristics of the deceased, to the point of identifying himself/ herself partially or totally with that person. This kind of depression and identity substitution, endemic to postmodernism, can be recognized in the variety of neo-avant-garde devices that have surfaced since the latter half of the 1990s: formal quotes from the vocabulary of geometrical abstraction, the adoption of politically radical concepts in critical texts, etc. The result has been to denude modernism of its meaning by transforming it into a form of nostalgic obsession.

Unable any longer to determine the direction of history, we have had to pronounce its end. The eternal reversions to modernist forms in the 1980s have been succeeded by the relativization of history itself through the medium of post-colonial thinking. This second postmodern period was less melancholy – but multiculturalist. It had its beginnings in the end of the Cold War. 1989 was the year not only of the collapse of the Berlin Wall but also of the exhibition that, for all the controversy it provoked, marked the symbolic inauguration of planetary art. Organized by Jean-Hubert Martin at the Centre Pompidou, Paris, it was entitled *Magicians of the Earth*. At this moment, history seemed to break free from a profound Ice Age imposed by the silent confrontation of the two political blocs. The grand modernist narrative was succeeded by that of globalization, which does not designate a cultural period properly speaking, but a geopolitical standardization and the synchronization of the historical clock. With the door thrown open to artistic traditions and cultures other than those foisted on the world by the West, post-colonial postmodernism followed along the trail blazed by the world economy, enabling a re-evaluation from the ground up of our visions of time and space: a 'horizontalization' of the planet on which we need to build today.

What better characterizes this period than the mythification of origins? The meaning of a work of art, for this second-stage postmodernism, depends essentially on the social background to its production. 'Where do you come from?' appears to be its most pressing question, and essentialism its critical paradigm. Identification with genre, ethnicity, a sexual orientation or a nation sets in motion a powerful machinery: multiculturalism, now a critical methodology, has virtually become a system of allotting meanings and assigning individuals their position in the hierarchy of social demands, reducing their whole being to their identity and stripping all their significance back to their origins. Thus postmodernism has moved on from the depression of the Cold War to a neurotic preoccupation with origins typical of the era of globalization. It is this thought-model that today finds itself in crisis, this multiculturalist version of cultural diversity that must be called into question, not in favour of a 'universalism' of principles or a new modernist esperanto, but within the framework of a new modern movement based on heterochrony, a common interpretation, and freedom to explore.

Modernism and heterochrony: From 'post' to 'alter'

Certain artists were hostile to the linear timeline of modernism based on a projection into the future. Such was the case with Marcel Duchamp, whose repertoire includes a vast catalogue of traditional craftwork, outdated or anachronistic (the croquet box of *Three Standard Stoppages* 1913–14, the door in *Etant donnés . . .* 1946–66, etc), thereby introducing a vision of contemporaneity very different from what was then in vogue. Reusing the tools of the past in order to confound the present, Duchamp went so far as to describe his masterpiece *The Bride Stripped Bare by Her Bachelors, Even* 1915–23 as a *retard en verre*: a 'delay in glass'. Duchamp's 'delay', more significant than it would seem, thus overleaps the opposition between futurist projection and nostalgic glances at the past, an opposition that structures our view of twentieth-century art. But there is more to modernity than a kind of futurism. It is significant that a number of today's artists operate in a space-time characterized by this 'delay', playing with the anachronistic, with multi-temporality or time-lag. We could say that the ageless drawings of Charles Avery, the paintings of Spartacus Chetwynd or Shezad Dawood, the iconographic materials of Olivia Plender, Peter Coffin, Matthew Darbyshire and Ruth Ewan, or Tacita Dean's and Joachim Koester's references to the origins of the cinema – like those of Navin Rawanchaikul to Bollywood posters – all deal in the aesthetics of heterochrony: their work displays none of the obvious signs of contemporaneity, save perhaps in the process of their constitution, in the assembling of their parts into meaningful networks. Here what is 'contemporary' is the structure of the work, its method of composition: the very fact that it brings together heterochronic elements – delay (analogous to 'pre-recorded') coexists with the *immediate* (or 'live') and with the anticipated, just as documentary coexists with fiction, not according to a principle of accumulation (postmodern baroquism), but with the aim of revealing our present, in which temporalities and levels of reality are intertwined.

Rails and networks: The 'viatorization' of forms

The predominant aesthetics of this concern with intemporality reside to all appearances in the massive usage of black and white, for instance in the 16mm silent films projected by Joachim Koester, the iconography of David Noonan, Tris Vonna-Michell or Charles Avery, the drawings of Olivia Plender, Tacita Dean's series *The Russian Ending*, or the entire universe of Lindsay Seers. Today, black and white labels images as belonging to the past and the world of archives – at the same time, however, guaranteeing the authenticity of their content, by the single fact that their technique pre-dates Photoshop. In the books of W.G. Sebald, the narrative is punctuated by similar photos, which, according to the author, are there to emphasize the truth of the story. With Sebald, then, narrative is not in conflict with image. But this is a different form of narrative from that employed by Wim Wenders, who sees images in the form of a line, in a fixed order, with a fixed chronology. The cinema, whose birth was contemporary with that of the locomotive, handles narrative spontaneously like 'a train passing in the night', to quote Francois Truffaut; that is to say, like narrative rails organizing the passage of images. What better metaphor for history as twentieth-century modernism perceived it than that of the train? Rosalind Krauss stated: 'Perspective is the visual correlative of causality: things arrange themselves one after the other according to rules'. If pictorial modernism has done away with the monocular, centrist (spatial) perspective, it has substituted for it 'a temporal perspective, i.e., history'.[12] There still remains the question, a far more difficult one, of whether the era of the worldwide web and global hypermobility is really giving rise to new ways of perceiving human space. The term 'postmodern' can be applied to art that is refractory to these two types of perspective: spatial and temporal. 'Altermodern', on the other hand, combines both; the space-time circumscribed by the oeuvre of the new generation of artists, from Koester to Chetwynd, via Avery or Dean, presents itself in the form of a Möbius loop. In their productions, perspective is simultaneously geographical (mobility, displacement and cultural nomadism as methods of composition) and historical (heterochrony as a spontaneous take on the world). Simon Starling or Darren Almond, for example, displace objects in space to illuminate their history; they could be said to 'viatorize' them (from Latin *viator*, 'traveller'). For them, historical memory, like the topography of the contemporary world, exists only in the form of a network. Signs are displaced, 'viatorized' in circuits, and the work of art presents itself in the form of this dynamic system.

But what is a network? A connected chain of distinct elements in time or space. Various materials can serve as a 'glue' to hold the component elements together, yet one of them today assumes a particular importance: storytelling. Among the artists who have contributed to the theoretical development of this concept, Philippe Parreno explains that 'Pre-production, production, post-production, these narrative instances depend upon each other. In the course of the chaining of these sequences, a narrative unfolds'.[13] Exhibiting a work composed as a network of signs – like a computer screen reacting to a sequence of hypertext links – allows us to bypass another form of contradiction that has become unproductive: that of form and narrative. Liam Gillick defines this new structure as a 'discursive framework' or a 'discursive model of practice'. This is not to be understood as an urge to replace form by the formulaic, for 'the discursive is what produces work but is also the produced work itself in the form of critical and impromptu exchanges'.[14] In the same way as Parreno, he envisages the production of a work of art as a form of sequencing, like the continuous passage of an image to a text, from a narrative to a sign. 'This discursive is a production cycle, rather than a fixed performative moment in time … It occupies the increasing gap between the trajectory of modernity (understood here as a flow of technologies and demographic development) and the somewhat melancholic imploded self-conscious trajectory of modernism'.[15]

A strategic universalism

If the postmodern critical process *par excellence* was the detailed explanation of signs by their origins, the vital thing today, starting from the standpoint of the extreme globalization of world culture, is to grasp afresh the emblematic gesture of modernity – the exodus. This may be defined as a wrenching separation from the traditions, customs, everything in fact that anchors an individual to a 'territory' and the habits of a culture petrified by fixed ways of doing and saying things. But what exactly is being transformed and carried off? To answer this question, we must re-examine the very notion of territory – cultural or otherwise – from the viewpoint of 'viatorization'.

For sociologist Marc Augé: 'Culture has never been a spontaneous product that any one territory could appropriate. This illusory definition resurfaces today because there no longer is any territory. It is one of the illusions maintained by globalization. Contemporary art acquiesces in this ambivalence, even when seeking to make it its subject'.[16] In a world every inch of which is under satellite surveillance, territory takes the form of a construction or a journey.

And so the artist, *homo viator*, turns nomad. They transform ideas and signs, transport them from one point to another. All modernity is vehicular, exchange-based, and translative in its essence; the variety apparently announcing its arrival today will become more extreme as it develops, for the first time in human history, on a planetary scale. And just as alterglobalization does not seek cumulative solutions to the steamrollering effect of economic globalization – rather a concatenation of singular responses within models of sustainable development – altermodern has no desire to substitute for postmodern relativism a new universalism, rather a networked 'archipelago' form of modernity. The movement is also taking shape under the urgent pressure to answer very basic questions: how do we live in this world that we are told is becoming 'global', but which seems to be buttressed on particular interests or tensed behind the barricades of fundamentalism – when not upholding icons of mass culture as role models? How to represent a power that is becoming ever more furtive as it slips into bed with economics? How, finally, to make art anything but a secondary type of merchandise in a system of values entirely oriented towards this 'general and abstract equivalent' that is money, and how can it bear witness against 'economic horror' without reducing itself to sheer militancy?

'When they created cities', argues J.M.G. Le Clézio, 'when they invented concrete, tar and glass, men invented a new jungle – but have yet to become its inhabitants. Maybe they will die out before recognizing it for what it is. The [Amazonian] Indians have thousands of years' experience of it, which is why their knowledge is so perfect. Their world is not different from ours, they simply live in it, while we are still in exile'.[17]

Notes

1   Wim Wenders, *La Logique des Images. Le Souffle de l'ange*, Paris 1995 p. 149.

2   Ibid.

3   Seth Price, 'Dispersion', 2001, on www.disputedhistory.com

4   'Fragmented Narratives', T. Vonna-Michell interviewed by Andrew Hunt, in *Untitled*, no. 45, Spring 2008, p. 27.

5   For a full description of the practice of chaining, in relation to the techniques of sampling and websurfing, see N. Bourriaud, *Postproduction*, New York 2002.

6   Peter Sloterdijk, 'La pensée sphérique', *BAM* No.2, Vies modes d'emploi, 2004, p. 192.

7   Bernard Stiegler, *Reénchanter le monde: le valeur-esprit contre le populisme industriel*, Paris 2006.

8   Douglas Crimp, with photographs by Louise Lawler, *On the Museum's Ruins*, Cambridge, Mass. 1993.

9   Ibid., p. 183.

10 Fredric Jameson. *Postmodernism, or the Cultural Logic of Late Capitalism*, Durham, NC 1991.

11 Slavoj Žižek, *Vous Avez Dit Totalitarisme?*, Paris 2004, p. 167.

12 Rosalind Krauss, 'A View of Modernism', in *Artforum*, Sept. 1972.

13 Philippe Parreno and Hans-Ulrich Obrist, *The Conversation-Pieces*, Cologne 2007.

14 Liam Gillick, 'Maybe it would be better if we worked in groups of three?', *Hermes Lecture*, Eindhoven 2008, p. 29.

15 Ibid., p. 30.

16 Marc Augé, *L'Art du décalage*, www.multitudes.samizdat.com, 5 June 2007.

17 Jean-Marie Gustave Le Clézio, *Haï*, Paris 1971, p. 36.

Digimodernism

Alan Kirby's idea of digimodernism began its life under a different name: 'pseudo-modernism'. (This coinage can be found in his essay 'The Death of Postmodernism and Beyond', in Part One of this book.) For Kirby, however, that term did not connote either the full extent or the precise nature of the shift away from the postmodern he had diagnosed. Deciding that 'pseudomodernity is finally a dimension of one aspect of digimodernism', he published a book in 2009, defining and exploring how a new digimodernist era had superseded postmodernity.

Like Robert Samuels's automodernism, digimodernism is a technologically inspired vision: it sees computers, mobile phones, and (so-called) interactive television as the vehicles driving the changes in the forms our culture and everyday lives take. These changes bear some superficial resemblances to the postmodern: for example, interactive media seem to embody such postmodernist ideas as Roland Barthes's 'writerly' text, with its transfer of agency from author to reader, or the non-linear, non-sequential nature of postmodern narrative – what, one might ask, is the internet if not a Borgesian labyrinth of forking paths, winding their unteleological ways through a Lyotardian diversity of petits récits*? Digital texts are by nature always coming into being, and are therefore open-ended, like the postmodern artwork as described by Lyotard. Furthermore, from the cameras in our phones to reality television, digimodernism shares postmodernism's preoccupation with the category of 'the real'.*

Kirby, however, does not share Samuels's ambivalence towards the new technological developments. Where Samuels flags up the sense of autonomy these new media bestow on their users as potentially positive, Kirby regards it as a tendentious step towards a solipsistic subjectivity he (problematically) compares to autism. Where some have regarded web-based platforms as forums for democracy and debate, Kirby sees instead the rise of a dumbed-down populism. Where postmodernism ironically juxtaposed the high with the low, digimodernism aggressively champions the low over the high – and it does so not ironically but sincerely, in the name of the (one time) postmodern value of anti-elitism.

Ultimately, then, the characteristics of digimodernism turn out to be significantly different from those of postmodernism, despite outward similarities that have obfuscated its distinctiveness as a new Jamesonian 'cultural dominant'. Digimodernism, as Kirby sees it, is the technologized face of a society given over to an unbridled consumerism – and in this respect, digimodernism resembles Lipovetsky's hypermodernism more closely than it does Samuels's automodernism.

It is certainly possible that Kirby's pessimistic criticisms of the digimodernist culture he describes may yet turn out to be premature, given the infancy of the technology he discusses. In the meantime, however, it remains a richly provocative analysis that offers, in a sense, an updated version of a basically McLuhanite position: the form *of the previous technology and culture (postmodernism's* bricolage, collaging, and sampling, *or its refusal of linearity, teleology, and sequence) has become the* content *of the new media technology, and will hold back the cultural expressions that use these new media until the potential for innovation in such media has been fully realized. Not till then will we be able adequately to judge the new digimodernist phase of our culture. Meanwhile, if 'the medium is the message', then is it surprising that digimodernist culture generates ephemeral, vapid, and throwaway texts, when the rapid pace of technological change guarantees that any attempt at using these media to make a lasting cultural contribution is doomed to built-in obsolescence? If this summary of Kirby's digimodernism is a valid one, then it is worth asking whether it is problematic that his diagnosis of a new 'cultural dominant' beyond the postmodern follows the same pattern of thought as Marshall McLuhan's work – a thinker firmly ensconced in the postmodern canon.*

The extract is from Alan Kirby, *Digimodernism: How New Technologies Dismantle the Postmodern and Reconfigure our Culture* (London: Continuum, 2009), pp. 1–3; pp. 50–54; pp. 58–72; pp. 139–50; pp. 223–4.

from Digimodernism: How New Technologies Dismantle the Postmodern and Reconfigure our Culture

Alan Kirby

Introduction

Now . . . bring me that horizon.
(Pirates of the Caribbean: The Curse of the Black Pearl, *2003*)[1]

Since its first appearance in the second half of the 1990s under the impetus of new technologies, digimodernism has decisively displaced postmodernism to establish itself as the twenty-first century's new cultural paradigm. It owes its emergence and preeminence to the computerization of text, which yields a new form of textuality characterized in its purest instances by onwardness, haphazardness, evanescence, and anonymous, social and multiple authorship. These in turn become the hallmarks of a group of texts in new and established modes that also manifest the digimodernist traits of infantilism, earnestness, endlessness, and apparent reality. Digimodernist texts are found across contemporary culture, ranging from 'reality TV' to Hollywood fantasy blockbusters, from Web 2.0 platforms to the most sophisticated videogames, and from certain kinds of radio show to crossover fiction. In its pure form the digimodernist text permits the reader or viewer to intervene textually, physically to make text, to add visible content or tangibly shape narrative development. Hence 'digimodernism', properly understood as a contraction of 'digital modernism', is a pun: it's where digital technology meets textuality and text is (re)formulated by the fingers and thumbs (the digits) clicking and keying and pressing in the positive act of partial or obscurely collective textual elaboration.

Of all the definitions of postmodernism, the form of digimodernism recalls the one given by Fredric Jameson. It too is 'a dominant cultural logic or hegemonic norm'; not a blanket description of all contemporary cultural production but 'the force field in which very different kinds of cultural impulses ... [including] "residual" and "emergent" forms of cultural production ... must make their way."[2] Like Jameson, I feel that if 'we do not achieve some general sense of a cultural dominant, then we fall back into a view of present history as sheer heterogeneity, random difference ... [The aim is] to project some conception of a new systematic cultural norm.'[3] Twenty years later, however, the horizon has changed; the dominant cultural force field and systematic norm is different: what was postmodernist is now digimodernist.

The relationships between digimodernism and postmodernism are various. First, digimodernism is the successor to postmodernism: emerging in the mid-late 1990s, it gradually eclipsed it as the dominant cultural, technological, social, and political expression of our times. Second, in its early years a burgeoning digimodernism coexisted with a weakened, retreating postmodernism; it's the era of the hybrid or borderline text (*The Blair Witch Project*, *The Office*, the *Harry Potter* novels). Third, it can be argued that many of the flaws of early digimodernism derive from its contamination by the worst features of a decomposing postmodernism; one of the tasks of a new digimodernist criticism will therefore be to cleanse its subject of its toxic inheritance. Fourth, digimodernism is a reaction against postmodernism: certain of its traits (earnestness, the apparently real) resemble a repudiation of typical postmodern characteristics. Fifth, historically adjacent and expressed in part through the same cultural forms, digimodernism appears socially and politically as the logical effect of postmodernism, suggesting a modulated continuity more than a rupture. These versions of the relationship between the two are not incompatible but reflect their highly complex, multiple identities.

On the whole I don't believe there is such a thing as 'digimodernity'. This book is not going to argue that we have entered into a totally new phase of history. My sense is that, whatever its current relevance in other fields, postmodernism's insistence on locating an absolute break in all human experience between the disappeared past and the stranded present has lost all plausibility. The last third of the twentieth century was marked by a discourse of endings, of the 'post-' prefix and the 'no longer' structure, an aftershock of 1960s' radicalism and a sort of intellectual millenarianism that seems to have had its day. Like Habermas, my feeling is that, ever more crisis ridden, modernity continued throughout this period as an 'unfinished project'. Although the imponderable evils of the 1930s and 40s could only trigger a breakdown of faith in inherited cultural and historical worldviews such as the Enlightenment, the nature and scale of this reaction were overstated by some writers. In so far as it exists, 'digimodernity' is, then, another stage within modernity, a shift from one phase of its history into another.

Certain other kinds of discourse are also not to be found here. I won't be looking at how digitization actually works technically; and I won't do more than touch on the industrial consequences, the (re)organization of TV channels, film studios, Web start-ups, and so on, which it's occasioned. I'm a cultural critic, and my interest here is in the new cultural climate thrown up by digitization. My focus is textual: what are these new movies, new TV programs, these videogames, and Web 2.0 applications like to read, watch, and use? What do they signify, and how? Digimodernism, as well as a break in textuality, brings a new textual form, content, and value, new kinds of cultural meaning, structure, and use, and they will be the object of this book.

Equally, while digimodernism has far-reaching philosophical implications with regard to such matters as selfhood, truth, meaning, representation, and time, they are not directly explored here. It's true that these arguments first saw the light of day in an article I wrote for *Philosophy Now* in 2006, but the cultural landscape was even then my primary interest.[4] In that article I called what I now label digimodernism 'pseudo-modernism', a name that on reflection seemed to overemphasize the importance of certain concomitant social shifts. The notion of pseudomodernity is finally a dimension of one aspect of digimodernism. The article was written largely in the spirit of intellectual provocation; uploaded to the Web, it drew a response that eventually persuaded me the subject deserved more detailed and scrupulous attention. I've tried to address here a hybrid audience, and for an important reason: on one side, it seemed hardly worth discussing such a near-universal issue without trying to reach out to the general reader; on the other, it seemed equally pointless to analyze such a complex, multifaceted, and shifting phenomenon without a level of scholarly precision. Whatever the result may be, this approach is justified, even necessitated, by the status and nature of the theme.

[...]

The digimodernist text

sea change: *(unexpected or notable) transformation*
watershed: *line of separation between waters flowing to different rivers or basins or seas . . . (fig.) turning-point*

(Concise Oxford Dictionary, *1982*)[5]

There are various ways of defining digimodernism. It is the impact on cultural forms of computerization (inventing some, altering others). It is a set of aesthetic characteristics consequent on that process and gaining a unique cast from their new context. It's a cultural shift, a communicative revolution, a social organization. The most immediate way, however, of describing digimodernism is this: it's a new form of textuality.

In this the passage from postmodernism to digimodernism bears no resemblance to the way that the former broke from its predecessor. Textually, *The Bloody Chamber* or *Pale Fire* differs from *The Waves* or *As I Lay Dying* only on the surface, as an evolution in the codes and conventions and the manner of their manipulation; in their depth they rely on the same textual functioning. The author creates and sequences a quantity of words; these solidify as 'the text'; the reader scrutinizes and interprets that inherited, set mass. The author precedes the material text, which may outlast him/her; the reader makes over their *sense* of what they receive but neither brings the words into being nor contributes to their ordering (I distinguish these two functions since 1960s' avant-gardism found ways [...] to give the reader some control over sequencing). Traditional texts were once thought to possess a hermeneutical 'secret', a fixed meaning placed there by the author which the reader was to locate and treasure; later, texts were seen as hermeneutical free-for-alls, their meanings multiple and scattered, which the reader chose to bring pell-mell into play. In either case the physical properties of the text remained solidified and inviolate: no matter how inventively you interpreted *Gravity's Rainbow* you didn't *materially* bring it into existence, and in this Pynchon's postmodern exemplum exactly resembled *Pride and Prejudice*.

The digimodernist text in its pure form is made up to a varying degree by the reader or viewer or textual consumer. This figure becomes authorial in this sense: s/he makes text where none existed before. It isn't that his/her reading is of a kind to suggest meanings; there is no metaphor here. In an act distinct from their act of reading or viewing, such a reader or viewer gives to the world textual content or shapes the development and progress of a text in visible form. This content is *tangible*; the act is physical. Hence, the name 'digital modernism' in which the former term conceals a pun: the centrality of digital technology; and the centrality of the digits, of the fingers and thumbs that key and press and click in the business of material textual elaboration.

Fairly pure examples of digimodernist texts would include: on TV, *Big Brother*, *Pop Idol*, *100 Greatest Britons*, *Test the Nation*, *Strictly Come Dancing*, and *Quiz Call*; the film *Timecode*; Web 2.0 forms like Wikipedia, blogs, chat rooms, and social networking sites; videogames such as *Mass Effect, Grand Theft Auto IV, BioShock, Final Fantasy XII,* and *Metal Gear Solid 4*; SMS messages; '6-0-6' and certain other kinds of radio phone-in; or the Beatles' album *Everest* [...]. Digimodernism is not limited to such texts or even to such a textuality; rather, it is more easily expressed as the rupture, driven by technological innovation, which permits such a form. They are not by virtue of their novelty 'great' texts; indeed, the quality of the digimodernist text is moot. The distinctiveness of their functioning interests us, not their ostensible content. Instead, it is in the functioning of such a textuality that the irreducible difference of the digimodernist becomes most palpable.

The digimodernist text displays a certain body of traits that it bequeaths to digimodernism as a whole. These will recur throughout the rest of the analysis. Such characteristics relate to the digimodernist textuality almost as a machine: considered as a system by which meaning is made, not as meaning. Postmodernist features denote either a textual content or a set of techniques, employed by an antecedent author, embedded in a materially fixed and enduring text, and traced or enjoyed by a willful reader/viewer. The traits of digimodernist textuality exist on a deeper level: they describe how the textual machine operates, how it is delimited and by whom, its extension in time and in space, and its ontological determinants. The surface level of what digimodernist texts 'mean' and how they mean it will be discussed later in the book. We can sketch the following dominant features:

Onwardness. The digimodernist text exists now, in its coming into being, as something growing and incomplete. The traditional text appears to almost everyone in its entirety, ended, materially made. The digimodernist text, by contrast, is up for grabs: it is rolling, and the reader is plunged in among it as something that is ongoing. For the reader of the traditional text its time is after its fabrication; the time of the digimodernist text seems to have a start but no end.

Haphazardness. In consequence, the future development of the text is undecided. What it will consist of further down the line is as yet unknown. This feels like freedom; it may also feel like futility. It can be seen as power; but, lacking responsibility, this is probably illusory. If onwardness describes the digimodernist text in time, haphazardness locates in it the permanent possibility that it might go off in multiple directions: the infinite parallel potential of its future textual contents.

Evanescence. The digimodernist text does not endure. It is technically very hard to capture and archive; it has no interest as a reproducible item. You might happily watch all the broadcast hours of *Fawlty Towers*; no one would want to see the whole of a *Big Brother* run again (retransmission has never been proposed), and in any event the impossibility of restaging the public votes renders the exact original show unreplicable.

Reformulation and intermediation of textual roles. Already evident, and explored at greater length in this chapter, is the digimodernist text's radical redefinition of textual functional titles: reader, author, viewer, producer, director, listener, presenter, writer. Intermediate forms become necessary in which an individual primarily the one acts to a degree like another. These shifts are multiple and not to be exaggerated: the reader who becomes authorial in a digimodernist text does not stand in relation to the latter as Flaubert did to *Madame Bovary*. These terms are then given new, hybridized meanings; and this development is not concluded.

Anonymous, multiple and social authorship. Of these reformulations what happens to authorship in the digimodernist text especially deserves attention. It becomes multiple, almost innumerable, and is scattered across obscure social pseudocommunities. If not actually anonymous it tends to a form of pseudonymity which amounts to a renunciation of the practice of naming (e.g., calling yourself 'veryniceguy' on a message board or in a chat room). This breaks with the traditional text's conception of authorship in terms tantamount to commercial 'branding', as a lonely and definite quantity; yet it does not achieve communality either.

The fluid-bounded text. The physical limits of the traditional text are easily establishable: my copy of *The Good Soldier* has 294 pages, *Citizen Kane* is 119 minutes long. Materially a traditional text – even in the form of a journalist's report, a school essay, a home movie – has clear limits; though scholars may discover new parts of a whole by restoring cut or lost material their doing so only reinforces the sense that the text's physical proportions are tangibly and correctly determinable (and ideally frozen). Embodying onwardness, haphazardness, and evanescence, the digimodernist text so lacks this quality that traditionalists may not recognize it as a text at all. Such a text may be endless or swamp any act of reception/consumption. And yet texts they are: they are systematic bodies of recorded meaning, which represent acts in time and space and produce coherently intelligible patterns of signification.

Electronic-digitality. In its pure form, the digimodernist text relies on its technological status: it's the textuality that derives from digitization; it's produced by fingers and thumbs and computerization. This is not to be insisted on excessively; however, this is why digimodernism dates back only to the second half of the 1990s. Digimodernism is not primarily a visual culture and it destroys the society of the spectacle: it is a manually oriented culture, although the actions of the hand are here interdependent on a flow of optical information unified through the auspices of the electronic.

Much more could be added here, but there is space for only two further clarifications. First, an ancestor of the digimodernist text is Espen J. Aarseth's notion of 'ergodic literature' in which, he argued as long ago as 1997, there is '*a work of physical construction* that the various concepts of "reading" do not account for … In ergodic literature, nontrivial effort is required to allow the reader to traverse the text'.[6] The description of pageturning, eye movement, and mental processing as 'trivial' is misleading, while the implication of textual delimitedness contained in 'traversal' has been outdated by technical-textual innovations. However, his account differs from mine most notably in its lack of a wider context. For I see the pure digimodernist text solely as the easily recognizable tip of a cultural iceberg, and not necessarily its most interesting element. These characteristics can be found diffusely across a range of texts that I would call digimodernist whose consumer cannot make them up; though digimodernism produces a new form of textuality it is not reduced to that, and many of its instances are not evanescent, haphazard, and so on. But the discussion had to start somewhere. Digimodernism can be globally expressed in seven words (the effects on cultural forms of digitization) and historically situated in eight (the cultural-dominant succeeding postmodernism prompted by new technologies). It can be captured, as I said, in a pun. Yet all in all it's a more complex development than this might suggest. Ergodic literature is then no more than the forerunner of a distinctive feature of digimodernism.

Second, this textuality has been described as 'participatory'. There's a political rhetoric to hand here, all about democracy, antielitism, the common man, and so on. Al Gore has celebrated Web 2.0 for offering such a mode of popular expression (debate, forums) and overcoming the top-down manipulation imposed by spectacular television.[7] But, as well as suggesting Gore hasn't watched TV since the 1980s (it has reinvented itself in the direction of Web 2.0), this way of thinking presupposes a cleaned-up, politically progressive but traditional text. 'Participation' assumes a clearly marked textual boundary (even if fuzzy a line is necessary to take part *in*), an equality of text-makers (you don't 'participate' by controlling), a communally visible and known group of intervenants, and a real-life situation (you can participate in theater but not in a novel). The participant too is condemned to action. Digimodernist textuality, as I hope I've made clear, goes beyond all this. The political consequences of digimodernism are more likely to be desocialization and pseudoautism than an upsurge in eighteenth-century notions of democratic practice.

[...]

The antilexicon of early digimodernism

One sign of the novelty of the digimodernist text is that none of the traditional words describing the relations of individuals with texts is appropriate to it. The inherited terminology of textual creation and reception (author, reader, text, listener, viewer, etc.) is awkward here, inadequate, misleading in this newly restructured universe. So new is it that even words recently developed to step into the breach (interactive, nonlinear, etc.) are unsatisfactory. Of course, in time this new kind of text will evolve its own seemingly inevitable lexicon, or perhaps existing words will take on new and enriched senses to bear the semantic load. Aiming to contribute nothing directly to this linguistic growth, I am going instead here to assess the wreckage of the current lexical state, thereby, I hope, helping to clear enough ground to open up the conceptual landscape a bit more to view. Like all dictionaries, what follows should really be read in any order: the reader is invited to jump nonsequentially around the entries, which inevitably overlap.

A is not exactly for Author

Central to postmodernism and to post-structuralism was their vigorous repudiation of the figure of the author. Roland Barthes in a famous essay published in 1968 declared that 'the birth of the reader must be at the cost of the death of the Author' and called for the latter's 'destruction' and 'removal' from the field of textual criticism.[8] Coupled with Michel Foucault's subsequent weak conception of the 'author-function', this stance became orthodoxy among post-structuralist critics.[9] Written selfconsciously 'in the age of Alain Robbe-Grillet and Roland Barthes', John Fowles's postmodern novel *The French Lieutenant's Woman* critiques and dismantles the myth of the Author-God, finally revealed as an 'unpleasant … distinctly mean and dubious' figure.[10] Postmodernist culture returns repeatedly to this debilitated or tarnished image of the author. Martin Amis's are obnoxious and louche: a priggish nerd with 'sadistic impulses' in *Money*, a murderer and murderee in *London Fields*, and twin pretentious morons in *The Information*: 'Like all writers, Richard wanted to live in some hut on some crag somewhere, every couple of years folding a page into a bottle and dropping it limply into the spume. Like all writers, Richard wanted, and expected, the reverence due, say, to the Warrior Christ an hour before Armageddon'.[11] As a symptom of this degeneration, almost all of the major fictions by one of the greatest of all postmodern authors, Philip K. Dick, are only, and read like, first drafts: messy, clunky, wildly uneven, desperate for polishing. Redeemed by their content, these texts' achievement implicitly junks the Romantic conception of the author as a transcendent donor of eternal beauty in favor of the haphazardly brilliant hack.

Digimodernism, however, silently restores the authorial, and revalorizes it. To do this, it abolishes the assumed singularity of authorship in a redefinition that moves decisively away from both traditional post-Enlightenment conceptions and their repudiation. Authorship is always plural here, perhaps innumerable, although it should normally be possible, if anyone wanted to, to count up how many there are. The digimodernist authorial is multiple, but not communal or collective as it may have been in premodern cultures; instead, it is rigorously hierarchical. We would need to talk, in specific cases, of layers of authorship running across the digimodernist text, and distributions of functions: from an originative level that sets parameters, invents terms, places markers, and proffers structural content, to later, lower levels that produce the text they are also consuming by determining and inventing narrative and textual content where none existed before. The differing forms of this authorship relate to this text at differing times and places and with varying degrees of decisiveness; yet all bring the text into being, all are kinds of author. Though a group or social or plural activity, the potential 'community' of digimodernist authorship (widely announced) is in practice vitiated by the anonymity of the function here. We don't even get Foucault's author as social sign: the digimodernist author is mostly unknown or meaningless or encrypted. Who writes Wikipedia? Who votes on *Big Brother*? Who exactly makes a videogame? Extended across unknown distances, and scattered among numerous zones and layers of fluctuating determinacy, digimodernist authorship seems ubiquitous, dynamic, ferocious, acute, and simultaneously nowhere, secret, undisclosed, irrelevant. Today, authorship is the site of a swarming, restless creativity and energy; the figure of the disreputably lonely or mocked or dethroned author of postmodernism and post-structuralism is obsolete.

If I is for Interactive, there's a love-hate relationship with 'inter'

The spread of the personal computer in the 1980s brought with it a new associated vocabulary, some of which, like 'interfacing' or going 'online', has been absorbed permanently into the language. If the emergence of the digimodernist text has had a comparable effect you might point to the discourse of 'interactivity' as an example. Videogames, reality TV, YouTube, and the rest of Web 2.0 are all supposed to offer an 'interactive' textual experience by virtue of the fact that the individual is given and may carry out manual or digital actions while engaging with them. I talk about the difficulties of the passive/active binary elsewhere, so will restrict myself here to the term's prefix, one that has, indeed, spread across the whole digital sphere.

The notion of '*inter*action' seems inevitable and exciting partly because it evokes the relationship (or interplay or interface) of text and individual as a dialectical, back-and-forth exchange. This very reciprocity can be seen, to an extent, as the kernel of digimodernism; the new prevalence of the 'interactive' nexus and of the prefix in general is a sign of the emergence of a new textual paradigm. Older terms like 'reader' or 'writer', 'listener' or 'broadcaster' don't convey that doubled give-and-take, its contraflow; they focus on one individual's role within an inert textual theater. The word 'interactive' then is as textually new as the digimodernism with which it is identical because it reflects the new textual dimension that has suddenly opened up: not only do you 'consume' this text, but the text acts or plays back at you in response, and you consequently act or play more, and it returns to you again in reaction. This textual experience resembles a seesawing duality, or a meshing and turning of cogs. Moving beyond the isolation of earlier words, 'interactivity' places the individual within a diachronic rapport, a growing, developing relationship based on one side's pleasure alone.

I like 'inter' both because it captures the historical rupture with the textual past in its new ubiquity, and because it highlights the structuration of digimodernism, its flow of exchanges in time. It's highly misleading, though, as well, because it suggests an equality in these exchanges. In truth, just as the authors of the digimodernist text vary in their levels of input or decisiveness, so the individual is never the equal of the text with which s/he is engaging. The individual can, for instance, abandon the text but not vice versa; conversely, the text is set up, inflected, regulated, limited and – to a large extent – simply invented well before s/he gets near it. Engaging with a digimodernist text, s/he is allowed to be active only in very constrained and predetermined ways. In short, the creativity of this individual arrives rather late in this textual universe.

A better understanding of digimodernist authorship would clarify the nature of interactivity too, which often seems reduced to a sort of 'manuality', a hand-based responsiveness within a textuality whose form and content were long ago set. Your 'digital' interventions occur here when, where, and how they are permitted to. But I won't let go of the glimpse of the new textual machinery that is conveyed by and contained within 'inter'.

L is sort of for Listener

Two versions of listening are familiar to us: the first, when we know we are expected to respond (in a private conversation, in a seminar, meeting, etc.); the second, when we know we will not respond (listening to music or a politician addressing a rally, etc.). The social conventions governing this distinction are fairly rigorously applied: they make heckling, the act of responding when not supposed to, inherently rebellious, for instance. Listening has then a double relationship with speech or other human sound creation, like music: it can only be done, obviously, when there is something to listen *to*; and it differs qualitatively according to whether the listener knows s/he is expected to respond. In one case, we can probably assume that s/he listens more closely, does nothing else at the same time; in the other s/he may start and stop listening at will, talk over the discourse, and so on. Varying contexts produce varying intensities of listening, though it remains always a conscious, directed act (distinct from the inadvertency or passivity of hearing). The corollary of this is that the grammar of what we listen to also embeds these social conventions. When we are expected to respond, the discourse offered will tend to the second person ('you'), either explicitly (e.g., questions, orders) or implicitly (e.g., a story that provokes the response 'something similar happened to me'). When not expected to respond we will probably listen to first-person plural modes ('we', the implicit pronoun of the stand-up comic) or third person ('s/he', 'they'), although politicians and others will sometimes employ rhetorically the second person to create an actually bogus sense of intimacy ('Ask not what your country . . .').

Radio, traditionally, offers sound to which we know we will not respond: third person, easily capable of being talked over or ignored or sung along to or switched off in mid-flow. DJs, like politicians, try to create warmth by generating the illusion that they are speaking to *you* (this is the whole art of the DJ) but without using literally a second-person discourse – their mode is also the comic's implicit 'we'. Digimodernist radio, in which 'listeners' contribute their texts, e-mails, and phone voices to the content of the show, gives us a different kind of listening, pitched halfway between the two familiar versions. We are neither expected to respond or unable to, but suspended between as *someone who could respond*, who *might* respond. We could, as easily as anybody else, send in a text or e-mail or call up the phone-in line and speak. And perhaps we do: some people will become regular callers to such programs or repeat contributors of written material, and their voices and writing take on in time the assured, measured delivery of the seasoned professional. In so doing, they achieve the conversational parity of the responding listener. It's noticeable that such programs permit their external contributors to make only very brief and concise points. This is usually explained by 'we've got a lot of callers' but in some instances, especially on sports phone-ins like those following an England soccer match, many of the callers make roughly the same point – they're not curtailed to allow space for a vast wealth of varying opinions. E-mails and texts are short too even though they tend to be better expressed and less predictable than the improvised speech of the presenter. This could again be due to the psychological effect being sought: the more people who contribute, the more it could be you contributing, both in terms of the show's mood and identity, and as a brute numerical fact.

Similarly, the discourse thrown up by digimodernist radio lies curiously stranded between the modes typical of the two traditional versions of listening. It consists, on one level, of the first-and-second person of ordinary conversation: I think this, why do you, and so on. Yet it cannot in fact be *about* either of them, partly because the external contributor, in digimodernist fashion, is virtually anonymous – to be 'Dave from Manchester' is to teeter on the brink of being anyone at all. So the content of the show becomes an intimate exchange about public matters, which is why it resembles stereotypical male conversation, like bar or pub talk (and the majority of contributors are always men). Accounts of personal experience are tolerated here, but only to clarify a general point. Unlike bar talk, this discourse has no chance of becoming oriented on private matters since, though intimately formulated, it belongs to a broadcast public discussion. The effect, finally, is that the exchanges feel neither really intimate (a faked I-you-I) nor generally interesting (they make no new intellectual discoveries but just stir around the quasi-knowledge and received wisdom of the presenter and their callers). It's an attractive model of spoken discourse because, synthesizing the traits of both common forms, it promises an unusual richness and potency. But it actually provides neither desired outcome of listening, neither personalization and intimacy, nor clarification and action. Listening to digimodernist radio does tend to be listening, but never the sorts we used to know.

N isn't yet for Nonlinear (a mess that needs clearing first)

Nonlinear: such a contemporary term! We are always hearing that new technologies prompt new, nonlinear experiences of texts, though this is a highly confused terminology. It's popular because it suggests freedom: to follow doggedly and obediently a 'line' is more oppressive than to scatter whimsically away from it (compare use of 'the beaten track', which everybody boasts of getting 'off' and nobody wishes to be seen 'on'). If linearity means to construct the textual experience as running necessarily from its beginning through its middle to its end, then some digimodernist forms are in fact ultralinear. Videogames, for instance, pass through these stages; although you can freeze your position within them for the next time, you will nevertheless simply resume your linear progression when you return. You can't do a bit near the end of the game, then a bit near the beginning; you follow a line. The innovation of videogames, it seems to me, is that they are multilinear: you follow, each time, a slightly *different* line, and these various strands lie virtually side by side as ghostly or actual lines taken. To a degree this is true of any game (it's certainly true of chess), but in videogames it's textually true: there are characters, plotlines, tasks, and so on, opened up along one line that are denied another. The multilinearity of videogames is precisely what differentiates them from other textual forms. A duller version of digimodernist ultralinearity is the DVD. If you had wanted, in the age of video, to show a class the similarities between the hat-passing scene in Beckett's *Waiting for Godot* and the lemonade stall sequence in the Marx Brothers' *Duck Soup*, you could have cued your two tapes just before the bits in question, then slid them into the seminar room VCR at the appropriate time. Try to do this with DVDs and you spend five minutes per film trudging through studio logos, copyright warnings (ironically), adverts and the rest of the rigmarole, because DVDs enforce a beginning-middle-end textual experience. Again, though, they are multilinear: whereas a video offers only one version of the movie, a DVD offers twenty, with different audio and/or subtitle settings, with the director's or a critic's commentary overlaid, and more. They sit side by side on the DVD, mostly ignored by the viewer; ultralinearity here is multilinearity.

What is often called nonlinearity is actually nonchronology, the jumping around in time of stories such as *Eyeless in Gaza*, *Pulp Fiction*, *Memento*, or *Waterland*. They are still, though, linear textual experiences. Reading and viewing are necessarily linear – you might skip, but you wouldn't jumble the chapters or sequences – whereas rereading and re-viewing will often focus on fragments, episodes, scenes; I've only read *Ulysses* from start to finish once, but I've read the 'Cyclops' section five times at least. To return to a text is to permit a nonlinear experience. Yet in practice this is only the replacement of a totalized linearity with a restricted one: I still tend to read the 'Cyclops' pages in order or, if I jump around, I read the lines in order – the linearity is ever more straitened, but indestructible.

As for new digimodernist forms, like the Internet, the terms that seem to me most apposite are antisequentiality and ultraconsecutiveness. By sequence I mean a progression in which each new term is logically produced by its predecessor or a combination of its predecessors (compare the Fibonacci sequence); by consecutiveness I mean a progression in which the new term is simply adjacent, in time or space, to the previous one without there necessarily being an overall systematic development. Clicking your way around the Internet or one of its sites, each shift of page takes you, inevitably, to one that is cyberspatially adjacent, even if that adjacency is found via the intermediation of a search engine. Moving from one page to the next contains its own logic, but a series of ten or twenty moves will produce a history with no overall logical arc; it's not random but it's not governed by a totalizing pathway either. The fact that it has no beginning, middle, and end (its mooted nonlinearity) is not very interesting for me, partly because, like rereading *Ulysses*, they are reproduced at more local, straitened levels, and partly because it's more useful to define it as a presence, an activity, than as a lack. Internet sweeps (what used to be called surfing) seem to me *necessarily* consecutive, condemned to the tyranny of the adjacent at the expense of the overall. They therefore bear two hallmarks: they are one-offs, virtually impossible to repeat, and, the corollary, they are intrinsically amnesiac – the brain cannot reconstruct them in the absence of a logical, overarching shape, so finds it difficult to remember them. Such sweeps tend to be antisequential, but not absolutely: each term may derive logically from the last, but a more complex, developed sequence becomes increasingly hard to discern. This is a complex field, where terminological precision is so far somewhat elusive, but stopping the habit of mindlessly boasting of nonlinearity would help.

P isn't for Passive (and Active is in trouble, too)

One of the most misleading claims the digimodernist text and its proselytizers can make is that it provides an *active* textual experience: that the individual playing a videogame or texting or typing Web 2.0 content is active in a way that someone engaged in reading *Ulysses* or watching *Citizen Kane* isn't. This is self-evidently something in its favor; no one wants to be 'passive'. It's typical of digimodernism that its enthusiasts make vigorous and inaccurate propaganda on its behalf; the vocabulary of 'surfing' the Internet common in the 1990s, where a marine imagery of euphoria, risk, and subtlety was employed to promote an often snail-paced, banal, and fruitless activity, seems mercifully behind us. But the hype differentiating the new technologies' supposedly terrific activeness from the old forms' dull passivity is still extant, and very misleading it is too.

It's true that the purer kinds of digimodernist text require a positive physical act or the possibility of one, and the traditional text doesn't. Yet this can't in itself justify use of the passive/active binary: you can't suppose that an astrophysicist sitting in an armchair mentally wrestling with string theory is 'more passive' than somebody doing the dishes just because the latter's hands are moving. Mere thought can be powerful, individual, and far-reaching, while physical action can become automatic, blank, almost inhuman; in terms of workplace organization, a college professor will be more active (i.e., self-directing) than a factory worker. The presence of a physical 'act' seems in turn to suggest the word 'active' and then its pejorative antonym 'passive', but this is an increasingly tenuous chain of reasoning. It's one of those cases beloved of Wittgenstein where people are hexed by language. Yet the mistake is symptomatic: how do you describe experientially the difference between the traditional and the digimodernist text? It's a tricky question, but one that at least assumes that there are such differences, which here is the beginning of wisdom.

P is also for a doubly different idea of Publishing

A friend of mine (though he's hardly unique) thinks that Web 2.0 offers the biggest revolution in publishing since the Gutenberg Bible. Anyone can now publish anything; it's democratic, open, nonelitist, a breaking down of the oppressive doors of the publishing cabal which for centuries repressed thought and decided what we could read; it's a seizing of the controls of the publishing world by the people for the people. If this were true, it would indeed be as exciting as my friend thinks. Sociologically, publishing has always defined itself as the sacrilizing of speech: whereas speech dies the instant it is spoken, and carries only to the geographical extent reached by the volume of the voice, the publishing of text enables utterances to endure for centuries, even millennia (though increasingly unstably), and to be transported to the furthest point on our planet, even beyond. Temporally and spatially published text is, at least potentially, speech equipped with wondrous powers, furnished with immense resources. It isn't surprising that such text has accrued a similarly wondrous and immense social prestige (even if, in practice, the great majority of it is soon destroyed). We all talk, but few of us talk to everyone forever. Publishing a book is the educated adult's version of scoring the touchdown that wins the Super Bowl. It's this glamour, this prestige that my friend assumes Web 2.0 lets everyone in on, and that he's gotten so excited about.

Leaving to one side for now the issue of whether everyone can or ever will access Web 2.0, let us imagine a world in which they do. The Web is indeed responsible for a stupendous increase in the volume of published material and in the number of published writers. Though held in electronic form rather than on paper, this text fulfills the definition of publication: it is recorded, in principle, for everyone forever. This is the first new idea of publishing. However, and more problematically, this innovation comes at the expense of a second: the loss of the social prestige associated with the publishing of text. It isn't only that so much UGC is mindless, thuggish, and illiterate, though it is. More awkwardly, nothing remains prestigious when everybody can have it; the process is self-defeating. In such circumstances the notion of a sacrilizing of speech becomes obsolete. To argue that the newly opened world of publishing is a newly devalued world seems patrician, antidemocratic, even (so help us God) 'elitist'. Furthermore, it's not strictly valid. Through, for instance, the placing of academic journals online, the Internet has also increased the quantity of easily accessible, highly intelligent, and well-informed written matter, and it sits cheek-by-jowl with the vile and ignorant stuff on search engine results pages. What will probably occur in the future will be a shift in our idea of publishing toward greater stratification and hierarchy, internally divided into higher and lower forms. The quantity of publication will continue to rise to unimaginable heights, but unendowed now with social prestige. How long it will take for the sacred aura of published text to go is anybody's guess, but the likelihood is that there will be nothing 'nonelitist' about it; differentiation will simply re-form elsewhere according to other criteria. This may be a meritocratic hierarchy, whereby text is judged for what it says rather than what it is, but I wouldn't want to bank on it.

R is, amazingly, for Reading (but don't rejoice yet)

Authors of best-selling jeremiads about contemporary society frequently bemoan a widespread decline in reading. Young people today don't know about books, don't understand them, don't enjoy them; in short, they don't read. Christopher Lasch, decrying in 1979 the 'new illiteracy' and the 'spread of stupidity', quoted the dean of the University of Oregon complaining that the new generation "'don't read as much'".[12] For Lasch himself, 'students at all levels of the educational system have so little knowledge of the classics of world literature', resulting in a 'reduced ability to read'.[13] Eight years later Allan Bloom remarked that 'our students have lost the practice of and the taste for reading. They have not learned how to read, nor do they have the expectation of delight or improvement from reading'.[14]

Such comments – repeated so regularly by commentators they have become orthodoxy – assume the prestige of publication: 'reading' will be of 'books' which will often be 'good', or at least complex and mindstretching. A quantitative decline in reading (fewer words passing intelligently before a student's eyes) can therefore be safely conflated with a qualitative decline (fewer students reading Shakespeare, Tolstoy, Plato). But the digimodernist redefinition of publishing goes hand in hand with a recasting of the sociocultural status of reading. In short, digimodernism – through the Internet – triggers a skyrocketing rise in quantitative reading as individuals spend hours interpreting written material on a screen; but it also reinforces a plunging decline in qualitative reading as they become ever less capable of engaging mentally with complex and sophisticated thought expressed in written form.

You do wonder what Lasch or Bloom would have made of the sight of a campus computer suite packed with engrossed students avidly reading thousands upon thousands of words. Yet although the Internet has brought about a vast sudden expansion in the activity of reading among young people, it has done so at the cost of heavily favoring one kind: scanning, sweeping across printed matter looking for something of interest. If literary research is like marriage (a mind entwined with the tastes, whims, and thoughts of another for years) and ordinary reading is like dating (a mind entwined with another for a limited, pleasure-governed but intimate time), then Internet reading often resembles gazing from a second-floor window at the passersby on the street below. It's dispassionate and uninvolved, and implicitly embraces a sense of frustration, an incapacity to engage. At times it's more like the intellectual antechamber of reading, a kind of disinterested basis to the act of reading, than the act itself. Internet reading is not, though, just scanning: it accelerates and slows as interest flickers and dies, shifts sideways to follow links, loses its thread, picks up another. What is genuinely new about Internet reading is the layout of the page, which encourages the eye to move in all two-dimensional directions at any time rather than the systematic left to right and gradually down of a book.[15] The screen page is subdivided by sections and boxes to be jumped around in place of the book page's immutable text and four margins. This, along with the use of hyperlinks, makes Internet reading characteristically discontinuous both visually and intellectually. It's interrupted, redefined, displaced, recommenced, abandoned, fragmentary. It's still unclear how the revolutionary layout of the Internet page will affect reading in its broadest sense, but there doesn't seem much good news here for advocates of training in sustained, coherent, consecutive thought. In the meantime it's noticeable that many student textbooks and TV stations have adopted the subdivided layout (oddly, when you can't actually click on anything).

The view that would probably be found among most people who had seen message-board comment on something they had published online would be that Internet reading is just bad: quick, slapdash, partial. Much comment is so virulent in tone it suggests a reader seething with a barely suppressed impatience to leap into print. As academics know, reading-to-write (e.g., book reviewing) is very different from just reading, and while alert subeditors will channel critics into some semblance of fair judgment, message boards impose no such intellectual quality control. But bad reading is as old as reading itself: *Lolita*, *Lucky Jim*, and Ian Fleming's James Bond novels are only the first examples that come to my mind of preelectronic texts widely misunderstood by their readers. This impatience and virulence are surely linked to the frustration inherent in reading-as-scanning. It presumably has a second cause as well, one that will affect the success or otherwise of the e-book should it finally ever be commercialized (it's been promised half my life). If Internet reading is on the whole qualitatively poor, as I think it is – it's often blank, fragmented, forgetful, or congenitally disaffected – then this can be explained by the unconscious intellectual unpleasantness of trying to make sense of something while having light beamed into your eyes. The glow of the screen pushes reading toward the rushed, the decentered, the irritable; while the eye is automatically drawn to the light it emits (explaining the quantitative surge), the mind is increasingly too distracted to engage with, remember, or even enjoy very much what it is given to scrutinize.

T definitely is for Text (but not that one)

Pace Barthes, digimodernism's emblematic text is very different than post-structuralism's key term. Derrida and Lacan were fascinated by the letter and the postcard; technological innovation produces a newer form. The text message, several billion of which are digitally created and sent every day, is by some criteria the most important 'textual' mode or recorded communication medium of our time. It's ubiquitous, near-permanent, a hushed element of the fabric of the environment; on the street, in cafés, bars, and restaurants, in meetings and lecture halls and stadia, on trains and in cars, in homes, shops, and parks, thumbs are silently darting over displays and eyes reading off what's been received: an almost-silent tidal wave of digital text crashing upon us every minute of our waking lives.

Manually formed, the text message concentrates, in a happy semantic coincidence, most of the characteristics of the digimodernist text. Constantly being made and sent, it exists culturally in the act of creation more than in finished form; though you see people texting all the time, the message inheres only in its formation and immediate impact (like a child's cry). Almost the whole lifespan of the text is comprised by its elaboration. It is ephemeral and evanescent, even harder to hold on to than the e-mail; biographers who depend professionally on stable, enduring private messages written and received by their subject look on the SMS and despair. It's almost anonymous: if the letter has no author (Foucault), it at least has a signatory, regularly elided by texts. Indeed, it's the lowest form of recorded communication ever known: if speech tends to be less rich, subtle, sophisticated, and elegant than writing, then the text places itself as far below speech again on the scale of linguistic resourcefulness. It's a virtually illiterate jumble of garbled characters, heavy on sledgehammer commands and brusque interrogatives, favoring simple, direct main clauses expressive mostly of sudden moods and needs, incapable of sustained description or nuanced opinion or any higher expression. Restricted mostly to the level of pure emotion (greetings, wishes, laments, etc.) and to the modes of declaration and interrogation, it reduces human interaction to the kinds available to a three-year-old child. Out go subclauses, irony, paragraphs, punctuation, suspense, all linguistic effects and devices; this is a utilitarian, mechanical verbal form.

The text is, of course, a very useful communicative tool, so useful there is no good reason to go without it. The danger lies in the effect it may exert, if used to excess, on all other forms of communication. Teachers who spot their teenage charges texting under their classroom desks have noted the use of similar verbal styles in their formal school work (e.g., writing 'cus' for 'because'). They may also identify in them a parallel tendency to a speech that is equally abbreviated, rushed, and fragmentary, reduced to simplistic and jumbled bursts of emotion or need. The comedy characters Vicky Pollard and Lauren Cooper, so successful recently in Britain as emblems of a certain kind of contemporary adolescent, speak with the expressive poverty and the breakneck fluency of the text message. The SMS is to discourse what fries are to nutrition: all depends on the wider communicative context.

T isn't for Typist, but it's very much for typing

Truman Capote famously and sourly remarked of Jack Kerouac's work: 'that's not writing, it's typing'. By this he meant that 'writing' was a creative and intelligent action, whereas 'typing' was mechanical, mindless, and reactive. In the world of work, this bifurcation was reflected in his day by the employment of women as 'typists' whose task was to uncomprehendingly and automatically convert the creative, intelligent outpourings of their male superiors. Challenged by feminism and by industrial restructuring, this hierarchy was finally demolished by the spread of the word processor in the 1980s. In the digimodernist age, everyone types all the time (to be a 'typist' is increasingly just to have a job). In this dispensation, typing is no longer the secondary and inferior adjunct to writing, but the sole method of recording discourse. There is no other term (more and more Capote's sarcasm will become unintelligible). What digimodernism therefore looks forward to is a world without writing, that is, one where nobody manipulates a pen or pencil to record discourse; it suggests a time when children will never learn how to write and be taught, instead, from infancy how to type. There is something scary about a society where no one writes, where no one knows how to hold and wield some sort of pen, since writing has always been the symbol of and identical with civilization, knowledge, memory, learning, thought itself. The idea, assumed by Capote, that writing's absence is somehow dehumanized, haunts us; not to teach a child how to write feels like consigning him or her to an almost bestial state. And yet there is no reason today to imagine that we are not heading toward such a world. Already the e-mail and SMS have largely superseded the phone call, which itself saw off the letter; we have passed from writing through speaking to typing, and while the newer form can coexist with its downgraded forerunner, something must logically at some stage become obsolete. Negotiating that may be a key challenge of our century. For now, we early digimodernists are stranded: we can write but have less and less need to, and we type but have never been trained to. It's a part of the characteristic helplessness of our age.

U is hardly for User (or up to a point)

The term 'user' is commonly found in expressions such as 'user-generated content' to describe someone who writes Wikipedia text or uploads YouTube clips or develops their Facebook page or maintains a blog. It has also been employed in TV, especially through the intriguing new portmanteau word 'viewser'. Yet it brings its own set of linguistic problems. The idea of 'use' suggests a means to an end (a spanner used to tighten a nut, an egg-whisk used to whisk an egg) whereby a tool plays an instrumental role in achieving a logically distinct objective. Here, however, it is difficult to identify such an objective since the acts in question appear to be their own end ('communication' is too vague an ambition, and incompatible with the anonymity of the Web). Equally, there's no identifiable tool involved: contrary to the egg-whisk or spanner, which were invented to answer an existing need, the computer predates and exceeds any of the applications of Web 2.0. Furthermore, 'usage' would seem grammatically to refer more to reading or watching material than creating it (compare 'drug-user', where the consumer and not the producer is denoted), rendering UGC a contradiction in terms.

Despite its final inadequacies, it's easy to see the initial attractiveness of the word. For one, it conveys the crucial digimodernist quality of a physical act, and it gives to this act the vital connotation of working a machine. True, it's misleading in that it distances us from the elaboration or manufacture of text or textual content, for which terms drawn from publishing (author, reader, etc.) have already been tried and found wanting. Filming your friends and putting the result on YouTube is so much more like writing a short story than it is like using a trouser-press that the rejection of a publishing jargon for a mechanistic one is unhelpful. Nonetheless, the word 'user' does succeed in taking the necessary step beyond the overspecificity of 'reader', 'filmmaker', 'writer' toward the polyvalent and shifting textual intervenant of digimodernism. This figure slides typically between maker and consumer, reader and writer, in a seamless complex singularity; and even in its vagueness 'use' does suggest both engagement with a technology and the inescapable multiplicity, the openness of that act.

V is no longer for Viewer (you might think)

Given all of this, can someone sitting on a couch in front of a digimodernist TV program really be called a 'viewer' any more? The term struggled initially into existence, finally being deliberately selected from an assortment of words indicating sight; it lacks naturalness, or once did, and while a change of terms several decades into a medium's existence seems unlikely, it already jars the ear in certain contexts with its incongruity. Some have suggested the portmanteau word 'viewser' to describe an engagement with TV that is both optical and manual, as in the combined act of watching and voting in *Big Brother* or otherwise actively participating in the editing and production of a show while gazing at it from outside. A clever pun, the term nevertheless inherits all the problems faced by 'user' – it's like correcting a car's faulty steering by removing a wheel. It should also be borne in mind that the viewer is far from obsolete, in two senses: first, many TV shows, like soaps and sitcoms, invite no manual action and imply a reception that can be defined optically; and second, even in the case of the digimodernist program the manual action relies on a prior optical experience – you only vote meaningfully on *Big Brother* after watching it, while many of its viewers won't vote at all. Viewing hasn't become *vieux jeu*: it's the essential condition of 'use', and not vice versa; more precisely, digimodernism builds beyond it.

However, there is no word at all (yet) for the individual who watches and votes, votes and watches in a spiraling weave of optical/manual actions. Digimodernist TV invents, then, an (extra)textual person for whom we do not have a name since their actions and standing are so new. And the attraction of the term 'viewser' is that it can be transferred to any Internet site privileging UGC: on YouTube or Wikipedia or message boards, an optical act (reading, watching) intertwines with a potential or real act of creating text. What do you call such a person? A reader, yes, a writer too, or some new term beyond both?

[...]

The rise of the apparently real

The apparently real, one of digimodernism's recurrent aesthetic traits, is so diametrically opposed to the 'real' of postmodernism that at first glance it can be mistaken for a simple and violent reaction against it. Postmodernism's real is a subtle, sophisticated quantity; that of digimodernism is so straightforward it almost defies description. The former is found especially in a small number of advanced texts; the latter is ubiquitous, a consensus, populist, compensating for any philosophical infirmity with a cultural-historical dominance that sweeps all before it. And yet there are also signs that the apparently real is beginning to develop its own forms of complexity.

For postmodernism, there is no given reality 'out there'. According to Baudrillard: '[t]he great event of this period, the great trauma, is this decline of strong referentials, these *death pangs of the real* and of the rational that open onto an age of simulation'.[16] The real is, at best, a social construct, a convention agreed in a certain way in a certain culture at a certain time, varying historically with no version able to claim a privileged status. Invented, the real is a fiction, inflected by preceding fictions; if the real is something we make up, it has also been made up by others before us. In Cindy Sherman's celebrated series of photographs *Untitled Film Stills* (1977–80), a solitary woman appears in a variety of urban settings in what seem to be images from 1950s–60s' movies: this one surely is from Hitchcock, that one must be Godard, doubtless this other something by Antonioni. But which movies? You can't quite remember ... Of course, this woman, variously dressed, wigged, and made up, immersed in her narratives of anxiety and ennui, alienation and off-screen perversity, is always Sherman herself; the photos can be seen as self-portraits of unreal selves. The films don't exist; the 'real' here is a movie, and not even a 'real movie' at that. The photos are fictions, or, rather, they are fictive fictions, invented fragments of what would be, if they existed, inventions. The plates of the real shift; '[t]here are so many levels of artifice' here as Sherman herself says, and what is finally represented is the act itself of representing a woman, or a woman's historicized act of self-presentation, in an ontological hall of mirrors redeemed by Sherman's wit, her subtlety, and exhilarating feminism.[17]

As a result, to believe in a reality 'out there' becomes a form of paranoia, the unwarranted ascription of meanings to a universe that cannot bear their load. Oliver Stone's film about the Kennedy assassination *JFK* (1991) mixes historical footage with fictional material shot thirty years later to propose a welter of conspiracy theories explaining what 'really' happened in November 1963. If the textual real is a mishmash of manufactured film sources, all equal, the functioning of the 'real world' is inevitably going to wind up seeming overdetermined and paranoid. Pynchon's *The Crying of Lot 49* (1965) follows Oedipa Maas's quest, similar in some respects to that of Stone's Jim Garrison, to uncover the 'truth' about what appear to be secret activities cascading through American life. She finally arrives at four possible conclusions: that there really is a conspiracy out there, or that she is hallucinating one, or that a plot has been mounted against her involving forgery, actors, and constant surveillance, or that she is imagining such a plot.[18] Pynchon doesn't resolve these multiple and incompatible versions of the 'real'. Other postmodernist novels and films, like *The Magus, Money, The Truman Show,* and *The Matrix,* would also dramatize fabricated realities involving professional actors and round-the-clock surveillance, and yielding similar interpretive options.

The aesthetic of the apparently real seems to present no such predicament. It proffers what seems to be real . . . and that is all there is to it. The apparently real comes without self-consciousness, without irony or self-interrogation, and without signaling itself to the reader or viewer. Consequently, for anyone used to the refinement of postmodernism, the apparently real may seem intolerably 'stupid': since the ontology of such texts seems to 'go without saying', more astute minds may think they cry out for demystification, for a critique deconstructing their assumptions. In fact, the apparently real is impervious to such responses. While it's true that a minimal acquaintance with textual practice will show up how the material of the apparently real has been edited, manipulated, shaped by unseen hands, somehow as an aesthetic it has already subsumed such an awareness. Indeed, though paradoxically and problematically, it seems to believe it has *surmounted* Sherman's and Pynchon's concerns, perhaps considering them sterile or passé. In 2007 it emerged that a number of apparently real British TV shows had in fact undergone devious trickery at the hands of their production companies or broadcasters. Newspapers reported this as 'scandal', the supposed betrayal of their audiences, while TV insiders explained that this aesthetic's reality was only *apparent,* as its name suggested, not absolute; viewers, unfazed, carried on watching them. The apparently real is, then, the outcome of a silent negotiation between viewer and screen: we know it's not *totally* genuine, but if it utterly seems to be, then we will take it as such.

In truth, apparently real TV, such as docusoaps and reality TV, has to be considered 'real' to a decisive extent to be worth spending time on. Its interest derives from its reality; reject the latter and you lose the former. The reality in question is narrowly material: these are genuine events experienced by genuine people; these are actual emotions felt by actual people. It's a shallow, trivial reality, the zero degree of the real: the mere absence of obvious lying; hence the importance of 'appearance' within the aesthetic, of visible seeming. This supremacy of the visual makes the aesthetic's natural environment television, film, and the Internet; the triumph of appearance carries it beyond the true/false dichotomy and the wrought 'fictiveness' of Weir or the Wachowski brothers.

The difference between the docusoap and reality TV, genres born in the 1990s, is not clear-cut, nor is it significant here. (Reality TV is sometimes distinguished by its celebrity participants or its pseudoscientific premises.) The child of the traditional documentary, the docusoap inherits all the *truth* of a form once defined in opposition to TV *fiction* (sitcoms, drama); to this it splices, in accordance with its name, the stuff of soap, of 'ordinary' life – these are true accounts, then, of everyday experience. People are filmed at work, on vacation or at home doing nothing very special; everything that is most recognizably stressful or tedious about contemporary life – learning to drive, getting married, renovating or cleaning or buying houses, checking in at airports, disciplining small children – is foregrounded. These semiuniversal (hence 'ordinary', that is, 'real') situations are portrayed from the perspective of 'ordinary' people, the supposedly humdrum individuals embroiled in them. This personalization and apparent intimacy are intended to convey an interior reality corresponding to the banally genuine exterior.

In either case, the digimodernism of reality TV and the docusoap is clear: *the participants improvise the immediate material*. Such shows create structures and manage recording processes around essentially extemporized content. They present haphazard material, captured and molded by a semi-invisible production company. Traditional TV (sitcoms, news, drama, etc.) monopolizes the creative roles; apparently real TV hands over the writing and direction – the fabrication of dialogue, the choice and sequencing of actions – to the wit, moods, and duties of the people taking part. As the production company don't back off completely, the 'reality' can only be apparent (what would've happened had they not been there?[19]); and yet the direction in which the content of the show will move genuinely does become haphazard in a manner similar to the openness of a Web 2.0 text. Web 2.0 depends so critically on the apparently real that it gives a name ('trolls') to those who reject it. Wikipedia, message boards, and social networking sites clearly require, in order to function at all, a level of sincerity in their users (impossible to measure objectively). Writing what you don't believe or know to be untrue defeats the object of these sites. The apparently real is prevalent on amateur YouTube clips, and underpins blogs: 'Honest blog writing is universally cited [*sic*] as a requirement of the genre ... all bloggers demand attempted truthfulness at all times'.[20] Indeed, newspapers, in a familiar move, have highlighted the 'scandal' of the 'sinister' machinations of businesses or institutions to pass themselves off online as 'real' (or 'viral'). The exception to this reliance might be chat rooms, where fictive selves wander free, but even they have a pressure toward encounters in the 'real' world that imposes on participants a permanent engagement with the appearance of their authenticity. In the world of the performing arts, David Blaine's shift from 'conjurer' of fabricated, 'magical' realities to the subject of apparently real feats of physical endurance is emblematic of the spirit of the times.

The apparently real may be thought such a naïve and simple-minded aesthetic that it vitiates any text it dominates, and examples of this can be found. *Jackass*, in both its TV and film formats, deploys the aesthetic as a kind of inverted pornography: instead of young people performing pleasurable acts for the (erotic) delight of watchers, *Jackass* has them perform agonizing ones for the (comedic) pleasure of its viewers. To gain any enjoyment from watching it's necessary to believe in the reality of its set-pieces; moreover, it's probably essential to feel that this reality outweighs any other consideration. At one point in *Jackass: The Movie* (2002) a cameraman genuinely throws up on-screen; the guys roar with laughter, doubtless because their aesthetic creed states that any actual, filmed physical suffering must be hilarious. This is the apparently real as personal degradation. Indeed, the aesthetic has often been exploited to record the harassment of members of the public; along with *Jackass* and myriad prank shows, perpetrators of 'happy slapping' attacks, where cell phones are used to film actual assaults on people for the later amusement of viewers, are also fond of this. The apparently real can in such cases become no better than a guarantee of suffering.

[...]

There are three concomitant observations that can be made about the textual functions of the apparently real: its deployment of a (pseudo)scientific discourse; its engulfing of the self ('addictiveness'); and its immersion in the present.

The postmodernist real favored a rhetoric of the literary: since the real was a fiction it made sense to read, to decipher it; similarly, it was conceptualized as written, created as an aesthetic object. The literary became the metaphorical model for interpretation through the text's supposedly fictive ontological status. The digimodernist turn toward a scientific discourse-repertoire is audible in the evening highlights shows during a run of *Big Brother*, where clips frequently start with a voice-over solemnly intoning something like: 'Day forty-seven in the *Big Brother* house' or '11.07 p.m. Dale, Bubble, and Mikey are in the bedroom. It is forty-three minutes since the argument in the kitchen'. This is the discourse of laboratory research, where records of results are kept carefully documenting dates, times, places, and the identities of participants. The function of this log-keeping is confirmed by *Big Brother*'s use of a resident academic psychologist whose role is to interpret the program's human interactions as though they formed part of some experiment s/he was conducting. Elements of the show's format, such as the isolation and continuous observation of the subjects being studied, do indeed suggest a putative experiment. Other docusoaps and reality TV shows have adopted this research-lab structure, adding to the isolation and surveillance a third essential feature, the introduction, whereby a foreign body is placed inside the observed environment to see what abreactions (explosions? assimilations?) would ensue. *Wife Swap* (2003–) is perhaps the most successful of such programs, and ends each time with an analysis of 'results' as if a genuine experiment has taken place leading to an advance in human understanding. Provided it was alien to its new surroundings anything could be introduced anywhere, with 'interestingly' unpredictable and filmable consequences; and so classical musicians were trained to perform as club DJs, regular families were inserted into the lifestyle of the Edwardians, and TV professionals dressed and ate as if in the 1660s.[21]

Though such shows adopted some of the methods and the language of anthropological or historical or sociopsychological investigations, it's unlikely that any finally made a contribution to knowledge. By the standards of actual scientists, the 'experiments' were inadequately prepared (insufficient samples, contamination of participants, no control group, etc.), while some of the 'experts' interpreting the 'results' seemed of dubious academic authority. In *That'll Teach 'Em* (2003), a documentary series made by Channel 4, a group of high-achieving teenagers was placed in an isolated house and subjected to the practices of a 1950s' private school: heavy uniforms, draconian discipline, period English food, daily organized sports, separation of the sexes, science practicals for the boys (stinks and bangs) and home economics for the girls (cooking), ferocious exams, and so on. They were filmed for a month and at the end the 'results' studied: the boys had fallen in love with science, they all hated the food and the uniform, each had lost on average about seven pounds in weight, they seemed happier and more natural, they had mostly failed the exams, and so on. Though fascinating and suggestive in itself, the show did not, as educationalists hastened to explain, actually produce any usable research findings: the discourse and rhetoric of the scientific experiment had been only that. The number and variety of programs during the 2000s ringing changes on the tropes of the experiment (isolation, observation, introduction, results, experts) have been so vast that sometimes viewers might have felt like apprentice anthropologists or psychologists themselves. If occasionally the rhetoric seemed a fig leaf for voyeurism and trash TV, the producers of such shows would defend them as offering 'insight' into, for example, 'gender differences', stealing the language of academics filling out an application for funding for their research. More elaborate uses of the apparently real would turn these tropes inside out. The stunts shown in *Jackass* or mounted by David Blaine could be read as grotesque parodies of medical research; *Borat*, as its subtitle makes clear, is a work of pseudoanthropology; the disappeared filmmakers [in *The Blair Witch Project*] were engaged on a university research *Project*.

Moral panic has also surrounded the digimodernist text's alleged addictiveness. It is commonly reported, both by researchers and the mass media, that such digimodernist forms as text messaging, e-mail, chat rooms, videogames, reality and participatory TV, and the Internet in general have addictive properties. It is, however, problematic to describe any form of text as addictive since it produces no heightened physical reaction (unlike drugs) and is rarely a trigger for intense emotion (unlike gambling); much digimodernist text may actually induce a sense of monotony. However, the keyboard trance is a recognizable phenomenon, whereby users click half-bored and semihypnotized endlessly from electronic page to electronic page, to no visible end. The digimodernist text does seem to possess the property of overwhelming the individual's sense of temporal proportion or boundaries; it can engulf the player or user or viewer, who experiences a loss of will, a psychological need for textual engagement that exceeds any realistic duration or rational purpose. Digimodernist texts can be hard to break off from; they seem to impose a kind of personal imperialism, an outflanking of all other demands on time and self. This derives from their apparent or experiential reality: combining manual action with optical and auditory perception, such a text overpowers all competing sources of the real.

There are two possible explanations for this: first, that our seeming impotence before the digimodernist text stems from its novelty and our consequent inexperience and incapacity to control the (semi)unknown; or second, that the digimodernist text truly affords an intensity of 'reality' which is greater and more engulfing than any other, including unmediated experience. Evidence is conflictual, and it may be too soon to say.

Finally, digimodernism's sense of cultural time also differs from that of postmodernism. Delighting in the quotation, the pastiche, and the hybridization of earlier texts, postmodernist culture was often backward-looking; historiographic metafictions such as Julian Barnes's *Flaubert's Parrot*, John Fowles's *The French Lieutenant's Woman*, and A. S. Byatt's *Possession* explored their very contemporary attitudes through an encounter with the textual past. Postmodernism also emphasized a new sense of history as constructed in the present, and, in novels like Toni Morrison's *Beloved* or Graham Swift's *Waterland*, a sense of the past as a haunting of the present. The apparently real and digimodernism are by contrast lost in the here and now, swamped in the textual present; they know nothing of the cultural past and have no historical sense. The difference is clear in cinema: where Baudrillard or Jameson identified a depthless 'nostalgia for a lost referential' in 1970s' films like *American Graffiti* and *Barry Lyndon*,[22] digimodernist historical movies like *The Mummy*, *Pirates of the Caribbean*, and *King Kong* make no effort to reproduce the manners and mores of the past. Instead, their actors behave like people from the 2000s, clad in vintage clothing and rushing through their CGI-saturated story. All attempts at mimicking past human behavior are given up by a digimodernism which assumes, in TV costume dramas like *Rome* (2005–07) and *The Tudors* (2007–), that people have always talked, moved, and acted pretty much as they do today, and have ever had today's social attitudes (equality for women, sexual outspokenness, racial tolerance). In short, digimodernism is, as the debate on addictiveness confirms, the state of being engulfed by the present real, so much so it has no room for anything beyond; what is, is all there is.

The apparently real also has a wider context, of course, evident in changing social notions of the textual hero. Classical Hollywood fashioned the 'star', the impossibly glamorous, absolutely remote, and seemingly perfect figure produced by and identical with its movies. By contrast, infused with a tarnished romanticism, post-1960s rock culture foregrounded the artist-hero, the on-the-edge voice of a generation grafted into his audience's context yet far more insightful and brilliant than you or me. The contemporary notion of the 'celebrity' is something else again. Its distinctive feature isn't that so many people portrayed as famous are almost completely unknown – an effect of the collapse of 'popular culture' into niches – but the virulence and loathing, the spitefulness of the discourse surrounding them. Celebrity magazines and TV programs picture famous women with their hair all messy, their makeup undone, their cellulite on show, or their grotesque weight gain (or loss) to the fore; lovingly dramatized are their relationship hells, their eating disorders, their career meltdowns, and their fashion disasters. You'd think the readers or viewers had a personal vendetta against them. What's happening is that the assumed 'realities' of the female reader/viewer (her supposedly actual anxieties) are projected as the apparent reality of the famous female; it's a globalized, textual version of a malicious idea of woman-to-woman gossip. In consequence, this discourse strips the 'celebrity' of everything but her fame: rather than see her as competent in some sense (talented at acting or singing, physically beautiful, etc.), she is constructed as exactly the same as anyone else, except famous. This is a prevalent coding: the aesthetic of the apparently real is a textual expression of the social death of competence.

[…]

Such a catalog of struggles and problematics within established media provokes a last, unanswerable question. Is digimodernism finally another name for the death of the text? Most of the crisis-ridden forms discussed here provide a closed, finished text: you buy, own, and engage a film or TV program or song as a total artistic entity, as a text-object. This objectivity endures over time, is authored, reproduced; it has become, in its material already-createdness, the definition of a text. Videogames and radio shows are markedly weaker in this regard; they are less culturally prestigious too; but socially they are thriving. The onward, haphazard, evanescent digimodernist 'text' may seem finally indistinguishable from the textless flux of life. Is digimodernism the condition of after-the-text? […] Kevin Kelly has dreamed of all books being digitized into 'a single liquid fabric of interconnected words and ideas' to be unraveled, re-formed, and recomposed freely by anyone for any reason.[23] There are signs across the media landscape of such a development. Yet, unquestionably, this would resemble a mass of unauthored and unlimited textualized matter. A text, though, must have boundaries and a history, in the same way that the distinction between 'life' and 'a life' ascribes to the latter physical circumscription and biography. With the reception and commodification of the individual text already imploding, will there be room under digitization for *a text*?

There are two optional answers to this. The first sounds a futuristic note of doomy jeremiad: early digimodernism will perhaps be remembered as the last time one could speak of a new, emergent form of textuality, before the singular object-text was drowned forever by the rising tide of undifferentiated text; the 2000s naively saluted a textual revolution before it revealed itself, in its totalitarianism, as the genocide of the text. The second entails turning away from texts and the consideration instead of history, or of contemporaneity placed in the long term. The survival of the object-text depends on the continued valorization of competence, skillfulness, and know-how, because these are, *ipso facto*, excluding forces: they delimit, isolate, close. These are social and moral issues, and so we come to the final chapter.

Notes

Editors' note: In the interests of internal consistency, the notes in this extract have been re-numbered to make them sequential.

1 Gore Verbinski (dir.), *Pirates of the Caribbean: The Curse of the Black Pearl* (Walt Disney Pictures, 2003).

2 Fredric Jameson, *Postmodernism, or, The Cultural Logic of Late Capitalism* (London: Verso, 1991), 6.

3 Ibid.

4 Alan Kirby, 'The Death of Postmodernism and Beyond' in *Philosophy Now*, November/December 2006, http://www.philosophynow.org/issue58/58kirby.htm Retrieved January 23, 2009.

5 Adapted from *The Concise Oxford Dictionary* (Oxford: Oxford University Press), 946, 1215.

6 Espen J. Aarseth, *Cybertext: Perspectives on Ergodic Literature* (Baltimore, MD: Johns Hopkins University Press, 1997), 1. Emphasis added.

7 Al Gore, *The Assault on Reason* (London: Bloomsbury, 2007).

8 Roland Barthes, 'The Death of the Author' in *Image Music Text*, trans. Stephen Heath (London: Flamingo, 1984), 148, 145.

9 Michel Foucault, 'What is an Author?' trans. Josué V. Harari, in *Textual Strategies: Perspectives in Post-Structuralist Criticism*, ed. Josué V. Harari (Ithaca, NY: Cornell University Press, 1979), 141–60. For a more recent view, see Seán Burke, *The Death and Return of the Author*, 2nd edition (Edinburgh: Edinburgh University Press, 1998).

10 John Fowles, *The French Lieutenant's Woman* (London: Vintage, 1996), 97, 388, 389.

11 Martin Amis, *Money* (London: Penguin, 1985), 247; Martin Amis, *The Information* (London: Flamingo, 1995), 300.

12 Christopher Lasch, *The Culture of Narcissism: American Life in an Age of Diminishing Expectations* (London: Abacus, 1980), 125, 127, 129.

13 Ibid., 150.

14 Allan Bloom, *The Closing of the American Mind: How Higher Education has Failed Democracy and Impoverished the Souls of Today's Students* (Harmondsworth: Penguin, 1988), 62.

15 For certain languages, like Arabic and Japanese, other directions are clearly involved.

16 Jean Baudrillard, 'History: A Retro Scenario' in *Simulacra and Simulation*, trans. Sheila Faria Glaser (Ann Arbor, MI: University of Michigan Press, 1994), 43. Emphasis added.

17 Cindy Sherman, *The Complete* Untitled Film Stills (New York: Museum of Modern Art, 2003), 9.

18 Thomas Pynchon, *The Crying of Lot 49* (London: Vintage, 2000), 117–18.

19 Baudrillard posed this question in 1981 about the subjects of the proto-reality TV show *An American Family*, first aired in 1973 ('The Precession of Simulacra' in *Simulacra and Simulation*, 28). Such shows used to appear once a decade; now they launch every week. When in 2008 Channel 4 screened a structural remake of the program that so exercized Baudrillard, a British TV critic noted presciently: 'it won't have the same impact . . . Reality shows, for want of a better expression, are now the norm' (Alison Graham, 'Déjà View' in London *Radio Times*, September 13–19, 2008, 47).

20 Hill, *Blogging for Dummies*, 268.

21 *Faking It* (Channel 4, 2000–05); *The Edwardian Country House* (Channel 4, 2002); *The Supersizers Go Restoration* (BBC2, 2008).

22 Baudrillard, 'History: A Retro Scenario', 44.

23 Kevin Kelly, 'Scan This Book!' in *New York Times*, May 14, 2006, www.nytimes.com/2006/05/14/magazine/14publishing.html?ex=1305259200&en=c07443d368771bb8& ei=5090 Retrieved October 10, 2008.

14

Metamodernism

The term 'metamodernism' has been advanced by cultural theorists Timotheus Vermeulen and Robin van den Akker, for whom it marks a twofold response to the demise of the postmodern on the one hand, and, on the other, to the global landscape of the early twenty-first century, which has entered a new state of political and cultural unrest. Although many commentators have come to the conclusion that these tendencies occurred in the aftermath of the terrorist attacks which took place on September 11, 2001, Vermeulen and Akker dismiss the suggestion that 9/11 led directly to the development of metamodernism. They argue that if anything, the fall of the Twin Towers worked only to re-emphasize postmodernist assumptions about the contemporary world. What they term 'metamodernism' is rather a cultural transition brought about, they claim, partly by a response to the early twenty-first century's large-scale economic crisis, precipitated by the implosion of the financial sector, and partly by the ecological challenges presented by climate change. In the face of these threats, Vermeulen and Akker argue, postmodernism's seemingly endless scepticism seems to have given way to a pervasive desire for answers.

While 'metamodernism' as a term seeks to give a clearer identity to the arts of the contemporary period, it is important to note that Vermeulen and Akker are at pains to examine the continuing presence of postmodernism in their discussion of metamodernism. Thus, while there is a general consensus amongst critics that postmodernism has come to an end or been left behind in some way, metamodernism shares with renewalism the view that many tendencies traditionally associated with postmodernism continue to linger on in contemporary culture, literature, and the arts, in ways that are problematic for any attempt to define or name that which follows the postmodern. Furthermore, Vermeulen and Akker also agree with Toth that these tendencies are in some way being morphed, or taking on a fundamentally new 'sens' or meaning. However, 'Notes on Metamodernism' goes a step further than The Passing of Postmodernism *through its provocative description of the structure of metamodernism, and in doing so offers a diagnosis of the aesthetic properties and values of art after postmodernism far more detailed than that which Toth gives in his somewhat sketchy descriptions of renewalism. Where Toth's renewalism saw a successor to postmodern literature in neo-realism, metamodernism finds it in neo-romanticism instead.*

In the following extract, Vermeulen and Akker suggest that artists in the twenty-first century are no longer portraying, as the postmodernists did, a world clouded by illusion, spectacle, simulacrum and irony. Instead, metamodernist artists, authors, architects, and the like, are formulating a new desire to embrace a sense of hopefulness about the contemporary world. Opposing the postmodern trend to voice doubts about reality, metamodernism seeks to emphasize positivity in a world which is patently lacking in it. Paradoxically, however, metamodernism does not seek simply to repudiate or surmount postmodern scepticism. Rather, according to Vermeulen and Akker, metamodernism simultaneously accepts and disregards the defeatist attitude of postmodernism. Much like remodernism, which emphasizes the importance of authenticity and the presentation of selfhood through art, metamodernism seeks to reclaim the status of the individual subject, and to foreground the subject as an agent of expression and of desire. It shares this feature not only with remodernism, but also with renewalism, performatism, and automodernism. However, Vermeulen and Akker's relocation of this emphasis differs categorically from the other formulations, in that metamodernism describes a process of searching for authenticity in contemporary art and literature, all the while knowing that this is an impossible act. A metamodern effort, then, is one that is made with hope and enthusiasm as it accepts the impossible, but believes in the possible in order to obtain a moral and political progression.

Vermeulen and Akker present the reader with an image of a pendulum that swings back and forth, on an unstable axis, between the two opposite poles of modernism and postmodernism. The oscillation of this pendulum, they suggest, is the very movement of metamodernism. In a nutshell, metamodernism oscillates between the irony, parody and pastiche associated primarily with postmodernism, and the modernist enthusiasm for purity and totality. This oscillation resembles the movement between the reachable and the unreachable, the presentable and the unpresentable, the beautiful and the sublime. Metamodernism in this sense is founded upon a central paradox, as it acknowledges postmodernist assumptions about reality, and yet it conveys a positive desire to move beyond the postmodern in order to locate the unreachable 'real' that modernism was looking for all along. Or in other words, it is both postmodernism and modernism, and at the same time neither of the two: thus, as Vermeulen and Akker argue, metamodernism is characterized by an in-between condition they term metaxis.

There are, however, a number of problems evident in this notion of metamodernism. As can be seen, it structures itself around the opposition between modernism and postmodernism: Vermeulen and Akker envisage these terms as opposing poles between which the motor force of metamodernism oscillates. But such a clear opposition between modernism and postmodernism has only rarely, if ever, been maintained: simply put, critics have never been able to agree where, when, or how modernism ended and postmodernism began, partly because the two were always far more alike than Vermeulen and Akker occasionally imply in this extract. Thus, though their image of the metamodern pendulum is a striking one, it is perhaps not a very propitious departure, since it means that metamodernism depends for its identity on a polarity between two extremes which were arguably never entirely distinct from each other to begin with. Moreover, if it is unhelpful for metamodernism to locate itself between two terms which are easily confused, this problem is compounded by the use of another term – romanticism. Vermeulen and Akker suggest that metamodernism quests for authenticity and meaning as against postmodern irony and scepticism, yet they seem to associate this aspect of it both with a residual modernism, and with an emergent form of neo-romanticism. This alliance is suspicious, because modernism often defined itself in stark opposition to the aesthetics of romanticism – indeed, this is arguably the founding gesture of modernism. All told, then, there is much that needs clarifying about the relationship between romanticism, modernism, and postmodernism, before metamodernism can become a meaningful and coherent term. Vermeulen and Akker's description of the pendulum, which swings between the modernist desire for sense and meaning and the postmodernist doubting of them, is a compelling characterization of contemporary culture. However, the disadvantage of Vermeulen and Akker's formulation is that it depends for its co-ordinates on its positioning between these rather loose terms.

Ultimately, though, if metamodernism appears both unable and unwilling to shed the skin of its postmodern predecessors, then this is a strength as well as a weakness. In the first place, it seems perfectly reasonable, and perhaps even commonsensical, to argue that the demise of postmodernism does not necessarily involve any seismic epochal shifts or dramatic end-of-an-era upheavals: if it did, it would no doubt be easier to achieve a consensus about what happened to postmodernism, and to identify what has supplanted it. Metamodernism scores highly in envisaging a role for a residual postmodernism fluctuating alongside an emergent new paradigm. At the same time, however, it is difficult to visualize it as the dominant concept through which we can assess the current situation post-postmodernism, or indeed label it a true successor to the postmodern: surely there are too many similarities between metamodernism and postmodernism to make this claim stick. Nevertheless, it certainly constitutes a positive challenge to the postmodern paradigm, and an interesting description of a contemporary cultural climate clouded in anxiety and uncertainty. Metamodernism might better be seen not as supplanting the postmodern but as engineering a structural transition process, one in which we are able to observe a recalibration of postmodernist assumptions about the contemporary world by placing them in dialogue with a resurgence of interest in modernism and a new incarnation of romanticism.

The extract is by Timotheus Vermeulen and Robin van den Akker, 'Notes on Metamodernism', *Journal of Aesthetics and Culture*, Vol. 2, 2010 (pp. 1–14).

Notes on Metamodernism

Timotheus Vermeulen and Robin van den Akker

The choice in this election is not between regions or religions or genders. It's not about rich vs. poor, young vs. old. And it is not about black vs. white. This election is about the past vs. the future. It's about whether we settle for the same divisions and distractions and drama that passes for politics today or whether we reach for a politics of common sense and innovation, a politics of shared sacrifice and shared prosperity. . . . Yes, we can. Yes, we can change. Yes, we can.

(Barack Obama, 'Yes, we can change', speech addressed at Democratic Assembly, 28 January 2008)

I'm noticing a new approach to artmaking in recent museum and gallery shows. . . . It's an attitude that says, I know that the art I'm creating may seem silly, even stupid, or that it might have been done before, but that doesn't mean this isn't serious. *At once knowingly self-conscious about art, unafraid, and unashamed, these young artists not only see the distinction between earnestness and detachment as artificial; they grasp that they can be ironic and sincere at the same time, and they are making art from this compound-complex state of mind.*

(Jerry Saltz, 'Sincerity and Irony Hug it Out', *New Yorker Magazine*, 27 May 2010)

The ecosystem is severely disrupted, the financial system is increasingly uncontrollable, and the geopolitical structure has recently begun to appear as unstable as it has always been uneven.[1] CEOs and politicians express their 'desire for change' at every interview and voice a heartfelt 'yes we can' at each photo-op. Planners and architects increasingly replace their blueprints for environments with environmental 'greenprints'. And new generations of artists increasingly abandon the aesthetic precepts of deconstruction, parataxis, and pastiche in favor of *aesth-ethical* notions of reconstruction, myth, and metaxis. These trends and tendencies can no longer be explained in terms of the postmodern. They express a (often guarded) hopefulness and (at times feigned) sincerity that hint at another structure of feeling, intimating another discourse. History, it seems, is moving rapidly beyond its all too hastily proclaimed end.

In this essay, we will outline the contours of this emerging structure of feeling. We will first discuss the debate about the alleged demise of 'the' postmodern and the apparent rise of another modernism. We will argue that this modernism is characterized by the oscillation between a typically modern commitment and a markedly postmodern detachment. We will call this structure of feeling *metamodernism*.[2] According to the Greek–English Lexicon the prefix 'meta' refers to such notions as 'with', 'between', and 'beyond'. We will use these connotations of 'meta' in a similar, yet not indiscriminate fashion. For we contend that metamodernism should be situated epistemologically *with* (post) modernism, ontologically *between* (post) modernism, and historically *beyond* (post) modernism. And finally, we will take a closer look at some tendencies that exemplify the current dominant sensibility, in particular the Romantic turn in contemporary aesthetics.

Some remarks, finally, on our approach. As the essay's title 'Notes on metamodernism' suggests, we intend what follows as a series of linked observations rather than a single line of thought. We seek to relate to one another a broad variety of trends and tendencies across current affairs and contemporary aesthetics that are otherwise incomprehensible (at least by the postmodern vernacular), by understanding them in terms of an emergent sensibility we come to call metamodern. We do not seek to impose a predetermined system of thought on a rather particular range of cultural practices. Our description and interpretation of the metamodern sensibility is therefore *essay*istic rather than *scient*ific, rhizomatic rather than linear, and open-ended instead of closed. It should be read as an invitation for debate rather than an extending of a dogma.

History beyond 'the end of history', art beyond 'the end of art' . . .

The postmodern years of plenty, pastiche, and parataxis are over. In fact, if we are to believe the many academics, critics, and pundits whose books and essays describe the decline and demise of the postmodern, they have been over for quite a while now. Some argue the postmodern has been put to an abrupt end by material events like climate change, financial crises, terror attacks, and digital revolutions. Others find that it has come to a more gradual halt by merit of less tangible developments, such as the appropriation of critique by the market and the integration of *différance* into mass culture. And yet others point to diverging models of identity politics, ranging from global postcolonialism to queer theory.[3] As Linda Hutcheon puts it, in the epilogue to the second edition of *The Politics of Postmodernity*: 'Let's just say it: it's over'.[4]

But if these commentators agree the postmodern condition has been abandoned, they appear less in accord as to what to make of the state it has been abandoned for. Hutcheon therefore concludes her epilogue with a pressing question – a question to which she herself does not yet know the answer:

> The postmodern moment has passed, even if its discursive strategies and its ideological critique continue to live on – as do those of modernism – in our contemporary twenty-first-century world. Literary historical categories like modernism and postmodernism are, after all, only heuristic labels that we create in our attempts to chart cultural changes and continuities. Post-postmodernism needs a new label of its own, and I conclude, therefore, with this challenge to readers to find it – and name it for the twenty-first century.[5]

Some theorists and critics have attempted to answer Hutcheon's question. Gilles Lipovetsky, of course, has claimed the postmodern has given way to the hypermodern. According to Lipovetsky, today's cultural practices and social relations have become so intrinsically meaningless (i.e. pertaining to past or future, there or elsewhere, or whatever frame of reference) that they evoke hedonistic ecstasy as much as existential anguish.[6] The philosopher Alan Kirby has proposed that the current paradigm is that of digimodernism and/or pseudomodernism. The cultural theorist Robert Samuels has further suggested that our epoch is the epoch of automodernism. And a number of critics have simply adopted the syntactically correct but semantically meaningless term post-postmodernism. Most of these conceptions of the contemporary discourse are structured around technological advances. Kirby's digimodernism, for instance, 'owes its emergence and pre-eminence to the computerization of text, which yields a new form of textuality characterized in its purest instances by onwardness, haphazardness, evanescence, and anonymous, social and multiple-authorship'.[7] And Samuels's automodernism presupposes a correlation between 'technological automation and human autonomy'.[8] But many of these conceptions – and Lipovetsky, Kirby, and Samuels's, however useful they are for understanding recent developments, are exemplary here – appear to radicalize the postmodern rather than restructure it. They pick out and unpick what are effectively excesses of late capitalism, liberal democracy, and information and communication technologies rather than deviations from the postmodern condition: cultural and (inter) textual hybridity, 'coincidentality', consumer (enabled) identities, hedonism, and generally speaking a focus on spatiality rather than temporality.[9]

Nicholas Bourriaud's suggestion, altermodernism, is probably the most well-known conception of the latest discourse. However, it also appears to be the least understood. In response to the exhibition of the same name Bourriaud curated at Tate Britain in 2009, Andrew Searle reported in *The Guardian* that 'Postmodernism is dead ... but something altogether weirder has taken its place'.[10] Similarly, the art critic for *The Times*, Rachel Campbell-Johnston, testified that 'Postmodernism is so last year but [that] its replacement ... is all over the shop'.[11] Bourriaud's accompanying essay invites a similar reaction: the precise meaning of altermodernism is as slippery and evasive as the structure of the argument is unclear. As we understand it, Bourriaud ultimately defines altermodernism as a 'synthesis between modernism and post-colonialism'.[12] According to Bourriaud, this synthesis is expressed, respectively, in heterochronicity and 'archipelagraphy', in 'globalized perception' as well as in nomadism, and in an incorporation and/or affirmation of otherness as much as in the exploration of elsewheres.

Many of Bourriaud's observations appear to be spot-on. The developed world has extended – and is still in the process of expanding – far beyond the traditional borders of the so-called West. Bourriaud argues that this development has led to a heterochrony of globalized societies with various degrees of modernity and a worldwide archipelago without a center; to globally intersecting temporalities and historically interrelated geographies. Consequently, he justly asserts, our current modernity can no longer be characterized by either the modern discourse of the universal gaze of the white, western male or its postmodern deconstruction along the heterogeneous lines of race, gender, class, and locality. He suggests that, instead, it is exemplified by globalized perception, cultural nomadism, and creolization. The altermodernist (artist) is a *homo viator*, liberated from (an obsession with) his/her origins, free to travel and explore, perceiving anew the global landscape and the 'terra incognita' of history.

Bourriaud's conception of altermodernism is at once evocative and evasive; it is as precise in its observations as it is vague in its argumentation. However provocative his writing may be therefore, it is also problematic. For instance, his notion of a 'globalized perspective' is somewhat difficult, for it implies a multiplicity and scope of (simulacral) vision neither phenomenologically nor physically possible (it appears to us to be more appropriate to speak of a 'glocalized perception', in which both the *a priori* of situation and situatedness are acknowledged). Similarly, his intriguing account of a progressive creolism is opposed to the retrospective multiculturalism of the artworks he illustrates it with. And his description of the restless traveler and the Internet junky as embodiments of altermodern art also seem rather anachronistic. For that matter, Saatchi's (long the personification of the postmodern, late capitalist art made flesh) recent shift away from the Young British Artists toward contemporary artists from the Middle- and Far East is far more telling – precisely because it implies an interest in a variety of 'glocalized perceptions'.

The main problem with Bourriaud's thesis however, is that it confuses epistemology and ontology. Bourriaud perceives that the form and function of the arts have changed, but he cannot understand how and why they have changed. In order to close this critical gap, he simply assumes (one could call this the 'tautological solution') that experience and explanation are one and the same. For Bourriaud, heterochronicity, archipelagraphy, and nomadism are not merely expressions of a structure of feeling; they become the structures of feeling themselves. And, indeed, it is because he mistakes a multiplicity of forms for a plurality of structures, that his conception of altermodernism – as expressed in the irregularity of the exhibition and the inconsistency of his writing – 'is all over the shop', never becomes wholly comprehensible let alone convincing.

Bourriaud perceives, say, seven types of fireworks, in seven kinds of disguises: one is red, one yellow, one blue, one is circular, one angular, and so on. But he cannot see that they are all produced by the same tension: an oscillation between metals, sulfurs, and potassium nitrates. We will call this tension, oscillating between – and beyond – the electropositive nitrates of the modern and the electronegative metals of the postmodern, metamodern.

From the postmodern to the metamodern

What do we mean when we say that 'the' postmodern has been abandoned for the metamodern? It has become somewhat of a commonplace to begin a discussion of the postmodern by stressing that there is no one such thing as 'the' postmodern. After all, 'the' postmodern is merely the 'catchphrase' for a multiplicity of contradictory tendencies, the 'buzzword' for a plurality of incoherent sensibilities. Indeed, the initial heralds of postmodernity, broadly considered to be Charles Jencks, Jean-François Lyotard, Fredric Jameson, and Ihab Hassan, each analyzed a different cultural phenomenon – respectively, a transformation in our material landscape; a distrust and the consequent desertion of metanarratives; the emergence of late capitalism, the fading of historicism, and the waning of affect; and a new regime in the arts.[13] However, what these distinct phenomena share is an opposition to 'the' modern – to utopism, to (linear) progress, to grand narratives, to Reason, to functionalism and formal purism, and so on. These positions can most appropriately be summarized, perhaps, by Jos de Mul's distinction between postmodern irony (encompassing nihilism, sarcasm, and the distrust and deconstruction of grand narratives, the singular and the truth) and modern enthusiasm (encompassing everything from utopism to the unconditional belief in Reason).[14]

We do not wish to suggest that all postmodern tendencies are over and done with.[15] But we do believe many of them are taking another shape, and, more importantly, a new *sens*, a new meaning and direction. For one, financial crises, geopolitical instabilities, and climatological uncertainties have necessitated a reform of the economic system ('*un nouveau monde, un nouveau capitalisme*', but also the transition from a white collar to a green collar economy). For another, the disintegration of the political center on both a geopolitical level (as a result of the rise to prominence of the Eastern economies) and a national level (due to the failure of the 'third way', the polarization of localities, ethnicities, classes, and the influence of the Internet blogosphere) has required a restructuration of the political discourse. Similarly, the need for a decentralized production of alternative energy; a solution to the waste of time, space, and energy caused by (sub)urban sprawls; and a sustainable urban future have demanded a transformation of our material landscape. Most significantly perhaps, the cultural industry has responded in kind, increasingly abandoning tactics such as pastiche and parataxis for strategies like myth and metaxis, melancholy for hope, and exhibitionism for engagement. We will return to these strategies in more detail shortly.

CEOs and politicians, architects, and artists alike are formulating anew a narrative of longing structured by and conditioned on a belief ('yes we can', 'change we can believe in') that was long repressed, for a possibility (a 'better' future) that was long forgotten. Indeed, if, simplistically put, the modern outlook *vis-à-vis* idealism and ideals could be characterized as fanatic and/or naive, and the postmodern mindset as apathetic and/or skeptic, the current generation's attitude – for it is, and very much so, an attitude tied to a generation – can be conceived of as a kind of informed naivety, a pragmatic idealism.

We would like to make it absolutely clear that this new shape, meaning, and direction do not *directly* stem from some kind of post-9/11 sentiment. Terrorism neither infused doubt about the supposed superiority of neoliberalism, nor did it inspire reflection about the basic assumptions of Western economics, politics, and culture – quite the contrary. The conservative reflex of the 'war on terror' might even be taken to symbolize a reaffirmation of postmodern values.[16] The threefold 'threat' of the credit crunch, a collapsed center, and climate change has the opposite effect, as it infuses doubt, inspires reflection, and incites a move forward out of the postmodern and into the metamodern.

So, history is moving beyond its much-proclaimed end. To be sure, history never ended. When postmodernist thinkers declared it to have come to a conclusion, they were referring to a very particular conception of history – Hegel's 'positive' idealism. Some argued that this notion of history dialectically progressing toward some predetermined Telos had ended because humankind had realized that this Telos had been achieved (with the 'universalization of Western liberal democracy').[17] Others suggested that it had come to a conclusion because people realized its purpose could never be fulfilled – indeed, because it does not exist. The current, metamodern discourse also acknowledges that history's purpose will never be fulfilled because it does not exist. Critically, however, it nevertheless takes toward it *as if* it does exist. Inspired by a modern naïveté yet informed by postmodern skepticism, the metamodern discourse consciously commits itself to an impossible possibility.

If, epistemologically, the modern and the postmodern are linked to Hegel's 'positive' idealism, the metamodern aligns itself with Kant's 'negative' idealism. Kant's philosophy of history, after all, can also be most appropriately summarized as 'as-if' thinking. As Curtis Peters explains, according to Kant, 'we may view human history *as if* mankind had a life narrative which describes its self-movement toward its full rational/social potential . . . to view history *as if* it were the story of mankind's development'.[18] Indeed, Kant himself adopts the as-if terminology when he writes '[e]ach . . . people, *as if* following some guiding thread, go toward a natural but to each of them unknown goal'.[19] That is to say, humankind, a people, are not really going toward a natural but unknown goal, but they pretend they do so that they progress morally as well as politically. Metamodernism moves for the sake of moving, attempts in spite of its inevitable failure; it seeks forever for a truth that it never expects to find. If you will forgive us for the banality of the metaphor for a moment, the metamodern thus willfully adopts a kind of donkey-and-carrot double-bind. Like a donkey it chases a carrot that it never manages to eat because the carrot is always just beyond its reach. But precisely because it never manages to eat the carrot, it never ends its chase, setting foot in moral realms the modern donkey (having eaten its carrot elsewhere) will never encounter, entering political domains the postmodern donkey (having abandoned the chase) will never come across.

Ontologically, metamodernism oscillates between the modern and the postmodern. It oscillates between a modern enthusiasm and a postmodern irony, between hope and melancholy, between naïveté and knowingness, empathy and apathy, unity and plurality, totality and fragmentation, purity and ambiguity. Indeed, by oscillating to and fro or back and forth, the metamodern negotiates between the modern and the postmodern. One should be careful not to think of this oscillation as a balance however; rather, it is a pendulum swinging between 2, 3, 5, 10, innumerable poles. Each time the metamodern enthusiasm swings toward fanaticism, gravity pulls it back toward irony; the moment its irony sways toward apathy, gravity pulls it back toward enthusiasm.

Both the metamodern epistemology (*as if*) and its ontology (*between*) should thus be conceived of as a 'both-neither' dynamic. They are each at once modern *and* postmodern and neither of them. This dynamic can perhaps most appropriately be described by the metaphor of *metaxis*. Literally, the term metataxis ($\mu\varepsilon\tau\alpha\xi\acute{\upsilon}$) translates as 'between'. It has however, via Plato and later the German philosopher Eric Voegelin, come to be associated with the experience of existence and consciousness. Voegelin describes metaxis as follows:

> Existence has the structure of the In-Between, of the Platonic *metaxy*, and if anything is constant in the history of mankind it is the language of tension between life and death, immortality and mortality, perfection and imperfection, time and timelessness, between order and disorder, truth and untruth, sense and senselessness of existence; between *amor Dei* and *amor sui*, *l'âme ouverte* and *l'âme close*; . . .[20]

For Voegelin thus, metaxis intends the extent to which we are at once both here and there and nowhere. As one critic puts it: metaxis is 'constituted by the tension, nay, by the *irreconcilability* of man's participatory existence between finite processes on the one hand, and an unlimited, intracosmic or transmundane reality on the other'.[21] Now, the debate about the meaning of metaxis is one of the longest running and most intriguing in the history of philosophy and deserves (and requires) much more attention than we can possibly offer here. The account we provide is therefore inevitably reductive, the arguments we lend from it inexorably precipitate. For our purposes, we intend the concept not as a metaphor for an existential experience that is general to the *condition humaine*, but as a metaphor for a cultural sensibility that is particular to the metamodern discourse. The metamodern is constituted by the tension, no, the double-bind, of a modern desire for *sens* and a postmodern doubt about the sense of it all.

Metamodern strategies

Let us take a closer look at some recent trends and tendencies in contemporary aesthetics to illustrate what we mean by metamodernism, and to demonstrate the extent to which it has come to dominate the cultural imagination over the last few years. Just as modernism and postmodernism expressed themselves through a variety of often competing strategies and styles, the metamodern also articulates itself by means of diverse practices. One of the most poignant metamodern practices is what the German theorist Raoul Eshelman has termed 'performatism'. Eshelman describes performatism as the willful self-deceit to believe in – or identify with, or solve – something in spite of itself. He points, for example, to a revival of theism in the arts, and the reinvention of transparency, kinesis and impendency in architecture.[22]

> Performatist works are set up in such a way that the reader or viewer at first has no choice but to opt for a single, compulsory solution to the problems raised within the work at hand. The author, in other words, imposes a certain solution on us using dogmatic, ritual, or some other coercive means. This has two immediate effects. The coercive frame cuts us off, at least temporarily, from the context around it and forces us back into the work. Once we are inside, we are made to identify with some person, act or situation in a way that is plausible only within the confines of the work as a whole. In this way performatism gets to have its postmetaphysical cake and eat it too. On the one hand, you're practically forced to identify with something implausible or unbelievable within the frame – to believe in spite of yourself – but on the other, you still feel the coercive force causing this identification to take place, and intellectually you remain aware of the particularity of the argument at hand. Metaphysical skepticism and irony aren't eliminated, but are held in check by the frame.[23]

The leading American art critic Jerry Saltz also has observed the surfacing of another kind of sensibility oscillating between beliefs, assumptions, and attitudes:

> I'm noticing a new approach to artmaking in recent museum and gallery shows. It flickered into focus at the New Museum's 'Younger Than Jesus' last year and ran through the Whitney Biennial, and I'm seeing it blossom and bear fruit at 'Greater New York', MoMA.
>
> P.S. 1's twice-a-decade extravaganza of emerging local talent. It's an attitude that says, *I know that the art I'm creating may seem silly, even stupid, or that it might have been done before, but that doesn't mean this isn't serious*. At once knowingly self-conscious about art, unafraid, and unashamed, these young artists not only see the distinction between earnestness and detachment as artificial; they grasp that they can be ironic and sincere at the same time, and they are making art from this compound-complex state of mind – what Emerson called 'alienated majesty'.[24]

Saltz writes exclusively about tendencies in American art, but one can observe similar sentiments across the European continent. Only recently, the established BAK Institute in the Netherlands initiated a group exhibition that was called 'Vectors of the Possible'. The exhibition, curator Simon Sheikh explained,

> examines the notion of the horizon in art and politics and explores the ways in which art works can be said to set up certain horizons of possibility and impossibility, how art partakes in specific imaginaries, and how it can produce new ones, thus suggesting other ways of imagining the world. Counter to the post-1989 sense of resignation, [it] suggests that in the field of art, it is the horizon – as an 'empty signifier', an ideal to strive towards, and a vector of possibility – that unites . . . and gives . . . direction. The art works in this exhibition can be seen as vectors, reckoning possibility and impossibility in (un)equal measures, but always detecting and indicating ways of seeing, and of being, in the world.[25]

And the much lauded up-and-coming Gallery Tanja Wagner introduced its opening exhibition with the remarkably analogous words:

> The works [at display] convey enthusiasm as well as irony. They play with hope and melancholy, oscilliate between knowledge and naivety, empathy and apathy, wholeness and fragmentation, purity and ambiguity, . . . looking for a truth without expecting to find it.[26]

Elsewhere, the cultural critic Jörg Heiser has perceived the emergence of what he calls 'Romantic Conceptualism'.[27] Heiser argues that the rational, calculated conceptual art of Jeff Koons, Thomas Demand, and Cindy Sherman is increasingly replaced with the affective and often sentimental abstractions of Tacita Dean, Didier Courbot, and Mona Hatoum. Where Demand reproduces the most concrete simulacra, Dean creates affective illusions that can never materialize. Where Koons obsesses over the obscene, Courbot is concerned with the increasingly obsolete. And whereas Sherman criticizes subjectivity, Hatoum celebrates the felt heterogeneity of identity. If the postmodern deconstructs, Heiser's Romantic Conceptualism is concerned with reconstruction.

The film critic James MacDowell, finally, has noted the emergence of the so-called quirky cinema associated with the films of Michel Gondry and Wes Anderson.[28] MacDowell describes quirky as a recent trend in Indie cinema characterized by the attempt to restore, to the cynical reality of adults, a childlike naivety – as opposed to the postmodern 'smart' cinema of the 1990s, which was typified by sarcasm and indifference. And yet others have recognized movements as diverse as remodernism, reconstructivism, renewalism, the New Sincerity, the New Weird generation, stuckism, Freak Folk, and so on. The list, indeed, of trends and movements surpassing, or attempting to surpass, the postmodern is inexhaustive.

Nicholas Bourriaud would undoubtedly argue that this multiplicity of strategies expresses a plurality of structures of feeling. However, what they have in common is a typically metamodern oscillation, an unsuccessful negotiation, between two opposite poles. In performatist attempts to defy the cosmic laws and the forces of nature, to make the permanent transitory and the transient permanent, it expresses itself dramatically. In Romantic Conceptualist efforts to present the ordinary with mystery and the familiar with the seemliness of the unfamiliar it exposes itself less spectacularly, as the unsuccessful negotiation between culture and nature. But both these practices set out to fulfill a mission or task they know they will not, can never, and should never accomplish: the unification of two opposed poles.

Neoromanticism

The world must be romanticized. *In this way its original meaning will be rediscovered. To romanticize is nothing but a qualitative heightening [Potenzierung]. In this process the lower self is identified with a better self. [. . .] Insofar as I present the commonplace with significance, the ordinary*

with mystery, the familiar with the seemliness of the unfamiliar and the finite
with the semblance of the infinite, I romanticize it.

(Novalis[29])

At the time of writing, metamodernism appears to find its clearest expression in an emergent neoromantic sensibility. This can hardly be called surprising. For Kant's negative idealism too was most successfully expressed by the early German Romantic spirit.[30] Now, of course, Romanticism is a notoriously pluralistic and ambiguous (and consequently uniquely frequently misinterpreted) concept. Arthur Lovejoy once noted that there are so many different, often differing definitions of the concept that we might rather speak of Romanticisms.[31] And Isaiah Berlin, one of our time's most adept critics of the Romantic worldview, observed that Romanticism, in short, is

> unity and multiplicity. It is fidelity to the particular … and also mysterious tantalizing vagueness of outline. It is beauty and ugliness. It is art for art's sake, and art as instrument of social salvation. It is strength and weakness, individualism and collectivism, purity and corruption, revolution and reaction, peace and war, love of life and love of death.[32]

However, essentially, the Romantic attitude can be defined precisely by its oscillation between these opposite poles.[33] Romanticism is about the attempt to turn the finite into the infinite, while recognizing that it can never be realized. As Schlegel put it, 'that it should forever be becoming and never be perfected'.[34] Of course, it is also specifically about *Bildung*, about self-realization, about *Zaïs* and *Isis*, but for our purposes, this general idea of the Romantic as oscillating between attempt and failure, or as Schlegel wrote, between 'enthusiasm and irony', or in de Mul's words, between a 'modern enthusiasm and a postmodern irony', is sufficient.[35] It is from this hesitation also that the Romantic inclination toward the tragic, the sublime, and the uncanny stem, aesthetic categories lingering between projection and perception, form and the unformable, coherence and chaos, corruption and innocence.

It is somewhat surprising that we appear to be among the first academics to discern in contemporary arts a sensibility akin to Romanticism. For in the arts, the return of the Romantic, whether as style, philosophy, or attitude, has been widely professed. In 2007 Jörg Heiser, co-editor of *Frieze*, curated an exhibition in Vienna and Nurnberg called 'Romantic Conceptualism'. A mere 2 years earlier, the Schirnhalle in Frankfurt hosted 'Ideal Worlds: New Romanticism in

Contemporary Art'. In addition, the TATE Britain has recently held a Peter Doig retrospective, while the MOMA looked back at the life and work of Bas Jan Ader. And then we have not even mentioned the multitude of galleries exposing the often-figurative paintings and photographs of twilights and full moons, ethereal cityscapes and sublime landscapes, secret societies and sects, estranged men and women, and strange boys and girls. It appears that, after all those years, the parody and pastiche of Jeff Koons, Jake and Dinos Chapman, and Damien Hirst, the ironic deconstruction of Cindy Sherman and Sarah Lucas, and the nihilist destruction of Paul McCarthy, are finally as out of place as they always pretended to be – but, in times where 'anything goes', hardly ever were.

This Romantic sensibility has been expressed in a wide variety of art forms and a broad diversity of styles, across media and surfaces. It has been visible in Herzog and de Meuron's negotiations between the permanent and the temporary; in Bas Jan Ader's questioning of Reason by the irrational; in Peter Doig's re-appropriation of culture through nature; and in Gregory Crewdson and David Lynch's adaptation of civilization by the primitive. It can be perceived in Olafur Eliasson, Glen Rubsamen, Dan Attoe, and Armin Boehm's obsessions with the commonplace ethereal, in Catherine Opie's fixation with the quotidian sublime. It can be observed in Justine Kurland, Kaye Donachie, and David Thorpe's fascination with fictitious sects, or in Darren Almond and Charles Avery's interest for fictional elsewheres. And one can see it in the plethora of works of artists anew attempting to come to terms with their unconsciousness (think, for example, of Ragnar Kjartansson's at once grotesque and heartfelt attempts to (re)create both his 'erotic fantasies of death, longing and eternity'[36] and the *Weltschmerz* stemming from his failure to do so entirely, or of Selja Kameric's attempts to retrieve an irrevocably irretrievable past, or of Michel Gondry, Spike Jonze, and Wes Anderson's attempts to rekindle the naivety and innocence of their childhood). What these strategies and styles have in common with one another is their use of tropes of mysticism, estrangement, and alienation to signify potential alternatives; and their conscious decision to attempt, in spite of those alternatives', untenableness.

Indeed, both Ader's attempts to unite life and death – and Reason and the miraculous, and self-determination and faith – and Rubsamen's efforts to unify culture and nature might have been more 'successful' had they employed other methods and materials. Ader could have equipped himself with a better boat in order to sail the seas (*In search of the miraculous*, 1975); and he could have trained himself better in the art of tree climbing in order to longer hang on to branches (*Broken fall*, 1971). Similarly, Rubsamen could have applied strategies of simulation and/or techniques of postproduction in order to make the electricity poles and lampposts (*I've brought you a friend*, 2007) look more like the magical trees and ethereal bushes they are supposed to resemble. The reason these artists haven't opted to employ methods and materials better suited to their mission or task is that their intention is not to fulfill it, but to attempt to fulfill it in spite of its 'unfulfillableness'. The point of Ader's journey is precisely that he might not return from it; of his tree climbing precisely that he cannot but fall eventually. Similarly, the point of Rubsamen's pursuit also is exactly that it cannot be fulfilled: culture and nature cannot be one and the same, nor can any one of them ever entirely overtake the other.

One should be careful, however, not to confuse this oscillating tension (a both-neither) with some kind of postmodern in-between (a neither-nor). Indeed, both metamodernism and the postmodern turn to pluralism, irony, and deconstruction in order to counter a modernist fanaticism. However, in metamodernism this pluralism and irony are utilized to counter the modern aspiration, while in postmodernism they are employed to cancel it out. That is to say, metamodern irony is intrinsically bound to desire, whereas postmodern irony is inherently tied to apathy. Consequently, the metamodern art work (or rather, at least as the metamodern art work has so far expressed itself by means of neoromanticism) redirects the modern piece by drawing attention to what it cannot present in its language, what it cannot signify in its own terms (that what is often called the sublime, the uncanny, the ethereal, the mysterious, and so forth). The postmodern work deconstructs it by pointing exactly to what it presents, by exposing precisely what it signifies.

The difference between the metamodern oscillation that marks contemporary art and the postmodern in-betweenness that signified much of the art of the 1990s, 1980s, 1970s, and 1960s is perhaps most visible in the work of those artists and architects who engage with everyday life, the commonplace, and the mundane. Postmodern works, like Rachel Whiteread's reconstructions, Daniel Buren's installations, or Martha Rosler's videos, deconstruct our assumptions about our lived spaces. Metamodern 'Romantic' works, such as Armin Boehm's city vistas, Gregory Crewdson's small townscapes, and yes, David Lynch's close-ups of suburban rituals, redirect – and indeed, heighten – our presuppositions about our built environment.

Boehm paints aerial views of commuter towns as at once enchanted and haunted. His oil painting, both tentative and figurative, both atonal and intensely colorful, with a darkness full of light, depicts places that are simultaneously the places we live in and places we have never experienced before. Crewdson photographs towns haunted by the nature they repress, disavow, or sublimate. In his work of tree-lined streets, white picket-fenced gardens, and picture-windowed houses are sites for inexplicable natural events, from local twilights to people shoveling earth into their hallways, and planting flowers in their lounges, to robins picking at limbs buried below ground. And Lynch's films too frequently thrive on moments that are, at once repulsive and attractive, beyond our grasp. They often tend toward the uncanny, abound with local animism, haunted houses, and surreal characters. A film like *Blue Velvet* (1995) not merely convinces us to distrust Reason. It persuades us to believe there are matters Reason cannot account for: a flickering light, a sadomasochistic relationship, a man wearing sunglasses at night, a blind man who can somehow see, the behavior of robins, an ear in the grass, and so on. The film presents these instances as haunting apparitions, within its texture as much as in its diegesis. They are woven into it, at times divulging the film's plot slowly, then again disrupting it abruptly. Each apparition signifies a narratively inexplicable (but, and that is the point, incredibly fertile) change in tempo, tune, and tone; alternating from comic to tragic, from romantic to horrific and back; turning the commonplace into a site of ambiguity, of mystery, and unfamiliarity, to us as much as to its characters.

In architectural practices this distinction between a metamodern oscillation and a postmodern in-between is even more pronounced – perhaps especially because an emergent metamodern style still needs to distinguish itself from the dominant postmodern discourse,[37] or perhaps especially because architecture cannot but be concrete. The works of 'starchitects' Herzog and De Meuron are exemplary here. Their more recent designs express a metamodern attitude *in and through* a style that can only be called neoromantic. A few brief descriptions suffice, here, to get a hint of their look and feel. The exterior of the De Young Museum (San Francisco, 2005) is clad in copper plates that will slowly turn green as a result of oxidization; the interior of the Walker Art Center (Minneapolis, 2005) holds such natural elements as chandeliers of rock and crystal; and the facade of the Caixa Forum (Madrid, 2008) appears to be partly rusting and partly overtaken by vegetation. While the above examples are appropriations or expansions of existing sites, their recent designs for whole new structures are even more telling. The library of the Brandenburg Technical University (Cottbus, 2004) is a gothic castle with a translucent facade overlain with white lettering; the Chinese national stadium (Beijing, 2008) looks like a 'dark and enchanted forest' from up close and like a giant bird's nest from afar[38]; the residential skyscraper at 560 Leonard street (NYC, under construction) is reminiscent of an eroded rock; the Miami Art Museum (Florida, under construction) contains Babylonic hanging gardens; the Elbe Philharmonic Hall (Hamburg, under construction) seems to be a giant iceberg washed ashore; and Project Triangle (Paris, under construction) is an immense glass pyramid that casts no shadows while it hovers over the city.

These buildings attempt to negotiate between such opposite poles as culture and nature, the finite and the infinite, the commonplace and the ethereal, a formal structure, and a formalist unstructuring (as opposed to deconstruction). Crucially, these attempts are unsuccessful as the buildings never so much seem to balance these distinct poles as oscillate between them. Fragile (bird's nest), disappearing (iceberg), or perishing (eroded rock) natural phenomena question the solidity of structures more or less built for permanence; while a mythical building (castle) from the days of old seems to be either resurrected from the past or mysteriously unaffected by time. Some edifices seem to be either left to the elements (oxidizing copper, rust) or seamlessly integrated with nature (overgrown walls, hanging gardens); yet others seem to defy the basic laws of geometry and gravity by means of their torsions. Lucid surfaces, radiating with light, give the most ordinary of sites a mysterious appearance; while ancient symbols (Pyramid) point toward transient cultures and the infinity of the cosmos.

Ader's, Thorpe's, Lynch's and Herzog & De Meuron's unsuccessful negotiations – the double-bind of both/neither – expose a tension that cannot be described in terms of the modern or the postmodern, but must be conceived of as metamodernism expressed by means of a neoromanticism.[39] If these artists look back at the Romantic it is neither because they simply want to laugh at it (parody) nor because they wish to cry for it (nostalgia). They look back instead in order to perceive anew a future that was lost from sight. Metamodern neoromanticism should not merely be understood as re-appropriation; it should be interpreted as re-signification: it is the re-signification of 'the commonplace with significance, the ordinary with mystery, the familiar with the seemliness of the unfamiliar, and the finite with the semblance of the infinite'. Indeed, it should be interpreted as *Novalis*, as the opening up of new lands in situ of the old one.

Conclusion: Atopic metaxis

Conceiving of the metamodern at the closing of a decade in which about every other philosopher, cultural theorist, and art critic has attempted to conceptualize the aftermath of the postmodern might be considered to be anachronistic, out of place, and – if one still feels the need to conceive it anew despite the multiplicity of attempts that conceptualized it priori – pretentious. It is therefore ironic that our inquiries into the discursivity by which current geopolitical tendencies can be explained and the sensibility by which the arts express themselves have led us precisely to those three concerns: a deliberate being out of time, an intentional being out of place, and the pretense that that desired atemporality and displacement are actually possible even though they are not.

If the modern thus expresses itself by way of a utopic syntaxis, and the postmodern expresses itself by means of a dystopic parataxis, the metamodern, it appears, exposes itself through a-topic metaxis. The Greek–English lexicon translates atopos ($\alpha\tau o\pi o\varsigma$), respectively, as strange, extraordinary, and paradoxical. However, most theorists and critics have insisted on its literal meaning: a place (topos) that is no (a) place. We could say thus that atopos is, impossibly, at once a place and not a place, a territory without boundaries, a position without parameters. We have already described metaxis as being simultaneously here, there, and nowhere. In addition, taxis ($\tau\acute\alpha\xi\iota\varsigma$) means ordering. Thus, if the modern suggests a temporal ordering, and the postmodern implies a spatial disordering, then the metamodern should be understood as a spacetime that is both – neither ordered and disordered. Metamodernism displaces the parameters of the present with those of a future presence that is futureless; and it displaces the boundaries of our place with those of a surreal place that is placeless. For indeed, that is the 'destiny' of the metamodern wo/man: to pursue a horizon that is forever receding.

Notes

1 The authors would like to thank Jos de Mul, Gry Rustad, Jonathan Bignell, and departmental colleagues for their invaluable comments to earlier versions of this essay.

2 Although we appear to be the first to use the term metamodernism to describe the current structure of feeling, we are not the first to use the term per se. It has been

used with some frequency in literature studies in order to describe a post-modern alternative to postmodernism as presented in the works of authors as far apart as, amongst others, Blake and Guy Davenport. However, we would like to stress that our conception of metamodernism is by no means aligned to theirs, nor is it derived from them. It is in so far related to these notions that it too negotiates between the modern and the postmodern; but the function, structure, and nature of the negotiation we perceive are entirely our own and, as far as we can see, wholly unrelated to the previous perception.

3   For an excellent consideration of the debate about the 'end of the postmodern', see Josh Toth's *The Passing of Postmodernism: A Spectroanalysis of the Contemporary* (Albany: SUNY Press, 2010).

4   L. Hutcheon, *The Politics of Postmodernism* (New York/London: Routledge, 2002), 165–6.

5   Ibid., 181.

6   G. Lipovetsky, *Hypermodern Times* (Cambridge: Polity Press, 2005).

7   A. Kirby, *Digimodernism: How New Technologies Dismantle the Postmodern and Reconfigure our Culture* (New York/London: Continuum, 2009), 1.

8   R. Samuels, 'Auto-Modernity after Postmodernism: Autonomy and Automation in Culture, Technology, and Education', in *Digital Youth, Innovation, and the Unexpected*, ed. T. Mcpherson (Cambridge, MA: The MIT Press, 2008), 219.

9   Although it should be noted here that Kirby is careful to point out that he appreciates temporality and spatiality equally.

10 A. Searle, 'The Richest and Most Generous Tate Triennial Yet', *The Guardian*, March 2, 2009. http://www.guardian.co.uk/artanddesign/2009/feb/02/altermodern-tate-triennial

11 R. Campbell-Johnston, 'Altermodern: Tate Triennal 2009 at Tate Britain', *The Times*, March 2, 2009, T2, 20–21.

12 N. Bourriaud, ed. *Altermodern. Tate Triennal 2009* (London: Tate Publishing, 2009), 12.

13 C. Jencks, *The Language of Post-Modern Architecture* (London: Academy Editions, 1991); J. F. Lyotard, *The Postmodern Condition: A Report on Knowledge* (Manchester: Manchester University Press, 1984); F. Jameson, *Postmodernism, or, The Cultural Logic of Late Capitalism* (Durham: Duke University Press, 1991); I. Hassan, *The Postmodern Turn: Essays on Postmodernism and Culture* (Columbus: Ohio State University Press, 1987), 84–96.

14 J. de Mul, *Romantic Desire in (Post)modern Art & Philosophy* (Albany: State University of New York Press, 1999), 18–26.

15 Our understanding of history, or rather historical periodization, is influenced by Raymond Williams's canonical description of dominants, emergents and residuals.

See R. Williams, *Marxism and Literature* (Oxford/New York: Oxford University Press, 1977), 121–8.

16 Consider, for example, the immediate differentiation between us (the so-called west) and them (the so-called axis of evil), the broadly shared sense of urgency – visible in the rhetoric of Bush and Blair among others – to 'defend western values', the general usage and acceptance of the frame of 'the gift of democracy' used in the build-up to the invasion of Iraq, the initial broad support for the Afghan War, and so on and so forth. This is not to say that there have not been critiques of this reflex, but it is only of late that these critiques have become more widely acknowledged, if not accepted.

17 F. Fukuyama, *The End of History and the Last Man*, (New York: The Free Press, 1992), 3.

18 C. Peters, *Kant's Philosophy of Hope* (New York: Peter Lang, 1993), 117. Our emphasis.

19 I. Kant, 'Idea for a Universal History from a Cosmopolitan Point of View', in *Kant On History*, ed. L. White Beck (Upper Saddle River: Prentice Hall, 2001), 11–12.

20 E. Voegelin, 'Equivalences of Experience and Symbolization in History', ed. E. Sandoz, vol. 12 of *The Collected Works of Eric Voegelin* (Baton Rouge: Louisiana State University Press, 1989), 119–20.

21 R. Avramenko, 'Bedeviled by Boredom: A Voegelinian Reading of Dostoevsky's *Possessed*', *Humanitas* 17, nos. 1 & 2 (2004): 116.

22 R. Eshelman, 'Performatism, or, What Comes After Postmodernism: New Architecture in Berlin', *Art-Margins* (April 2002), http://www.artmargins.com/index.php/archive/322-performatism-or-what-comes-after-postmodernism-new-architecture-in-berlin

23 R. Eshelman, *Performatism, or the End of Postmodernism* (Aurora: Davies Group, 2008), 3.

24 J. Saltz, 'Sincerity and Irony Hug It Out', *New York Magazine*, May 27, 2010, http://nymag.com/arts/art/reviews/66277/

25 BAK, 'Press Statement Vectors of the Possible' (August 2010), http://www.bak-utrecht.nl/?click [pressrelease]

26 Galerie Tanja Wagner, 'Press Statement The Door Opens Inwards' (September 2010), http://www.tanjawagner.com

27 J. Heiser, ed. *Romantic Conceptualism* (Bielefeld: Kerber, 2008).

28 J. MacDowell, 'Notes on Quirky', *Movie: A Journal of Film Criticism* 1:1 (2010), http://www2.warwick.ac.uk/fac/arts/film/movie/contents/notes_on_quirky.pdf

29 Novalis, 'Fragmente und Studien 1797–1798', in *Novalis Werke*, ed. G. Schulz (Munchen: C.H. Beck, 2001), 384–5. Our translation.

30 Although we would argue that Kant's negative idealism inspired early German
   Romanticism, we by no means intend to say that they are alike or even
   comparable. For Kant, there is no purpose in history or nature, but he imagines
   one nevertheless in order to progress. For the early German Romantics, nature has
   a purpose; they simply can never grasp it. To explain this difference by way of the
   donkey-and-carrot parable: the Kantian donkey never manages to eat the carrot it
   chases because the carrot is virtual; the early German Romantic donkey never
   manages to eat the carrot merely because, although actual, it is too far away.

31 A. Lovejoy, 'On the Discrimination of Romanticisms', *PMLA* 39, no. 2 (June 1924).

32 I. Berlin, *The Roots of Romanticism* (Princeton: Princeton University Press,
   2001), 18.

33 Ibid., 101–5.

34 F. von Schlegel, 'Atheneum Fragments', in *Friedrich Schlegel's Lucinde and the
   Fragments*, ed. P. Firchow (Minneapolis: University of Minnesota Press, 1975), 175.

35 J. de Mul, Ibid., 25.

36 A. Coulson, 'Ragnar Kjartansson', *Frieze* 102 (October 2006) http://www.frieze.
   com/issue/review/ragnar_kjartansson/

37 Now, we should stress once more that we do not intend to say that
   metamodernism expresses itself solely by means of neoromanticism.
   Contemporary architecture, for instance, has to our knowledge not often been
   associated with Romanticism. Furthermore, the one critic that has compared
   recent architectural practices with a Romantic spirit, Reed Kroloff, has mistakenly
   reduced that Romantic spirit to some kind of soothing sensuality and pastel
   patterning. One might argue that this lack of address might to some extent be
   explained by the uneasy fit between architecture and Romanticism. Architecture,
   after all, is the art of the 'permanent'; Romanticism is the attitude of the transient.
   Or one may suggest that architecture, as the applied art most affected by the
   fluctuations of the industrial and financial markets and the shifting priorities of
   political decision making, simply requires more time, money, and political
   intervention in order to take form more than other arts do. But the lack of address
   could also simply indicate that metamodern architecture has so far expressed itself
   primarily by means of other topoi. Of course, there is widespread agreement that
   contemporary architecture is no longer postmodern. The end of the postmodern
   is most clearly signaled here by the return to commitment. The growing awareness
   of the need for sustainable design has led to an ethical turn in the attitude toward
   the built environment. Roof gardens and solar panels are heavily subsidized,
   carbon neutral buildings and ecologically friendly neighborhoods are widely
   commissioned, and, yes, even entirely green cities are being designed from scratch.
   Necessitated by a competitive market, urged by demanding politicians, and

inspired by the changing Zeitgeist, architects increasingly envision schemes for a sustainable urban future. But it is also, as we intend to show, increasingly paired to a new form.

38 N. Ourossoff, 'Olympic Stadium with a Design to Remember', *The New York Times*, May 8, 2008, http://www.nytimes.com/2008/08/05/sports/olympics/05nest.html

39 Several Internet critics have made similar observations. M. Van Raaij of *Eikongraphia* (http://eikongraphia.com/) commented the following on the 'erosion iconography' of the residential skyscraper in NYC: 'It is beautiful in its celebration of nature. There is however also something apocalyptic and frightening about the reference to decay. It reminds me of the sublime landscapes in romantic painting: beautiful, yet horribly desolate and uninhabitable'. And K. Long of *Icon Eye* (http://www.iconeye.com/) described Cottbuss' Castle, accordingly: 'It is possible to photograph this building as if it were a classical folly, stumbled upon by a German romantic painter in an idealized German landscape. Schinkel or Caspar David Friedrich would understand the references'.

Conclusions

15

Note on the Supplanting of 'Post-'
David Rudrum

Surveying the writings collected in this volume, probably the most obvious place from which to start the task of summing up would be the simple observation that three quarters of the positions anthologized in Part Two set out to supplant the postmodern by prefixing the root '-modern' with something other than 'post-'. The significance of this observation seems at first blush pretty clear: the excising of the 'post-' from 'postmodern' can most plausibly be read as indicating a consensus that, by the early twenty-first century, the postmodern moment has passed into history. So the task of this conclusion is therefore to weigh up whether things really are as simple as that.

Nobody ever liked that prefix 'post-', even though it became the late twentieth-century's favourite way of coining a critical designation (as in '-colonial', '-feminist', '-industrial', '-Marxist', and even, oxymoronically, '-theoretical'). Back in 1987, Brian McHale opened his classic study of postmodernist fiction with a survey of popular discontent at the term which still holds relevance today, a quarter of a century later, and which wasn't entirely new even back then: he quotes Richard Kostelanetz, writing in 1982 that: 'Post is a petty prefix, both today and historically, for major movements are defined in their own terms, rather than by their relation to something else.... No genuine avant-garde artist would want to be "post" anything' (Kostelanetz 1982: 38). There was a gaggle of puns about being 'lost in the post', or sounding 'the last post', and so on. So it is not surprising that, after a decade or two in which 'New' replaced 'post-' (as in 'New historicism', 'New aestheticism', 'New textualism', and plenty of others), there is now a race to be 'first past the post'. Whatever else they may demonstrate, remodernism, digimodernism, metamodernism, automodernism, hypermodernism, altermodernism, and similar coinages collectively demonstrate a loss of patience with that 'post-'. Not before time.

But focusing on the disappearance of the 'post-' and arguing about which new prefix ought to supplant it overlooks something important: the persistence of the '-modern'. Surely at least one possible conclusion to draw from the sheer number of newly prefixed '-modernisms' on offer is that the postmodern thesis about modernity having come to an end was simply false. How else to account for a situation in which, after four or five decades of polemical analyses according to which the project of modernity had been abrogated or wound up, it would appear that some form of '-modernism' still remains the most ubiquitous way of characterizing the culture of the present?

One obvious riposte to this question might simply be to reject its premise – that is, to assert that postmodernity is still alive and well, and has some way to go before it becomes a thing of the past. Peter Zima argues this position, on the following grounds:

> The chronological argument is relatively simple: if modernity as an historical period begins with the Enlightenment, i.e. sometime in the 17th century, and lasts for about three centuries, until the Second World War, then postmodernity is unlikely to end after fifty years or so. In this context, titles announcing the end of postmodernity – e.g. *After Postmodernism* – seem to stem from rash conclusions.
>
> (Zima 2003: 13)

Such a view, when simply stated, appears to have the ringing endorsement of common sense behind it. But it involves dismissing as wrongheaded more or less all the writings collected in this anthology, on grounds no more compelling than that it is simply too soon for today's critics and theorists to overturn the diagnoses of the preceding generation. Note, moreover, the importance of Zima's 'if': it is predicated on the acceptance of a rather textbookish notion of postmodernity, which is precisely what I am about to question.

Consider Klaus Stierstorfer's slightly more nuanced assessment of the situation. Prudently asserting that 'there is, obviously, no simple answer to whether postmodernism is over or which new paradigm may have begun' (Stierstorfer 2003: 9), he goes on to suggest that:

> If indeed such a transition beyond postmodernism were currently taking place, it would, in view of the heavy in-fighting during the earlier discussion, seem a curiously quiet exit, unworthy of a moment which had been expected to end Western noetic systems and bring to grief centuries of misplaced confidence in truth, values, morality, representation, reality and a host of other

quasi sacrosanct traditions – most of which can presently be observed to be leading a vigorous afterlife.

(Stierstorfer 2003: 2)

Stierstorfer is saying two important things here: first, that since the death throes presaging the demise of postmodernity have been fewer and less rambunctious than its birth pangs, it is worth regarding them with some scepticism; and second, that many of the hallmarks of the modernity that postmodernity was said to supplant are in fact disconcertingly intact. The first point may indeed raise the question of whether postmodernity has come to an end. But the latter surely begs the question of whether the explanation for this might be because it never really started. Stierstorfer's account requires us to accept a somewhat paradoxical narrative in which, amid a good deal of critical and philosophical posturing, an end to modernity was declared by the postmodern generation, only for a subsequent generation of critics to announce a new wave of '-modernisms' as soon as the dust had settled. Modernity, I contend, is no such stop-and-start affair. The best way of resolving this paradox is to recognize that the glitch in this narrative is there because our conception of postmodernity is, and always was, deeply flawed. Clearly, then, it is worth asking when and why 'post-' ceased to be an appropriate prefix to 'modern'. But if no clear answer can be found to this question – and the diversity of opinion in Part One of this anthology rather suggests that it cannot – then it is also worth asking whether it ever was.

To put it another way: the range of prefixes recently attached to '-modern' aim to supplant the 'post-' modern, and to name something new. But a different way of looking at it might be to suggest that since 'post-' was never a sensible prefix in the first place, what is needed is a suitable prefix that would better describe late twentieth-century '-modernism'; one that need not be predicated on a rift between the late twentieth and the early twenty-first century. Consider, for example, the following description of the postmodern by Mike and Nicholas Gane: 'The postmodern, if it stands for anything at all, embraces ... plurality, dissensus, or, more generally, anything *dis-* (that which is apart or away from, that which is removed or expelled from, that which is the reversal of action)' (Gane & Gane 2007: 128, my emphasis).

This is a well-made point. The embracing of the prefix 'dis-' was so widespread that you could read more or less any critical essay that drew upon postmodern aesthetics, or choose at random a journal article discussing postmodern ideas in more or less any sphere of the humanities, and keep a running tally of how many times it used vocabulary such as 'displacement', 'dislocation', 'dissolution', 'disjuncture', 'disrupt', 'dismantling', 'discontinuity', 'disembodiment', 'disorder', 'disillusion', and, of course, 'disbelief [in grand narratives]'. The extent to which the postmodern is bound up with this prefix is even plainer to see in any undergraduate's bibliography. Scanning the titles of classic texts in the formulation of postmodernism will yield (for example): dismemberment (Hassan); dissemination (Derrida); disaster (Blanchot); disappearance (Virilio); dispositifs (Lyotard, and, albeit in a slightly different sense, Foucault); discourse (Foucault, and, albeit in a slightly different sense, just about everybody else). That many of the undergraduates who read these texts will go on to apply the terms to 'Dis-ney' or 'Dis-co' may be a facetious point, but the fortuitous etymological coincidence underscores the question: was the idea of *post*modernity not a misnomer for something better conceived of as a *dis*modernity?[1]

I do not imagine that Jean-François Lyotard, who did more than virtually anyone else to coin the term 'postmodern', would have dismissed this suggestion too lightly. His lucid 'Note on the Meaning of "Post-"', from which my own title borrows so heavily, expresses impatience with the misunderstanding that 'the "post" of postmodernism has the sense of a simple succession, a diachronic sequence of periods in which each one is clearly identifiable', because 'this idea of a linear chronology is itself perfectly "modern"' (Lyotard 1992b: 76). So in these terms, those who claim to diagnose a new era following postmodernity, which was itself an era following modernity, succeed only in demonstrating that their outlook is still rooted in that of the modern – a view based on the linear and on progress. More to the point, though, Lyotard's essay concludes with the assertion that 'the "post" of "postmodern" does not signify a movement of *comeback*, *flashback*, or *feedback*, that is, not a movement of repetition but a procedure in "ana-": a procedure of analysis, anamnesis, anagogy, and anamorphosis that elaborates an "initial forgetting"' (Lyotard 1992b: 80). It seems, then, that even Lyotard himself sensed that there were better prefixes than 'post-' to describe the features of our modernity that most interested him. Thomas Docherty, one of the best exegetes of the postmodern I know, has taken up this suggestion and mooted what he calls an 'anagrammatology', adding 'anachrony' to its features (Docherty 1996: 112). But it seems to me that what Lyotard is at least hinting at here is that the *post*modern might as well (or perhaps rather better) be prefixed *ana*modern.

The advantage of this formulation is that it avoids the implication that the postmodern was a new and distinctive epoch following some moment conceived as the death or end of modernity (whatever that might mean – do we really know what it is to be modern, and what it would mean for modernity to come to an end?). Bear in mind here the oft-cited way Lyotard asks and answers the question: 'What then is the postmodern? ... It is undoubtedly part of the modern' (Lyotard 1992a: 12). According to Lyotard, then, 'postmodernism is not modernism at its end, but in a nascent state, and this state is recurrent' (Lyotard 1992a: 15). The postmodern, that is, is not an epoch that follows the modern, but a moment of crisis, fissure, or rupture within it, and it is part of the very fabric of modernity that such moments will come back up again (and again). Since 'back', 'up', and 'again' are the principal meanings of the prefix 'ana-', it is not unreasonable to propose that we have never been *post*modern. Ours is better termed the *ana*modern condition.

Looked at this way, it begins to appear that certain ways of debating the demise of the postmodern are in fact counterproductive: all they succeed in achieving is perpetuating the (in my view misguided) picture of the postmodern as a discrete and distinct entity, readily and neatly separable from the modernism that went before it, and whatever '-ism' is said to succeed it. Lyotard is quite right that this is a surprisingly 'modern' view of the postmodern. As Mike and Nicholas Gane have put it:

> The very idea that the postmodern has to *mean* something, that this meaning has to be *clear*, and that any movement that is postmodern in orientation is to be necessarily one and *unified* in aim is already to work from modernist value presuppositions, and to promote these over any alternative perspective.
>
> (Gane & Gane 2007: 127–8)

And so it is hard to avoid the conclusion that evaluating the downfall of the postmodern in terms that invoke the chronological succession of clearly defined eras or epochs is rather missing the point. Instead of demonstrating that postmodernity is over, such debates succeed rather in ducking the question of how much (or how little) intellectual impact postmodernity has had in the longer term, and hence in ducking the question of whether postmodernity can really be said to have come into being properly at all. Such debates, moreover, are counterproductive in another, more obvious way: as Josh Toth has suggested in his discussions of the persistent ghost of postmodernism, by writing obituaries and epitaphs on the postmodern, by interminably proclaiming and analysing its death, one actually prolongs its (after)life.

However, it does not follow from this that the numerous attempts to supplant the postmodern presented in this anthology are misguided. In the first place, the *term* 'postmodern' needs supplanting, since it offers a misleading picture, and many of the coinages on offer herein present some very promising alternatives to it. In the second place, if Lyotard's idea of the postmodern as a moment of rupture or crisis in the fabric of the modern holds good, then what is being described by many of the positions in this anthology could well be the healing of such a rupture, the closing of a fissure, which is paradoxically experienced as a new moment of crisis in modernity. What I mean is that a majority of the attempts to describe what comes after the postmodern concur in ascribing to it many of the values which postmodernity supposedly dispensed with: for example, spirituality and sincerity, authenticity and autonomy. Values such as these are reasserted vocally, albeit in different degrees and combinations, by remodernism, performatism, automodernism, metamodernism, and renewalism. Many of these positions explicitly look to new incarnations of earlier styles and schools of art: neo-realism for renewalism; neo-romanticism for metamodernism; and some form of neo-modernism for remodernism. What this suggests to me is not that the postmodern has come to an end, and a new era has begun instead: what it suggests is that the postmodern was merely an expression of a sense of crisis within the modern, and that this particular sense of crisis has now abated. So endemic had that sense of crisis become, however, that its resolution is being experienced as something new, something disconcerting, and indeed, as the end of an era or the start of a new one. The desire to name this new era is therefore understandable, even laudable. But what is being named need not be conceived of as a *successor* to the postmodern; rather as a *reappraisal* of it.

To put it differently: consider the following two critical positions, which, interestingly enough, can be found in the same volume of essays. Pelagia Goulimari, editor of *Postmodernism: What Moment?*, asserts in her introduction to this indispensable book that 'any triumphal celebration of the postmodern against the modern is out of place' (Goulimari 2007: 1), and that 'the postmodern, in its relations of continuity with the modern, is here to stay' (Goulimari 2007: 2). A hundred pages later, Douglas Kellner takes the contrasting view that 'In general, utilizing the term "postmodern" in a meaningful way requires that one develop a systematic contrast with the "modern"' (Kellner 2007: 107–8). For Goulimari, the postmodern is continuous with the modern; for Kellner, it contrasts with it. Each is a sensible position, with much to recommend it, and many readers of that volume will doubtless have found themselves hard pressed to decide which is the more persuasive. If forced to choose, I would incline more towards Goulimari's view of things, but nevertheless find myself wondering: if contrasting the postmodern against the modern is 'out of place' because of the 'relations of continuity' between them, then why continue to distinguish between them?

The beginning of wisdom in this matter is to heed Jacques Rancière's warning that 'The simplistic opposition between the modern and the postmodern prevents us from understanding the transformations of the present situation and their stakes' (Rancière 2009: 128). For Rancière, 'There is no postmodern rupture' (2009: 36; the assertion is repeated on p. 42), nor is it necessary to invent one: 'There is no need to imagine that a "postmodern" rupture emerged' (Rancière 2009: 49). That is not to suggest that Rancière is trying to gloss over some important historical and cultural developments: certainly, the culture, art, philosophy, and literature of the late twentieth century exhibit deep-seated differences in form and emphasis from their early twentieth-century counterparts. But Rancière's point is that these differences are attributable not to the ending of the modern era and the dawning of another era post-modernity, but rather to deep-seated paradoxes and ambiguities within the modern conception of the aesthetic, and to different ways in which artists and writers explore them – the changing accentuations and the probing of new facets of modernity's problematic notion of the aesthetic. For Rancière, the modern aesthetic, as formulated largely by Romantics such as Schiller, is predicated on 'a contradiction that is originary and unceasingly at work' (Schiller 2009: 36), and it is simplistic to suppose that modernity is so monolithic an entity that successive generations of artists are incapable of experimenting with its aesthetic precepts in contradictory ways. Hence, where Lyotard envisages a series of postmodern crises or ruptures 'in the modern' (Lyotard 1992a: 15), establishing a newly nascent state of modernity, Rancière is at pains to argue that these crises are in some ways anticipated in modernity's very conception of the aesthetic, and that hence there is nothing 'post' about them at all.

To enlarge on this point, consider the differences of emphasis in the work of Lyotard (arguably the aesthetician-in-chief amongst the postmodernists) and Nicolas Bourriaud (whose sharply rising prominence marks him out amongst a new generation of art theorists). For Lyotard, the aesthetic of the postmodern famously hinges on exploring the limits of presentation, so as to demarcate what lies beyond the boundaries of that concept. Postmodern art, for Lyotard, bears witness to the unpresentable. By contrast, according to Bourriaud's influential work *Relational Aesthetics*, art of the 1990s and beyond seeks to explore questions of community, reconnecting social bonds and discovering new forms of sociability, by creating 'everyday micro-utopias' (Bourriaud 2002: 31). A lineage traceable from Malevich's black square to Daniel Buren's striped canvases offers ample examples of the former; Rirkrit Tiravanija's 2012 contribution to La Triennale *Soup/No Soup*, which consisted of inviting people to Paris's Grand Palais to dine on soup, would be a good example of the latter. Behind Lyotard's ideas stands his engagement with the Kantian sublime; Bourriaud's is related, albeit in complicated and indirect ways, to the Hegelian position that sees art as imbued with the spirit of the community that made it. Whereas the former sees the experience of art as an experience of the unavailable and the unspeakable, the latter seeks to make the experience of art so available and so accessible that its separation from the sphere of life becomes hard or impossible to sustain.

There is, of course, nothing new about this stand-off. It is, more or less, the same debate that was had earlier in the twentieth century between Adorno and Lukács, itself an inflection of the long-standing debate between autonomy and commitment in the arts. But for Rancière, it is in fact a non-debate. It is rather a tangling up of 'two strands of the same originary configuration, namely that which links the specificity of art to a certain way of being of the community' (Rancière 2009: 25). Since at least the Romantic period (and, Rancière argues, even earlier – since Plato's *Republic*) the idea of the aesthetic – that is, the designation of something as 'art' – sets it apart from what is *not* art – that is, 'life' – which means that the very idea of art involves a demarcation of a space in the ordering of life, and is in this sense a political designation. It is political because setting apart something from 'life' that is called 'art' inevitably posits the question of the relationship between the two, and that question cannot but be political. To seek to efface the distinction between life and art, to strive to make life and art one (posing the question: 'One what?') is an inherently political gesture. Equally, to set art apart from life, whether to minister and preach to life from art's pedestal, or to pursue beauty for its own sake, is no less a political gesture. That is why, in the above debate, each side regularly denounces the other's complicity in the political stakes: Adorno, Lyotard, and indeed most champions of autonomous art are decried for their political retreat into solipsism and navel-gazing; Bourriaud, Lukács, and many advocates of committed art are regularly accused of a political descent into populism and ephemerality. So, for Rancière, it is simply not the case that Bourriaud's relational aesthetics have heralded a new era that has supplanted the postmodern, any more than Lyotard's postmodern sublime itself heralded a new era that supplanted modernity, because the story of modern art 'has only ever been a long contradiction between two opposed aesthetic politics, two politics that are opposed but on the basis of a common core linking the autonomy of art to the anticipation of a community to come, and therefore linking this autonomy to the promise of its own suppression' (Rancière 2009: 128). According to Rancière, then, 'What we must therefore recognize both in the linear scenario of modernity and postmodernity, and in the academic opposition between art for art's sake and engaged art, is an originary and persistent tension between the two great politics of aesthetics' (Rancière 2009: 43–4).

If there is anything new about the contrast between Lyotard's and Bourriaud's views, it lies in the fact that they seek to describe and engage with what Josh Cohen has called 'self-annihilating artworks'. It is important that when Lyotard regards certain paintings as bearing witness to the catastrophes of modernity, the witness that they bear is a *silent* witness, hence his vocabulary foregrounds the unpresentable, the unspeakable. As Cohen puts it, 'nothing is shown by these artworks, and yet they do not show us nothing' (Cohen 2006: 222). Equally, Bourriaud's view of art as a 'social experiment' or a 'social interstice' (Bourriaud 2002: 11, 16) is predicated on the risk of dissolving or abrogating any notions of 'art' as a sphere distinct from 'life', from which it is only a small step to dissolving or abrogating the very idea of 'art' altogether (thus, in response to the perennial philistinism of the 'Is this Art?' question, one can imagine an artist in Bourriaud's relational mould responding 'I hope not'). For Rancière, this suggests that we are faced not with two successive epochs – the postmodern and whatever lies beyond it – but rather with 'two opposed types of politics: … the logic of art becoming life at the price of its self-elimination and the logic of art's getting involved in politics on the express condition of not having anything to do with it' (Rancière 2009: 46). It is a basic error to place these two conflicting political viewpoints into a chronological narrative of different periods in the history of art, because 'the notions of modernity and postmodernity misguidedly project, in the form of temporal succession, antagonistic elements whose tension infuses and animates the aesthetic regime of art in its entirety. This regime has always lived off the tension between contraries' (Rancière 2009: 42).

Even if one does not accept the political dimension that underpins Rancière's view, it is nevertheless hard to deny his central point: that in place of a succession of breaks or ruptures, it is very possible to draw an axis of continuity between postmodernism and the modernism that preceded it, and from modernism to the romanticism it claimed to supplant. A similar view was convincingly argued by Gerald Graff back in 1973, before the idea of the postmodern had even achieved widespread currency. Graff's essay, superbly entitled 'The Myth of the Postmodernist Breakthrough', sets out 'to challenge the standard description of postmodernism as representing a sharp break with romantic-modernist traditions' (Graff 1977: 218), arguing that 'Postmodernist anti-art was inherent in the logic of the modernist aesthetic, which in turn derived from the romantic attempts to substitute art for religion' (Graff 1977: 221). To make this point, he cites Coleridge, whose 'famous assertion, crucial in the development of modern criticism, that a good poem should "contain in itself the reason why it is so and so, and not otherwise"' (Graff 1977: 229) Graff takes to be an exemplary statement of the aesthetic issues involved. By surveying what a Wittgensteinian might call a series of intermediate cases, we soon see that this (romantic) idea shares its conceptual orbit with Cleanth Brooks's (modernist) asking of the question 'What does poetry communicate?' (to which his implicit answer is, 'itself'), which in turn is none too distant from Jacques Derrida's (postmodernist) view that '*il n'y a pas de hors-texte*'. Obviously, no small amount of oversimplification and distortion is inevitable in such a sketchy view of the positions involved here, but the point is that Graff closely anticipates Rancière's argument in his view that 'postmodernism should be seen not as breaking with romantic and modernist assumptions but rather as a logical culmination of the premises of these earlier movements' (Graff 1977: 219). Hence, amidst all the rhetoric of the death of postmodernism, it is worth remembering that it is still, and it always has been, open to question whether postmodernism actually had a birth to begin with.

If the line of thought pursued by Rancière and Graff is right, then it may be tempting to leap to the conclusion that, in seeking to describe the demise of the postmodern and its replacement, the essays and manifestos collected in this volume, and indeed the anthology itself, are basically a colossal waste of their authors' ink and their readers' time. But, tempting though this conclusion may be, it is premature, and even facile. I return to my point about how the majority of writings in Part Two prefix the 'modern' in six new ways: 'Re-', 'Hyper-', 'Alter-', 'Meta-', 'Digi-', and 'Auto-'. Let me add that the remaining two positions are no less indebted to the modern: what is performed in performatism, and what is renewed in renewalism, if not a certain way of interpreting the 'modern', and indeed of *being* modern? Jointly and severally, then, what the positions set out in Part Two demonstrate is that, following a few decades in which an orthodoxy we called postmodernism became (to borrow a term from Jameson) a 'cultural dominant', there is now an expanding number of different and diverse ways of experiencing and exploring our modernity. In this respect, the collective significance of these positions is clearly greater than their individual significances: together, they illustrate that the modern is an ongoing experience with an increasing array of different inflections. As Bourriaud might argue, the contemporary subject is something of an explorer, in the position of negotiating his or her path between these various modernisms.

This argument can best be encapsulated by drawing on a recent quotation from arch-postmodernist Charles Jencks, which Alan Kirby's writings brought to my attention:

> Very interesting in this regard is the recent work of Charles Jencks, the author of an important study of postmodernism in architecture and the arts first published in 1986 and regularly updated since. The book's fifth edition, released in 2007, argues for the displacement of postmodernism, after thirty years, by a new cultural era called critical modernism beginning in 2000. This refers 'both to the continuous dialectic between modernisms as they criticize each other and to the way the compression of many modernisms forces a self-conscious criticality, a Modernism-2'.
>
> (Kirby 2009: 44–5)

Putting the issues in these terms clarifies things: firstly, Jencks describes the present formation of contemporary culture – correctly, in my view – in terms of a critically interanimating encounter between many different modernisms. However, if what supplants postmodernism is a new critical modernism, so that modernism is what comes after postmodernism as well as what went before it, then postmodernism begins to appear not as an epoch, style, or movement distinct from modernism, but as a kind of rupture, or cleft, or fold within it. Surely postmodernism was *itself* such an era of 'critical modernism' – a phase in which culture reflected critically on the experience of the modern – which is in turn now being criticized, in the name of the modern, from a refreshing variety of numerous new directions.

Confirmation of this diagnosis can be found in the resurgent importance of the idea of 'modernity' in recent work by an array of distinguished thinkers, some of whom did much to inaugurate the idea of postmodernity. No less a commentator than Fredric Jameson has turned from mapping out postmodernity to theorizing what he dubs a 'singular modernity' (Jameson 2002). Zygmunt Bauman, whose work gave currency to the idea of postmodernity in the social sciences, has abandoned the term in favour of what he now calls 'liquid modernity' (Bauman 2000). Indeed, a survey of new developments in sociology reveals that 'postmodernity' as a label for the state of the present has been rejected by Ulrich Beck in favour of what he initially named a 'new modernity' (Beck 1992), but later, in collaboration with Anthony Giddens, elucidated as a radicalized or 'reflexive modernity' (Beck, Giddens & Lash 1994). In other words, the same tendency can be found in the social sciences as in the arts and humanities: the notion that postmodernity constituted a winding-down of modernity has been widely jettisoned as premature, though what has replaced it is no one term for a catch-all modernity, but rather an array of overlapping new conceptions of modernity – perhaps even a number of new modernities.

However, faced with a view of the contemporary that envisages a plurality of different new ways of experiencing and interpreting the modern, one anticipates the followers of Fredric Jameson objecting that 'If we do not achieve some general sense of a cultural dominant, then we fall back into a view of present history as sheer heterogeneity, random difference, a coexistence of a host of distinct forces whose effectivity is undecidable' (Jameson 1991: 6). I would counter this by suggesting that it is not clear whether the 'present history' of the early twenty-first century actually *has* a 'general sense of a cultural dominant'. Surveying the positions in this volume, though, we could certainly identify a number of shared key themes: I have already mentioned the emphases on authenticity, sincerity, and spirituality that supplant the postmodern shibboleth of irony, for example. But these emphases are inflected in a variety of importantly different ways. As another example, take the rise of digital information and communication technology, which is held by many of the writers anthologized herein to define a new era following the postmodern. Automodernism and digimodernism, in particular, single it out as a definitive characteristic of twenty-first-century culture. But they are divided as to its significance, with Alan Kirby taking a dim view of its populism and consumerism, while Robert Samuels equally valorizes its enabling potential for new forms of autonomy. The point is that taking the idea of the digital age – or any other idea, come to that – as a defining new 'cultural dominant' simply does not produce a coherent or unified account of 'present history' (if that phrase is anything more than a contradiction in terms).

This being so, I had originally intended to suggest a new prefix of my own, and that prefix was going to be 'epi-'. My conclusion was going to propose the term 'epimodern', not just to designate the present cultural moment of the early twenty-first century, but also to apply it retrospectively to that of the late twentieth century, in order to replace the term 'postmodern'. My reasoning was that the prefix 'epi-' has a range of meanings: it can mean 'after', 'beyond', or even 'post-', with obvious usefulness in supplanting the term 'postmodern'. But it can also mean 'near', 'next to', 'beside', or 'attached to', all of which can be taken to indicate proximity and continuity with the modern. It can moreover mean 'over', 'upon', and 'around', suggesting an experience of modernity which is surrounded or surmounted by another experience of modernity. And, most crucially for my purposes, in certain senses it means 'within' and 'emerging from', thus dispensing with the need to envisage dramatic breaks between the modern and the postmodern, and the postmodern and its successors. The term 'epimodern', taken this way, would indicate a variety of different modes of adjacency, reflecting the variety of different yet overlapping ways of experiencing modernity that is suggested by the writings in this volume.

However, a bit of googling soon revealed, disappointingly, that 'epimodernism' is not a neologism of my own invention: the word has already cropped up in a small number of discussions, some dating back thirty years. I refrain from using this term, though, not from any sense of sour grapes at not being the first to coin it, but rather because, on reflection, it would be counterproductive to the aim of highlighting the variety of different experiences of our modernity if I sought to encompass them all within one single term. It is not necessary to decide which prefix ought to replace the 'post-' in postmodernity, any more than it is necessary or desirable to try to pick or predict which of the newly prefixed '-modernisms' in this volume will ultimately supplant the postmodern. (I suspect that none of them will, at least not individually.) Nor is it necessary to come up with yet another prefix that would better describe our present cultural condition by subsuming or reconciling these various new '-modernisms' on offer. Their diversity is their strength.

The conclusion I draw from the writings in this anthology, then, is finally this. That the overwhelming majority of attempts to supplant the postmodern consist in large measure of attaching a new prefix to the word 'modern' strikes me as a clear indication that we are not yet done with our modernity; and that such a number of new prefixes are being mooted (such as 're-' and 'dis-'; 'alter-' and 'auto-'; 'hyper-' and 'meta-'; 'ana-' and 'digi-'; you might also have come across 'geo-' and 'neo-', too)[2] suggests to me that there is a broadening variety of ways in which we experience or negotiate our modernity – or, alternatively, a broadening *awareness* that there is, and probably always has been, a variety of modernities. It was always simplistic to assume that for some reason they all came to an end suddenly, whether that was in May 1968, or when the Pruitt-Igoe housing project was dynamited, or at any other time. By the same token, it is no more sensible to assume that some new modernity was born when the Berlin Wall fell, or when American Airlines flight 11 crashed into the North Tower of the World Trade Center on September 11, 2001, or at some other arbitrarily selected moment of historical significance. Instead, it might be worth suggesting that – with a nod to Bruno Latour – we have never been postmodern.[3] Hence, I predict that debating the end of postmodernity will ultimately prove futile, but no more and no less futile than debating its origins and its birth. What the newly prefixed modernisms to be found in this anthology suggest to my mind is that what supplants postmodernity is a realization that we never left modernity behind in the first place, and that the discourses seeking to formulate or describe the late twentieth century as an era that was somehow (though there was never much clarity as to *how*) 'post-'modernity amount to little more than half a century of groping down a blind alley.

Notes

1 In fact, the term 'dismodernism' is already in use in disability studies, thanks to the work of Lennard J. Davis. (See Davis 2002.)

2 Neomodernism, as formulated by British artist Guy Denning, appears to be an offshoot of remodernism (see http://www.neomodern.org), though the same term has been used to mean completely different things in architectural and philosophical circles. It does not appear to have attained a high level of currency in any of these three fields, hence its lack of inclusion in the present volume. For geomodernism, see Doyle and Winkiel (2005).

3 It is important to clarify what is being suggested by this admittedly rather glib phrase: I am certainly not endorsing an unquestioning logic whereby, because Latour has argued that modernity is a myth, it necessarily follows that postmodernity must be, too. Quite the reverse: I am suggesting instead that, in spite of our best efforts, we have not yet found an exit to modernity.

References

Bauman, Zygmunt (2000), *Liquid Modernity*, Cambridge: Polity.
Beck, Ulrich (1992), *Risk Society: Towards a New Modernity*, trans. Mark Ritter, London: Sage.

Beck, Ulrich, Giddens, Anthony, and Lash, Scott (1994), *Reflexive Modernization: Politics, Tradition and Aesthetics in the Modern Social Order*, Cambridge: Polity.

Bourriaud, Nicolas (2002), *Relational Aesthetics*, trans. Simon Pleasance & Fronza Woods with Mathieu Copeland, Dijon: Les Presses du Réel.

Cohen, Josh (2006), 'No Matter: Aesthetic Theory and the Self-Annihilating Artwork', in David Rudrum (ed.), *Literature and Philosophy: A Guide to Contemporary Debates*, 221–30. Basingstoke: Palgrave Macmillan.

Davis, Lennard J. (2002), *Bending Over Backwards: Disability, Dismodernism and Other Difficult Positions*, New York: New York University Press.

Docherty, Thomas (1996), 'Ana-', in *Alterities: Criticism, History, Representation*, 112–26, Oxford: Oxford University Press.

Doyle, Laura and Winkiel, Laura (eds) (2005), *Geomodernisms: Race, Modernism, Modernity*, Bloomington: Indiana University Press.

Gane, Mike and Gane, Nicholas (2007), 'The Postmodern: After the (Non-)Event', in Pelagia Goulimari (ed.), *Postmodernism: What Moment?*, 127–38, Manchester: Manchester University Press.

Goulimari, Pelagia (2007), 'Introduction' in *Postmodernism: What Moment?*, 1–13, Manchester: Manchester University Press.

Graff, Gerald (1977), 'The Myth of the Postmodernist Breakthrough' in Malcolm Bradbury (ed.), *The Novel Today: Contemporary Writers on Modern Fiction*, 217–49, Manchester: Manchester University Press. First published 1973.

Jameson, Fredric (1991), *Postmodernism, or, The Cultural Logic of Late Capitalism*, London: Verso.

Jameson, Fredric (2002), *A Singular Modernity: Essay on the Ontology of the Present*, London: Verso.

Kellner, Douglas (2007), 'Reappraising the Postmodern: Novelties, Mapping, and Historical Narratives' in Pelagia Goulimari (ed.), *Postmodernism: What Moment?*, 102–26, Manchester: Manchester University Press.

Kirby, Alan (2009), *Digimodernism: How New Technologies Dismantle the Postmodern and Reconfigure our Culture*, London: Continuum.

Kostelanetz, Richard (1982), 'An ABC of Contemporary Reading', *Poetics Today*, 3 (3): 5–46.

Latour, Bruno (1993), *We Have Never Been Modern*, trans. Catherine Porter, Cambridge, MA: Harvard University Press.

Lyotard, Jean-François (1992a), 'Answering the Question, What is the Postmodern?', in *The Postmodern Explained*, trans. Don Barry, Bernadette Maher, Julian Pefanis, Virginia Spate, and Morgan Thomas, 1–16, Minneapolis: University of Minnesota Press.

Lyotard, Jean-François (1992b), 'Note on the Meaning of "Post-"', in *The Postmodern Explained*, trans. Don Barry, Bernadette Maher, Julian Pefanis, Virginia Spate, and Morgan Thomas, 75–80, Minneapolis: University of Minnesota Press.

McHale, Brian (1987), *Postmodernist Fiction*, London: Routledge.

Rancière, Jacques (2009), *Aesthetics and its Discontents*, trans. Steven Corcoran, Cambridge: Polity.

Stierstorfer, Klaus (2003), 'Introduction: Beyond Postmodernism – Contingent Referentiality?' in *Beyond Postmodernism: Reassessments in Literature, Theory, and Culture*, 1–10, Berlin: Walter de Gruyter.

Zima, Peter V. (2003), 'Why the Postmodern Age Will Last', in Klaus Stierstorfer (ed.), *Beyond Postmodernism: Reassessments in Literature, Theory, and Culture*, 13–27, Berlin: Walter de Gruyter.

16

The Anxieties of the Present

Nicholas Stavris

I will not begin by suggesting that we have now entered into a new epoch after postmodernism. To do so would be to beg the question, by concluding before beginning that the postmodern (whether as Lyotard's 'condition' or as Jameson's 'cultural dominant') is now at a complete end. Rather, strange as it may seem, I contend that the writings in this collection point towards the continuation of postmodernism, because collectively they demonstrate a realization that what we called 'postmodernism' was even more problematic than was at first thought. It is understandable that this exasperating realization may lead some to abandon their faith in the idea of the postmodern, or may give the impression that we are better off moving on from it. But it is clearly not over, as Linda Hutcheon would have us believe. We are not simply now within some new phase of the social or the aesthetic, one that is distinctly separate from postmodernism. Wherever we are now logically follows on from that which preceded it, in the same way that postmodernism grew out of modernism.

I would instead suggest that the writings in this anthology cast the early twenty-first century as a transitional period of development which clearly seeks to distinguish itself from the postmodern, but at the same time has no choice but to carry with it many of postmodernism's prevailing characteristics. This sense of transition is, I will argue, created out of the fears and anxieties of the current moment. Indeed, the demand for ascribing a term to where we are now is one that stems from the uncertainties of contemporary culture. This constant attempt to name or re-name our current moment is testament to the anxieties of the present, just as equally as it was testament to giving structure and cohesion to a postmodernism that always purported to resist form and meaning. Since the turn of the twenty-first century, then, we have been witnessing a series of perhaps inevitable attempts by artists and cultural theorists alike to assign meaning to our current existence in response to perceived moments of crisis.

The anxieties that engulf contemporary culture are observed throughout this anthology and are continuously discussed in relation to the end of postmodernism. One of the obvious difficulties that the authors in this collection have faced in their investigations, alongside there being an ongoing awareness of the continued existence of postmodernism even after its demise, is the unanimous agreement that as a cultural entity, it was so misunderstood to begin with. Due to the fact that postmodernism has largely lacked tangibility as to its overall timeframe and definition, it has become increasingly difficult for cultural theorists to centre a conclusive investigation into its replacement. Despite these difficulties, the arguments set out in this anthology show that there is a race to locate the current situation within the global and cultural landscape. For one reason or another, there now appears to be a demand for categorization, and the collection of theories that have been presented here seek to establish a prevailing coinage of this new epochal moment.

Anxiety about our existence as cultural subjects inside this vast spectrum of universal confusion is nothing new. It permeates our physical and spiritual awareness about our past, present, and future. For the postmodernists, anxiety became less of a concern: it hid 'beneath the general demand for relaxation and appeasement' (Lyotard 1992: 9). As Lyotard made clear, postmodern culture was – rightly or wrongly – associated with the desire for a more relaxed global landscape, and this was expressed in the art world and the cultural establishment: 'Together, artist, gallery owner, critic and public indulge one another in the Anything Goes – it's time to relax' (Lyotard 1992: 5). Today, it is no longer a time for such relaxation: faced with a contemporary culture of anxiety, artists attempt to overcome the uncertainties of the human condition in the twenty-first century by reaching out for a renewed period of sincerity. Authenticity is the new focus for the present day artist. The assertion that 'Anything Goes' is no longer the case, nor is it a commonly felt sentiment: the desire for relaxation has been replaced by the desire to formulate some kind of grip on reality, one which was challenged during postmodernism. This development has occurred in response to a culture of fear.

That is not to say that this fear is fear of something specific, nor that there is a consensus about what we should be afraid of; perhaps fear need not be fear 'of' anything at all. The twenty-first century began with a moment of apocalyptic hysteria – the dreaded 'Millennium Bug' – and since then, it seems that the very future of Western culture, and perhaps the world itself, has constantly been under threat from some none-too-well understood source or other, whether that be mass epidemics (SARS, avian flu, ebola), financial meltdown, climate change, or terrorism. Of course, the heyday of postmodernism was itself something of a golden age of fear: from mutually assured destruction to reds under the bed, cold war paranoia was one of American postmodernism's formative influences. But this was a different kind of anxiety: there was a consensus as to what the threat was and where its source lay. Sadly, reaching a similar consensus about (for example) the all-too-real danger of climate change, or the extent of the threat posed by terrorism, remains intractably difficult.

There are several key factors which underscore my point that twenty-first-century culture is engulfed by a climate of anxiety. Some of these have been observed and discussed by the writers in this anthology. Vermeulen and Akker, for example, have argued that the development from the postmodern to the metamodern has occurred in response to a 'threefold threat'; that of 'the credit crunch, a collapsed center and climate change' (Vermeulen & Akker 2010: 5). With an unstable economy and a severe lack of faith in government leadership across the board, alongside the ever pressing issues concerning global warming, deforestation, and fuel consumption, contemporary culture is driven by anxiety. Further to this, there is also a great deal of debate which has come about in recent years surrounding the loss of selfhood, identity, and freedom of the individual, which according to Alan Kirby and Robert Samuels, among others, is largely down to the advancements made in technology. While Samuels doesn't necessarily share Kirby's pessimism about technology, particularly regarding the way we now use the internet, he too highlights the fear of digitization and its effects on the individual. Though I doubt digimodernism or even automodernism are likely to become the prevailing 'isms' in the aftermath of the postmodern, their observations about contemporary culture are nevertheless true of our age. As the individual becomes more and more immersed in the digital world, the loss of individuality becomes increasingly apparent. However, Gilles Lipovetsky's concerns about hypermodern culture offers perhaps the most compelling study into how contemporary culture is fuelled by anxiety. The hypermodern individual is constantly being thrust in a forwards trajectory, ever short of time, and exploited by consumerism and profit. On the other hand there is a greater sense of freedom on the part of the subject, who can, as Lipovetsky suggests, organize their own life and make choices that will reinvigorate their sense of self-worth. The hypermodern existence however is an anxious one, constantly under threat and concerned primarily with an uncertain future.

In addition to these concerns, the anxiety of contemporary culture has been widely discussed in relation to the aftermath of the attacks on the World Trade

Center in New York in 2001. Whilst there are differences of opinion in the debate surrounding 9/11 and its role in the death of postmodernism, one thing we can be sure about is that the way the west perceived the world took a dramatic turn on that date. Anxiety has been the defining characteristic of the post-9/11 era and it would be foolish to ignore the importance of the pervasive rhetoric of 'terror' that followed when attempting to define our current situation post-postmodernism.

With so many contributing factors to the uncertainties of the contemporary era, it is difficult to pinpoint the exact origin of the responses that have been taking place. But it doesn't necessarily matter; the reaction – a forceful reassertion of selfhood – is more vociferous than any diagnosis of its sources. In a world that seems constantly under threat, and where selfhood, identity, individuality, and reality are always being called into question, we have seen a strong cultural response, from literature, art, architecture, and other art forms. The result is a strong resurgence in the presentation, or rejuvenation, of selfhood and identity, and a concomitant rejection of the postmodern idea of the 'Death of the Subject'. As Patricia Waugh makes clear in a chapter from an anthology published in 2013, which examines the relationship between contemporary culture and modern science, with the end of postmodernism there is a 'renewed interest in retrieving the self' (Waugh 2013: 31). With this in mind, it seems that we are now in a state of slow recovery from postmodernism, as we attempt to locate and give meaning to our present condition. This search for meaning can be found in artistic attempts to recapture reality, and presents a shift from postmodern scepticism surrounding authenticity. In his observations about the postmodern condition, Lyotard suggested that the desire for authenticity and sincerity came second to the demand for an oppositional challenge to the rules governed by traditional forms of presentation:

> Our demands for security, identity and happiness, coming from our condition as living beings and even social beings appear today irrelevant in the face of this sort of obligation to complexify, mediate, memorize and synthesize every object, and to change its scale. We are in this techno-scientific world like Gulliver: sometimes too big, sometimes too small, never at the right scale. Consequently, the claim for simplicity, in general, appears today that of the barbarian.
>
> (Lyotard 2001: 1614)

We are still living in this 'techno-scientific world', now even more so than ever before. However, what has been steadily unfolding is a demand for simplicity, authenticity, and sincerity, a demand that is supplanting postmodern concerns for fragmentation and distortion. It is now the artist that embraces cultural hyperreality and fragments traditional notions of artistic representation or narrative who becomes the barbarian.

The desire to achieve sincerity has been argued by theorists such as Josh Toth, Timotheus Vermeulen, and Robin van den Akker to be one of the primary factors in the new and emerging epoch or era we are now entering. It is this desire to break away from postmodern scepticism that could be viewed as a response to the anxieties that encapsulate the present situation in contemporary culture. As Adam Kelly suggests, postmodernist tactics such as irony and scepticism have been rejected 'in favour of a renewed sincerity' (Kelly 2013: 66). This transition is described by Douglas Kellner as a 'Dramatic metamorphosis' (Kellner 2007: 104). The artist is no longer concerned with postmodern displacement strategies; instead, their primary aim is to convey a transition, a positive desire on the part of the subject to reclaim wholeness and selfhood in a globalized culture that is clouded in uncertainty. Further to this, our occupation of a cultural landscape that strives for freedom and autonomy is met with a realigned focus on truth which deviates from postmodern scepticism about reality, and can be seen in some of the fiction that has been produced in the wake of postmodernism.

Waugh, who has commented on some of the contemporary fiction which has come out of the past decade, suggests that we are seeing a response to anxiety in recent works which are engulfed in fears about our cultural existence: 'The contemporary novel shows a continuing preoccupation with what it feels like to live in a biomedicalized, neo-corporate, late capitalist, post-postmodern culture and with the relations between the economic and the neurobiological as they play out in psychopathologies of contemporary everyday life' (Waugh 2013: 31).

Waugh reflects here upon recent fiction that presents a strong awareness of contemporary anxieties, fiction that pays particular attention to the desire for selfhood and autonomy in a present-day culture that is powered by consumerism and technological growth. The relationship between the 'economic and the neurobiological' is not only applicable to the novels which Waugh discusses, but is also in keeping with many of the theories surrounding the development away from postmodernism. Where Alan Kirby regards the networked world of the digital era as a primary factor in the loss of individuality and autonomy, Waugh depicts a sense of 'estrangement' in contemporary fiction as a result of economic uncertainty, and views such fiction as being highly concerned with 'conditions of mental disturbance and depression' (Waugh 2013: 31). Waugh argues that contemporary works which portray the loss of selfhood, identity and autonomy in contemporary culture do so in response to 'a pervasive mood of weariness which colors the entire world' (Waugh 2013: 32). Interestingly, Waugh also highlights this as a response to postmodernism, as she suggests: 'In the current cross-disciplinary quest to recover from what Raymond Tallis calls "neuromania" and "Darwinitis" as well as from postmodernism, there seems to be a renewed interest in retrieving the self through examining those processes and structures of feeling that give rise to its loss' (Waugh 2013: 31).

With this in mind, loss and estrangement are at the heart of contemporary fiction, and while novels that Waugh closely examines, such as Tom McCarthy's *Remainder*, Jonathan Coe's *The Terrible Privacy of Maxwell Simm*, and Jonathan Franzen's *The Corrections* can clearly be seen to have grown out of postmodernism, they have taken on a new shape, or new *sens* as Vermeulen and Akker would suggest. They are works of fiction that reflect upon the disassociated self, and the characters presented in these texts are engulfed in personal estrangement throughout. Interestingly, as Waugh makes clear, novels such as these are driven by the recovery process, with their characters taking on the role of the recovering patient.

Waugh argues that these novels can still be associated with postmodernism even after its disappearance; what has changed is the overall mentality of their characters: 'These are primarily novels about loss, inadequacy, and weariness in which the dominant mood is depressive (though sometimes comic-depressive) rather than apocalyptic, manic or addictive' (Waugh 2013: 31). The authors of these works, according to Waugh, are no longer displaying the doubt about meaning which embodied postmodern scepticism; instead they are focusing on the retrieval of the self which disappeared during postmodernism.

Waugh's assessment here mirrors the thoughts of Vermeulen, Akker, and Toth, who regard the current period of contemporary culture as displaying continuing attributes associated with the postmodern, albeit with a change in emphasis, focusing instead on the notion of desire. In response to the anxieties that have been discussed, authors are apparently moving towards a renewed sense of sincerity, and it is this response that can be seen to be the breakaway moment from postmodernism. Yet the characters in these texts are still part and parcel of the global landscape of capitalism, profit, consumerism, and digitization, all of which continue to limit their sense of selfhood, identity, and autonomy.

Thus, the contemporary novel is arguably contradictory in nature, and authors are showing an increased awareness for the ways in which contemporary culture is perpetually located within the space of both freedom and incarceration. As Robert Samuels indicates, if we are finding ourselves increasingly more confined within the space of the digital world, losing touch with the self through the rise of digitization, we are at the same time developing a new sense of freedom that wasn't there before. We are contributing authors of new texts, in Kirby's opinion, and collaborators in the vast network of digital information. We are constantly told that we can access anything we want via the internet and communicate to almost anyone we want at the click of a button yet, at the same time, we are still confined as subjects within a consumerist, capitalist culture. The notion of freedom is intrinsically and paradoxically tied up in the arena of consumption and as such, as Lipovetsky claims, we are forever attempting to overcome our anxieties about self-deficiency through the act of self-renewal.

The tension between incarceration and freedom which Lipovetsky discusses is the crux of the various other theories concerning contemporary culture set out in this book. It mirrors the argument between the end of postmodernism, the entry into a new and emerging epoch, and the ongoing presence of postmodernism within it. It is this tension that can be found in contemporary literature today. In Waugh's terms, authors such as Jonathan Franzen, Jonathan Coe, and Tom McCarthy, who can be viewed as key contributors to this new 'period' of literary history, saturate their fiction with existentialist enquiries and at the same time reveal a central desire to locate their characters outside the now unfavourable confines of the postmodern novel. These authors depict a contemporary culture that resists anxiety and characters that embrace the paradox that we can now associate with twenty-first-century life. However, within these novels is the underlying participation with the knowledge that has stemmed from postmodernist assumptions about reality, hyperreality, and the decentred self. In them we also see a response to the uncertainty that exists today in the aftermath of postmodernism.

The transition in contemporary fiction from the use of postmodern tendencies such as irony, pastiche, and satire into a new heralded position of sincerity goes hand in hand with the return to realist modes of discourse discussed by Toth, Vermeulen, and Akker. For Toth, the postmodern has been rejected in favour of a renewed interest in realism. He refers to this return as a form of neo-realism or renewalism, and suggests that authors of the twenty-first century are now embracing the impossibility of presenting reality with a renewed belief in overcoming that impossibility. A similar argument has been made by Vermeulen and Akker, who refer to this transition as a return to neo-romanticism. Both stances depict the new epoch as being patently aware of the ongoing presence of postmodernism in contemporary works of fiction and art, and yet at the same time convey this awareness alongside depicting a central desire to overcome it. Both stances, renewalism and metamodernism, suggest cultural aesthetics are engaged in a paradoxical strategy of reclaiming representation, all the while maintaining the knowledge of the impossibility of presenting reality. The desire for sincerity in response to contemporary anxieties can also be viewed as related to the development or return to past modes of narrative and artistic discourse – a return, that is, which eschews the irony of the indirect encounter with the past on offer in postmodern pastiche.

That is not in any way to claim that experimental narrative fiction has fallen out of favour in the early years of the twenty-first century. Far from it. Novelists are still finding new ways of grappling with the form of the novel, and twisting it into unprecedented shapes. Consider Mark Z. Danielewski's *House of Leaves* (2000), in which the book's paratextual apparatus – its footnotes and appendices – do at least as much to drive the narrative forward as the body of the text: this experiment both recalls and outdoes Nabokov's postmodern classic *Pale Fire*. Another case in point would be T.M. Wolf's remarkable novel *Sound* (2012), which appropriates a form not unlike that of the music score, with lines like staves running across the page, so that the words spoken by a character can be represented simultaneously yet distinctly from the thoughts they think, the memories they recall, and the fantasies they entertain. Apparently, experimental fiction is still a path through which novelists can achieve acclaim, success, and recognition: Jennifer Egan's appropriation of the form of a PowerPoint printout did not prevent her 2010 novel *A Visit from the Goon Squad* from winning a Pulitzer Prize, any more than Eimear McBride's rediscovery of Joycean stream of consciousness in *A Girl is a Half-Formed Thing* (2013) stood in the way of an impressive array of awards. Experimental fiction is alive and well. There is, perhaps, a point to be made about the way that most of these experiments are experiments in capturing selfhood or reality, rather than in inducing postmodern scepticism about it (*à la* John Barth, say). But there is nevertheless a more symptomatic point to be made, too: erstwhile experimental writers of postmodernist fiction have been turning away from this genre, towards more mimetic modes of narrative fiction. There doesn't appear to be a corresponding trend in the opposite direction.

The fiction of Jonathan Franzen is particularly interesting in regards to the development away from postmodernism into a supposedly new era of fiction writing. If a shift has occurred from postmodernism into something after-postmodernism, Franzen's writing, it could be suggested, highlights this transitional moment. Franzen is an author who, in his early career, was seen as a postmodern writer, as Robert Rebein has stated: 'in his first two books, *The Twenty-Seventh City* (1988), and *Strong Motion* (1992), Franzen often seemed to be striving specifically to become, along with his friend David Foster Wallace, the next great po-mo writer' (Rebein 2007: 201).

In contrast, with the arrival of his third novel, *The Corrections* (2001), Franzen could be seen to have rejected his postmodern past in favour of 'a realist tradition' (Rebein 2007: 201). However, where Waugh has accredited this move towards realism as a result of the desire for self-reclamation, Rebein has suggested that authors such as Franzen have had no choice but to move away from postmodern literature if they are to become successful writers.

Rebein provides an in-depth discussion concerning the possible reasons for Franzen's choice to 'switch sides', including his personal struggles as a writer after his second novel and the failure of postmodernism to keep up with a 'revitalized realism' (Rebein 2007: 220). However, Rebein concludes his chapter concerning this development by addressing the relationship between Franzen's rejection of postmodern writing and the rise of technology, which has led to the slow decline of reading fictional literature on a global scale. As he explains, 'Even larger than the trend from postmodernism to realism, however, is the one from fiction to nonfiction, or indeed from reading to non-reading forms of entertainment' (Rebein 2007: 220). With the growth in technology, he suggests, people are turning away from the act of reading novels, an act which is becoming lost in the 'frenetic pace of contemporary culture' (Rebein 2007: 204). For authors such as Franzen, Rebein discusses, the tendencies associated with postmodernism as a cultural framework for the act of structuring a novel no longer have a place in a culture which is already beginning to reject the very format of traditional literature itself. Referring to the thoughts of author Philip Roth, Rebein reflects upon the troubling notion that reading literature is becoming lost as a cultural pastime: 'many of our most influential writers have come to the belief that we are now living in a "post-literate" age in which the act of reading itself is being retooled or phased out altogether' (Rebein 2007: 220).

In terms of technological advancements, it is certainly plain to see that literature is succumbing to digital enhancements, and that electronic communications, web pages, texting, Facebook updates, Twitter feeds, and blogs are the primary modes of textuality in use in contemporary society. This is also an issue directly discussed by theorists Alan Kirby and Robert Samuels. With so great an interest in these recent developments, Rebein suggests, traditional literature such as fiction novels are becoming outdated, and if we are indeed living in a hypermodern culture, as Lipovetsky believes, where stress, constant movement, consumerism, technology, and speed are the foundational components of modern life, the act of reading literary novels is something that contemporary culture is finding less and less time for.

That said, the notion that reading is no longer viewed as a valuable use of time is somewhat misleading. Reading, it could be argued, is now part and parcel of contemporary life as we know it today. The ways in which people exist inside technological environments such as Facebook and Twitter for example indicate not a lack of reading altogether, but a metamorphosis of the written word. This is not an entirely new transition; twenty years ago, the birth of email led to a dramatic alteration in the way we communicate and in the way we read. Chatrooms introduced a culture of pseudonymity and ephemerality that began to change our conceptions of identity and selfhood. Social media sites have now taken this a step further, altering communication to the extent that acquaintanceship is no longer a requisite for sustained social interaction. Seemingly, more and more people are functioning in an online community in which the act of reading is more alive than ever, and a vital component in modern life.

Nevertheless, Roth's observations about a decline in the reading of literature certainly go hand in hand with a hypermodern state of cultural noise, as the basic necessity for reading is lost in the stampede of mental and physical exhaustion: 'Literature requires a habit of mind that has disappeared. It requires silence, some form of isolation, and sustained concentration in the presence of an enigmatic thing' (Roth, quoted in Rebein 2007: 220–1). Silence and solitude are not often characteristics we could associate with contemporary culture today, and as such, Roth has a point. Franzen himself has addressed this issue in his collection of essays *How To Be Alone* (2002). Rebein reflects upon the fact that if indeed there is an increase in the lack of 'serious reading' in the twenty-first century, postmodernism is not the ideal choice for contemporary authors, 'with its wilfully tricky plots, buried illusions, and uncompromising opacity' (Rebein 2007: 221). In his opinion at least, reading postmodernist fiction is going to prove too much for a culture that lacks the concentration and isolation of mind required for it, and authors such as Franzen are going to have far more luck as writers in presenting to their audience novels that show a progressive return to realist modes of fiction.

However, it is important to point out that 1) much of the fiction which has come about in the past decade is not necessarily less intellectually demanding than postmodernist literature; and 2) even if this were so, apparently it still hasn't dissuaded the Danielewskis of this world from continuing with the project of experimental narrative fiction. In other words, today's authors who are returning, as Toth argues, to a form of neo-realism, are also (and thereby) bombarding their readers with challenging questions about selfhood, identity, and time – otherwise put, they are enquiring into the workings of the human condition in progressively demanding ways, whilst simultaneously presenting fictional narratives which highlight the anxieties that humanity is currently faced with. Authors such as Franzen, then, are not necessarily making fiction easier to read; on the contrary, they express contemporary culture's complex desire to locate reality within a landscape that is being continuously reshaped and becoming increasingly more difficult to define.

Rebein's analysis of Franzen's deliberate choice to embrace realism and reject his postmodern past conflicts with the thoughts of Ben Marcus, who criticizes authors such as Franzen for contributing to a lack of ambition within the literary world. While Marcus agrees that literature today swings mainly in favour of realism, that it is 'by far the reigning style of contemporary literature' (Marcus 2005: 41), he concludes that Franzen's rejection of a form of writing that has long since been left behind by the consuming masses, is a failure on the part of the author to challenge his readers by going against the grain (Marcus 2005: 41). Marcus argues that 'a writer with ambition is now called "postmodern" or "experimental" and not without condescension'. He reflects upon the notion that if a writer is to be experimental, they are immediately placing their work at the mercy of the firing squad; 'You hate your audience, you hate the literary industry, you probably even hate yourself. You stand not with the people but in a quiet dark hole, shouting to no one' (Marcus 2005: 40). Marcus goes on to describe Franzen's *The Corrections* as a novel that ultimately defines him as a conformist in spite of his postmodern assertiveness which was so evident during his early career:

> Engrossing, operatic, and ably choreographed, the book was nevertheless a retreat for Franzen into the comforts of a narrative style that was already embraced by the culture. His ambition clearly was to belong to the establishment rather than stand out from it, to join a well-defined team rather than strike out on his own.
>
> (Marcus 2005: 43)

While this is a strong criticism of Franzen, Marcus echoes the words of Lyotard, who imagined that the postmodernist would become the rejected artist, 'destined to lack credibility in the eyes of the devoted adherents of reality and identity, to find themselves without a guaranteed audience' (Lyotard 1992: 4). In terms of popularity, Franzen has certainly achieved recognition for his ability as a contemporary fiction writer, and it seems likely that this is in part down to his supposed shift from postmodernist to realist. But is it true to say that this shift reflects a dumbing down or a lack of ambition? I would argue that *The Corrections* and his 2010 novel *Freedom* are, on the contrary, laudably bold in their attempts to encapsulate the anxieties that exist in culture today. *Freedom* observes contemporary culture from the perspective of several different characters who are engulfed with perpetual fears about isolation and solitude, constantly striving for meaning in a world that refuses to slow down. Told from varying viewpoints, truth is never straightforwardly available, and with overlapping narratives that slide back and forth through time, with characters that grow as their individual timelines progress, not only is it problematic to suggest that it is a novel which lacks ambition; it is a novel which reports on the entrapment of the contemporary subject who seeks emancipation from the uncompromising and frenetic pace of the world around them.

Franzen's *Freedom* can be seen to be part of an ongoing but incomplete transition away from postmodernism, as can the fiction of Jonathan Coe and Tom McCarthy, authors who appear to strive for the continued need for experimentation in literature while reflecting upon the anxieties that exist in contemporary culture. Waugh places both authors in the same bracket, analysing their novels as attempts to present the reclamation of selfhood and identity. However, McCarthy's *Remainder* (2005), and Coe's *The House of Sleep* (1997) and *The Terrible Privacy of Maxwell Simm* (2010), appear to present this desire for a return to true authenticity or identity, while knowing that this desire is elusive; a renewed wish to embrace reality, knowing that estrangement has taken its place. It is this desire which reflects the demand for sincerity that exists in contemporary culture today. McCarthy's *Remainder* explores the loss of selfhood and identity as a result of serious trauma. The protagonist, who has come into a large amount of money in compensation for an unknown accident, spends the entirety of the novel funding a search for his lost connection to reality. Narrative – mostly re-enactment – is the key component in this novel, and it is deliberately unstable at best. It functions in a way which lacks credibility and persistently questions traditional formulations of storytelling, and ultimately, it is a novel that strives to embrace the impossibility of mimesis, of presenting the impossibility of presenting reality.

Coe's *The Terrible Privacy of Maxwell Simm* works in a similar way to *Remainder*, revealing the personal struggle of its main protagonist, who is lost in the network of contemporary capitalist society. He is bound by the desire to form relationships, to make connections, and arguably his most stable relationship is with the satellite navigation system in his car, which conjures up the reliance of culture on technological interaction. Aware of his own inadequacies, he seeks above all else to find structure, coherence, and a return to his own personal being. He is, for the duration of the novel, an outsider from his sense of self, as the novel takes on the form of what Waugh terms 'Syndrome Fiction', where 'the self experiences itself as disembodied, outside itself and looking in' (Waugh 2013: 33). In his 1997 novel *The House of Sleep*, Coe also deals in the reclamation of selfhood, and observes the contemporary fascination with identity. Trauma is at the heart of the narrative, as with *Remainder*, and the novel explores the experimentation of identity in response to a traumatic past, and an unstable present that is clouded in uncertainty. This particular novel, which propels the reader back and forth through time, draws to a climax with the revelation that one of its primary characters has altered his sex to become female so that he can be with the love of his life, whom he believes is a lesbian, only to discover that she no longer is. Gender and identity are collapsed in *The House of Sleep*, a novel that explores the instability of present day selfhood, but also reflects the contemporary exploration of gender issues. The nature of both gender and identity in this novel reveals the breakdown of selfhood in contemporary culture, and at the same time announces the contemporary desire to embrace the self, to return to a humanist ideal of meaning, specifically in terms of the concept of lost identity. It is perhaps an earlier example of an attempt to explore identity in ways that reflect contemporary culture as it swerves away from postmodernist irony. It is also a novel that strives to purport on the difficulty of existing in a contemporary world that both incarcerates and celebrates individual freedom.

All of these works of fiction take on the task of moving past postmodernism through a refocused concern for the self, for identity and reality. While these issues are not necessarily distinct from postmodernism, their overall tone reveals a sense of transition. There is a renewed demand for the authentic, a demand that wasn't necessarily there during postmodernism. The postmodern concern for the impossibility of mimesis continues but in a way which is now being reformed and reshaped. Without completely rejecting postmodernism, with its seemingly blurred assumptions about reality, authors such as Coe and McCarthy appear to reach something of a middle ground between the reality of human existence and postmodern experimentation. The point, then, is not a simple assertion that realism is a newly dominant mode for twenty-first-century fiction, supplanting the experimental postmodern novel – clearly, new experimental fiction is being written to acclaim and success. The point is rather that an aesthetic of (some form of) realism is a better means of connecting with the pervasive sense of anxiety that fuels contemporary culture.

As has been suggested throughout the writings presented herein, there is an ongoing presence of postmodernism in contemporary culture, and a persistence of experimentation across the arts. Franzen's apparent switch from postmodernist to realist, however, can be taken as evidence of a development away from postmodernism as a mode for expressing the culture of the present. As Peter Boxall clarifies, 'Right across the spectrum of writers ... one can see the emergence of new kinds of realism, a new set of formal mechanisms with which to capture the real, as it offers itself as the material substrate of our being in this world' (Boxall 2013: 10). Contemporary realism, as Boxall makes clear, is woven into the fabric of the contemporary climate. Such 'mechanisms' continue to grow out of the remains of postmodernism.

In some ways, then, perhaps postmodernism is more relevant than ever. Mary K. Holland convincingly remarks upon the ongoing nature of postmodernism, suggesting that 'if ... the essential change marked by postmodernism amounts to intense antifoundationalism, particularity, and subjectivity of truth and belief, then the literature we are seeing in the nascent twenty-first century is still fundamentally postmodern, rather than something wholly beyond postmodernism' (Holland 2013: 200).

As I have argued, the ways in which we exist today show us how disassociated from the real world we have become – just as postmodern thinkers like Baudrillard already predicted, 'in a hyperspace without atmosphere' (Baudrillard 2001: 1733). However, this existence, one which is moulded on the absence of reality, has generated a reaction that postmodernism could hardly have anticipated: the demand for a new period of sincerity. Artists are now exploring that demand, and we are witnessing various attempts to take hold of reality in the face of the anxieties of our contemporary world – attempts that, Holland makes clear, do not abandon postmodernism per se; instead, they reshape it into what she calls a 'newly humanist postmodernism' (Holland 2013: 200). So it is not by forgetting postmodernism that this embrace of reality, selfhood, and identity can be achieved. This can only be done by rethinking and working through its central aesthetic tenet: the impossibility of presenting reality.

References

Baudrillard, Jean (2001), '*from* The Procession of Simulacra' in Vincent B. Leitch et al. (eds), *The Norton Anthology of Theory and Criticism*, 1729–41, London: Norton. First published 1981.

Boxall, Peter (2013), *Twenty-First Century Fiction*, Cambridge: Cambridge University Press.

Coe, Jonathan (1998), *The House of Sleep*, London: Penguin Books.

Coe, Jonathan (2010), *The Terrible Privacy of Maxwell Simm*, London: Penguin Books.

Danielewski, Mark Z. (2000), *House of Leaves*, New York: Pantheon.

Egan, Jennifer (2011), *A Visit from the Goon Squad*, London: Corsair.

Franzen, Jonathan (2002a), *The Corrections*, London: Fourth Estate.

Franzen, Jonathan (2002b), *How To Be Alone*, London: Fourth Estate.

Franzen, Jonathan (2010), *Freedom*, London: Fourth Estate.

Holland, Mary K. (2013), *Succeeding Postmodernism: Language and Humanism in Contemporary American Culture*, New York: Bloomsbury.

Hutcheon, Linda (2007), 'Gone Forever, But Here To Stay: The Legacy of the Postmodern' in Pelagia Goulimari (ed.), *Postmodernism: What Moment?*, 16–17, Manchester: Manchester University Press.

Kellner, Douglas (2007), 'Reappraising the Postmodern: Novelties, Mapping, and Historical Narratives' in Pelagia Goulimari (ed.), *Postmodernism: What Moment?*, 102–26, Manchester: Manchester University Press.

Kelly, Adam (2013), 'From Syndrome to Sincerity: Benjamin Kunkel's Indecision' in T. J. Lustig and James Peacock (eds), *Diseases and Disorders in Contemporary Fiction: The Syndrome Syndrome*, 66–80, New York: Routledge.

Kirby, Alan (2009), *Digimodernism: How New Technologies Dismantle the Postmodern and Reconfigure our Culture*, London: Continuum.

Lipovetsky, Gilles (2005), 'Time in Conflict, and Chrono-reflexivity' in *Hypermodern Times*, trans. Andrew Brown, 48–53, Cambridge: Polity. Originally Published as *Les Temps Hypermodernes* (Paris: Grasset, 2004).

Lustig, T. J. and Peacock, James (eds) (2013), *Diseases and Disorders in Contemporary Fiction: The Syndrome Syndrome*, New York: Routledge.

Lyotard, Jean François (1992), 'Answering the Question: What is the Postmodern?' in *The Postmodern Explained to Children*, 1–9, Sydney: Power Publications.

Lyotard, Jean François (2001), 'Defining the Postmodern' in Vincent B. Leitch et al. (eds), *The Norton Anthology of Theory and Criticism*, 1609–15, London: Norton. First published 1986.

Marcus, Ben (2005), 'Why Experimental Fiction Threatens to Destroy Publishing: Jonathan Franzen, and life as we know it', *Harpers Magazine*, Oct: 39–52.

McBride, Eimear (2014), *A Girl is a Half-Formed Thing*, London: Faber.

McCarthy, Tom (2011), *Remainder*, London: Alma Books.

Rebein, Robert (2007), 'Turncoat: Why Jonathan Franzen Finally Said "No" to Po-Mo' in Neil Brooks and Josh Toth (eds), *The Mourning After: Attending the Wake of Postmodernism*, 201–22, New York: Rodolpi.

Remnick, David (2000), 'Into the Clear: Philip Roth Puts Turbulence in its Place', *The New Yorker*, 8 May: 76–89.

Samuels, Robert (2007), 'Auto-Modernity after Postmodernism: Autonomy and Automation in Culture, Technology, and Education', in Tara McPherson (ed.) *Digital Youth, Innovation, and the Unexpected*, 219–40, Cambridge, MA: MIT Press.

Vermeulen, Timotheus and Akker, Robin van den (2010), 'Notes on Metamodernism', *Journal of Aesthetics and Culture*, 2: 1–14.

Waugh, Patricia (2013), 'The Naturalistic Turn, the Syndrome, and the Rise of the Neo-Phenomenological Novel', in T. J. Lustig and James Peacock (eds), *Diseases and Disorders in Contemporary Fiction: The Syndrome Syndrome*, 27–46, New York: Routledge.

Wolf, T. M. (2012), *Sound*, London: Faber.

Index

CPSIA information can be obtained
at www.ICGtesting.com
Printed in the USA
LVHW022124280119
605528LV00016B/296